The BP exhibition

Sunken cities
Egypt's lost
worlds

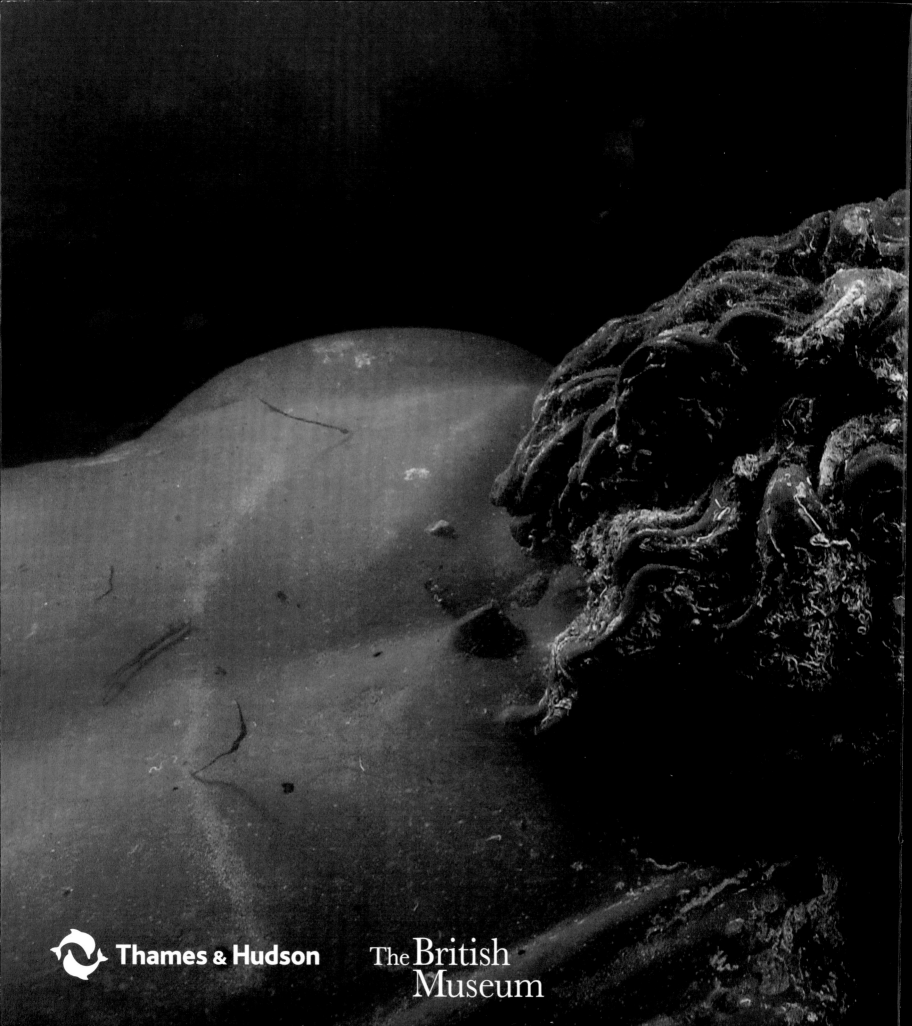

Thames & Hudson The British Museum

The BP exhibition

Sunken cities
Egypt's lost worlds

Edited by Franck Goddio
and Aurélia Masson-Berghoff

This publication accompanies the BP exhibition *Sunken cities: Egypt's lost worlds* at the British Museum from 19 May to 27 November 2016. It has been produced with the Hilti Foundation and the Institut Européen d'Archéologie Sous-Marine, in collaboration with the Ministry of Antiquities of the Arab Republic of Egypt.

The exhibition at the British Museum has been made possible by the provision of insurance through the Government Indemnity Scheme. The British Museum would like to thank the Department for Culture, Media and Sport and Arts Council England for providing and arranging this indemnity.

First published in the United Kingdom in 2016 by Thames & Hudson Ltd, in collaboration with the British Museum.

Sunken cities: Egypt's lost worlds © 2016 The Trustees of the British Museum/Thames & Hudson

Text © 2016 The Trustees of the British Museum

Designed by Maggi Smith

A catalogue record for this book is available from the British Library

ISBN 978-0-500-29237-2

Printed and bound in Italy by Graphicom

To find out about all our publications, please visit **www.thamesandhudson.com**.
There you can subscribe to our e-newsletter, browse or download our current catalogue, and buy any titles that are in print.

p. 1: Cult statue of the deified Ptolemaic queen Arsinoe II, see p. 93

pp. 2–3: Bust of Neilos, personification of the Nile's flood, as discovered underwater, see p. 208

pp. 6–7: Colossal statue of a Ptolemaic king dressed as an Egyptian pharaoh, see p. 98

p. 8: The god Serapis (detail showing gilding and painting remains), see p. 81

pp. 12–13: Reconstruction of the seaport Thonis-Heracleion, criss-crossed by canals and basins, with its Egyptian temples and harbour installations

Contents

Director's foreword

Sunken Cities is the British Museum's first major exhibition focused on underwater archaeology. The European Institute for Underwater Archaeology (Institut Européen d'Archéologie Sous-Marine or IEASM, Paris), led by Franck Goddio, has been working off the Mediterranean coast of Egypt, near Alexandria, for the last twenty years. The resulting rediscoveries of Thonis-Heracleion and Canopus have challenged our perceptions of ancient Egypt. At the interface with the Mediterranean world, these two cities thrived on the exchange and flow of people, goods and ideas, from around 300 years before Alexander the Great arrived in Egypt. Their prime location at the mouth of the Nile's Canopic branch, once the guarantor of their incredible wealth and dynamism, was also a fragile and unstable landscape between land and sea. The cities then sank beneath the sea, as canals silted up and other catastrophic events (perhaps earthquakes or tidal waves) compelled their inhabitants to abandon the area.

We are delighted to bring to the public these once lost worlds, brought to light through modern technologies, with the exhibition and this accompanying book informed by the latest research of a multidisciplinary team. From colossal and stunning statues to fine metalware and gold jewellery, the spectacular finds are presented for the first time in the UK, in a narrative that explores the encounter between ancient Egypt and Greece. New insights into the quality and unique character of the art of this period are revealed, alongside a better understanding of the deep and meaningful interconnections between Greek and Egyptian communities in Egypt at this time. Displayed side by side, Egyptian, Greek and 'hybrid' artworks convey the colourful multicultural world in which the inhabitants of these cities lived. They make us appreciate that Egypt was not an isolated civilization. The exhibition also serves to highlight the Museum's research project in Naukratis, a bustling international harbour town closely connected to Thonis-Heracleion.

The exhibition and book are the results of a collaboration between the British Museum and IEASM, and we are thankful to all involved. We are particularly grateful for the exceptional loan of objects from the Egyptian Ministry of Antiquities, allowing us to show masterpieces of the Egyptian Museum in Cairo and several museums in Alexandria, some of which have never before left Egypt. The outstanding objects on loan from Egypt are supplemented by a select group of objects from the British Museum's collection. The exhibition is only made possible through the generous support of BP, one of the British Museum's longest-standing corporate partners. We also wish to express our gratitude to the members of IEASM, foremost Franck Goddio, and the Hilti Foundation for their help and input throughout this project.

Hartwig Fischer
Director, British Museum

Sponsor's foreword

Discovery is part science and technology, part human endeavour. To discover oil and gas offshore we survey the rocks beneath the ocean from ships on the surface. From such marine seismic surveys we can create detailed, three-dimensional maps of the rock formations thousands of metres below. And from these maps our geologists can identify the places where hydrocarbons might be found.

It should be no surprise then that we feel a strong affinity with the maritime archaeologists who have created and studied their own maps of the Mediterranean seabed to discover the lost cities of Thonis-Heracleion and Canopus. We may work at different depths, but like our fellow marine explorers, BP knows the Nile Delta and the waters off the Mediterranean coast well, having explored and worked in Egypt for over fifty years.

Our many discoveries have been providing the people of this historic country with energy since the 1960s. We continue to invest in Egypt's future through our exploration and production activities, which are creating jobs and new industries, and through our social programmes which are supporting education and local communities. We remain committed to play our part in unlocking Egypt's true energy potential and to grow production safely, reliably and efficiently.

Egypt today is as vivid as in those ancient times, when its people walked among the colossal statues of Thonis-Heracleion and worshipped at the temples in Canopus. The artefacts on show in this exhibition are as striking and inspiring as any Egyptian antiquities and it is my great pleasure that BP is helping the British Museum to share them with you.

I hope that you enjoy the exhibition and the information provided in this accompanying publication.

Bob Dudley
Group Chief Executive, BP

Foreword from the Hilti Foundation

When the Hilti Foundation began working with Franck Goddio and the European Institute for Underwater Archaeology in Egypt almost twenty years ago, nobody anticipated the significance this project would gain over the years, nor its impact. What started with an exploratory underwater mission gradually developed into one of the most highly regarded and sustained projects in the field of underwater archaeology.

Founded and financed for many years by the Martin Hilti Family Trust, the Hilti Foundation is now supported jointly by the Trust as well as the international Hilti Group – a manufacturer and supplier of state-of-the-art technological products, systems and services for the construction and associated industries. The Foundation, based at the company's headquarters in Liechtenstein, sponsors selected sustainable projects and initiatives, especially in the cultural, social and educational fields.

Franck Goddio's research projects are a key aspect of the cultural and scientific work of the Hilti Foundation today. The Foundation's interest is focused primarily on two purposes: the scientific analysis of Goddio's findings in close collaboration with the Oxford Centre of Maritime Archaeology at the University of Oxford, which also enables young scientists to study underwater archaeology, and on the opportunity to make the results of this work accessible to wider audiences through publications and exhibitions.

We are pleased and proud to see the latest research findings produced by Franck Goddio and his team exhibited for the first time in the UK at the British Museum. We are also proud that our long-term sponsorship of this research has helped to make it possible. In keeping with the Foundation's mission statement to building a better future our partnership is closely connected with our belief that knowledge of the past is fundamental to gaining a better understanding of the present.

Michael Hilti
Member of the Board of the Hilti Foundation

HILTI FOUNDATION

1   Rediscovering Thonis-Heracleion and Canopus

Franck Goddio and Damian Robinson

Beneath the waters of Abukir Bay, at the edge of Egypt's northwestern Nile Delta, lies a vast submerged landscape. Facing the Mediterranean – the 'Sea of the Greeks'[1] – this was the very edge of Egypt in ancient times, a region that was neither fully land nor sea: a landscape of lakes and marshes dotted with islands and sandbanks. A mosaic from Palestrina, Italy, provides a contemporary glimpse of this Nilotic landscape of wild exoticism, as it seemed to the Romans (fig. 2).[2] This aquatic region, with all its harbours, temples and towns, eventually subsided and sank beneath the waters of the bay.

Here, over 1,000 years later, were found the lost cities of Thonis-Heracleion and Canopus, submerged yet preserved beneath the sea. Their recent rediscovery, made possible only through the use of the latest technologies, is transforming our understanding of the relationship between ancient Egypt and the Greek world, and the unique importance of these cities.

2   Scenes of the Nile. Mosaic (detail) from the sanctuary of Fortuna (Isis) in Palestrina, Italy, end of 2nd century BC. Museo Nazionale Prenestino, Palazzo Barberini

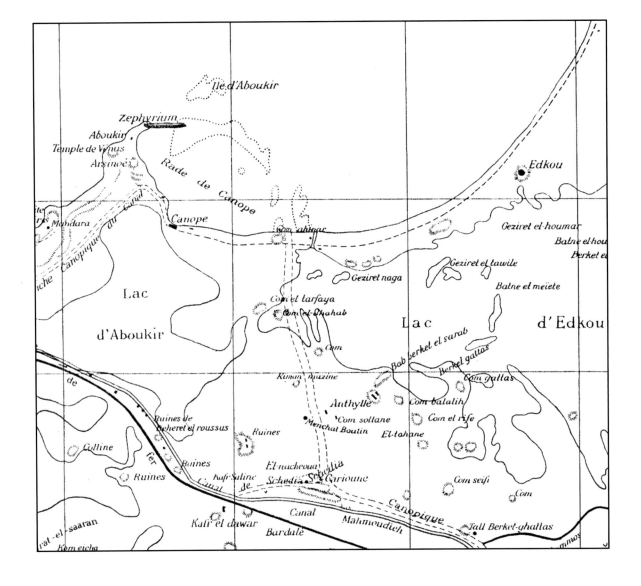

3 Detail from Mahmud Bey el-Falaki's map of the environs of Alexandria showing the hypothetical line of the Canopic branch of the Nile and the position of the town of Canopus

The Canopic region and the cities

In antiquity the westernmost branch of the Nile, the Canopic, flowed 30 kilometres east of Alexandria.[3] This region was well known in the ancient world, because of its key role as the place where travelling Greeks came into close contact with Egyptian civilization. These early meetings are echoed in an ancient Greek myth that described this region as the place where the half-god Herakles first set foot in Egypt.[4] The tale gave the Canopic branch of the Nile its alternative name: the Heracleotic.

As Greek peoples became increasingly familiar with this area, so it became incorporated into their stories. The earliest, and still quite scanty, references to Egypt are found in the works of Homer, whose characters were subsequently incorporated into later texts. The Greek historian Herodotus wrote that, after abducting Helen from her husband King Menelaos of Sparta, the Trojan prince Paris was forced by adverse winds to seek shelter in a temple to Herakles at the end of the Canopic branch of the Nile: 'Now there was on the coast (and still is) a temple of Herakles'.[5] Such stories no doubt helped to fix this region into the imagination of the Greeks and also to affirm their long-standing influence upon it. For example, the city of Canopus was said to owe its name to Menelaos' pilot Canobos, who died there.[6]

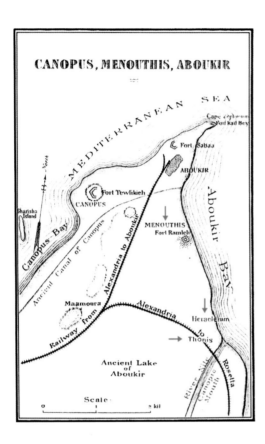

CANOPUS, MENOUTHIS, ABOUKIR

4 Map published by Jules Faivre (1918) illustrating the presumed locations of the towns of Thonis, Heracleion and Menouthis on the modern Abukir shoreline (indicated by red arrows)

overleaf
5 Red granite column shafts from Canopus

Contained within these ancient sources are snippets of geographical information and the names of cities and important buildings that became lost over time. For example, the Decree of Canopus mentions a city called Heracleion, situated in the Canopic region, where a god called 'Amun-Gereb' was worshipped alongside Herakles, the half-god who gave his name to the town.[7] It was to the easily understood texts of the Greco-Roman period – particularly in the years before hieroglyphs were translated – that scholars and explorers turned for clues to help them locate these lost cities. The Greek geographer Strabo, for instance, provides a first-hand account of the main settlements lying along the narrow strip of coastline roughly eastwards of Alexandria,[8] and various other ancient authors noted distances to other local sites.[9] In combination, these texts helped scholars such as Mahmud Bey el-Falaki, the astronomer of the Viceroy of Egypt, to create in 1866 a regional map with Canopus located on the coast of Abukir Bay, which also guided his excavations (fig. 3).[10] In the early twentieth century, Evaristo Breccia and Jules Faivre suggested locations for Thonis, Heracleion and Menouthis along the eastern shore, with Canopus near modern Fort Tawfiq on the west of the Abukir peninsula (fig. 4).[11]

The presence of ruins on the coastline, however, indicated that ancient sites might also be submerged out in the bay; so the distances given in the ancient texts might extend out across the sea. The French Egyptologist Georges Daressy's 1929 map consequently suggested that Canopus was located on the Abukir peninsula with Menouthis, Thonis and Heracleion offshore.[12]

This reasoning was proved correct when in 1933 Group Captain Cull, commander of the British R.A.F. base at Abukir, thought he glimpsed ruins in the bay while taking off from the aerodrome. He alerted Prince Omar Toussoun, a scholar of the Delta, to look over the site. Finding nothing, Toussoun asked local fishermen if they had any knowledge of submerged ruins. Following their directions, the prince located an important archaeological site about 2 kilometres off the present shore, composed 'of marble columns and red granite' (fig. 5).[13] His discoveries, including a white marble statue representing Alexander the Great, were the basis of future research on the Canopic region, proving that part of a once-inhabited area had been submerged.

New research

Following this pioneering work in the waters of Abukir Bay, a half-century passed before research into the sunken cities of the Canopic coast restarted with the work of the Institut Européen d'Archéologie Sous-Marine (IEASM), the European Institute for Underwater Archaeology. The IEASM was initially attracted to the bay by the French warships sunk at the Battle of the Nile in 1798, but it was the potential to unlock the mysteries of the sunken ancient landscapes that drew them back to Egypt once the warship excavations were complete. In 1992 new work began in the Portus Magnus, the eastern harbour of Alexandria;[14] it was extended in 1996 into the waters of Abukir Bay and continues to this day.[15] This research is undertaken in cooperation with the

Egyptian Ministry of Antiquities (formerly known as the Supreme Council of Antiquities) and supported by the Hilti Foundation. Its aims are to locate, identify and excavate the major ancient sites that vanished into the sea: the Portus Magnus in Alexandria Bay,[16] and the cities of Canopus and Thonis-Heracleion in the western part of Abukir Bay. The latter was previously thought to be two separate towns, but further investigation has proved that both names refer to the same city: 'Thonis' the Egyptian rendering, and 'Heracleion' the Greek.

Rediscovering ancient sites in the Canopic region is a challenging task. References to the towns in the ancient texts are often cursory, merely mentioning their existence and that of certain buildings and monuments. Furthermore, the distances and directions from one place to the other are difficult to interpret, since the points from which they were measured are rather ill defined. In Abukir Bay itself, very poor visibility in the water makes it very difficult for divers to search for archaeological remains. Here, at the mouth of the Nile, large amounts of sediment are discharged into the Mediterranean, making the water murky and concealing everything under a layer of sand. In only a very few locations – such as the area where Toussoun discovered the granite

6 Diver investigating a sunken vessel (ship 17) discovered in the Central Port of Thonis-Heracleion

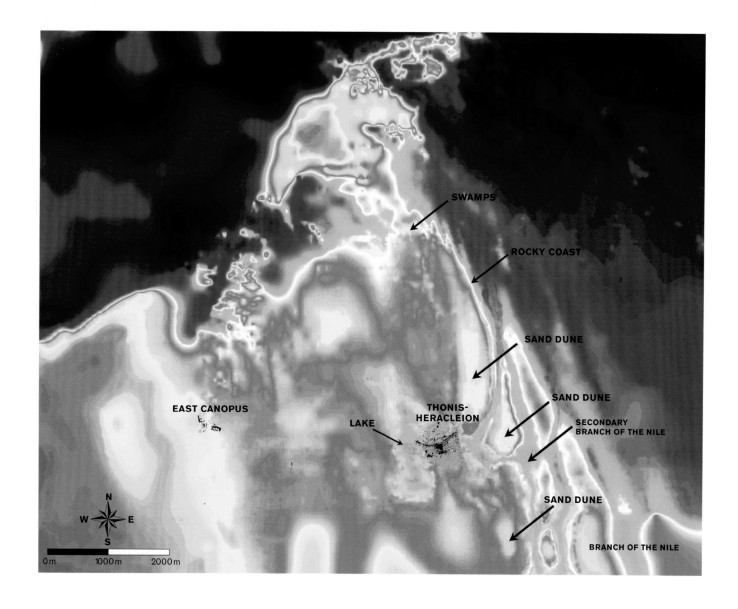

SWAMPS

ROCKY COAST

SAND DUNE

SAND DUNE

EAST CANOPUS

THONIS-
HERACLEION

LAKE

SECONDARY
BRANCH OF THE NILE

SAND DUNE

N
W · E
S

0 m   1000 m   2000 m

BRANCH OF THE NILE

7 Bathymetric chart of the submerged Canopic region according to the results of geophysical, geological and archaeological research. The areas above sea level today are shaded in brown

columns – do the remains of ancient buildings still protrude from the seabed. Finally, the region in question is enormous – 110 square kilometres. All these challenges meant that a methodology had to be developed that could gather information about the submerged landscape efficiently and target promising areas for excavation.

Recognizing that the best way to study a submerged landscape was by first making a series of detailed maps, the initial stage of the new research did not put divers into the water, but instead used a range of survey techniques.[17] One of these was side-scan sonar, which directs pulses of sound energy at the seabed and analyses the echo that is bounced off it to create a detailed bathymetric map. The technique highlighted features that stuck out of the largely sandy bottom – such as the remains of buildings – but at the larger scale it also revealed the overall shape of the submerged landscapes and some of the geographical features within them, such as the ancient course of the Canopic branch of the Nile (fig. 7).

The majority of the archaeological remains, however, are buried. The nuclear magnetic resonance (NMR) magnetometer proved to be particularly effective in looking at what lies beneath the modern seabed.[18] This technique relies upon detecting localized differences in the Earth's magnetic field created

9 The colossal statue of Hapy, the personification of the Inundation of the Nile, being raised from the waters of Abukir Bay (see pp. 102–3)

by buried structures. When the results from the magnetometer were analysed at the scale of the entire survey area, they showed a series of strong magnetic anomalies in particular locations. Subsequent investigations revealed that they were large-scale geological faults. These faults were created when the weight of buildings, coupled with extra pressure from unusually heavy floods or tidal waves, caused the sediments underneath to fracture (fig. 8).[19] Such faults, therefore, not only revealed the location of potential settlements, but also provided an explanation for their submergence (see p. 30). When the newly discovered sites were investigated in detail, the NMR technique again proved particularly effective in locating objects such as the large pieces of granite that made up the remains of the stele of Ptolemy VIII (p. 96).[20] It also further substantiated the presence of geographical features that had already been indicated by the side-scan sonar. Additionally, a sub-bottom profiler was used to reveal slices through the geological strata beneath the seabed, which indicated areas of thick sediment layers that correspond to the ancient Canopic branch of the Nile and to several ancient canals. This technique also confirmed that the areas with strong magnetic fields, which corresponded to geological faults, also had disturbed sedimentary layers.

8 A diver investigates fissures caused by the liquefaction of clay. This photograph was taken following the removal of a 2.5-metre thick layer of sediment

10 Transporting the colossal statue of a Ptolemaic pharaoh through the streets of Alexandria

Together, the different survey techniques enabled the research team to determine the outline of the submerged Canopic region and to identify the mouth and the course of the Nile's former westernmost branch. It confirmed that the area lost beneath the waters of Abukir Bay was an immense piece of land, a little over 10 by 10 kilometres in size. The survey also provided information about what this region once looked like, with a rocky strip of coastline protecting a fragile aquatic landscape of islands, canals, lakes and marshland, called a *hone* in ancient Egyptian.[21] Finally, the survey led to suggestions for the locations of the major lost cities. Using the information generated by the extensive survey work, carefully targeted underwater excavations could begin in these sunken ancient towns. This exciting work of discovery is still ongoing today.

Less than 10 metres deep, Abukir Bay is easily accessible using conventional SCUBA (self-contained underwater breathing apparatus) equipment. During each excavation season the research vessel *Princess Duda* anchors over the area to be investigated. The vessel provides not only a home for the archaeological dive team, but also space for researchers working on the many objects brought up, and facilities for their conservation and storage under carefully controlled conditions.

The excavations are conducted by small teams of divers working in shifts, which generally last around two hours. The dive time is limited both by the amount of air in the divers' cylinders and the physically demanding nature of the work. The first task is to remove the overlying blanket of sand, using a waterdredge, a tool that resembles a huge underwater vacuum cleaner. Sucking away the sand reveals the first archaeological layer, which may be parts of temples or other such monumental stone buildings, pieces of statuary, or ships sticking out of the clay of the former harbour basins. The work underwater is conducted to the same high standards as an archaeological dig on land. Just as much time is devoted to conservation and documentation – written descriptions, drawing and photography – as to discovery.

Artefacts found during the excavations are carefully bagged, labelled and then taken to the surface. Once the objects reach the deck of the ship, the team's conservator ensures that they are cleaned and stored in ways that do not damage them. Following this, the artefacts may be studied by the finds team on board the ship, or – more likely – await transportation back to the storage and conservation facility of the Ministry of Antiquities in Alexandria (fig. 10). It is here that artefact specialists from the Ministry, the University of Oxford or the IEASM's other scholarly partners can examine the objects in detail and prepare reports, doctoral theses and publications. Together, a large multinational team is studying the finds and the cities they came from and is slowly piecing back together what life was like on the Canopic coast of ancient Egypt.

Canopus

Northeast of the modern port of Abukir, an area containing numerous remains was identified in 1999, including some that clearly corresponded to Toussoun's 1933 discoveries. The site shows a 150-metre-long line of ruins, with broken smooth red granite shafts of columns, limestone building blocks and other architectural elements. Artefacts from the Byzantine period (AD 330–641), including jewels, crosses, coins and seals, indicated the remains of a large Christian establishment, probably built within a formerly pagan sanctuary.

Just to the northwest of the Byzantine structure, the survey and excavations revealed beneath almost 2 metres of sand the well-preserved foundations of an Egyptian temple built of limestone blocks, bordered by a canal on its

southern face (figs 11, 12). The remains of the temple walls stretched for over 103 metres, suggesting that it was a major shrine, the largest Egyptian temple found so far in the region.[22]

Between the temple and the Christian complex, further excavations revealed a dump of statues, maybe thrown there to be cut up and reused. In addition to the heads of pharaohs and broken sphinxes, a remarkable marble head of the god Serapis was found (p. 130). Dating from the Ptolemaic period (323–31 BC) when Egypt was under Greek rule, it belonged to a statue over 4 metres high, presumably the principal cult statue of the temple of Serapis (the Serapeum) at Canopus.[23] The dump further revealed the headless effigy of a queen (p. 92),[24] a fine Roman bust of the personification of the Nile, Neilos (p. 209),[25] and two Osiris-Canopus jars, one of which is shown on p. 133.[26] The discovery of the side walls of an important shrine, the so-called 'Naos (shrine) of

12   A diver examines and records
the measurements of the foundation
blocks of the large temple's
enclosure wall so that an accurate
plan of it can be drawn

the Decades' (p. 137), completed the long archaeological history of this object, separate pieces of which have been found over a period of 222 years.[27]

The large temple and cult statue of Serapis found next to a Christian monument are highly significant when studied in combination with the ancient texts describing the region. They indicate that the Christian complex near the great pharaonic shrine of the Serapeum corresponds to the Martyrium of Saint John and Saint Cyril.[28] The identification of the sanctuary as the Serapeum of Canopus was further confirmed by the discovery of the main temple of Thonis-Heracleion, because the distance between the two sanctuaries corresponds to that mentioned in the ancient texts.

The excavation of these imposing monumental buildings in Canopus neatly characterizes the type of 'settlement archaeology' that has been preserved underwater. Large stone buildings are not unduly affected by their submersion – in sharp contrast to the homes of the great majority of the population. Houses would have been built out of mudbrick, which dissolves in seawater, and so they have not been preserved. Consequently, evidence of everyday life in the Canopic cities is much more ephemeral, and therefore difficult to study. Much remains to be done to understand domestic life in these cities.

Thonis-Heracleion

Thonis and Heracleion are mentioned as apparently separate cities in ancient Egyptian and Greek sources. One such source is the trilingual Decree of Canopus, issued in Egypt in 238 BC. The Egyptian versions of the text refer to the 'temple of Amun-Gereb', which is called the 'sanctuary of Heracleion' in the Greek version, making it clear that Amun-Gereb was venerated at

Heracleion. Excavations on the site, however, provided evidence to prove that Thonis and Heracleion were, in fact, the same town.

In 2001, to the east of Canopus, about 6.5 kilometres from the coast, the IEASM discovered a harbour town on the west bank of the former mouth of the Canopic branch of the Nile.[29] The whole site consists of several islands, with channels crossing it, connecting the eastern harbours with a large Western Lake (fig. 14).[30] The widest transverse waterways were called by the research team the 'North Canal' and 'Grand Canal'. The numerous port basins were interconnected by a network of north–south channels. Access to the Nile was through wide openings in the lines of sand dunes that provided a sheltered anchorage.

The underwater excavations uncovered the remains of a large sanctuary located on the central island, built from limestone blocks. On the site two monuments were brought to light that were crucial in identifying the town. The first is a pink granite naos (shrine) whose few remaining inscriptions revealed that it housed the principal god of the temple, Amun-Gereb (p. 105).[31] This proved that the deity worshipped in the large sanctuary, the great temple of this town, was Amun-Gereb and, through the comparison of the Egyptian and Greek versions of the Decree of Canopus, that the name of the town was Heracleion.

A second discovery in the area of the temple was an intact granodiorite stele (p. 51)[32] bearing a decree by pharaoh Nectanebo I (r. 380–362 BC). The wording of the decree matches that on a stele from nearby Naukratis, which

13 A diver documents the bow section of a processional barge (ship 11) deliberately scuttled in the Grand Canal in Thonis-Heracleion (see pp. 188–89)

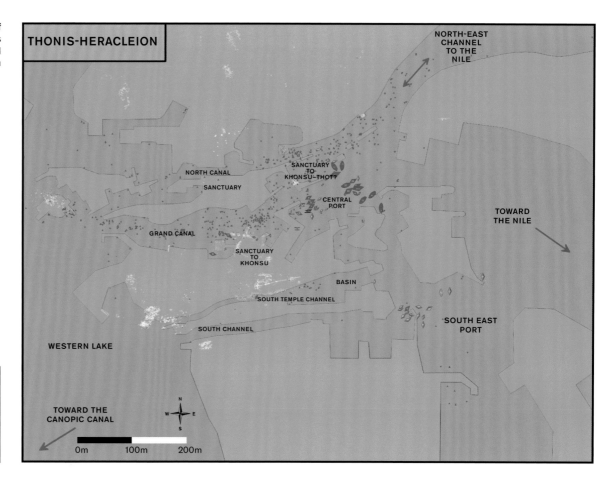

THONIS-HERACLEION

NORTH-EAST CHANNEL TO THE NILE

NORTH CANAL

SANCTUARY

SANCTUARY TO KHONSU-THOT?

CENTRAL PORT

TOWARD THE NILE

GRAND CANAL

SANCTUARY TO KHONSU

BASIN

SOUTH TEMPLE CHANNEL

SOUTH EAST PORT

SOUTH CHANNEL

WESTERN LAKE

TOWARD THE CANOPIC CANAL

N W E S

0m   100m   200m

LAND NOW SUBMERGED
WATER IN ANCIENT TIMES
□ LIMESTONE BLOCK
▼ ANCIENT ANCHOR
◆ ANCIENT SHIP

was found and deciphered in the nineteenth century and records a donation to the temple of Neith of Sais. The stele found by the IEASM in Abukir Bay indicates the Egyptian name of the town where it was erected: 'The-*hone*-of-Sais', that is, Thonis. The simultaneous discovery of these two inscribed objects – the shrine of Amun-Gereb and the stele of Thonis-Heracleion – solved a mystery of historical geography. The archaeological site that the IEASM had located was both the Heracleion of the Greeks and the Thonis of the Egyptians.

Other significant artefacts were found in the area of the temple. Close to the shrine of Amun-Gereb, a large basin of red granite was discovered, a so-called 'garden tank'[33] intended for the secret rituals known as the Mysteries of Osiris (p. 170; see chapter 4). Three colossal red granite statues over 5 metres high, representing a king, a queen and Hapy, god of fertility, abundance and the flooding of the Nile, are clear evidence of the temple's scale (pp. 98–103).[34] Beautifully crafted statues of gods and royalty, numerous bronze statuettes of divinities and ritual instruments were also found, and they clearly illustrate the forms of cult and the rituals that took place within the sanctuary.[35]

Excavation in the Grand Canal along the north side of the temple has revealed a substantial collection of artefacts that appear to have been ritually deposited in the waters.[36] Many of these, such as bronze ceremonial ladles, known as *simpula*, and ritual lead models of barques (boats), were clearly associated with the Mysteries of Osiris, and help to illustrate the sacred character of this great waterway. Furthermore, *simpula* were also discovered within the area of the temple of Amun-Gereb, which confirms that they were used in the Egyptian Osirian rituals during the celebration of the Mysteries.[37]

Many discoveries corroborate the statement by the ancient writer Diodorus that Thonis-Heracleion was Egypt's main *emporion* (trading port) on the Mediterranean Sea,[38] controlling the traffic towards the inland trading port of Naukratis some 77 kilometres further up the Canopic Branch of the Nile. Thonis-Heracleion was active from at least the seventh century BC, rising to pre-eminence as the major trading centre in the fifth to fourth centuries BC, from which time the Decree of Sais indicates that customs duties were levied there.[39] Archaeological evidence suggests that the customs administration centre was located near to the entrance of the northern channel during the early years of the city, and was transferred to the central island close to the main temple around the fourth century BC. The harbour bottom clearly demonstrates the intensity of maritime activity, with findings of over 750 ancient anchors and sixty-nine ships (figs 13, 14), the majority dating from the sixth to the second centuries BC.[40]

Located at the edge of the 'Sea of the Greeks', Thonis-Heracleion guarded the western entrance to Egypt[41] and controlled maritime traffic.[42] Once customs were cleared, goods could either be transported directly upriver to locations such as Naukratis or trans-shipped onto Egyptian river barges – *bari* – for this journey (pp. 58–59).[43] Goods from inland areas could also be transported to Thonis-Heracleion via the Western Lake, which was connected by a 3.5 kilometre canal to Canopus.[44] The port thus served as an interface between Egypt and the world beyond its shores, redistributing imports and assembling cargoes of locally produced goods for export. A network of canals assured easy communication between the port basins, Canopus and the inland areas.

The excavations have revealed a sizeable assemblage of pottery and coins, the analysis of which reveals that supply of both to the city abruptly stops at the same time at the end of the second century BC.[45] This also coincides with the erection by Ptolemy VIII Euergetes II of a colossal stele of red granite in the north of the settlement in around 118 BC (p. 96). Shortly afterwards the main temples on the central island were destroyed in a catastrophic natural event (see below). After the destruction of its major temples, the city appears to have been largely abandoned, although there is evidence of a small population remaining until the end of the eighth century AD, particularly on the central island, where a former temple was converted into a Christian religious centre, as indicated by finds of Byzantine architectural elements, jewellery and coins.[46]

Why are the cities now underwater?

How did this landscape become submerged beneath the waters of Abukir Bay? Various causes have been suggested including seismic (earthquakes and tsunamis), hydrological (floods and variations in sea level) and geological (subsidence). Research by the IEASM and teams working alongside them has revealed that, rather than one single cause, the sites in the Canopic region were subjected to elements of all three, which operated on differing timescales.[47] On the one hand there was the slow subsidence of the land that affects this part of the southeastern Mediterranean basin due to movements of the Earth's crust. There was also the long-term subsidence of the edge of the Nile Delta owing to compaction of the underlying water-saturated deposits. Together these processes would have brought about the gradual submersion of the land in the area of the Canopic cities. In addition, over the last 2,000 years the sea level has risen in the local area by 1 to 1.5 metres.[48]

The archaeological remains out in the Abukir Bay, however, are all located at a depth of around 7 metres and so clearly there was another reason behind the submergence of the sites. Core samples taken from the sediments under the bay identified the characteristic signs of 'liquefaction', whereby the ground surface literally turns from a solid into a liquid. This collapse also resulted in the fractures of the underlying sediments that were discovered by the NMR magnetometer. This was the cause of the collapse of the major temples of Thonis-Heracleion at the end of the second century BC, although it was a very localized episode of liquefaction that only appears to affect parts of the central island. The heavy temple buildings put excessive pressure on the clay soils on which they were built. The additional weight of a particularly severe flood or tsunami could have been enough to compress the sediments further and expel water contained in their clay matrix, which would quickly cause them to lose their volume and collapse with disastrous consequences.[49] It is also possible that earthquakes could have triggered similar catastrophic sedimentary failures.[50] Such collapses could both affect relatively small areas of the landscape, such as parts of the central island, as well as much larger regions, and it is likely to have been a combination of both that resulted in the disappearance of a major part of the Canopic region under the surface of the sea. The dating evidence from both Canopus and Thonis-Heracleion suggests that this occurred towards the end of the eighth century AD, although whether both cities were lost at the same time or during two different episodes of sedimentary collapse is a question for future research.

The research continues

Significant progress has been made in understanding the submerged cities of the Canopic coast, but the team is only at the beginning of a much longer journey to fully comprehend these sites. Perhaps as little as five per cent of the area has been investigated to date, and much remains to be done. While the early years of research aimed at understanding the topography of Thonis-Heracleion, current studies are now able to address specific questions. One of these concerns the location of the temple of Herakles that Herodotus visited during his voyage (c. 450 BC).[51] Excavations of the temple of Amun-Gereb and the sanctuary of Khonsu-Herakles on the central island showed that cultic activity there only began in the fourth century BC, after Herodotus' visit.[52] So where was the temple seen by Herodotus? Excavations have revealed that the city shifted towards the south over the centuries of its life, and consequently the oldest parts of Thonis-Heracleion are in the north of the settlement.[53] Excavations here have revealed the remnants of monumental buildings that appear to have been abandoned and dismantled.[54] Is the temple of Herakles to be located somewhere among these buildings in the north? Only future work can tell us for sure.

Another question concerns the traces of Greek religious activity in the city. Despite Thonis-Heracleion's dual Egyptian–Greek name, the temple architecture discovered there so far is resolutely Egyptian in its style, even for buildings dating from the Ptolemaic period. Are we to believe that there were no Greek sanctuaries in the city? The gold foundation plaque of a gymnasium dedicated by Ptolemy III[55] would suggest otherwise. The cities of the Canopic coast have yet to reveal many secrets.

15   The Thonis-Heracleion stele,
lifted from the sea. See p. 51

2 Egypt and Greece: early encounters

Aurélia Masson-Berghoff and Alexandra Villing

Traders and mercenaries

To ancient Greeks, Egypt was a strange yet fascinating land. Unbelievably fertile, its desert landscape was mysteriously inundated every year by the Nile flood. It was the home of ancient magic and wisdom, containing some of the greatest monuments ever built by humankind, with a history stretching back an unimaginable length of time, yet also in some respects fundamentally alien and incomprehensible.[1] We find traces of the Greek fascination with Egypt already in the work of the early Greek poet, Homer; in the *Odyssey* he marvels at Egypt as the 'land where the earth, giver of grain, bears the richest yield of herbs'[2] and in the *Iliad* describes Egyptian Thebes as a city of a hundred gates, 'where treasures in greatest store are laid up in men's houses'.[3]

Following the Late Bronze Age (about 1500–1100 BC), which saw considerable trade and exchange between the Minoan kings of Crete and Egyptian pharaohs,[4] Egypt went through a period of internal turmoil and maintained only limited contact with the Greek world.[5] When stability returned with the 25th dynasty (760–656 BC), Egypt first interacted with the Nubian Kingdom of Kush (in modern Sudan) where the 25th-dynasty pharaohs originated.[6] It was not until the seventh century BC, a period of fundamental socio-political change, that Egypt once more opened itself to substantial contact with the wider Mediterranean, sharing interests in trade and military security. Under the new Egyptian pharaohs of the 26th dynasty (664–525 BC), also known as the Saite dynasty from their capital city Sais, the Nile Delta developed into a cross-cultural contact zone.[7]

Close relations between the two great civilizations of Egypt and Greece were initiated by the founder of the Saite dynasty, Psamtik I (r. 664–610 BC) (fig. 16). Greek mercenaries were drafted into his army to consolidate his power and help defend the country's borders. Greek goods were traded to Egypt, and Egyptian goods to Greece. Diplomatic gifts were exchanged, and Greek aristocrats visited Egypt. Around 600 BC, the Athenian statesman Solon described in a poem how he dwelled 'at the Nile's mouth, by Canopus' shore'.[8] Thonis-Heracleion and Naukratis, where Greek traders were allowed to settle, became international ports. This was the beginning of a long history of close entanglement between Egypt and Greece that persisted through two periods of Persian rule in Egypt (525–402 and 342–332 BC), culminating in Alexander the Great's (r. 336–323 BC) defeat of Persia and establishment of a Greek dynasty in Egypt.

16   Plaque with Horus name of Psamtik I
664–610 BC
Thonis-Heracleion
Bronze. H. 11 cm | W. 7 cm
Maritime Museum, Alexandria SCA 1392

Import and export

According to the Greek historian Diodorus Siculus, it was Psamtik I who began
to promote Egyptian trade with the Mediterranean and admitted Greek and
Phoenician traders into Egypt.[9] Psamtik I's new capital, Sais, was located in
the western Nile Delta, and it was the westernmost branch of the Nile, called
the Canopic branch, that was developed as the main route for traffic and trade
from the late seventh century BC onwards, long before the foundation of the
port of Alexandria by Alexander the Great. At the entrance to the Canopic
branch, the sea port Thonis-Heracleion flourished as a trade harbour and
customs station. Some 100 kilometres farther upstream an inland harbour,
Naukratis,[10] was established, probably connected with nearby Sais by a canal.
The large amount of imports discovered at both sites[11] indicates that the two
ports were key nodes in the networks of trade and exchange that linked Egypt
with the Mediterranean. At least as far as Naukratis,[12] and possibly beyond, the
Canopic branch was navigable even for large ships. This is suggested by recent
geomorphological work (which examines the evolution and configuration of
landforms), but also by historical sources. The victory stele of king Amasis
(r. 570–526 BC), for example, records 'seagoing ships, filled with countless
Greeks, sailing on the Anu canal'. These were Greek mercenaries in the service of Amasis' predecessor.[13] Continuing further upstream, ships would have
reached Memphis, the ancient capital at the apex of the Delta, and the sites of
Upper Egypt. The neighbouring Bolbitine branch of the Nile may also have
provided direct access between Thonis-Heracleion and Sais.[14] Thus the fluvial
waterway system of the Delta constituted the vital backbone for extensive trade
links[15] which generated wealth that benefited not just the western region of the
Delta but the whole of Egypt.

   Just how busy the well-appointed harbour of Thonis-Heracleion, with its
numerous basins and canals,[16] must have been is evident from the work of the
European Institute for Underwater Archaeology.[17] So far this has uncovered
sixty-nine ships dated between the sixth and the second centuries BC, as well
as over 700 anchors (see pp. 58–59).[18] Many of the ships that called here would
have been Greek ships on their way upstream to Naukratis, which had a unique
position functioning at once as a royal Egyptian port (*pr-mryt*, meaning 'the
domain of the port') and a Greek port of trade (*emporion*). The community of
Greek traders who lived here side by side with Egyptians[19] enjoyed privileges,

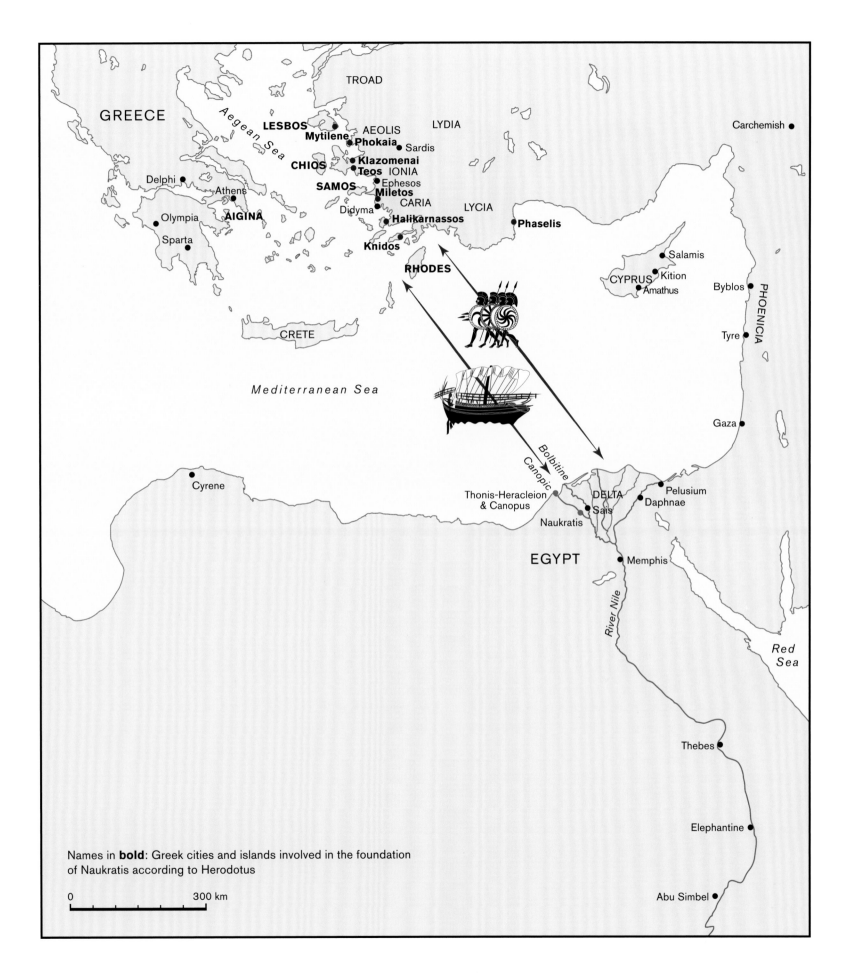

TROAD

GREECE

LYDIA

Carchemish •

Aegean Sea

LESBOS
Mytilene   AEOLIS
     Phokaia   Sardis •
CHIOS   **Klazomenai**
     Teos   IONIA
Delphi •   **SAMOS**   Ephesos •
Athens •   **Miletos**
         Didyma •   CARIA   LYCIA
Olympia •   **AIGINA**   **Halikarnassos**
Sparta •   **Phaselis**
         Knidos

         RHODES

Salamis •
CYPRUS   Kition •
     Amathus •
          Byblos •   PHOENICIA

CRETE

Tyre •

Mediterranean Sea

Gaza •

Bolbitine
Canopic

Cyrene •

Thonis-Heracleion
& Canopus •   DELTA   Pelusium •
          Daphnae •
     Naukratis •   Sais •

EGYPT   Memphis •

River Nile

*Red
Sea*

Thebes •

Elephantine •

Names in **bold**: Greek cities and islands involved in the foundation
of Naukratis according to Herodotus

0   300 km

Abu Simbel •

but was also tightly controlled by the Egyptian state. Their institutional framework was provided or sanctioned by the pharaoh.[20] As we know from the Greek historian Herodotus,[21] who visited Naukratis around the mid-fifth century BC, traders from twelve Greek islands and city-states were represented here (see fig. 17), including Aigina, Miletos, Samos, Phokaia and Rhodes, all of them major seafaring and trading powers.

Besides people, the trade that passed through Thonis-Heracleion and Naukratis included a variety of commodities. Significant quantities of metals (copper, tin and iron) are listed among the imported goods brought to Egypt on Greek and Phoenician ships in a fifth-century BC tax register, alongside wine, oil, wool and wood (the latter a scarce commodity in Egypt and long imported, especially from Lebanon).[22] Wine and oil would have been carried in pottery jars, and archaeological discoveries show that from around 640–630 BC Greek transport amphorae began to penetrate much of Egypt (p. 52).[23] Greek painted pottery, in contrast, was not a major trade item, although certain wares, especially perfume flasks, became popular from the fifth century BC (p. 53). Phoenician amphorae (for wine) and Cypriot amphorae (for wine and oil) also formed a significant proportion of the early imports, and were sometimes accompanied by kitchen pottery.[24] Silver was imported in the form of coins, but at first only used as weighed bullion.[25] Among the many coins found at Thonis-Heracleion and Naukratis, *tetradrachms* minted in Athens are particularly numerous (fig. 18); imitations were minted locally at Thonis-Heracleion in the fourth century BC.[26] Silver formed the basis of economic exchanges and of the Egyptian taxation system,[27] and Egypt – lacking its own resources – had to import this precious metal, mostly from the Greek world. Copper and lead, although far less precious, played an important role in the production of countless commodities in Egypt and were most likely sourced from Cyprus and Greece.[28] Lead ingots have recently been discovered in Thonis-Heracleion, probably originating from the mines of Laurion in Greece.[29] Since lead is a by-product of silver mining, the unique and wide corpus of lead objects[30] uncovered in Thonis-Heracleion may indirectly reflect the scale of the silver trade.

Egyptian exports to Greece included vital supplies of grain, but also natural resources such as alum and natron, which were especially important in fabric dyeing.[31] In addition, Egypt was well known for semi-luxury goods such

18 Athenian *tetradrachms* with the head of Athena and the owl
450–406 BC
Found in Naukratis; from Athens
Silver
W. 16.54–16.76 g
British Museum 1905,0309.1–3

as papyrus, perfume and amulets.[32] Some of these were produced at Naukratis itself. Workshops in the town catered for both local and global demand; their products included widely exported perfume flasks (p. 56) as well as scarabs and amulets, which were valued across the Mediterranean world for their protective properties (p. 54). Metal production took place at Naukratis[33] as well as Thonis-Heracleion,[34] though much of this was probably for local use. The discovery at both sites of an impressive number of weights conforming to a variety of different standards (Egyptian, Greek, Phoenician and Persian) provides further evidence for the thriving commercial activities in these bustling harbour towns.[35]

To facilitate the collection of import and export taxes and to control the influx and movements of foreigners, the Egyptian authorities attempted to restrict traders to certain routes and areas.[36] Both Thonis-Heracleion and Naukratis benefited from this, notably from the strict rules that limited access to the Canopic branch and that were probably in place under pharaoh Amasis and perhaps earlier. According to Herodotus:

> *Naukratis was in the past the only trading port in Egypt. Whoever came to any other mouth of the Nile had to swear that he had not come intentionally, and had then to take his ship and sail to the Canopic mouth; or if he could not sail against contrary winds, he had to carry his cargo in bar-boats [*bari*][37] around the Delta until he came to Naukratis. In such esteem was Naukratis held.[38]*

Such measures appear to have been abolished during the Persian periods (the Persians conquered Egypt twice, in 525 and again in 342 BC). Yet this did not hinder profitable commerce, for Naukratis and Thonis-Heracleion continued to flourish.[39] During the 30th dynasty (380–342 BC), the last native dynasty, deposed by the Persians and followed by Macedonian and later Ptolemaic kings of Greek origin (323–31 BC), the entry restrictions may have been reinstated.[40] According to the royal decree of Nectanebo I (r. 380–362 BC), all goods imported from the Mediterranean sea ('Sea of the Greeks') were subject to customs fees at Thonis-Heracleion, while at Naukratis taxes were levied on 'all things that appear', meaning anything traded or produced at Naukratis (p. 51).[41]

Greeks and Carians in pharaoh's army

From as early as the seventh century BC, foreign mercenaries played an important role in Egyptian history. Many of them were Greeks from the region of Ionia (parts of the Aegean coast of modern Turkey and the Greek islands opposite, see fig. 17) and the island of Rhodes, as well as Carians, close neighbours of the Ionians who were renowned as warriors.[42]

Greek and Carian mercenaries were first employed around 670–660 BC by the pharaoh Psamtik I to help him usurp power from his rival kings and shake off foreign domination.[43] Later Greek authors gave a mythical cast to their arrival: an oracle is said to have told the pharaoh that 'men of bronze coming from the sea' would come to his aid. Soon after this a group of Ionians and

Carians put ashore in Egypt, 'voyaging for plunder', and astounded locals by their unfamiliar appearance. They were equipped with the impressive bronze armour of the Greek *hoplites* (fig. 19), the citizen soldiers of the independent Greek city-states, who were well trained from frequent armed clashes between rival cities. Psamtik seized his chance and put them on his payroll.[44] We know of the rich rewards that awaited them (gold and the gift of a 'city') from the inscription on an Egyptian statue that a returning mercenary, Pedon, dedicated in the early sixth century BC to a sanctuary in his native Ionia.[45]

Alongside other foreigners (including Phoenicians, Cypriots, Aramaeans and Jews),[46] Greeks and Carians soon became a fixture in the Egyptian army. As expert sailors and shipbuilders, Greeks and Carians would also have contributed to building up the Egyptian navy under Necho II (r. 610–595 BC).[47] Some were probably stationed at Thonis-Heracleion, where Greek armour (fig. 20) and evidence for the production of lead sling bullets – a common weapon in Greek warfare – have been found.[48] Serving under their own generals, these soldiers took part in perilous campaigns that led them all over Egypt and beyond. We catch glimpses of them about 605 BC at the battle of Carchemish in Syria, fighting for the pharaoh Necho II alongside Assyria and against Babylonia,[49] and sailing more than 1,000 km up the river Nile during Psamtik II's (r. 595–589 BC) Nubian campaign in 593 BC. Stopping off at the grand temple of Abu Simbel (fig. 21), a troop of men from Rhodes and the Ionian cities of Teos and Kolophon, under their own Greek commander, scratched their names on the colossal statues of Ramses II, creating some of the earliest preserved 'tourist' graffiti (fig. 22).

Foreign mercenaries also continued to be deployed in internal power struggles. This could lead to conflict and anti-foreign sentiment. In his fight against the usurper Amasis, pharaoh Apries (r. 589–570 BC) had relied on a fleet of Greek warriors with which he threatened to take over Amasis' stronghold at Sais.[50] Following his victory, Amasis moved Greek mercenaries from

19 Stele showing a Greek *hoplite*
525–500 BC
Naukratis
Limestone
H. 39 cm | W. 30 cm
British Museum 1900,0214.21

20 Greek helmet of the 5th–4th century BC before restoration
Thonis-Heracleion
Bronze
H. 34 cm | W. 23.5 cm
Maritime Museum, Alexandria SCA 1026

21 The temple of Abu Simbel

22 Graffiti left by Greek soldiers on the legs of the colossal statues of Ramses II at Abu Simbel

their garrisons in the eastern Delta to Memphis and appointed them as his royal guards, as well as restructuring and granting privileges to the Greek port of Naukratis: these were clever strategies to win the Greeks over, while at the same time keeping them under tight control. Similarly the diplomatic gifts that Amasis (see p. 70) and other pharaohs made to sanctuaries in Greece and that the Greeks interpreted as signs of 'philhellenism' (that is, his friendly feelings towards Greeks) were also strategically aimed at promoting alliances and the loyalty and supply of mercenaries.[51]

The role of religion: identity and interaction

Religion and religious spaces (sanctuaries) played an important role in the lives of Egyptians and Greeks, as well as in their relations with each other. For the foreign people who visited or inhabited the Nile Delta, and for the Egyptians who were their hosts, religion could be a means of retaining one's own identity and culture. But it could also provide a means of adapting to a foreign environment and negotiating new paths in a meeting of cultures.

Greek sanctuaries and cosmopolitan offerings at Naukratis

From the seventh century BC, Naukratis became a key node in the Mediterranean network of trade and travel routes that linked Egypt with Greece, Cyprus, the Phoenician coast, North Africa, Sardinia, Etruria and Spain. It is the Greek sanctuaries of Naukratis (figs 23, 24) that tell us much about these connections

23 Between 1884 and 1903, Flinders Petrie and David Hogarth excavated the sanctuaries and cemetery of Naukratis

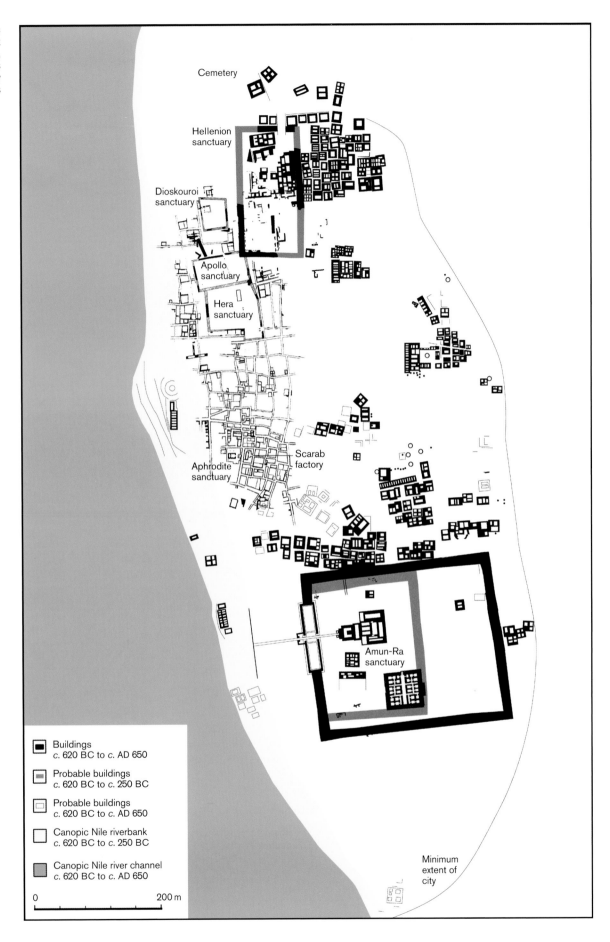

24 Plan of Naukratis incorporating all fieldwork by Petrie, Gardner, Hogarth, Coulson, Leonard, Thomas and Villing and preliminary geophysics results

Cemetery

Hellenion sanctuary

Dioskouroi sanctuary

Apollo sanctuary

Hera sanctuary

Scarab factory

Aphrodite sanctuary

Amun-Ra sanctuary

Minimum extent of city

Buildings
c. 620 BC to *c.* AD 650

Probable buildings
c. 620 BC to *c.* 250 BC

Probable buildings
c. 620 BC to *c.* AD 650

Canopic Nile riverbank
c. 620 BC to *c.* 250 BC

Canopic Nile river channel
c. 620 BC to *c.* AD 650

0   200 m

and the people that created them. Already Herodotus underlines the sanctuaries' significance when he tells us that

> *Amasis became a friend of the Greeks [philhellene] and granted them a number*
> *of privileges; to those who came to Egypt he gave Naukratis as a city [polis] to*
> *live in. To those who sailed there but did not want to live there he gave lands on*
> *which they might erect altars and sanctuaries to the gods.*[52]

While the rediscovery and early excavation of Naukratis (between 1884 and 1903) by pioneering archaeologists Sir William Matthew Flinders Petrie and David Hogarth (fig. 23) have shown that, in fact, Naukratis had existed since the time of Psamtik I, nearly a century before Amasis,[53] they have also amply confirmed the importance of religion for the city from its earliest days. A considerable area of the town of Naukratis – home to over 10,000 people at its peak[54] – was occupied by sanctuaries, both Greek and Egyptian (fig. 28). For ancient Greeks, sanctuaries were an essential feature of any trading port. Here, traders and travellers could seek or acknowledge divine protection for perilous sea journeys and important business deals, and find familiar and secure spaces to engage in contact and conviviality. For those that stayed longer, shared rituals helped forge a new local community.

At Naukratis, some of the Greek sanctuaries were dedicated to deities traditionally worshipped as patrons of seafaring, such as the Dioskouroi, the twin sons of Zeus, and Aphrodite, the goddess of love but also guardian of safe voyages. Others were 'branches' of the main sanctuaries of the traders' mother cities, and ensured divine sanction for the foreign venture as well as locally flying the city's 'flag'. They included the sanctuaries of Hera, of Apollo, and of Zeus (the latter not yet located in excavations). The largest of the sanctuaries was the Hellenion, a joint foundation by nine Greek cities and also the heart of the port's Greek administration (see p. 64).

Rich finds from all these sanctuaries show that they were heavily frequented. From the early days of the port, the highly mobile Greek elites – especially those from the powerful trading cities of East Greece – flocked to Naukratis, combining the quest for profit with the pleasure of feasting in the company of the local high-class courtesans, *hetairai*, said to be of exceptional beauty (see p. 52).[55] During ritual festivities, wine would have been drunk and animals such as sheep, goats or pigs slaughtered, a portion burned on the altar for the god and the remainder consumed by the feasting community. We hear how one trader based at Naukratis, Herostratos, invited 'his relations and closest friends to a feast in the temple' of Aphrodite, to celebrate his safe arrival after a stormy sea voyage (see p. 60).[56] Yet the attraction of Egypt was not just economic. A visit to Naukratis, the gateway to rich and ancient Egypt,

25 Bowl of Sostratos
Late 7th century BC
Chios, Greece
Pottery
H. 17.7 cm | D. 38.8 cm
British Museum 1888,0601.456

26 Cypriot horse-and-rider figure
c. 600–525 BC
Found in Naukratis, sanctuary
of Aphrodite. Probably made
in the region of Salamis
Terracotta
H. 9.8 cm | L. 9.4 cm | W. 4.3 cm
British Museum 1911,0606.1

27 Egyptian figure of Horus-the-child on a horse
c. 450–350 BC
Limestone
Naukratis, Hellenion sanctuary,
H. 10 cm | L. 11.75 cm
British Museum 1900,0214.27

The figure has a Greek inscription
mentioning a nymph.

also promised intellectual gain, social 'capital' and prestige.[57] In the fifth century BC, Herodotus travelled to Egypt seeking to understand history and tracing the roots of his own culture. Many philosophers were said to have travelled to Egypt, such as, in the fourth century BC, Plato, who supposedly financed his voyage by selling Athenian olive oil.[58]

From around 630/620 BC, the traders and travellers that came to Naukratis brought figurines as gifts for the gods and fine pottery for feasting and dedication in the town's sanctuaries. Many thousands of pottery fragments have been uncovered by archaeologists, often bearing the dedicator's name or that of the deity.[59] One example is the fine bowl, made on the Greek island of Chios, that Sostratos dedicated to Aphrodite (fig. 25). Sostratos was a member of a prominent family of traders that operated across the Mediterranean, including Italy, and amassed a great fortune. According to Herodotus,[60] their riches even surpassed the wealth of yet another intrepid Greek sea captain, Kolaios. He supposedly made a massive profit in Spain in the 630s BC, after accidentally being blown off course during a trading voyage to Naukratis.

Offerings in the Greek sanctuaries originated not just from across the Aegean Sea but also from Cyprus (figurines), Phoenicia (cosmetics containers carved from Red Sea shells), and Italy (pottery). Cypriot figurines (fig. 26), most of them probably dedicated by Greeks, were especially popular dedications between the late seventh and the late sixth century BC. While few offerings of clearly Egyptian type are known from the Greek sanctuaries of Naukratis, a typical Egyptian 'offering spoon' was presented in the Aphrodite sanctuary,[61] and several Egyptian limestone figures of Horus-the-child (the son of Isis and Osiris) on horseback – one of them bearing a fragmentary Greek inscription – were found in the area of the Hellenion sanctuary (fig. 27).[62] Their findspot was not far from the sanctuary of the Dioskouroi, the Greek twin deities who are also often shown as riders. Excavations by the British Museum in 2014 and 2015

28 Reconstruction of the international harbour town of Naukratis with its Egyptian and Greek temples

uncovered large amounts of sixth-century BC Egyptian pottery associated with this cult, suggesting that the Greek sanctuaries of Naukratis were less purely 'Greek' than previously thought (fig. 28).[63]

In fact, Naukratis was at least as much an Egyptian as a Greek town, a point that has sometimes been neglected by scholars fascinated with the site's Greek aspects. We see this also in the town's religious life: not only Greek sanctuaries but also Egyptian temples and cults flourished at Naukratis from the 26th dynasty onwards, no less than they did in Thonis-Heracleion and Canopus.

Egyptian temples and animal devotion

The main Egyptian deity revered in Naukratis was the ram-headed god Amun-Ra Baded, a local manifestation of Amun of Thebes (fig. 29).[64] Greeks identified him with the Greek god Zeus Thebaios, as shown by the Greek inscription on a fourth-century BC statue base discovered outside the sanctuary's entrance.[65] By the Ptolemaic period, Amun-Ra Baded's majestic sanctuary dominated the landscape of Naukratis (figs 24, 30).[66] Yet his cult goes back as far as the sixth century BC.[67] He, his wife Mut and their son Khonsu formed a divine triad that was worshipped not only at Naukratis but also at Thonis-Heracleion. We see them represented in a procession of deities that adorns a pyramid-shaped bronze inscribed with the name of pharaoh Amasis (p. 70).[68]

Animal worship was a significant trend in Egyptian religion from the 26th dynasty onwards, which led to a dramatic proliferation of animal mummies buried in religious complexes.[69] The most ancient and important of these complexes was at Saqqara, the sacred necropolis close to Memphis, and featured underground galleries and sanctuaries dedicated to various deities.[70] Mummified bulls were interred there from the reign of Amenhotep III (r. *c.* 1391–1353 BC),

29 Sculptor's model in the shape of a ram
c. 450–350 BC
Naukratis
Limestone
H. 6.9 cm | W. 10.2 cm | D. 11.35 cm
British Museum EA 27528

30 Reconstruction of the magnificent temple-precinct of Amun-Ra Baded

but the burials of ibises, hawks, dogs and cats appeared much later, during the Late Period (664–332 BC). Each species was buried in its own 'House of Rest' (animal mummy cemetery), some by the millions. Thonis-Heracleion and Naukratis were not isolated from such practices.

In 2012, the IEASM team at Thonis-Heracleion uncovered a small shrine dedicated to the composite god Khonsu-Thoth.[71] This deity, also much revered in Naukratis, combined the functions of the avenger and healer god Khonsu with the god of justice Thoth.[72] Thirteen small limestone sarcophagi[73] were found near the shrine. They probably once contained the mummified remains of falcons and ibises (figs 31, 32). These birds were sacred to Khonsu and Thoth, who, when worshipped as individual deities, were often depicted in bird form.[74] A bronze plaque associating Amasis with Khonsu-Thoth (fig. 33) was discovered in the same area, and Amasis is known to have founded various animal cemeteries across Egypt, including one for ibises.[75] It is significant that the limestone sarcophagi and the bronze plaque naming Amasis were all found clustered at the harbour entrance north of the central island (fig. 14), at the mouth of the northeast channel which once connected with the Canopic branch. Here, Khonsu-Thoth, 'keeper of gates, entrances and passages, letting through the righteous and warding off the nefarious', ritually protected Egypt's maritime border.[76] This is one of the earliest occupied areas in Thonis-Heracleion and was abandoned at the end of the fifth century BC when the northeast channel silted up.[77]

Bronzes representing animals were common in animal cemeteries, although not as common as bronzes of the god Osiris, his wife Isis and their son Horus-the-child.[78] Bronze fittings added to the animal mummy, and bronze 'votive boxes' or 'mummy-cases' that were supposed to contain an animal mummy, were sold to worshippers by weight, sometimes costing the equivalent

31 Group of sarcophagi, probably for ibis or falcon mummies
664–525 BC
Thonis-Heracleion
Limestone
L. *c.* 35 cm
Maritime Museum, Alexandria: SCA 1513, 1514, 1517

32 The sarcophagi as they were found, having been excavated from under 1.8 m of sediment

**33 Plaque naming the pharaoh
Amasis and the Egyptian god
Khonsu-Thoth**
570–526 BC
Thonis-Heracleion
Bronze
H. 10 cm | W. 8.5 cm
Maritime Museum, Alexandria SCA 1310

34 Ibis figure
6th–2nd century BC
Thonis-Heracleion
Bronze
H. 10 cm | W. 8.8 cm | D. 3.3 cm
Maritime Museum, Alexandria SCA 1087

of several months' salary for an average worker.[79] A large find at Naukratis[80] comprised one hundred of these boxes, mainly topped by figures of reptiles. Except for one large box (p. 68), all were small, often less than 5 centimetres in length. The large and heavy Egyptian mongoose 'mummy-case', discovered in the same context, must have been worth a small fortune.[81]

Herodotus considered animal devotion a curiosity and probably exaggerated some traits of this worship, which was so alien to the Greeks.[82] Similarly, Diodorus Siculus, who visited Egypt around 59 BC, found practices related to sacred animals 'astonishing and beyond belief'[83] and spent a portion of his book on Egypt describing animal worship there and the reasons behind it. For many Greeks such practices, looked at from the outside, served to illustrate the differences that set themselves apart from others. They were cited to paint a picture of Egyptian life as an upside-down version of Greek reality:[84]

> *I couldn't bring myself to make an alliance with you; neither our manners nor our customs agree, but stand far apart from each other. You worship the cow, whereas I sacrifice it to the gods. You hold the eel to be a great divinity, we regard it as by far the greatest delicacy. You eat no pork, but I like it very much. You worship the dog, I beat it when I catch it eating my food. … If you see a cat in any trouble, you cry, but I am perfectly happy to kill and skin it. You see the field-mouse as mighty, for me it doesn't count at all.*[85]

Herodotus recounted that hawks and ibises were revered to the extreme that 'whoever kills an ibis or a hawk, with intention or without, must die for it'.[86] Yet, from one single cemetery in the religious complex of Saqqara alone, over four million ibis mummies have been excavated, and millions more were uncovered in Abydos.[87] Some were just dummies or contained only a few bones of the animal,[88] or bits and pieces of other species (including human!),[89] but some contained a complete animal, as should have been the rule[90] (p. 69), or even multiple animals wrapped together.[91] The creatures rarely died a natural death,[92] and during life were probably held captive in harsh conditions.[93]

The role and value of an animal mummy varied greatly. Sacred bulls, such as the Apis bull revered in Memphis (see p. 121),[94] had a status far above the millions of other animals buried in the cemeteries. The Apis bull was seen as the living incarnation of a god: carefully selected and unique until it died, it was deified after its death and usually buried in a solid, expensive container.[95] Other animals could be seen as offerings dedicated to gods that were associated with specific animals,[96] or as messengers between mortals and gods.[97]

A shared religion?

In societies such as ancient Greece or Egypt, where multiple gods were worshipped, equating gods with similar characteristics, or even adopting a new god, were ways in which people from different cultures could engage with each other and find common ground. Even though they differed in some aspects, Greeks

'Nearly all the names of the gods came to Greece from Egypt'

(Herodotus, *Histories* II.50)

and Egyptians recognized similarities between many of their gods.[98] They would have learned about each other's religions in different ways, ranging from everyday contact and observation to conversations between Egyptian priests and curious Greeks and religious 'sightseeing' or pilgrimage. Graffiti in the temple of Osiris at Abydos show that, just like Egyptians, foreigners visited important Egyptian shrines – from ordinary soldiers to emperors such as Hadrian.[99]

Mercenaries in particular participated in Egyptian cult, even if foreigners were probably excluded from some sacred spaces and knowledge.[100] Thus Greeks and Carians dedicated Egyptian-style figures to Egyptian gods, sometimes with inscriptions noting an equation with a deity from their own pantheon.[101] At Memphis, one of the most ancient but also cosmopolitan of Egyptian cities, their funerary rites combined traditional Egyptian with traditional Greek and Carian elements (p. 57). By the fourth century BC it was the descendants of these mercenaries at Memphis, known as Hellenomemphites and Caromemphites, who, as fellow-soldiers, played a key role in introducing the conquering Alexander the Great and his successor Ptolemy I Soter I to Egyptian culture.[102]

Yet it is outside the great public sanctuaries and cemeteries, in the more private sphere of the household, that everyday beliefs and ritual practices would have been shared and absorbed most deeply. At Naukratis numerous Egyptian terracotta and stone figurines were found in the port's residential areas. Nude women, phallic representations of Horus-the-child or images of the dwarf-god Bes make up a repertoire of figures associated with protection, fertility and cyclical renewal that is typical of contemporary Egyptian sites, including Thonis-Heracleion (see pp. 210–11).[103] They suggest that Egyptian religion, and notably rituals related to fertility and the Inundation of the Nile, were practised here at least from the sixth or fifth century BC onwards, indicating a mixed Greek–Egyptian population and probably mixed marriages. Ethnically mixed marriages were not unusual in Late Period Egypt and commonly involved Egyptian women and foreign settlers.[104]

With their intimate knowledge of both cultures, resident mercenaries and traders, alongside other 'cultural brokers' such as translators, played a crucial role in facilitating exchange and understanding between Greece and Egypt. They also would have carried Egyptian ideas and knowledge back into the Greek world: myths about the origins of the gods, ideas about the afterlife, skills in medicine and architecture, and techniques of craftsmanship.[105]

**The Decree of Sais
on the Thonis-Heracleion stele**
380 BC
Thonis-Heracleion
Black granodiorite
H. 1.99 m | W. 88 cm | D. (max) 33 cm
National Museum of Alexandria 285, SCA 277

Tax and trade

In the first year of his reign, the pharaoh Nectanebo I (r. 380–362 BC) issued a royal decree regarding the taxation of trade passing through Thonis-Heracleion and Naukratis. This royal decree is known from two almost identical stelae, both in pristine condition. One was unearthed in 1899 in the sacred enclosure dedicated to Amun-Ra Baded in Naukratis;[106] the second was retrieved from the seabed more than a hundred years later in the sanctuary of Amun-Gereb in Thonis-Heracleion.[107]

The decree stipulates that a portion of tax must be given to the sanctuary of Neith, the patron goddess of Sais, the capital of Egypt in the 26th dynasty. This is visually represented by the semicircular section, or lunette, at the top of the stele, which shows a symmetrical scene of the king making offerings to Neith. To the right, the king appears with the red crown, which symbolizes his dominion over Lower Egypt (the Delta), and he carries a tray supporting ritual vases and bread loaves. To the left, he wears a *tcheni* crown – composed of two tall ostrich feathers set on a sun disc framed by horizontal ram's horns – and offers a wide necklace ending with falcons' heads, the gold *usekh*-collar. In the centre are two back-to-back representations of Neith, probably depicting two cult statues of the goddess. Neith, the 'Mistress of Sais', is seated on a throne wearing the red crown and a long tight-fitting dress. She holds a *was*-sceptre (a symbol of power) in one hand and an *ankh*-sign (a symbol of life) in the other. A winged sun disc with two *uraei* (sacred cobras and emblems of supreme power) crowns the scene.

Below, the hieroglyphic text is arranged in fourteen columns. The most important passage refers to special taxes levied on imports and exports. Nectanebo I declares that an additional tenth of the taxes due to the royal treasury on all goods coming from the Mediterranean[108] to Thonis-Heracleion and those exported from Naukratis are to be donated to the temple of Neith in Sais.[109] The decree only specifies precious commodities: silver and wood (both 'timber' and 'processed wood'), of which Egypt had little, appear alongside gold. Royal donations to a sanctuary were customary in Egypt and similar taxes on merchandise existed previously.[110] Nectanebo's decree counters the one issued by the Persian king Cambyses II (r. 530–522 BC), son of Cyrus the Great (r. 559–530 BC), following the Persian invasion of Egypt in 525 BC. The fact that Cambyses halved or even put an end to such donations partly explains the bitter memories Persian rule left in Egypt.[111]

The decree stipulates where this version of the stele should be set up: 'at the mouth of the Mediterranean sea, in the town by the name of The-*hone*-of-Sais', thus providing the Egyptian name of Thonis-Heracleion. '*Hone*' can be understood as the delta formed at the mouth of major branches of the Nile, which corresponds precisely to the landscape of Thonis-Heracleion.[112] In the same place on the other stele is a reference to Naukratis.

The quality and intricacy of the design and the text, using multiple stylistic features of the past and cryptic scripts, mark these stelae as masterpieces of the 30th dynasty. They were probably produced together in a temple workshop at Sais, under the scrutiny of the priests of Neith. [AMB]

'His Majesty [Nectanebo I] decreed: let there be given one-tenth of the gold, of the silver, of the timber, of the processed wood and of all things coming from the sea of the Hau-Nebut [Mediterranean Sea], of all goods that are reckoned for the benefit of the royal domain in the town named hone *[Thonis-Heracleion], as well as one-tenth of the gold, of the silver, and of all things that appear in the domain of the port called Keredj [Naukratis] on the bank of the Anu [Canopic branch?], which are reckoned for the benefit of the royal domain, to become divine offerings to my mother Neith … This shall be recorded on the present stele to be set up at the mouth of the sea of the Hau-Nebut in the town by the name of The-*hone-of Sais.'*[113]

Cargoes of wine

This Greek amphora[114] once contained wine from Klazomenai, a Greek city on the west coast of Turkey and one of the cities trading through Naukratis. From around 640–630 BC such amphorae began to reach Egypt, appearing across the Nile Delta and as far south as Luxor. Wine from Klazomenai and the Greek islands of Chios, Samos and Lesbos was especially popular.

Many of the traders that visited Egypt were probably members of the Greek elite, for whom a visit to rich and exotic Egypt brought both profit and prestige. One of them was Charaxos, the brother of the poetess Sappho of Lesbos. Around 600 BC Charaxos is said to have travelled to Naukratis with a cargo of Lesbian wine – only to fall in love with a local courtesan, spending a fortune on releasing her from slavery. Sappho's poems record her mockery of this, but also show her anxiety 'for Charaxos to arrive home, bringing his ship undamaged' and 'laden' with profit.[115]

Imported wine was destined for both resident foreigners and the Egyptian elite, who had for some time been consuming wine from Phoenicia and the Levant as well as producing wine themselves.[116] Wine was placed in rich tombs and consumed and offered at festivals and rituals, and Egyptian temples such as the sanctuary of Neith at Sais received imported wine and oil directly as a portion of tax.

This amphora has been repaired, showing that Egyptians valued Greek amphorae not just for their contents but also as containers, to be repaired and reused. Herodotus describes how he saw Greek and Phoenician transport amphorae being gathered at Memphis and filled with water for people in the desert.[117] [AV]

A Greek wine amphora from Egypt
c. 550–500 BC
Tell Dafana (Daphnae)
Pottery
H. 75 cm
British Museum EA 22343

Greek scent

This small pottery *lekythos* (oil flask), decorated with the image of a panther,[118] was designed to hold small amounts of perfumed oil. Such juglets were mass-produced in Athens' flourishing pottery workshops in the late fifth and fourth centuries BC and were popular both at home and abroad.[119]

Greek, especially East Greek fine-ware pottery had reached Thonis-Heracleion from around 630 BC, most of it brought by East Greek traders on their way to Naukratis. But Persia's conquest of Egypt in 525 BC and its crushing of the Ionian revolt in 494 BC, together with the rise of Athens after the defeat of the Persians in 480–479 BC, transformed trade and politics in the eastern Mediterranean. At this time, Athenian products dominated the fine-ware pottery trade.

The limited range of shapes found at most Egyptian sites (mostly small oil flasks, drinking cups and a few large mixing bowls) shows that Athenian pottery was not high-status dining ware here, as it was elsewhere in the Mediterranean.[120] Instead, it reflects different social practices and a special interest in imported perfume, a prestigious commodity used in both religious and personal life. Perfume vessels traditionally constitute a major category among fine-ware pottery imports in Egypt, and some, such as Athenian *lekythoi*, were also copied by local potters. [AV]

An Athenian perfume bottle
c. 410–400 BC
Thonis-Heracleion
Pottery
H. 8.3 cm | D. 5.4 cm
National Museum of Alexandria SCA 247

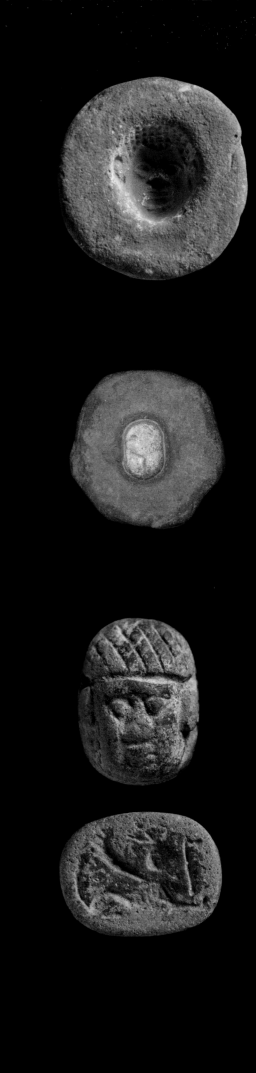

Amulets and amulet moulds
600–570 BC
Naukratis

Moulds in terracotta
1.6 to 4 cm
British Museum 1920,0417.2;
1965,0930.902; 1965,0930.917;
2012,5020.1; EA 26902; EA 26918

Amulets in faience and Egyptian blue
1 to 1.45 cm
British Museum EA 27570; EA 29961;
EA 30705; EA 66443; EA 66452;
EA 66487; EA 66493; EA 66514

The 'Scarab Factory'

Small Egyptian amulets, in the form of scarab beetles or Egyptian gods and symbols, were popular not just among Egyptians but also Greeks and Phoenicians. Designed to be worn or carried for protection, they could also function (in the case of scarabs and scaraboids) as seals, since their bases were inscribed with designs and/or hieroglyphs.

In 1885, the archaeologist Flinders Petrie uncovered the discarded waste of a workshop in the vicinity of the sanctuary of Aphrodite in Naukratis.[121] This workshop, known as the 'Scarab Factory', was active mainly between 600 and 570 BC. It specialized in the mass production of amulets, primarily in the form of scarab beetles in faience (quartz ceramic with a glaze) and 'Egyptian blue' (a synthetic pigment). Amulets, hundreds of associated moulds and some raw material used in the production were discovered in the rubble.

Terracotta moulds in a variety of shapes and sizes were used to form the back of the amulets, by pressing faience paste into them; traces of the paste are sometimes preserved. Shapes include scarabs but also scaraboids in the form of simple domes, lions, rams' heads (common motifs in Greece as well as Egypt) and Black African heads, the latter in particular catering to Greek ideas of foreign and far-away Egypt. There are also moulds for amulets of the *wedjat*-eye, the sacred eye of Horus and a powerful protective charm, and of the dwarf-god Bes, guardian of pregnant women and children.

The highly varied stamped or incised motifs on the underside of scarabs and scaraboids also betray inspiration from different cultures. They include the Egyptian human-headed sphinx, the winged horse Pegasus from Greek mythology, and orientalizing creatures, such as griffins. Some of the hieroglyphs name Amun, the principal Egyptian god revered in Naukratis since the 26th dynasty (664–525 BC);[122] others are degraded, suggesting that the true meaning escaped the craftsmen who produced them. It is possible that the employees of this workshop were as cosmopolitan as the town of Naukratis itself, including Egyptians and Phoenicians (both with a strong tradition of producing faience amulets) and Greeks.

Greek traders and other visitors to Naukratis provided a ready market for the workshop's products. Greeks had been familiar with both Egyptian and Phoenician-made Egyptian-style amulets since the tenth century BC. They were attracted not only by the potent protection offered by these amulets from an ancient civilization famous for its powerful magic, but also by the social prestige these exotic goods carried.[123] Egyptian amulets were used especially for protecting women and children and were placed in tombs or dedicated in sanctuaries. The products of the Naukratis workshop were distributed as far as the Levant, Tunisia, southern Russia, Greece, Italy, Spain, Libya and Cyprus. They chart the wide range of the trading networks that linked Egypt with the Mediterranean world via Naukratis. [AMB]

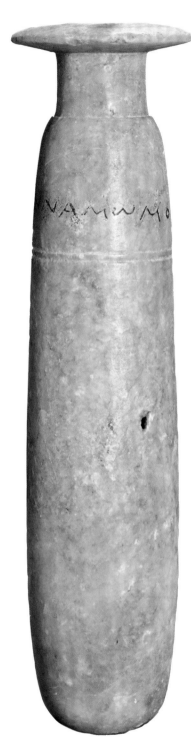

Egyptian perfume

Egyptian perfume was highly prized in the ancient world, and elegant Egyptian perfume containers, or *alabastra*, are frequent finds in Greek and Etruscan tombs.[124] The Greek inscription on this *alabastron* identifies the type of perfume it once contained: 'cinnamon' (κιννάμωμον). The vessel has an elongated shape with a narrow neck and a wide flat mouth, ideal for containing and dispensing precious liquids. It is made from alabaster, the yellow-white and partly translucent stone that gave these vessels their name.

Alabastra had a long tradition. In the late eighth and seventh centuries BC, such containers were usually limited to royal tombs or palaces,[125] but from the sixth century onwards they became distributed more widely across the Mediterranean, as part of a thriving international trade in semi-luxuries.[126]

Naukratis was an important centre for the trade in *alabastra*, but also for their production, at least from the late sixth century BC onwards. Thousands of drill cores, characteristic leftovers of their production, as well as fragments of unfinished calcite vessels, were discovered in the sanctuary of Apollo.[127]

Alabastra were probably traded with their content, which included prized perfumes, unguents or oils used in medical prescriptions. The names of spices or herbs used in their manufacture are sometimes inscribed on them, for example fenugreek, sweet marjoram or – as here – cinnamon.[128] According to the Roman writer Pliny the Elder, unguent of cinnamon was exceedingly expensive.[129]   [AMB]

Imported *alabastron*
323–31 BC (Greek period)
Egypt
Gypsum alabaster
H. 20.3 cm
British Museum 1895,1020.5

Drill cores
Late 6th–early 5th century BC
Naukratis
Calcite ('Egyptian alabaster')
H. 0.8 to 3 cm
British Museum EA 27628

'Hybrid' tombstones

Foreigners living in Egypt often adopted the Egyptian way of life and death, at least in part. This is especially true for mercenaries and their families. One example is Piabrm, a woman who was buried in Saqqara, the vast sacred burial ground of Memphis (close to modern Cairo), one of the most ancient and important, as well as cosmopolitan, cities in Egypt. Piabrm's tombstone mixes Egyptian, Greek and Carian elements. Such culturally 'hybrid' tombstones are typical for Saqqara, and were also erected for Greeks and later for Aramaeans and Persians.[130] They show how foreigners adhered to Egyptian customs while retaining their own cultural identity.

At the bottom we see Piabrm on a funerary bed, surrounded by mourners. This laying out of the body and lamenting of the dead was the first stage in a traditional Greek burial, and is shown here in a typically East Greek manner. One of the mourners seems to be cutting his forehead with a knife, in a special Carian mourning ritual.[131] The upper two scenes relate to Egyptian funerary cult. In the centre, the ibis-headed god Thoth approaches the sacred Apis bull, who is protected by the winged arms of the goddess Isis standing behind. The top image shows a man worshipping the enthroned god Osiris, accompanied by Isis, the deity's wife and sister. The scene is crowned by the winged sun disc with two *uraei* (sacred cobras and emblems of supreme power), similar to the carving on Nectanebo I's stele from Thonis-Heracleion (p. 51). This mixture of Greek and Egyptian elements also extends to the stele's shape and style: flat, round-topped stones decorated in low relief (and once colourfully painted) are typically Egyptian, but the style of carving betrays an Ionian craftsman. The fact that the carver replaced Osiris' usual attribute, the crook, with the *was*-sceptre, a symbol of power, suggests he was familiar with a special royal form of Osiris particularly revered in Memphis.[132] He also introduced some other unusual features, such as adding a table with food offerings in front of the bier.

An inscription on the stele tells us the name of the deceased, Piabrm, and that of her father or husband, Usold.[133] Both names are Carian. The Carian people of southwestern Anatolia (modern Turkey) had been well-known suppliers of mercenaries to Egypt since the seventh century BC, as had their close neighbours, the Greeks of the

region around Miletos (Ionia).[134] Usold probably belonged to the elite Carian and Ionian troops that the pharaoh Amasis (r. 570–526 BC) had stationed at Memphis as his bodyguards;[135] they and their descendants later populated whole town quarters. It is here at Memphis that they came to know and participate in the rituals of the sacred Apis bull, the centre of which was at Saqqara, and the closely related cults of Osiris and Isis (see Chapter 3).[136]   [AV]

Tombstone of a Carian woman
c. 540/530 BC
Saqqara/Memphis
Limestone
H. 63 cm | W. 31 cm | D. 10 cm
British Museum EA 67235

Thonis-Heracleion: a hub of maritime trade

According to the Greek historian Diodorus Siculus, 'Thonis ... in early times was the trading port of Egypt',[137] a statement that is amply borne out in the material evidence excavated by the IEASM. The importance of international trade to the port can be seen in its inhabitants' ready access to foreign ceramics, which appear in far greater number than local Egyptian pottery in the excavations from the very earliest phases of occupation.[138] These ceramics undoubtedly arrived in Thonis-Heracleion in the holds of trading ships from Greece and the Levant that put into the port after making landfall in Egypt, but whose ultimate destinations may have been locations further upriver, such as Naukratis.

In the waterways surrounding the port, archaeologists have found an astonishing maritime assemblage that clearly demonstrates both the presence of foreign ships and the role played by local Egyptian vessels. So far over 700 ancient anchors and sixty-nine ships and boats have been discovered in Thonis-Heracleion. While the majority of the vessels date to between the sixth and second centuries BC, the presence of a few ships from before this time also suggests that the location may have been used as a harbour since the Third Intermediate Period (fig. 14).[139]

Not all of the vessels that have been discovered are shipwrecks; in fact the majority of them were reused at the end of their sailing lives to create elements of port infrastructure, such as wharfs and piers, as well as pontoon bridges (also known as floating bridges), and others appear to have been scuttled in a quiet area of the port.[140] There is also a small temple boat that was deliberately sunk in a sacred location at the entrance to the Grand Canal, most likely as part of the rituals associated with the Mysteries of Osiris (see pp. 139–47). The deliberate decision to reuse some of these vessels and abandon others means that this collection is not simply a 'snapshot' of all of the different types of ships and boats in use in the Nile Delta, and while some of the anchors clearly indicated the presence of seagoing ships, missing from the ship assemblage are the military galleys, perhaps of Greek design, that would have used the port and defended Egypt's shores from invaders and pirates.   [DJR]

Ships and anchors from Thonis-Heracleion

Many of the anchors that archaeologists have discovered in the port are from ships of its likely trading partners, Greece and Phoenicia; fig. 35, for example, shows the wooden and lead stock from a one-armed wooden anchor, a type that is well known throughout the Mediterranean,[141] with examples coming from both the Greek world, such as the shipwrecks of Porticello and Tektaş Burnu,[142] and from the coast of Israel, such as that from the Ma'agan Michael wreck.[143] For these Levantine examples, however, it has been suggested that they may not have been from Phoenician vessels but from ships from the central and western Mediterranean that were engaged in commercial or military activities along the Syro-Palestine coast, or else from Phoenician ships using foreign anchors.[144]

Foreign vessels, however, appear to be largely absent from the group currently under investigation in the Central Port and Grand Canal, with only two ships made from the wood of non-native trees.[145] The local origin of the majority of these vessels is further demonstrated by the unique way in which many of them appear to have been constructed and it is likely that they were built in a shipyard at the port.[146] One such local vessel is the *baris*. One of these has been fully excavated,[147] and work on a second is under way (fig. 36).[148] The *baris* is a type of flat-bottomed river barge that was perfectly adapted to the sailing environment of the river system.[149] It is possible that many of them from Thonis-Heracleion were part of a fleet associated with the temple and as such they would have been involved in the collection and redistribution of goods on its behalf.[150] As well as transporting local goods, the *baris* would also have played a role in moving foreign merchandise around the Delta.[151] This type of vessel was consequently an essential part of the maritime economy and would have been a familiar sight transporting goods along the Nile and around its Delta, as well as in the port of Thonis-Heracleion, located on the shore of the 'Sea of the Greeks'.   [DJR]

35   A Kapitan Type II wooden anchor stock with lead inserts from Thonis-Heracleion, dated to between the fifth and third centuries BC

36   The prow of ship 43, a *baris* barge, from Thonis-Heracleion under excavation

Nursing mother

This figure of a nursing mother was found with Cypriot votive offerings down a well within the sanctuary of Aphrodite in Naukratis. Finely carved from Cypriot limestone, the statuette depicts a woman seated on a throne holding a nude boy to her left breast; he, in turn, is embracing the woman. She is wearing the typical elite Cypriot fashion (a long dress with overfold, veil, necklace and pendant) of the sixth century BC. The figure was originally painted, with traces of red and black pigment remaining. The motif is taken from the Egyptian tradition of the goddess Isis nursing the baby Horus (see p. 199), depicted here with his typical side-lock of hair. Egyptian iconography had long influenced Cypriot figurative art. The Isis-like figure may have been reinterpreted by the person who dedicated it as Aphrodite, even though the equation between Isis and Aphrodite is common only in later periods.

Greeks offered many gifts, including representations of Aphrodite, at her sanctuary in Naukratis, where she was recognized as a patron of sailors. Many of the offerings came from Cyprus, which was an important hub on the East Greek trade routes of the seventh and sixth centuries BC, and the mythological birthplace of Aphrodite. The importance of the sanctuary of Aphrodite, which was one of the earliest structures built at Naukratis, is well illustrated by the story related by Athenaeus of the trader Herostratos of Naukratis, who, at the time of

the twenty-third Olympiad … having sailed round many lands, … touched also at Paphos in Cyprus. There he bought a statuette of Aphrodite, a span high, of archaic style, and went off with it to Naukratis … and having sacrificed to the goddess, and dedicated the image to Aphrodite, he called his friends and relations to a banquet in the temple itself.[152]

[RT]

Cypriot statuette of a seated goddess nursing a baby (Isis and Horus?)
c. 550 BC
Naukratis, sanctuary of Aphrodite, found in a well
Limestone
H. 11.9 cm | W. 7.5 cm | L. 5.1 cm
British Museum 1888,0601.31

Nude male figures

Cypriot stone figures of nude beardless youths (known as *kouroi* in Greek) were popular votive offerings at Naukratis. *Kouroi* stand in a frontal position, with left leg advanced. The pose is derived from Egyptian sculpture and was copied by Greek and Cypriot sculptors. The earliest Cypriot figures of youths from the beginning of the sixth century BC, while distinctly Cypriot, often had Egyptianizing features. The limestone sculpture of the youth holding a lion with yellow fur before him is distinctly Cypriot in style and technique, yet nude male figures were a Greek subject and not common for Cyprus. The figure's identity remains debated. Cypriot 'lion tamers' are also known from other East Greek sanctuaries such as Knidos, Miletos and Samos as well as from Salamis in Cyprus. They are often considered the representation of a hero, and depictions of heroes wrestling lions are a common theme in Cypriot and Near Eastern art.

The finely carved alabaster youth shows the influence of the East Greek style on Cypriot *kouroi* figurines during the middle of the sixth century BC, and may have been made specifically for Greeks. In his hair he wears a band or diadem which was painted with vermilion, as were his lips. His skin was painted red-brown, and his eyes, eyebrows, moustache, long hair and pubic hair are black. The figure was found in three fragments around the altar of Aphrodite.

Cypriot figures of nude male youths were popular votive offerings across the eastern Mediterranean. They have been found in Cypriot and Phoenician cities (Byblos, Amrit, Sidon), but were particularly common within the sanctuaries of the Greek cities on the islands of Samos, Rhodes, Delos and Chios and on the western coast of Turkey (Knidos, Ephesos, Miletos). Both figures illustrated here come from the sanctuary of Aphrodite, but similar pieces were dedicated at all the major Greek sanctuaries at Naukratis. Within the sanctuaries, male and female figures appear to be represented in approximately equal proportions, suggesting that they may have been dedicated by, or on behalf of, both men and women. [RT]

Cypriot nude male youth (*kouros*)
c. 580–560 BC
Naukratis, sanctuary of Aphrodite, found near her altar
Gypsum alabaster
H. 25.7 cm | W. 8.8 cm | D. 4.4 cm
British Museum 1888,1006.1

Cypriot sculpture of nude youth or hero wrestling a lion
c. 600–560 BC
Naukratis, sanctuary of Aphrodite
Limestone
H. 21.3 cm | W. 6.4 cm | D. 4.2 cm
British Museum 1888,0601.27

The first temple of Apollo at Naukratis

The earliest stone temple for Apollo at Naukratis was built around 560 BC, when the Greek cities represented at Naukratis erected their first monumental temples. Its columns and decorative features were carved from limestone; its walls were either limestone or stuccoed mudbrick.

Only a few fragments of this temple survive today. Together with archaeological investigations of the sanctuary and comparisons with other Ionian temples, they help us to imagine what the sanctuary of Apollo might have looked like (fig. 37).[153] Around 15 by 8 metres wide at the front, the temple was built in the Ionic order, in a style closely resembling the great temples of Samos and the region of Miletos. Similar to other Ionian temples of comparable size, Apollo's temple at Naukratis probably had columns at the front and within its porch. Their intricate floral friezes were ultimately inspired by Egyptian art.

The temple would have housed a cult statue, while in front of the temple stood the main altar, around which most of the cult activities took place, including animal sacrifices. Subsidiary buildings, such as roofed halls, would have provided shelter for the feasting community. As with all Greek sanctuaries, the free space would have been cluttered with offerings: statues on columns, statuettes around the altar, and trinkets and garlands suspended from trees.

[AV]

The sanctuary of Apollo was one of the main Greek sanctuaries of Naukratis and flourished from the early days of the site. According to Herodotus,[154] it was founded by traders from the Ionian city of Miletos, where the god Apollo and his oracle shrine at nearby Didyma had a central role in civic life and politics – including sanctioning Milesian settlements in foreign lands, such as Naukratis.

Beautifully carved with a palmette above a 'bead-and-reel' band, this fragment of a cornice (decorative moulding) is one of the few surviving relics of the early Greek buildings of Naukratis. It could be from a large altar, or from a second phase of the temple of Apollo itself, which would have replaced the first temple (built around 560 BC).

The sixth century BC was the great age of Ionian temple building: inspired by the monumental architecture of Egypt and other Near Eastern civilizations and adopting some of their technical know-how, the wealthy Ionian cities began to vie with each other in building ever more elaborate temples and altars to their gods. The temple of Hera with its massive altar on the island of Samos, the Milesian temple of Apollo at Didyma and the Artemision of Ephesos were masterpieces of engineering and the biggest and most sophisticated buildings ever attempted in Greece: the Samian Hera temple measured over 100 metres in length and featured more than a hundred columns, some 18 metres high.

The temples of Naukratis were on a smaller scale, but they were designed by the same architects and built by the same craftsmen in a typically Ionian style, and were finished with great care and expense. The Apollo temple used marble that was probably imported from Ephesos (in modern-day Turkey) and once would have been colourfully decorated. Scientific analysis has recently identified traces of its original painted decoration, including hematite (red) and 'Egyptian blue', one of the oldest known synthetic pigments.   [AV]

Architectural moulding from the Archaic Greek sanctuary of Apollo
c. 530–510 BC
Marble
Naukratis, from the Apollo sanctuary
H. 22 cm | W. 13 cm | L. 8 cm
British Museum 1886,0401.41

37   Reconstruction of the sanctuary of Apollo at Naukratis

The Hellenion: a Greek 'cooperative' in Egypt

The Hellenion was the most famous and most frequented sanctuary of Naukratis, but it is also the most significant and enigmatic. A large, rectangular, multi-chambered structure,[155] the Hellenion was, according to Herodotus, jointly founded by nine otherwise fiercely independent East Greek cities which represented the three ethnic groups of Greece: Ionians, Dorians and Aiolians. Here they jointly appointed the chief officers of the Greek *emporion* (port), but also worshipped gods such as Aphrodite Pandemos ('common to all') and the 'gods of the Hellenes', an exceptionally early expression of a common Greek identity that emerged precisely in this period, fostered by the phenomenon of the Greek diaspora abroad.[156]

As a sanctuary, commercial headquarters and communal space for Greek traders, the Hellenion was not entirely dissimilar to the sanctuary of Amun-Ra, which would have had economic and administrative functions for the Egyptians, and which dominated the town's south as the Hellenion did the north.   [AV]

Votive female bust
c. 450–350 BC
Naukratis, Hellenion sanctuary
Terracotta
H. 17.8 cm | W. 18.3 cm | D. 13.3 cm
Fitzwilliam Museum, Cambridge GR.3.1898

Colourfully painted heads or busts of women were popular offerings to the gods in the Hellenion sanctuary of Naukratis.[157] They were made from a mould and have an open back. In this fine example, the woman's delicate face is painted white, with red lips and dark eyes. A light blue diadem decorated with rosettes sits atop her wavy red hair, which is arranged in the fashionable classical style of the period.

At Naukratis, such busts appear from the late sixth century BC onwards. Their dedication is a typically East Greek ritual practice, common in Ionia and on the island of Rhodes. Most examples were found in the Hellenion, where Aphrodite was worshipped alongside other gods, but some were also dedicated in the main Aphrodite sanctuary of Naukratis. Whether they represent Aphrodite, another goddess or the mortals who offered them, remains the subject of debate.

The busts found at Naukratis were mostly imported from Ionia and Rhodes, though local workshops also produced their own versions. They highlight the important role the island of Rhodes (one of the founding members of the Hellenion) played in commerce with Egypt from the fifth century BC.   [RT]

Cypriot female sphinx

This incense burner[158] takes the form of a seated sphinx carrying a bowl on its head; the teats on the belly show that it is female. It is carved in a style that combines Greek and Cypriot elements. The plinth and the creature's forefeet are broken and the piece is worn from exposure to seawater.

The mythical sphinx was a mixed being, part-human and part-lion. In ancient Egypt it had a long history as the male incarnation of the pharaoh and a powerful guardian figure. Greek and Cypriot culture transformed it into a winged, female monster associated especially with the border between life and death.

Burning fragrances was important in both Egyptian and Cypriot cult. Incense burners carried by sphinxes and, less frequently, other figures are well known from Cypriot sanctuaries and palaces from the early fifth century BC onwards; close parallels are found especially at Amathus.[159]

[DJR, from ZK]

Cypriot incense burner
Early 5th century BC
Thonis-Heracleion
Limestone
H. 24.2 cm | W. 9 cm | D. 12 cm | Diam. of bowl 13.5 cm
National Museum of Alexandria SCA 270

Saucer with mythical beasts
6th–4th century BC
Thonis-Heracleion
Lead
Diam. 5 cm
Maritime Museum, Alexandria SCA 907

An 'Easterner' at Thonis-Heracleion

This fragment of a statuette represents a male head wearing a stiff, pointed cap. There would originally have been four cone-shaped protrusions extending in a row down the cap's front (only three now survive), and the cap has earflaps, which are tied on the centre of the forehead with a bow. The face is smooth and clean-shaven with large almond-shaped eyes, carved in a style that indicates that the statuette was produced on Cyprus.

The head may depict an elite Cypriot male. Possibly a temple offering, it would have been dedicated during a visit to the port, perhaps during the first Persian period (525–404 BC). Alternatively, given the peculiarities of the cap, the head may represent a Semitic deity, perhaps Baal or Herakles-Melqart. Both of these 'foreign' gods had Egyptian equivalents (Baal was identified with Amun and Melqart with Herakles) and had temples in Thonis-Heracleion. Whether the head represents an elite male or a god, it is a clear sign of the cultural, religious and commercial exchanges that took place between the port-city and Cypriot–Phoenician communities such as that at Kition, on the southern coast of Cyprus.[160]   [DJR, from SH & DF]

Head of a Cypriot statuette
Late 5th–early 4th century BC
Thonis-Heracleion
Limestone
H. 12.9 cm
Maritime Museum, Alexandria SCA 1394

Votive bronzes

These two bronzes were discovered in a large cache, or hoard, of votive objects in Naukratis in 1885, during Flinders Petrie's first season at the site. The cache offers important insights into Egyptian religious beliefs and practices in this international harbour town.

On the top of the rectangular votive box is an elongated eel, its wavy body detailed by fine incisions. The small end of the box is open. The large hollow-cast figure represents an Egyptian mongoose. The animal is depicted standing with its front paws raised in an attitude of prayer. The box and the figure are now empty, but they probably once contained the mummified remains of the animals represented (although this was not always the case with such bronzes).

Found in the southern part of Naukratis not too far from the great Egyptian temple of Amun-Ra, the votive cache contained a great variety of bronzes but also some other objects. The latest dateable finds in the cache belong to the late fifth century and first half of the fourth century BC, but others may be as early as the sixth century BC. Dozens of bronze figures depict Egyptian deities, particularly the Osirian triad of Osiris, Isis and Horus. Votive boxes, however, are most numerous, all topped by figures of animals, particularly lizards, snakes and eels. Reptiles, eels and the Egyptian mongoose were sacred to the Egyptian solar and creator god Atum. They could also be early evidence for the local cult of the snake Shena – 'the One who repels'. There is evidence for this cult at Naukratis in the Ptolemaic period (323–31 BC).[161] [AMB]

Votive box and mummy-case
c. late 5th–early 4th century BC
Naukratis
Bronze
Votive box: L. 35.5 cm | H. 3.5 cm
Mummy-case: H. 31.5 cm | W. 10.2 cm
British Museum EA 27581 (votive box)
and EA 16040 (mummy-case)

Ibis mummy
Ptolemaic period (323–31 BC)
Saqqara, Egypt
Linen, resin, bone
H. 42 cm | W. 16 cm
British Museum EA 68219;
1971,0227.153

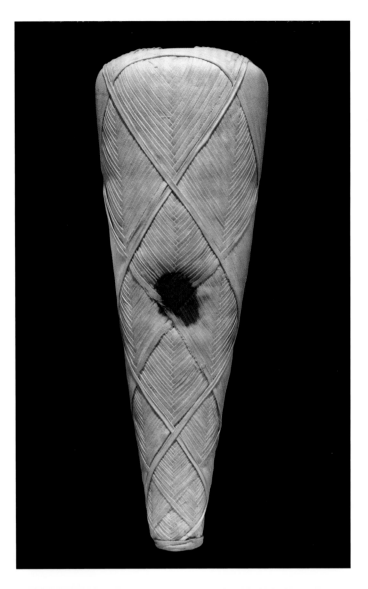

Animal worship

This carefully wrapped mummy contains the remains of an ibis, a bird now extinct in Egypt but one of the most important animals worshipped by the ancient Egyptians. The ibis was associated with Thoth, the god of wisdom, writing and mathematics, and the patron of all scribes. The mummy came to light in Saqqara, south of Cairo, where several graveyards for sacred animals have been discovered.

The linen wrappings of the mummy are arranged in a neat diamond pattern and a patch of resin is visible in the centre of the mummy. During the Late and Ptolemaic periods, millions of animals were mummified but this specimen is exceptionally carefully arranged and in an excellent state of preservation.

Using modern technology, the mummy has been X-rayed, allowing an examination of its contents without causing any damage. It proved to contain a completely preserved ibis bird, with the down-curved beak and the long legs of the animal clearly visible on the X-ray image.

Many bird mummies were only filled with parts of the animal such as bones, feathers or eggs; others were basically fakes, consisting only of mud, sand or bandages. This seems to imply that the outer appearance of an animal mummy was considered more important than its content. The ibis mummy preserved at the British Museum is, therefore, exceptional, as detailed attention was clearly paid to both the careful mummification of the bird and its meticulous wrapping. [DR]

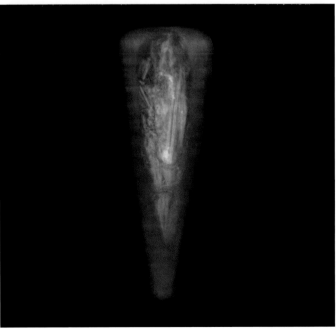

Amasis, the philhellene

The Greek historian Herodotus described Amasis (r. 570–526 BC) as a philhellene, a 'friend of the Hellenes', a pharaoh who sought to strengthen his diplomatic links with the Greeks by a variety of means. Not only did Amasis provide the Greek traders in Naukratis with privileges, but he also married a Greek noblewoman of Cyrene, Ladike, and sent valuable gifts to several Greek sanctuaries.[162] For the rebuilding of the famous Greek oracle shrine of Apollo at Delphi he sent a large consignment of alum, a valuable Egyptian trading commodity. The Samian Heraion received two wooden statues of himself.

In addition to a painted picture of himself he dedicated a gilded statue of the goddess Athena at Cyrene.[163] Sparta[164] and the temple of Athena at Lindos on Rhodes each received a linen corselet with fine golden and cotton embroideries, and Rhodes in addition two (gilded?) stone statues. He was not the first pharaoh to give such gifts: Necho II (r. 610–595 BC) had dedicated a linen corselet he had worn in battle to the oracle sanctuary of Apollo at Didyma near Miletos, presumably acknowledging the help of Ionian mercenaries.[165]

[AMB]

This small bronze pyramid-shaped object was discovered in the foundation level of the temple of Khonsu-Thoth, located on an island at the entrance of the North Canal of Thonis-Heracleion. On one of the narrower sides of the artefact the kneeling pharaoh Amasis presents vases as an offering. The king is identified by his cartouches (oval frames containing his royal names) engraved above him. Opposite, a winged goddess holds an ostrich feather in each hand. The wider sides have two registers displaying some of the Egyptian divinities venerated in Thonis-Heracleion, marching in file: Min, Amonet, Thoth, followed by a canine god, probably Anubis, and a falcon-headed god; in the second register are Amun, Mut and Khonsu, as well as Isis, Nephthys and Wadjit. No parallel or counterpart of this type of object is known; the style of the engraving is original and very different from the habitual classicism of the Saite period, when artistic styles deliberately harked back to older Egyptian traditions. The engraving is vivid, and the entire decoration offers an astonishing impression of liveliness and movement.

[ASvB]

Pyramidal object
26th dynasty (Saite period)
Thonis-Heracleion
Bronze
H. 13 cm | W. 8.5 cm
Maritime Museum, Alexandria SCA 1575

3   Greek kings and Egyptian gods

Aurélia Masson-Berghoff and Franck Goddio

39   Youthful posthumous portrait of Alexander the Great
2nd–1st century BC
Alexandria
Marble
H. 37 cm
British Museum 1872,0515.1

Alexander the Great

Alexander's conquest of Egypt in 332 BC marked the beginning of three centuries of Greco-Macedonian rule, but it was only one step in Alexander's long campaign against Persia. The Satrap of Egypt, who governed the country on behalf of the Great King of Persia Darius III (r. 336–330 BC), surrendered without resistance – the first respite for Alexander and his troops after three years of war. Despite his short stay in Egypt, from late autumn 332 to late spring 331 BC, Alexander had a deep impact on the country.[1] He most famously founded Alexandria, the remarkable port-city built by leading Greek architects.

Even though he was a foreign conqueror, Alexander III of Macedon (r. 336–323 BC) was hailed as a liberator by the Egyptians. The last native pharaoh, Nectanebo II (r. 360–342 BC), had been defeated by Darius. Persian rulers were quite unpopular in Egypt, and they are sometimes shown treating Egyptian temples and their priests poorly. Alexander's reign, in which he presented himself as a pious ruler who performed the traditional duties of a pharaoh, came as a welcome alternative. Lodging in the residence of the pharaohs in Memphis, he engaged in Egyptian ritual practices, including sacrifices to the local royal god, the Apis bull, and was probably crowned pharaoh in Memphis.[2] Alexander initiated construction or restoration projects at major temples, notably in the Theban region. The barque shrine (a resting place for the sacred boat in which the god's statue was carried in processions) he built in the heart of the temple of Luxor is particularly significant; this temple was dedicated to the cult of the royal *ka*, the divine aspect of kingship shared by all pharaohs. The priests must have recognized Alexander as a legitimate ruler of Egypt to allow him to be associated with such a cult.[3]

Alexander's actions reveal his desire for acceptance within Egypt, although he was keen to maintain his Greek heritage. He carried out the crucial duties of a pharaoh, but at the same time organized athletic and poetic competitions in the Greek tradition in Memphis, with participants from all over the Greek world.[4] Alexander appointed both Greeks and Egyptians to important official positions. He went as far as to cross the Libyan Desert to reach the oracle shrine of Zeus-Ammon, an Egyptian god with Greek and Libyan components, renowned among Greeks since the early fifth century BC.[5] When the famous oracle recognized Alexander as the son of Zeus-Ammon, his rule of a great empire that embraced multiple cultures gained divine sanction.

73

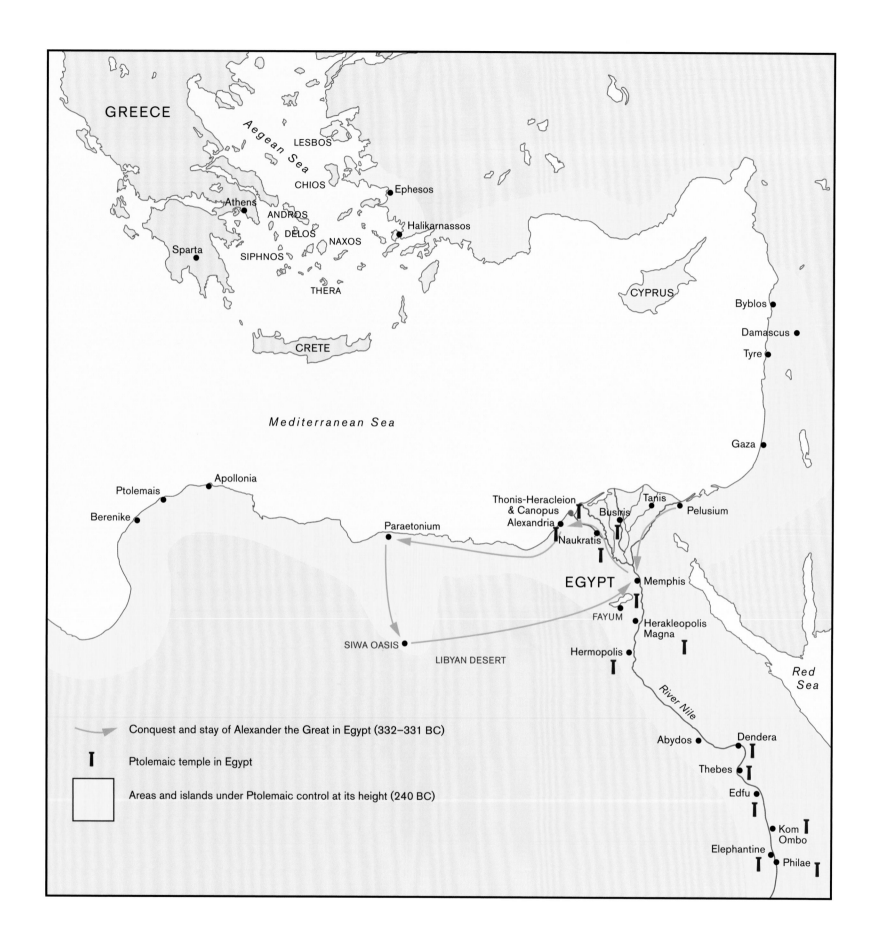

GREECE

Aegean Sea

LESBOS

CHIOS

Athens ANDROS

DELOS

Sparta SIPHNOS NAXOS

Ephesos

Halikarnassos

THERA

CYPRUS

CRETE

Mediterranean Sea

Byblos

Damascus

Tyre

Gaza

Apollonia

Ptolemais

Berenike

Paraetonium

Thonis-Heracleion
& Canopus
Alexandria

Tanis

Busiris

Pelusium

Naukratis

EGYPT

Memphis

FAYUM

SIWA OASIS

LIBYAN DESERT

Hermopolis

Herakleopolis
Magna

River Nile

*Red
Sea*

Abydos

Dendera

Thebes

Edfu

Kom
Ombo

Elephantine

Philae

⟶ Conquest and stay of Alexander the Great in Egypt (332–331 BC)

▐ Ptolemaic temple in Egypt

☐ Areas and islands under Ptolemaic control at its height (240 BC)

Images of Alexander, created both during his lifetime and after his death, project him as a ruler over many different cultures. In Egyptian temples, his image follows the traditional pharaonic style (fig. 42), strikingly different from the Greek-style idealized portrait from Alexandria (fig. 39). Both, however, were intended to visually convey a notion of Alexander as a seemingly superhuman being, far from the more naturalistic style of his contemporaries.[6]

In the steps of Alexander and the pharaohs: the Ptolemies

At the death of Alexander in 323 BC, his empire was divided among the generals who followed him on his epic conquest.[7] In the ensuing struggle, a trusted general and friend of Alexander, Ptolemy son of Lagos, took over Egypt, a territory that he and his successors expanded (fig. 40). Crowned pharaoh in 305 BC, Ptolemy I Soter I founded a new dynasty which lasted until the reign of Cleopatra VII (r. 51–30 BC). Alexander played a crucial legitimizing role for the new kings of Egypt. Ptolemy I seized his corpse on its way back to Macedonia and had him buried in Egypt – first in Memphis, then later in the new capital Alexandria, although Alexander had wished on his deathbed to be buried in the temple of his father Zeus-Ammon.[8] Alexander's tomb, the *Sema*, became the focus of an important dynastic cult.[9] Unfortunately, it has never been found.

The Ptolemies transformed Alexandria into one of the greatest intellectual and cultural centres of the ancient world, adorning the cosmopolitan city with monumental architecture and sculptures, such as the iconic buildings of the Lighthouse and the Royal Library. The nearby cities of Thonis-Heracleion and Canopus benefited from sumptuous construction programmes too. Numerous

41   The Ptolemaic temple
of Hathor at Dendera

temples across Egypt were built, renovated or enlarged, including some of those that are the best preserved today: Dendera (fig. 41), Edfu and Philae.

The new dynasty used pharaonic tradition to facilitate acceptance of the transition of power, satisfying the influential Egyptian priesthood.[10] Complex religious beliefs and rituals surrounded the pharaohs, and the Ptolemies swiftly mastered their divine role. Skilled in using art as an agent of ideology, the Ptolemies made use of statues '... to represent themselves in multiple ways to multiple groups, and in doing so they maintained the traditions and styles of each'.[11] The places where royal statues were displayed determined stylistic choices. Statues of pure Egyptian or partially Greek style were particularly prevalent in temples, while Greek royal sculptures seemed to be more confined to town contexts.[12] In order to appeal to all communities the Ptolemies appeared both as Greco-Macedonian kings and Egyptian pharaohs. The head of a late Ptolemaic king[13] discovered in Canopus (fig. 42) is a traditional pharaonic-style sculpture. The king wears the *nemes* with *uraeus*, the customary headcloth of pharaohs with a rearing cobra.[14] This stylized head belongs to a sphinx, which possibly once guarded the entrance to a temple. In contrast, Greek-style portraits of the king convey the image of a wealthy, righteous and cultured statesman who shows concern for his subjects.[15] This naturalistic-seeming style was relatively rare and particularly clustered in Alexandria and the Canopic region, probably reflecting the special treatment these cities received from the royal house, and the presence there of Greek communities. The more stylized pharaonic depictions dominate the sculptural landscape of Ptolemaic Egypt.

Numerous works of art, shrines and decrees honouring the ruling family demonstrate the growth of the royal cult under the Ptolemies. The famous Rosetta Stone,[16] now in the British Museum, bears a decree written in three scripts – hieroglyphic, demotic and Greek. The decree established the divine cult of Ptolemy V Epiphanes, a token of gratitude from Egyptian priests for restoring cosmic order (*maat*) by fulfilling his cultic duties.[17] It records that a statue of Ptolemy V, 'made in the native way', should be set up in each temple in the most prominent place and alongside the chief god of the temple. The royal cult enhanced rather than replaced that of the Egyptian deities, 'blurring the line between ancestral gods and mortal rulers'.[18] The royal cult was not limited to Egypt, reaching even beyond the kingdom of the Ptolemies; similarly, it was not limited to the male ruler. The cult of the queen was key to royal propaganda.[19] The politically and religiously charged office of mother, wife or daughter of pharaoh meant that in pharaonic times these women were depicted wearing the divine attributes of goddesses (such as the crown usually worn by the goddess Hathor, who represented joy, feminine love and motherhood, and who was often combined or even merged with Isis in the first millennium BC), and sometimes they enjoyed a long-lasting cult.[20] The Ptolemies were significantly more systematic than their predecessors at using religion to enthral their Greek and Egyptian subjects. Arsinoe, daughter of Ptolemy I Soter I, became particularly popular with both communities and was worshipped throughout the Ptolemaic

42 Head of a sphinx representing a Ptolemaic king
c. 2nd–1st century BC
(late Ptolemaic period)
Canopus
Quartzite
H. 38 cm | W. 31.5 cm
Bibliotheca Alexandrina Antiquities Museum
SCA 166

43 The colossal queen being
reassembled underwater following
preliminary cleaning

The Ptolemies

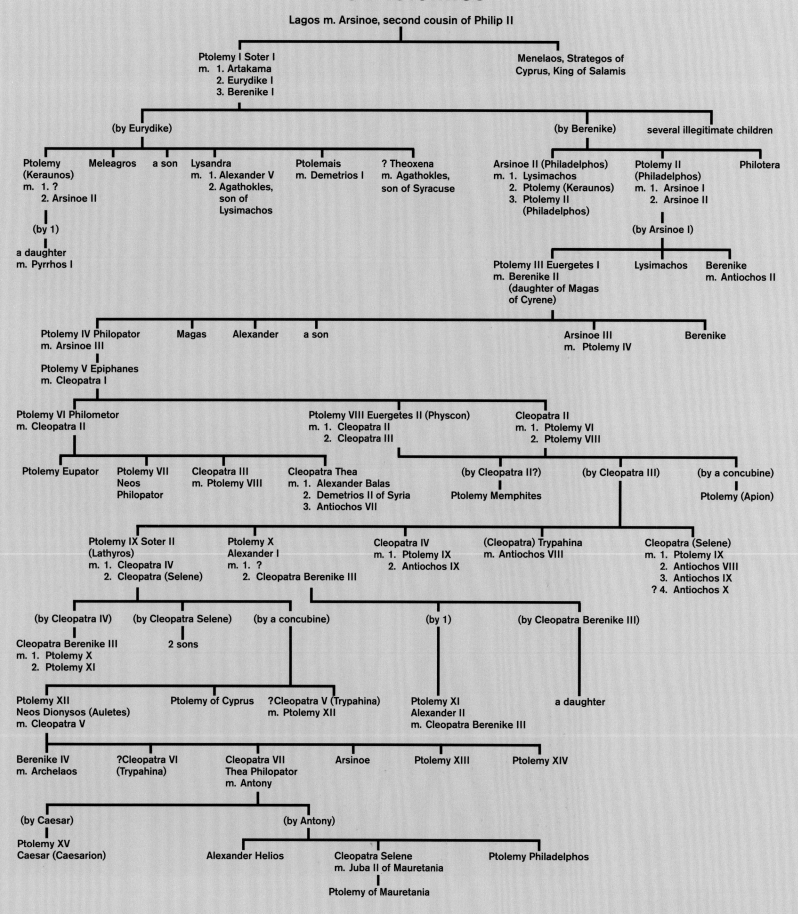

Lagos m. Arsinoe, second cousin of Philip II

Ptolemy I Soter I
m. 1. Artakama
    2. Eurydike I
    3. Berenike I

Menelaos, Strategos of
Cyprus, King of Salamis

(by Eurydike)

(by Berenike)   several illegitimate children

Ptolemy
(Keraunos)
m. 1. ?
    2. Arsinoe II

Meleagros   a son   Lysandra
m. 1. Alexander V
    2. Agathokles,
       son of
       Lysimachos

Ptolemais
m. Demetrios I

? Theoxena
m. Agathokles,
son of Syracuse

Arsinoe II (Philadelphos)
m. 1. Lysimachos
    2. Ptolemy (Keraunos)
    3. Ptolemy II
       (Philadelphos)

Ptolemy II
(Philadelphos)
m. 1. Arsinoe I
    2. Arsinoe II

Philotera

(by 1)

a daughter
m. Pyrrhos I

(by Arsinoe I)

Ptolemy III Euergetes I
m. Berenike II
(daughter of Magas
of Cyrene)

Lysimachos   Berenike
m. Antiochos II

Ptolemy IV Philopator
m. Arsinoe III

Magas   Alexander   a son

Arsinoe III
m. Ptolemy IV

Berenike

Ptolemy V Epiphanes
m. Cleopatra I

Ptolemy VI Philometor
m. Cleopatra II

Ptolemy VIII Euergetes II (Physcon)
m. 1. Cleopatra II
    2. Cleopatra III

Cleopatra II
m. 1. Ptolemy VI
    2. Ptolemy VIII

Ptolemy Eupator

Ptolemy VII
Neos
Philopator

Cleopatra III
m. Ptolemy VIII

Cleopatra Thea
m. 1. Alexander Balas
    2. Demetrios II of Syria
    3. Antiochos VII

(by Cleopatra II?)

Ptolemy Memphites

(by Cleopatra III)

(by a concubine)

Ptolemy (Apion)

Ptolemy IX Soter II
(Lathyros)
m. 1. Cleopatra IV
    2. Cleopatra (Selene)

Ptolemy X
Alexander I
m. 1. ?
    2. Cleopatra Berenike III

Cleopatra IV
m. 1. Ptolemy IX
    2. Antiochos IX

(Cleopatra) Trypahina
m. Antiochos VIII

Cleopatra (Selene)
m. 1. Ptolemy IX
    2. Antiochos VIII
    3. Antiochos IX
  ? 4. Antiochos X

(by Cleopatra IV)

Cleopatra Berenike III
m. 1. Ptolemy X
    2. Ptolemy XI

(by Cleopatra Selene)

2 sons

(by a concubine)

(by 1)

(by Cleopatra Berenike III)

Ptolemy XII
Neos Dionysos (Auletes)
m. Cleopatra V

Ptolemy of Cyprus

?Cleopatra V (Trypahina)
m. Ptolemy XII

Ptolemy XI
Alexander II
m. Cleopatra Berenike III

a daughter

Berenike IV
m. Archelaos

?Cleopatra VI
(Trypahina)

Cleopatra VII
Thea Philopator
m. Antony

Arsinoe   Ptolemy XIII   Ptolemy XIV

(by Caesar)

Ptolemy XV
Caesar (Caesarion)

(by Antony)

Alexander Helios   Cleopatra Selene
m. Juba II of Mauretania

Ptolemy Philadelphos

Ptolemy of Mauretania

kingdom.[21] Her third marriage was to her brother Ptolemy II Philadelphos (r. 285–246 BC), a union considered sacred by the ancient Egyptians. She gained divine status after her death, becoming a Greco-Egyptian goddess, identified as Isis by the Egyptians, and Hera and Aphrodite by the Greeks. A stunning sculpture discovered at Canopus represents the deified queen as the perfect embodiment of her dual religious nature (p. 93).

Gods, temples and royal legitimacy at Thonis-Heracleion

The cult of the god Amun spread from Thebes throughout Egypt from the time of the 18th dynasty (1570–1293), if not earlier,[22] carrying with it the idea that it was Amun who raised pharaoh to the kingship. At Thonis-Heracleion, his cult was celebrated as early as the reign of the Saite king Amasis (570–526 BC). A small bronze engraved object shows this king, identified by his cartouches, in the process of making offerings (p. 70). It displays two rows of divinities headed by Amun, his wife Mut and their son Khonsu, followed by other gods worshipped in the town. In the Ptolemaic period a monumental temple was dedicated to Amun, Lord of Gereb at Thonis Heracleion.

The earliest evidence for the epithet 'gereb' associated with Amun (Amun-Gereb) appears on the trilingual Decree of Canopus, issued in the year 238 BC, which declared Ptolemy III and Berenike as *Euergetes*, 'Benefactors'. The term *gereb* is found on the walls of Ptolemaic temples, particularly at Karnak and Edfu, where it is associated with the Egyptian word for inventory or inheritance, relating to the kings in these scenes. It is also related to the word *mekes*, which can designate a sceptre of power, but also (and especially) means the case containing the papyrus scroll that lists the inventory of royal property – that is, the realm of Egypt, and the whole universe, over which pharaoh exerts supremacy. Consequently, Amun-Gereb was the god who handed over the *gereb* and the *mekes* and thereby conferred royal sovereignty and legitimacy.[23]

The underwater excavations at Thonis-Heracleion have brought to light three imposing artefacts directly connected with Amun-Gereb. The first is a pink granite shrine, whose surviving inscriptions demonstrate that it housed the principal god of the temple, Amun-Gereb (p. 105).[24] The second object is a colossal bilingual stele in Egyptian and Greek, dating from the reign of Ptolemy VIII Euergetes II. Despite the highly eroded text, the epithet ' … Lord of the Gereb' can be read in the Egyptian version, the Greek text being indecipherable (p. 96).[25] The stele also provides evidence for the cult of the goddess Mut, wife of Amun, and their son Khonsu in the same sanctuary. Lastly, excavations near to the boundary of the great temple uncovered the headless, inscribed torso of an individual of the Ptolemaic period (p. 109). The inscriptions reveal that he was a benefactor of the 'Lords of Gereb',[26] meaning that he had made donations to the temple. The plural 'Lords of Gereb' on the torso includes Khonsu-Herakles, and draws attention to the increasing importance of Amun's son in the dynastic functions of the temple of Thonis-Heracleion.

For the Egyptians, Khonsu-the-child, son and heir of Amun, was the divine image of the terrestrial heir from the New Kingdom (1550–1077 BC). For Greeks in Egypt, Khonsu was equated to Herakles, the deified hero of outstanding strength. This connection (noted by Herodotus in the fifth century BC) is the origin of the name of the temple of Thonis-Heracleion, and subsequently also of the town. The Ptolemies claimed descent from Herakles on their father's side and Dionysos (the Greek equivalent to Osiris) on their mother's. Claims of divine descent helped justify their right to rule, and this explains their continuing interest in the temples of Thonis-Heracleion, where Amun-Gereb

45   Head of Herakles wearing a lion-skin (perfume bottle)
6th century BC
Naukratis
Terracotta
H. 7.5 cm | W. 6.8 cm
British Museum 1886,0401.1402

and Khonsu-Herakles, the 'Lords of Gereb' who granted royal legitimacy, were worshipped. The generosity of the Ptolemaic kings is evident from the outstanding statuary and the abundance and richness of the artefacts found in the temple. Their benevolence is also the source of the town's continued prosperity as a religious centre into the second century BC, despite Alexander's decision of 331 BC to move all international harbour activities to his new city of Alexandria.[27]

The presence of a temple of Herakles in the Canopic region is well attested in ancient literature. Herodotus mentions it,[28] saying that servants of the Greek prince Paris (en route to Troy c. 1200 BC; see p. 16) left their master and took refuge in this temple, which offered the right of asylum (security and protection in the temple). This ancient right is also mentioned on the bilingual stele of Ptolemy VIII mentioned above (and see p. 96).

Excavations in Thonis-Heracleion have revealed a sanctuary attributed to Khonsu-Herakles in the northern part of the area of the temple of Amun-Gereb. However, it cannot be the one that Herodotus mentioned (and possibly visited) in 450 BC, as it had not been built at that time. A very fine and complex bronze headdress (p. 120) of a type often worn by Khonsu, and big enough to have adorned his cult statue, came to light in this later sanctuary, as did a pink granite naos (shrine) which might have contained it (fig. 46). A highly original and remarkably well-preserved votive deposit dating from the 30th dynasty was also found in the northeast corner of the sanctuary. It included a faience statuette of the child god with his wooden shrine, surrounded by protective amulets of high quality (pp. 118–19). Khonsu-Herakles' popularity is revealed by the great number of statues, statuettes and amulets of child divinities discovered all over the area of the temple, and throughout the town and its surroundings.[29]

A dynastic creation? Serapis and the two faces of a cult

Late accounts tell us that Ptolemy I Soter I was visited in a dream by an anonymous god who ordered him to bring the god's cult statue from Sinope, a Black Sea port in what is now northern Turkey, to Alexandria.[30] The identity of the god remained a mystery, combining attributes of Hades, the Greek god of the underworld, and Zeus, the king of gods, until the statue reached Alexandria and was recognized as Serapis. Dreams, oracles, arduous negotiations between kings, unexplained illnesses and miracles surround the origin of Serapis' cult statue.[31] According to copies and descriptions, it represented the god as a mature bearded figure, seated on a throne, holding a sceptre and wearing a *kalathos* (a corn measure symbolizing abundance and fertility) on his head (fig. 47), with the three-headed dog Cerberus by his side.

Serapis is neither an imported god nor a pure Greco-Macedonian creation. His name and associated beliefs derive from Osiris-Apis, the long-revered bull of Memphis[32] and a special form of Osiris in that area.[33] The Apis bull was selected with much care[34] to be the living incarnation of Ptah – an Egyptian creator god and chief deity in Memphis – and a symbol of royal succession.

46 Naos of Khonsu-the-child
4th–2nd century BC
Thonis-Heracleion
Pink granite
H. 110 cm
Maritime Museum, Alexandria SCA 456

**47 Serapis bust with *kalathos*
from Alexandria**
2nd century BC
Alexandria, from the Serapeum
Marble
H. 81 cm
Graeco-Roman Museum, Alexandria
22158

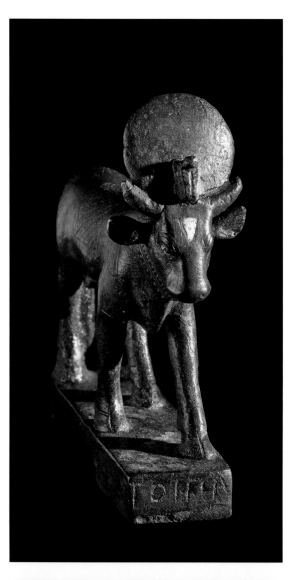

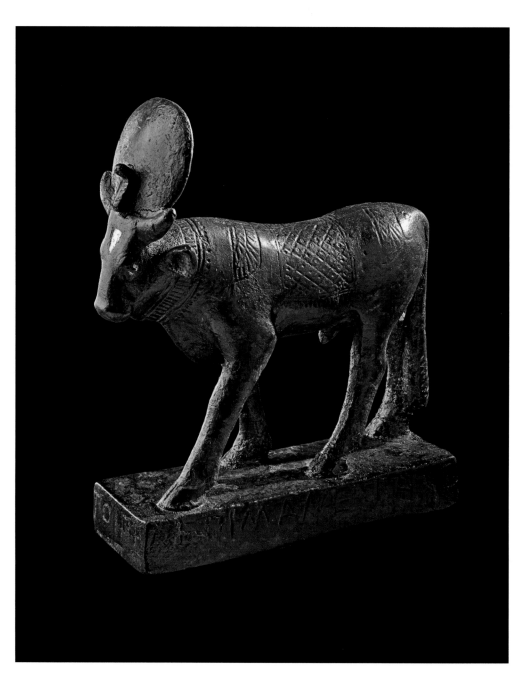

48 Statuette of the sacred Egyptian Apis bull
500–450 BC
Memphite region
Bronze
H. 10 cm | L. 8.7 cm
British Museum 1898,0225.1

The statuette has a Greek dedication to
'Panepi' (the name deriving from a popular
designation of the god Apis) by a Dorian
named Sokydes.

At his service were priests as well as a harem of cows! After death, Apis was transformed into Osiris-Apis. The bull's mummified body was carried in procession to the Serapeum, a large religious complex at Saqqara, the sacred burial ground outside Memphis.[35] In both life and the afterlife the sacred bull combined many roles,[36] royal (the bull was crowned in Memphis, like a pharaoh), funerary and mantic (he could deliver oracles and interpret dreams).

Since the 26th dynasty (664–525 BC), Greeks and other foreigners residing in the Memphite region showed a particular interest in Apis,[37] as evidenced by a bronze bull bearing a Greek dedication (fig. 48).[38] Alexander the Great sacrificed to Apis when he arrived in Memphis.[39] His pious behaviour contrasts with that of the Persian conqueror of Egypt, Cambyses (r. 530–522 BC), who was charged by ancient historians with slaughtering the Apis bull.[40] The Ptolemies followed Alexander's example and worshipped sacred animals.

The transfer from Osiris-Apis to Serapis is sometimes attributed to Alexander the Great himself,[41] although textual and archaeological evidence points more towards the beginning of the Ptolemaic period.[42] Serapis appears as a Greek version of Osiris-Apis, merging the aspects and roles of major gods of the Greek Pantheon – Zeus, Hades, Dionysos (god of wine, vegetation, pleasure and festivity), and Asklepios (god of medicine). This 'new' universal god became the patron deity of Alexandria, as well as the protector of the Ptolemaic dynasty.

Serapis' temples in Egypt and beyond

Serapis had little impact on Egyptians. The cult of and devotion to Osiris-Apis in Memphis was not replaced, nor did it decline under the Ptolemies. The new god was aimed at Greeks living in Egypt, binding together Greek communities, both the newly settled and those founded long before. And so Serapis' cult mainly developed where Greeks were the dominant presence, such as at Alexandria, Canopus, in the Fayum, and in various other places in the Ptolemaic realm and beyond.[43]

As patron of the Ptolemaic capital and dynasty alongside the Egyptian goddess Isis, Serapis had a religious complex at Alexandria that benefited from royal patronage. Although this Serapeum was razed to the ground by Christians in AD 391, it is possible to reconstruct the classical Ptolemaic temple it housed, which combined Greek-style architectural elements.[44] Its underground galleries, in contrast, betray Egyptian influence, imitating a similar arrangement to that of the Serapeum of Memphis.[45] Statues of Ptolemaic rulers in Greek style[46] discovered at the site indicate strong links with the royal court. Sets of foundation plaques marked the corners of the enclosure wall and the temple of Serapis. According to the bilingual dedications inscribed on these plaques, Ptolemy III Euergetes I (r. 246–222 BC) and Berenike dedicated the temple and domain to Osiris-Apis (in the hieroglyphic text) and to Serapis (in the Greek text).[47] The connection between the two gods is further emphasized by the magnificent Apis bull dedicated here to Serapis (p. 126) by the Roman emperor Hadrian (r. AD 117–138). The formal sanctuary of Ptolemy III possibly replaced an earlier Serapeum.[48] The earliest dedications from the site were offered to Isis and Osiris, the latter being closely associated to Serapis in his funerary function.[49] This confusion between Osiris and Serapis[50] echoes that between Osiris and Osiris-Apis.[51] The sacred enclosure which contained the Serapeum of Canopus may have been recently rediscovered by the IEASM, which uncovered the impressive remains of a stone wall at least 100 metres long.[52] The healing powers of Serapis were particularly

**49   Gilded wood statue of
Osiris with inlaid eyes**
323–31 BC (Ptolemaic period)
Minia (Upper Egypt)
Sycamore
H. 1.52 m | W. 44 cm
Bibliotheca Alexandrina Antiquities
Museum 633

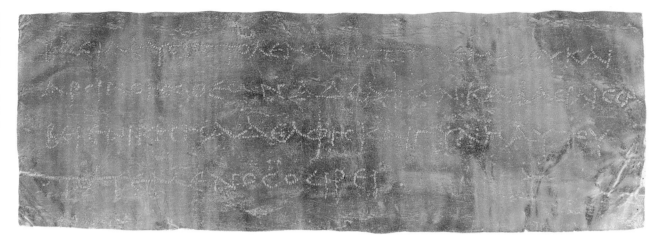

50 Foundation plaque
246–221 BC
Canopus
Gold
L. 17.1 cm | W. 5.8 cm
British Museum 1895,1030.1

This foundation plaque bears a
dedication of a sanctuary to
Osiris by Ptolemy III.

**51 Amulet in the shape of a
Greek-style temple**
332–31 BC (Ptolemaic period)
Canopus
Lead
L. 1.2 cm
Maritime Museum, Alexandria
SCA 470

renowned at Canopus, where healing by incubation (sleeping within a sanctuary, to obtain divinely inspired dreams) was practised.[53] A gold foundation plaque from Canopus bearing the dedication of a sanctuary (*temenos*) to Osiris by Ptolemy III could well pertain to this sacred enclosure or to a contemporary religious complex (fig. 50).[54] This would mean that the (re)construction of the Serapeum of Alexandria would have coincided with the building or reconstruction of this sanctuary at Canopus, the temple of which was possibly also of classical Greek architectural style, as shown on an amulet discovered in Canopus (fig. 51). This amulet, however, could depict another building from Canopus, for example an Iseum, a temple dedicated to Isis.[55]

It is evident from ancient texts that even by the reign of Ptolemy II Philadelphos (r. 285–246 BC) Serapis' cult had spread beyond Egypt and as far as the coasts of Anatolia (western Turkey) and the Caspian Sea.[56] The foundation of a sanctuary dedicated to Serapis – alone or with his consort Isis – was sometimes prompted by an individual's repeated dreams and could result from private initiatives.[57] For example, a letter written in 257 BC by a certain Zoilos, living in the realm of the Ptolemies but outside Egypt, urges Apollonios, a high financial officer under Ptolemy II, to build a Serapeum. Zoilos explains that the god appeared to him through dreams and that he fell ill as a result of not complying immediately with the god's wishes. Zoilos stresses that if Apollonios were to fulfil the god's order, it would be profitable to his health and would make him appear illustrious in the king's eyes. In fact, Ptolemaic kings and queens themselves fostered their identification with the divine Serapis, regarded as King Osiris and his consort Isis. This explains why the cult of Serapis was able to develop so successfully alongside the royal cult: pleasing the god would please the king.

Water-clock depicting Alexander the Great
331–323 BC
Tell el-Yahudiya (Egypt)
Black granodiorite
H. 37 cm | W. 38 cm | Th. (of lip) 6 cm
British Museum EA 933

Coin portraying Alexander the Great
Late 4th century BC
Minted in Alexandria
Silver
Diam. 30 mm | Wt 15.7 g
British Museum 1876.0505.33

Silver coin of Alexander

This coin features an idealized portrait of Alexander the Great with a ram's horn. The sacred *aegis* of Zeus, an impenetrable goat skin fringed by snakes, is tied around his neck, and he wears an elephant scalp as a headdress, commemorating his victories in India. On the coin's reverse is the Greek goddess Athena, with her warrior attributes. Tracing back his lineage to the hero Herakles (and thence to his father, Zeus himself), Alexander considered Athena to be his special patron, as she was Herakles'. The ram's horn is traditionally associated with Alexander's journey to the oracle of Zeus-Ammon in the Siwa Oasis, in the Libyan Desert, where he was recognized as the son of this Greek-Egyptian-Libyan god.[58] Recently, scholars have linked the horns with Apollo Karneios, another ram-horned deity revered in Libya.[59] In either case, depicting Alexander with such divine attributes was meant to blur the 'boundary between ruler and god'.[60]

This coin was one of the earliest minted by Ptolemy I Soter I (r. 323–285 BC), and was intended to associate his reign with that of Alexander. Several of Alexander's successors issued coins with his portrait. Horned Alexander was one of his most widely circulated and iconic images throughout the Greek period.   [AMB]

Alexander the Great: a pious pharaoh

Water-clocks such as this one were used in temples by priests who had to perform nightly rituals at specific hours.

The fine sunken relief incised on the outer surface of this fragmentary water-clock shows Alexander the Great dressed and acting as a pharaoh. He appears twice, wearing a triangular-fronted kilt with a bull's tail hanging from the back, symbolizing the strength of the pharaoh. In each scene, he is escorted by one Egyptian deity and is making an offering to another. He presents a globular wine vessel to the Theban lunar god Khonsu (right) and a cup filled with burning incense to an unidentified male god (left). Of the accompanying gods, only the goddess Ipet can be identified. Both Khonsu and Ipet

are patron deities of specific months in the year. The figured frieze is surmounted by a row of stars and framed by two horizontal lines of hieroglyphic text at the bottom and a third one at the top. Alexander's Egyptian names appear in cartouches with the traditional pharaonic titles 'King of Lower and Upper Egypt' and 'Son of Ra'.

Dots, regularly spaced and arranged in vertical lines, are incised on the inner surface, each line set above a large hieroglyphic sign; the only surviving ones are an *ankh*-sign (life), a *djed*-pillar (stability) and a *was*-sceptre (power). There were originally twelve signs, each corresponding to one month. The marks helped to measure night hours as the water level decreased, dripping through a small hole pierced in the base.   [AMB]

Horus protecting pharaoh

This remarkable statue shows the divine falcon, Horus, protecting Nectanebo II (r. 360–342 BC), the last native pharaoh of Egypt. The falcon's eyes were originally inlaid with glass, but only its left eye is completely preserved today.

While the wings and the body of the bird are sculpted in a rather simple manner, the head and the feet are impressively carved. The projecting piece left on the falcon's head proves that the statue was once crowned by a headdress. The king depicted between the bird's legs is wearing a long kilt, his palms resting flat against it, and his legs are placed together. He is shown in the pose of a king in prayer before a god and – like every other Egyptian pharaoh – as the reincarnation of the sky god who appeared as a falcon.

Although no inscription confirms the name of the king, it is highly likely that the statue can be identified as Nectanebo II. It forms part of a series of seven statues of this type, discovered in various towns in Egypt, of which five give the name of this king. These statues might be part of a royal cult, as there is evidence for priests of 'Nectanebo II-the-Falcon' – the cult may have been set up for him after his victory against the Persians, though they overthrew him again eight years later.   [DR]

Statue of Horus protecting pharaoh
c. 350 BC
Egypt
Limestone and glass
H. 55 cm
Egyptian Museum, Cairo JE 33262

Coins of Ptolemy I

These five gold coins (*hemidrachms*) were discovered in the temple of Khonsu with a group of gold jewellery.[61] They portray Ptolemy I on the obverse. Around his neck he wears the protective *aegis* of Zeus, a divine attribute previously only shown worn by a mortal on Alexander the Great's coinage (see p. 86). On the reverse, the inscription 'of King Ptolemy' (in Greek) frames the image of an eagle riding a thunderbolt. Both are attributes of the Greek god Zeus and became symbolic of the Ptolemies on their coinage. These particular coins were issued by Ptolemy I Soter I (r. 323–285 BC) and his successor Ptolemy II Philadelphos (r. 285–246 BC). Similar imagery is used on their silver coins.

Silver and gold coins formed the backbone of the Egyptian economy in Ptolemaic times, while bronze coinage was used in day-to-day transactions. Ptolemy I instigated a monetary policy that allowed him to significantly increase the royal revenue. The weight of the coins was reduced in comparison to the Attic standard and these coins became the only type to circulate within the Ptolemaic kingdom. This restrictive regulation meant that every non-Ptolemaic coin was melted upon its arrival in Egypt. The policy was applied well after the end of the Ptolemaic dynasty, through to the Roman empire.[62]

The obverses of Greek coins had traditionally been reserved especially for a city's patron god or hero. In Ptolemaic Egypt, by contrast, this place was now occupied by a portrait of the king, the royal couple or sometimes the queen, thus associating 'money with piety' and emphasizing the 'divine affiliation of the minting authority'.[63] Coinage played an important role in the spread of royal portraiture and associated propaganda, being its most public expression throughout the kingdom. [AMB]

Coins portraying Ptolemy I Soter I
305–247 BC
Thonis-Heracleion
Gold
Diam. 9–10 mm | Wt 1.7–1.8 g
Graeco-Roman Museum, Alexandria
SCA 304, 307, 312, 313, 318

Head of a pharaoh

This magnificently sculpted head of a pharaoh came to light during underwater excavations at Canopus. The skilful surface treatment and exploitation of the raw material mark it as a product of 3,000 years' expertise in carving hard stone. The chin was once adorned by the artificial royal beard, which has broken off, and the king's mouth is relatively small with well-defined corners. All that remains of his almond-shaped eyes are the now-empty sockets, which were once inlaid – a rather uncommon feature in royal statues. The subtle eyebrows lead to a delicate nose with a slender bridge. His forehead is adorned by the sacred rearing cobra, the *uraeus*, protruding from his *nemes*, the traditional headcloth of the pharaohs.

Although no inscriptions are preserved, the style of the head suggests it dates to the Early Ptolemaic Period, as royal heads with a similarly executed slender *uraeus* have come to light from this era.[64] The king, although a foreigner, is represented here entirely as a pharaoh and in accordance with ancient Egyptian traditions. This portrait perfectly illustrates the determination of the Ptolemaic kings to present themselves to their Egyptian subjects as the legitimate successors to the rulers of the last native dynasties. [DR]

Head of a pharaoh
3rd century BC
Canopus
Granodiorite
H. 35 cm | W. 30 cm | D. 29 cm
Bibliotheca Alexandrina Antiquities Museum SCA 167

Arsinoe II: from tragic queen to goddess

At the young age of fifteen, the eldest daughter of Ptolemy I Soter I, princess Arsinoe (*c.* 316–270/68 BC), married Lysimachos, the ruler of Thrace, Macedon and part of Asia Minor, in a highly political union.[65] Lysimachos, a sixty-year-old surviving companion of Alexander the Great, died twenty years later in a battle against Seleukos, another of Alexander's generals. Arsinoe remarried her half-sibling Ptolemy Keraunos, although this second marriage was short and ended in a failed conspiracy and the murder of her two younger sons by Keraunos.

Arsinoe later fled to Egypt where she was unexpectedly thrust back into political life when she married her full brother Ptolemy II Philadelphos. There is evidence for brother–sister unions in pharaonic tradition, although it is sporadic,[66] but this marriage was the first of a series of such unions in the Ptolemaic dynasty. It emphasizes the divine status of the ruling couple as an earthly incarnation of the divine siblings Osiris and Isis, who form the archetype of the royal couple. With this propagandistic coup, Ptolemy II anchored the Greco-Macedonian dynasty in the most sacred Egyptian founding myth. To the Greeks, such a union could also find a mythological justification with Zeus and Hera, the Greek divine ruling couple. A number of Greek poets at the court of Ptolemy II referred to Zeus and Hera to celebrate Ptolemy II and Arsinoe II's marriage.

Ptolemy II established and disseminated his wife's cult after her death, and possibly slightly earlier. The extensive veneration for Arsinoe was shared by both Egyptians and Greeks.[67] She was worshipped as one of the Divine Siblings alongside Ptolemy II himself, but also as a goddess on her own. In 270 BC, Ptolemy II issued a decree (the Decree of Mendes) that all temples of Egypt should host a cult statue of the divine Arsinoe. She was incorporated into Egyptian cult and temples, sometimes identified with the goddess Isis. Ptolemy II erected a sanctuary to her at Alexandria. For its vault, the architect Timochares planned to use lodestone, a stone with magnetic properties. According to Pliny, this was 'so that the iron statue [of Arsinoe] contained in it might have the appearance of being suspended in mid-air'.[68]

A number of Greek courtiers at the court of Ptolemy II mention in poems a shrine for Arsinoe-Aphrodite Zephyritis at Cape Zephyrion, between Alexandria and Canopus, built on the order of Kallikrates of Samos, Supreme Commander of the Ptolemies' powerful fleet. One of the newly discovered poems of Poseidippos (*c.* 310 –240 BC) declaims:

> *Whether you plan to cross the sea by ship or make fast the*
> *stern-cable from the shore, say 'hail' to Arsinoe of Fair Sailing,*
> *and call the goddess-queen from her temple, which Boiskos' son,*
> *the nauarch [admiral], Samian Kallikrates dedicated especially*
> *for you, sailor.*[69]

Ptolemaic sea power reached new heights under Ptolemy II, when Egypt had the largest fleet in the eastern Mediterranean. 'Kallikrates sought through this coastal shrine to identify the queen with the maritime Aphrodite, who held particular significance for sailors.'[70] Sea ports bearing Arsinoe's name and hosting her cult, as patron goddess of sailors, proliferated throughout the Ptolemaic kingdom. [AMB]

The imagery attributed to Arsinoe II is abundant, mainly posthumous, and associated with her cult, and there are examples in pharaonic, Greek and Greco-Egyptian styles. This masterpiece from Canopus is Greco-Egyptian, an 'intimate fusion of two aesthetics put in the service of a religious project'.[71]

The sculpture represents the queen as an incarnation of Aphrodite, the goddess of beauty believed to grant 'fortunate sailing'.[72] The surface of the black, hard stone has been rubbed to achieve a polished appearance. The striding pose is rather traditional and formal, but the masterful wet drapery provides vitality to the composition, a dynamism accentuated by the lack of a back pillar. The long pleated dress, which leaves her shoulders bare, and the shawl knotted above her left breast embrace tightly the curves of her body.[73] The sensual rendering of her flesh is revealed through the play of the transparent garment. The style is reminiscent of Greek masterpieces such as *Venus Genetrix* and dancing *Maenads* credited to the famous sculptor Kallimachos of Athens (second half of the fifth century BC), which show a similar treatment of the fine, clinging drapery.

Since, by royal decree, a statue of the queen had to be placed in all temples of Egypt, this slightly over-life-size sculpture might have been the cult statue of Arsinoe in the Serapeum of Canopus.[74]   [AMB]

Statue of Arsinoe II
3rd century BC
Canopus
Black granodiorite
H. 1.5 m | W. 0.55 m | D. 0.28 m
Bibliotheca Alexandrina Antiquities Museum
SCA 208

Queen and goddess

This over-life-size statue, discovered in several pieces, depicts a Ptolemaic queen dressed as the Egyptian goddess Isis. Her almond-shaped eyes were once inlaid and, together with her tight-lipped mouth, give her a rather stern facial expression. Her hair is parted in the middle and arranged in short strands, and she wears a diadem adorned by the royal *uraeus* (sacred rearing cobra). In her left hand the queen is holding a musical instrument called a *sistrum*, while in her right she holds an *ankh*-sign, the symbol of life.[75]

The statue shows characteristics of both Egyptian and Greek art. The queen's pose, standing with the left foot advanced, is typically Egyptian, as is the choice of a local stone (rather than the marble favoured by the Greeks), and the presence of a back pillar, which in this case has no inscription to help us identify the monarch. Clearly of Greek influence, on the other hand, are the corkscrew locks falling over her back and shoulders and the garment she is wearing. It is the so-called 'Isis garment', wrapped around her body and fastened between her breasts in a large knot (the Isis-knot), creating a cascade of plaits that barely hide the anatomy of the queen.

Representations of female members of the royal family from Egypt are numerous, and many of them are outstanding in terms of the quality of the carving, clearly underlining the influential role queens played in the politics of the Ptolemies. On the basis of stylistic comparison, this statue might represent a queen of the second rather than the third century BC, as Greek influence in royal statuary seems to increase from the early towards the mid-Ptolemaic period. Some scholars believe this sculpture to be the effigy of Cleopatra III (r. 142–101 BC) whose life story might explain her sombre expression. After having been married to her much older uncle Ptolemy VIII, with whom she had five children, she ruled jointly after his death with her mother Cleopatra II and her son Ptolemy IX. She expelled him from Alexandria and replaced him, as co-regent, with her second son Ptolemy X – only to be murdered by him six years later.   [DR]

**Queen (possibly Cleopatra III)
dressed as Isis**
2nd century BC
Thonis-Heracleion
Granodiorite
H. 2.2 m | W. 60 cm | D. 40 cm
National Museum of Alexandria SCA 283

Monumental stele

This monumental stele, inscribed in hieroglyphs and Greek, is broken into numerous fragments and has been badly damaged by erosion. A quarter of the total document is legible, in particular at the upper left corner. Unfortunately the beginning of each line of hieroglyphs is lost and only a few letters of the accompanying Greek text remain.[76]

The stele was erected under the joint reign of Ptolemy VIII Euergetes II and his two wives, Cleopatra II and III (that is, during the periods 141/140–131 or 124–116 BC). The three are depicted in the left part of the corner that is still preserved, officiating before Amun, the king of the Egyptian gods, his wife Mut, the Egyptian mother goddess, and a line of deceased and deified Ptolemaic kings. The presence among these kings of Ptolemy VII Neos Philopator (Memphites) suggests that the stele was probably created shortly after 118 BC. In that year, his deification was used as a means of reconciling factions in the ruling family (he had been murdered in 130 BC).

The text is presented in the traditional manner, highlighting the king's generosity as well as his prowess in war. The surviving narrative tells initially of Ptolemy's gifts to the temples in northern Egypt and refers to previous troubles in the region where the king restored order. It also mentions the ancient right of asylum, which the temple is said to have lost, and reports a request to regain this right and to recover land formerly owned by the temple, 'from the time of the ancestors until the year 44 of Amasis' (that is, 526 BC, just before the first period of Persian domination of Egypt).[77] It is paradoxical that this stele is among the latest-dated objects to be found at Thonis-Heracleion, yet it refers to the earliest period of the town, and indeed recollects the Trojan War episode of the servants of Paris seeking asylum in the town's temple (see p. 80). The very existence of this gigantic stele is obvious proof that the priests' request was granted. Ptolemy VIII ruled in favour of the priests and had the decree delivered to them: hence the creation of this stele.

The stele was found, not on the Central Island, but in the far north of the city: perhaps near the site of the earlier temple of Herakles mentioned by Herodotus.[78] The search for this temple will be a focus of future excavations.   [DJR, from CT and FG]

Stele of Ptolemy VIII Euergetes II
2nd century BC, most likely shortly after 118 BC
Thonis-Heracleion
Red granite
H. 6.1 m | W. 3.1 m | D. 40 cm | Wt 15.7 t
Maritime Museum, Alexandria SCA 529

A Ptolemaic ruling couple

These colossal statues represent a king and queen depicted upright and striding forwards, both with their backs against a pillar. The role of these statues was the same as those erected at temples by the pharaohs of the New Kingdom (see p. 39): they stood before the facade of the temple of Amun-Gereb in Thonis-Heracleion, watching over it and allowing the king's subjects to worship him.

Found in five separate pieces and measuring 5 metres tall, the king is practically complete. His dress is extremely simple and classical: bare-chested, he wears the traditional *shendyt* kilt with the double crown – the *pschent* – which symbolizes the unification of the two lands of Egypt, the Delta and the Nile Valley. It is adorned on the front with the *uraeus* (rearing sacred cobra). Overall, the statue is traditionally Egyptian, drawing inspiration from the New Kingdom but also the later 26th and 30th dynasties. In his right fist the king holds a small cylinder, possibly the *mekes* case containing the inventory of Egypt that conferred legitimate sovereignty, emphasizing the dynastic function of the temple of Amun-Gereb in front of which the statue stood.

The queen's body was found broken into three pieces and is missing the right shoulder, arm and left knee. She wears the crown of Hathor and

Isis (cow horns, sun disc and feathers), which was worn by royal wives. It was made separately from the head. The queen wears the classical three-part wig with minutely detailed braids, and a finely pleated dress, which ends just above the ankles. Around her shoulders there is a shawl whose end hangs diagonally between her breasts and joins the sash, to which a knot attaches it.

Three colossal statues have been found in Thonis-Heracleion, which may suggest they were arranged as a triad of the king, the god Hapy and a female. This grouping suggests that the colossal female statue is a representation of Isis or, more likely, a queen fully assimilated with the goddess, so as to create a conceptually balanced composition of two deities flanking the king.

All three statues were either repaired or re-carved in antiquity. Since early Ptolemaic portraits take care not to suggest the Greek origin of the royal house, the face was sometimes re-carved when royal portraiture displayed Greek elements. The two distinct semicircular eyebrows suggest that the re-carving was done after the reigns of Ptolemy V–VI, and the broad face and thin lips recall the features of Ptolemy VIII. Was the king re-carved at the time of the erection of the colossal stele of Ptolemy VIII (p. 96) during the final years of Thonis-Heracleion?　　　　[DJR, from JY & EL]

Statues of Ptolemaic king and queen
Early Ptolemaic period (possibly reign of Ptolemy II)
Thonis-Heracleion
Red granite
King: H. 5 m | W. 1.5 m | D. 75 cm | Wt 5.5 t
Queen: H. 4.9 m | W. 1.2 m | D. 75 cm | Wt 4 t
Maritime Museum, Alexandria SCA 279 and SCA 280

left and overleaf
Colossal statue of a pharaoh, reassembled underwater after excavation and preliminary cleaning

Fertility figures

This uninscribed colossal statue is a typical fertility figure. The statue shows a fat male, who holds before him an offering table with a central lip for a water channel at the front. The offering table rests on his forearms and the palms of his hands. He has a tripartite wig of the type normally worn by male deities, above which rises a clump of papyrus, representing the heraldic plant of Lower Egypt; this was particularly associated with the god Hapy, the personification of the Inundation of the Nile. The principal function of such fertility figures was to bring offerings to the temple, and the statue's striding pose expresses this sense of movement. Like almost all Egyptian statues of any size, the figure has a back pillar; this runs up to the top of the heraldic papyrus clump. Unlike many large and prestigious statues, however, this one is not inscribed. The face itself has a bland, idealized character that is common to much Late Period and early Ptolemaic statuary. The figure may have been made in the fourth or third century BC.

The colossus was found broken into seven pieces and also bears many marks of damage or alteration between its original creation and final abandonment, notably on the front of the right shoulder and the adjacent wig. The statue may have fallen over to its right, perhaps after an earth tremor or episode of sedimentary liquefaction (see Chapter 1). The damaged surfaces were then re-carved, so presumably the whole statue was re-erected.

Fertility figures are not deities in a straightforward sense. They personified fertile aspects of nature and the cultivated land, supplying offerings to the temple for the king to present to the gods, who in turn provided for Egypt's well-being. So they belong more with the king, as representative of this world, than with the gods. Many such effigies – but none on this scale – were engraved on the walls of temples, conveying the message of royal and divine provision for the country. Although this statue is almost identical in scale to the colossal statues of the king and queen also discovered in Thonis-Heracleion (p. 98), it is uncertain whether the three formed a set. Fertility figures were typically grouped in pairs, but at this site no trace of a companion has been found. Perhaps this was because the statue of Hapy, as a representation of the Nile Inundation, was set up at one of the river's mouths.   [DJR, from JB-K]

Statue of a fertility figure (probably Hapy)
4th or 3rd century BC
Thonis-Heracleion
Red granite
H. 5.4 m | W. 1.05 m | D. 90 cm | Wt 6 t
Maritime Museum, Alexandria SCA 281

Naos of Amun-Gereb

A naos, or shrine, was an architectural structure that contained the cult statue of a god or goddess, and represented a physical manifestation of this deity. It was the focal point of most ceremonies performed in a temple. These shrines, typically erected in the most western and sacred part of the building, could be made of stone, wood or metal and were sealed with wooden doors.

This particular shrine was discovered in Thonis-Heracleion.[79] Although heavily worn, its remaining inscriptions give the epithets of the principal god of the temple, Amun-Gereb, so the shrine must once have housed his cult statue. The cartouches that give the name of the pharaoh who erected this chapel are also damaged, but judging by the length of the cartouches it was probably a Ptolemaic king, most likely one between Ptolemy III and Ptolemy VIII. The name of the god given on the shrine, Amun-Gereb, was already known from the Egyptian text in the Decree of Canopus (see Chapter 4, p. 143). The name of the temple of Amun-Gereb is written as 'sanctuary of Heracleion' in the Greek part of the decree, confirming the identification of the city.

The shrine shows some fragmentary inscriptions yielding an interesting piece of cult-political information: they inform us that it was here, in Thonis-Heracleion, that the pharaoh received his divine power to rule over the country from Amun himself. This is in line with pharaonic ideology in which it was the god who chose the royal heir, thus legitimizing each king's reign – an aspect of crucial importance for sovereigns of foreign origin, such as the Ptolemies. [DR]

Shrine of Amun, lord of Gereb
4th–2nd century BC
Thonis-Heracleion
Pink granite
H. 1.74 m | W. 1.0 m | D. 93 cm
Maritime Museum, Alexandria SCA 457

Crown of Amun
4th–2nd century BC
Thonis-Heracleion
Bronze
H. 15.1 cm
Maritime Museum, Alexandria SCA 967

The two faces of Amun

Amun, king of the Egyptian gods, is often depicted as a man wearing a flat-topped crown surmounted by two tall feathers (left). Part of such a crown (above) was discovered in the temple of Amun-Gereb in Thonis-Heracleion, probably a fitting for a large figure of this god. Amun could also be represented in the form of a ram, his sacred animal (see p. 107). Greeks were sometimes taken aback by the animal shape of many Egyptian gods and the general reverence Egyptians seemed to show towards animals. [AMB]

'One comes [...] to a sanctuary of commensurate size, though it has no statue, or rather no statue of human form, but only of some irrational animal'

Strabo, Greek geographer and historian, *Geography* (64 BC–AD 24)

Figure of Amun-Ra
Ptolemaic period (332–31 BC)
Egypt
Bronze
H. 29.8 cm
British Museum 1913,0308.4

Limestone plaque

Plaque representing Amun as a ram
6th century BC
Thonis-Heracleion
Limestone
H. 9 cm | L. 11.5 cm | D. 0.4 cm
Maritime Museum, Alexandria SCA 1579

This finely chiselled limestone plaque depicts two rams' heads, one on each side of the slab. It was excavated just to the northeast of the sanctuary of Khonsu-Thoth,[80] and dates to the sixth century BC. The function of the object is difficult to determine. It could have been a sculptor's model, possibly intended as an offering, or – given its iconography and place of deposition – an object with ritual significance.

The horns and ears of the heads identify the animals as rams, and they are clearly representations of Amun, the patron god of Thonis-Heracleion. The image was used in the port-city, for example, as a symbol of the temple of Amun-Gereb on a coin weight.[81]   [DJR, from DF]

Sphinx

The sphinx – a human-headed lion – was a major sculptural form in Egypt, and avenues of sphinx statues were traditionally used to create monumental processional ways to the main entrances of temples. This example depicts the traditional pose: the forefeet lie flat with the rear legs tucked up, and the tail curls over the rear thigh. It wears the traditional royal *nemes* headcloth topped by the *uraeus* (rearing sacred cobra), indicating that it is a representation of a monarch, although the absence of an inscription makes the exact identification of the king difficult. Given the similarity of its form and facial features to examples from the time of Nectanebo I (380–362 BC) or Nectanebo II (360–342 BC), the sphinx probably dates to this period.[82]

The sphinx was found in three pieces – the head was found inside the sanctuary of the temple of Amun-Gereb, whereas the other two body pieces were found over 200 metres away to the north. It is likely that this was the result of modern-day trawling activity in Abukir Bay, which has also disturbed other pieces of statuary, moving them away from the area of the temple.   [DJR, from ZK]

Sphinx
4th century BC
Thonis-Heracleion
Granodiorite
H. 98 cm | W. 58 cm | L. 1.47 m
Maritime Museum, Alexandria SCA 282

Benefactor statue

This fragmentary votive statue of a man has been eroded during its immersion underwater. The torso and leg section were found years apart and it is hoped that future excavations will discover the missing head and legs. The dimensions of the piece suggest that it was either slightly under life-size or simply of a small male figure. The statue is an interesting mixture of pharaonic and Greek traditions in terms of the style of dress and the form of the sculpture and the inscription.

The man wears an unfringed garment which does not quite conceal the paunchiness of his body underneath. The drapery is of a delicate material, since details such as the nipples are visible. The shawl of the statue has three folds, over which is engraved a hieroglyphic inscription with the signs of typical Ptolemaic workmanship: 'The noble (?) beneficent who did what was beneficial to the two lords of *Gereb* N [...] sons of [...]'.[83]

The name of the man is unclear, as is that of his father,[84] but from the inscription it is discernible that he had been a benefactor, or *euergetes*, to the principal deities of the temple of Thonis-Heracleion, Amun-Gereb and his son Khonsu-Herakles, the two 'Lords of the Gereb'. This unknown benefactor was probably a member of the port-city's elite, who had been allowed to place his statues within the sacred sanctuary of the great temple. The inscription echoed the same father–son relationship as the gods of the temple and was part of a dynastic strategy to keep the benefactor's name and that of his father alive after death. Here the local elite were using the temple and its relationship to the 'Lords of the Gereb' in the same way as the Ptolemies, to secure the future of their dynasty, both on Earth and in the afterlife.

[DJR, from ZK & JY]

A temple benefactor
4th–2nd century BC
Thonis-Heracleion
Granodiorite
H. 64 cm | W. 20 cm | D. 22 cm
Maritime Museum, Alexandria SCA 455

Oil lamp
4th–2nd century BC
Thonis-Heracleion
Bronze
L. 14.1 cm
Maritime Museum, Alexandria
SCA 1568

Incense burner
4th–2nd century BC
Thonis-Heracleion
Bronze
Diam. 13 cm
Maritime Museum, Alexandria
SCA 1086

Bowl
4th–2nd century BC
Thonis-Heracleion
Bronze
Diam. 25.2 cm
Maritime Museum, Alexandria
SCA 406

Pot
4th–2nd century BC
Thonis-Heracleion
Bronze
Diam 27.9 cm
Maritime Museum, Alexandria
SCA 407

Mirror

This mirror has a large, flat oval section, which is a typically Egyptian shape; at least one side of it would have been reflective. A stepped tang projects from one edge and a handle, perhaps of wood, ivory or another perishable material, would have been attached to this.

The weight of this mirror makes it too heavy to be held in one hand. Relief decoration in Egyptian art shows offerings of mirrors to the gods,[85] and so perhaps this example was bought or commissioned as a votive gift. Like every other mirror discovered at Thonis-Heracleion, it was deposited in the sacred waters of the Grand Canal alongside other ritual objects.[86]   [DJR, from ZK]

Brazier

This brazier is made up of a conical section riveted in four places to a large plate with a rim. Two handles are attached to the outer edge of the plate, making it easily portable. This is a functional object that has little in the way of decoration. It has been identified as a brazier due to its similarity to other Greek examples, where the indentation in the centre of the plate would have been used for coals, with the vessel to be heated resting on either a small tripod or grille above. It is unknown whether this brazier was used in the preparation of food in a household in Thonis-Heracleion or for burning other substances in an Egyptian or Greek temple.

[DJR, from ZK]

Large brazier
4th century BC
Thonis-Heracleion
Bronze
H. 23 cm | Diam. 46 cm
Maritime Museum, Alexandria SCA 912

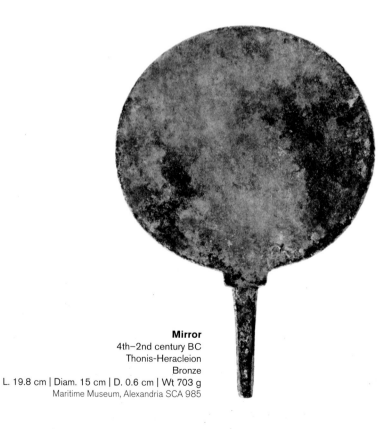

Mirror
4th–2nd century BC
Thonis-Heracleion
Bronze
L. 19.8 cm | Diam. 15 cm | D. 0.6 cm | Wt 703 g
Maritime Museum, Alexandria SCA 985

Basins

Bronze basins
4th–2nd century BC
Thonis-Heracleion
Bronze
H. 11.9 cm | Diam. 42.1 cm | Wt 291.4 g
Maritime Museum, Alexandria SCA 911

4th–2nd century BC
Thonis-Heracleion
Bronze
H. 17 cm | Diam. 25.3 cm | Wt 111.6 g
Maritime Museum, Alexandria SCA 900

Basins, either with or without handles, and without specific markings, are usually classified as hand basins. The two shown here have sides that taper outward slightly towards the top, with a flared rim. They were produced by hammering a single piece of bronze into the required shape.[87] Hand basins, usually in association with metal ewers (jugs or pitchers), were used in ritual ablutions (the ceremonial act of washing), in the world of medicine, and for more general purposes in the home.

These basins were found in the Grand Canal amongst the destruction horizon caused by the devastating collapse of the temple wall into the waters. Other examples of basins found at Thonis-Heracleion also come from the Grand Canal, and may have been placed in the waters deliberately as ritual deposits.[88]   [DJR, from ZR]

Offering drinks to the gods

This type of bowl is mentioned by Athenaeus as an oriental drinking cup often used for pouring libations (ritual drinks offered to the gods).[89] The findspots of these examples, around the main temple of Thonis-Heracleion and in the Grand Canal, also suggests a ritual use. Such vessels were very popular under the Achaemenid rulers of Persia, and their use spread outwards with Persian expansion, soon becoming

incorporated into local repertoires in many parts of their empire. By the mid-fourth century BC this was the favoured Macedonian form of small drinking bowl, and by the Ptolemaic period (332–31 BC) it had been adopted almost all over the Greek-speaking world, playing an integral part both in banquets and in day-to-day drinking.[90] The shape was very popular in both expensive gold or silver and cheaper bronze or ceramic.

Each of these bowls has a ridge that marks a break between the rounded, footless, lower part of the vessel and the relatively straight upper part. The majority of bowls from Thonis-Heracleion have little decoration beyond a single or double pressed line around the bottom of the neck. A few are decorated with embossed designs: a central rosette surrounded by leaf-like fluting stretching up the sides of the bowl (as illustrated overleaf).[91]   [DJR, from ZR & DF]

Achaemenid Persian bowls
5th–2nd century BC
Thonis-Heracleion
Bronze

H. 6.5 cm | Diam. 12.5 cm | Wt 277 g
Maritime Museum, Alexandria SCA 586

H. 8.2 cm | Diam. 10.6 cm | Wt 213 g
Maritime Museum, Alexandria SCA 216

overleaf
Diver with a drinking cup, decorated with a rosette
Maritime Museum, Alexandria SCA 904

A bronze masterpiece

During the first millennium BC, the number of royal statues multiplied and true masterpieces were produced in bronze as the craft of metalworking flourished. This statuette of a pharaoh in the classic marching pose shows him wearing the *shendyt* kilt and crowned by the high *khepresh* blue crown, with pointed circles and a *uraeus* (rearing sacred cobra) with one symmetrical loop. His fists would once have held the insignia of power, the cane and the *ankh*-sign symbolizing life. With eyes close to the narrow root of the nose, his firm oval face appears fleshy, with a full mouth and chin. The muscles on his slender body are carefully modelled, as are the fine details and realistic features, such as the collarbones, knees and lower legs.

The name of the pharaoh is incised on his belt buckle, possibly in an oval cartouche, with hieroglyphs that are difficult to decipher. The use of three hieroglyphs is typical of Saite (26th-dynasty) kings. The most likely reading is 'Neferibre', one of the royal names of Psamtik II (r. 595–589 BC).

This statuette was discovered in the sanctuary of the temple to Amun-Gereb on the Central Island of Thonis-Heracleion.[92] The temple was built between 450 and 380 BC, suggesting that the statuette had perhaps been transferred from an older temple located in the north of the city.[93]

[JB-K]

Pharaoh with *khepresh* crown
26th–29th dynasty (664–380 BC)
Thonis-Heracleion
Bronze
H. 21 cm | W. 5.5 cm | D. 5.8 cm | Wt 1,033 g
Maritime Museum, Alexandria SCA 1305

Foundation deposit for Khonsu-the-child

This statuette of a child-god and his wooden shrine, surrounded by amulets, were discovered at the northeast corner of the temple of Khonsu, in the north of the temple of Amun-Gereb. The faience statuette and the amulets were all made in the same style and were produced with the intention that they would be used as a group.[94]

Shown standing naked, the child-god bears a *uraeus* (rearing sacred cobra) on his forehead and displays the classical side-lock of hair and the finger on the mouth that identifies him as Khonsu-the-child, rather than adult Khonsu. This Egyptian lunar deity was assimilated by the Greeks to Herakles, the deified hero who gave his name to the temple, and to the town of Thonis-Heracleion. Renowned for his mastery of the waters, Herakles also gave his name to the branch of the Nile on which the port-city was located, the Heracleotic (now known as the Canopic) branch. Khonsu, son of Amun and Mut, was seen by the Egyptians as the image of the divine and terrestrial successor. In his left hand, the god seems to hold a cylindrical object – the 'testament of the gods' – that marks him as the predestined heir to the throne, and he appears as the very symbol of the dynastic function of the temple of Amun called 'of the Gereb' in Thonis-Heracleion, the seat of the perpetuation of royal power and monarchic legitimacy.

The amulets surrounding the young god originally were of a turquoise green colour before the seawater altered it. These objects protect and give new life and energy to the god, and each of them has a specific role and meaning: a twin vase, a little papyrus column, the god Shu with the sun on his head bearing the sky like Atlas (not illustrated), the *uraei* and the *wedjat*-eye. When they are viewed as a group it is clear that the statuette and amulets were carefully chosen to tell two very clear stories about the temple and its locality. Firstly, they emphasize the dynastic function attributed to the temple where they were discovered. Secondly, they throw light on the major role of Herakles, the emblematic divinity of both the port-city and this region at the edge of the 'Sea of the Greeks'.

Very efficiently protected by his amulets against the course of the centuries, gigantic natural seismic events and human pilfering, the enchanting child has emerged almost intact from the bottom of the ocean after more than 2,000 years. [ASvB & DF]

Shrine with statuette and amulets
30th dynasty (380–342 BC)
Thonis-Heracleion
Faience and wood
Wooden naos: H. 13 cm (SCA 583)
Faience statuette and amulets: Khonsu H. 7.9 cm (SCA 562); papyrus-shaped column H. 13 cm (SCA 565); double vase *hes* H. 7.3 cm (SCA 559); *wedjat*-eye H. 4 cm | W. 5 cm (SCA 558); *uraei*: left H. 4.2 cm (SCA 555), right H. 4.15 cm (SCA 552); faience plaque L. 8.4 cm | W. 3.6 cm (SCA 560); Shu H. 5.8 cm (SCA 553) (not illustrated).
Maritime Museum and National Museum of Alexandria.

A crown fit for a cult statue

This complex headdress was found in the sanctuary of Khonsu-Herakles at Thonis-Heracleion, near a pink granite shrine.[95] Called a *hem-hem* crown, it consists of two horizontal twisted ram's horns, on which are placed three bunches of papyri, each surmounted by a solar disc, and flanked on either side by an ostrich feather and a *uraeus* (sacred rearing cobra) topped by a solar disc.[96] The crown is set on a *nemes*, the royal pleated headcloth, which has two forward parts framing the face and a rear one plaited into a braid. A large *uraeus* rears its head on the frontal head band. On the right side of the *nemes*, a tang allowed the juvenile side-lock of hair, characteristic of child deities, to be attached. There are two more holes underneath each horn to suspend four hanging cobras.[97]

The name *hem-hem,* meaning 'the roaring', is related to the function of the figure wearing it: to terrify the enemy. Such crowns are often borne by child-gods[98] and divine heirs in their role of fighting evil, and particularly by Khonsu, who was assimilated to Herakles by the Greeks.[99]

Judging from the size of the headdress, the figure wearing it must have been some 50 to 70 cm high. That would be the right size for the cult statue that might have been housed in the shrine of Khonsu (see p. 80), beside which the headdress was found.   [ASvB]

Headdress of Khonsu-the-child
30th dynasty–early Ptolemaic period
(4th to 3rd century BC)
Thonis-Heracleion
Bronze
H. 15 cm | W. 10 cm
Maritime Museum, Alexandria SCA 401

Gold coin

The obverse of this coin features a beardless Melqart, the Phoenician god that the Greeks identified as Herakles. He is covered by a lion-skin and carries his bow and club.[100] On the reverse, a lion leaps onto the back of a stag and sinks its teeth into the base of the wild animal's neck. This subject, drawn from old Asiatic or Egyptian traditions, was taken up in the fifth century BC by the dynasty from Kition in Cyprus. The Phoenician inscription that appears above and in front of the scene reads *L MLK PMJTN* ('King Pumiyaton') and dates the issue of the coin to the eight or ninth year of his reign (either 355/354 or 354/353 BC).

The coin is part of a remarkable series of gold coins from Cyprus, of which Pumiyaton produced the greatest quantity.[101] Scientific analysis of the gold suggests that Egypt was the source for much of it[102] – at a minimum 5,000 kilograms – suggesting a considerable flow of Cypriot goods in the other direction to pay for it, much of which would have passed through the port of Thonis-Heracleion.

[DJR, from JY, BL and AM]

Statue of Khonsu
Late Period (664–332 BC)
Thonis-Heracleion
Bronze
H. 21.5 cm
National Museum of Alexandria 294, SCA 387

Statuette of Harpokrates
4th–2nd century BC
Thonis-Heracleion
Bronze
H. 18 cm
Maritime Museum, Alexandria
SCA 1268

Cypriot *hemistater* coin
355/354 or 354/353 BC (reign of Pumiyaton)
Thonis-Heracleion
Gold
Diam. 1.37 cm | Wt 4.10 g
National Museum of Alexandria SCA 287

Gold jewellery: votive offerings?

This collection of gold jewellery (see right and overleaf) was recovered during excavations in temples on the Central Island in Thonis-Heracleion, with the exception of one ring (SCA 1128) which is from Canopus. The pieces are most likely votive offerings to the temples, and the styles of the jewellery are significant for what they reveal about the people who dedicated them. Much of it is Greek in style, with the exception of items such as the sickle-shaped earrings (SCA 297, SCA 14372)[103] or the *uraeus* fragment (SCA 14333), a motif which was reserved for gods and royalty and, as such, had probably decorated an Egyptian cult statue. Earrings with tapered gold sheet hoops (four twisted tubes for SCA 298), with a sleeve and a sheet-gold animal head at the broader end, were commonly selected pieces for deposition. Lions' heads are most common (SCA 298), but other animals or mixed griffin-lion heads are also found (SCA 288, SCA 1408).[104] Such jewellery was popular in the Greek world from the fourth to second centuries BC, with prototypes going back to the fifth century BC. Rings such as that with the oval stone (SCA 290) were also widespread throughout the Greek world and similar examples date from the later third or early second century BC.[105] Other examples refer specifically to Greek deities, as seen by the ring with a round bezel engraved and punched with a winged figure of Nike (the Greek personification of victory), standing next to a seven-tiered incense holder (SCA 286).[106] The nearest parallels are western Greek from the late fourth and early third century BC.

While the temples to which these pieces were donated were Egyptian in their architecture and in the gods worshipped, the jewellery itself is more cosmopolitan, reflecting contemporary Greek styles and the mixing of elements of Egyptian and Greek cultures during the Ptolemaic era.

[FG, from YS]

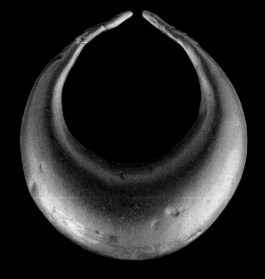

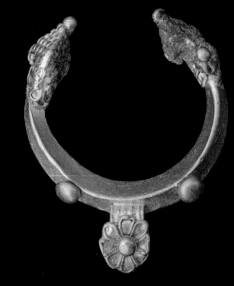

Jewellery
4th–2nd century BC
Thonis-Heracleion
Gold

Earrings
Sickle-shaped
made of sheet gold with filling material
D. 2.65 cm
Graeco-Roman Museum, Alexandria SCA 297

D. 2.5 cm
National Museum of Alexandria 1623, SCA 14372

Granulations and floral decoration
D. 2 cm
National Museum of Alexandria 1621, SCA 14174

Animal-headed
D. 1.9 cm | Th. 0.89 cm
Graeco-Roman Museum, Alexandria 32231, SCA 298

D. 1.9 cm | Th. 0.38 cm
National Museum of Alexandria 318, SCA 288

D. 3.2 cm
National Museum of Alexandria SCA 1408

Rings
Ring with a round bezel and a punched depiction of Nike:
D. 2.97 cm | Th. 2.8 cm
National Museum of Alexandria 314, SCA 286

Ring engraved with an unidentified Greek divinity
D. 1.3 cm
National Museum of Alexandria 1599, SCA 1344

Ring with a pyramid of eighteen granules:
D. 1.71 cm
Graeco-Roman Museum, Alexandria 32239, SCA 308

Ring with an oval glass or stone dark red cabochon:
Ring: D. 2.68 cm | Th. 1.89 cm
Cabochon: H. 1.45 cm | W. 0.96 cm | Th. 0.35 cm
National Museum of Alexandria 315, SCA 290

Ring of one twisted wire ended with a Herakles knot (for protection), found in Canopus:
1st century BC−1st century AD
D. 1.56 cm | Th. 0.48 cm
Graeco-Roman Museum, Alexandria 32344, SCA 1128

Other jewellery
Bird-shaped pendant:
L. 1.7 cm
National Museum of Alexandria 1558, SCA 1204

Uraeus fragment
L. 3.8 cm
National Museum of Alexandria SCA 14333

The Apis bull

The cult of the sacred bull, Apis, the most important of all animal cults in Egypt, was probably initiated in Memphis. Ancient historians inform us that priests carefully selected a living bull on the basis of certain markings. According to Herodotus, the sacred Apis bull had to be 'black, with a white square on its forehead, the image of an eagle on its back, the hair on its tail double, and a scarab under its tongue'.[107] The living animal was a representative of the god Ptah (the patron god of Memphis) on Earth, but also closely linked to the cult of the living king.

This life-size statue depicts Apis in his full vitality and strength. His head is crowned with the sun disc with a *uraeus* (rearing sacred cobra) between his horns. The sculpture is naturalistic in style, with details of the bull's muscular body, the folds of his dewlap, and the hair on his forehead clearly defined. A Greek inscription adorns the pillar that supports the belly of the bull. It hints at the statue's time of production during the emperor Hadrian's visit to Egypt in AD 130: '[To Zeus Helios the great] Serapis and to the gods worshipped in the same temple on the occasion of the venerable emperor Caesar Trajan Hadrian our patron, the city …'.

When the Apis bull died, its body was mummified and it turned into Osiris-Apis. The death of the animal was announced all over the country and the whole nation contributed to its costly burial. When a new Apis was found everyone in the country rejoiced, and the Roman writer Pliny even informs us that 'gold and silver goblets were thrown into the Nile on his birthday'.[108] This devotion can be explained by the powerful abilities ascribed to Apis. He was, among other things, capable of interpreting dreams, telling fortunes, making prophecies and delivering oracles, all of which ensured that a large number of pilgrims from all over Egypt regularly visited his sanctuary.

Memphis, the residence of the pharaohs during most of pharaonic history and the home of the creator god Ptah, was the main place of worship of the Apis bull, though his temple has yet to be discovered among the ruins of the ancient capital. The mummified animals were buried in Saqqara, the necropolis (cemetery) of Memphis on the western bank of the Nile. Numerous bulls were interred in huge stone sarcophagi (stone coffins) deposited in extensive underground galleries. Appreciating the close link between the cult of Apis and the living king, but also wishing to ensure a good relationship with the Egyptian priesthood, Alexander the Great did not hesitate to offer valuable sacrifices to the Apis bull when he arrived in Memphis in 332 BC.

His successor, Ptolemy I (r. 323–285 BC) brought the cult of Apis to Alexandria, where he was worshipped by the Greeks in the (human) form of the god Serapis. A bilingual foundation plaque discovered in his sanctuary at Alexandria indicates that the Egyptian name Osiris-Apis was the official counterpart of the Greek Serapis (see p. 129). However, images of the god Apis in animal form continued to be produced in Ptolemaic and even Roman times. The emperor Hadrian (r. AD 117–38), whose visit to Egypt left a profound impression on him (see pp. 224–26), promoted the cult of Apis, and even more the one of Serapis, and rebuilt the Serapeum in Alexandria.

[MSD]

Colossal statue of the Apis bull
AD 117–38 (reign of emperor Hadrian)
Alexandria; found in 1895 near the northeast corner of the atrium of the underground passages of the Serapeum
Black diorite
H. 1.9 m | L. 2.05 m
Graeco-Roman Museum, Alexandria 351

Serapis statue
2nd century BC
Discovered in Theadelphia (Batn Ihrit),
El Fayum in 1932
Sycamore wood
H. 1.81 m
Graeco-Roman Museum, Alexandria 23352

Statue of Serapis

This wooden statue depicts the god Serapis, the Greek version of the Egyptian god Osiris-Apis. He is seated on a throne, wearing a tunic that falls in a loose fold on his chest. The mantle is brought over the god's left upper arm and covers his lower torso. When the statue was complete, the left hand would have held a staff while the right hand rested on the three-headed dog Cerberus, the 'hellhound' who guarded the entrance of the Greek underworld to prevent the dead from escaping. The god's head would once have been crowned by a *kalathos* – a basket symbolizing abundance and fertility – of which only the lower part is preserved. Serapis is depicted with long curled hair, a full beard divided in two vertical coiled locks on the chin and a moustache. The statue was originally painted and gilded, as indicated by the remains of black pigment on the eyes and hair, as well as off-white layers on his face and body.

This statue was a Roman reproduction of the great cult statue of Serapis, the patron deity of Alexandria. The original cult statue, executed in Greek style, was attributed to the Athenian sculptor Bryaxis. According to some ancient historians, the god arrived in Alexandria from Sinope in the Black Sea region. Serapis, however, assumes the functions of Egyptian deities revered in Memphis, the creator god Ptah and the royal deified bull Osiris-Apis. He combines the attributes of major Greek gods, notably Hades the 'Lord of fertility and of the Underworld', Zeus the supreme god of the Greeks, Asklepios the god of healing and Dionysos the god of wine and vegetation. The cult of Serapis was probably introduced by Ptolemy I Soter I (r. 323–285 BC), possibly to please the priesthood of Memphis, but mainly to win over the Greek communities living in his kingdom. Serapis was venerated in various Egyptian towns where there were Greek communities – such as Theadelphia in the Fayum, where this statue was discovered – but became particularly popular in Alexandria, where he acted as a patron deity, and in Canopus.

He was worshipped together with his wife Isis and their child Harpokrates (Horus-the-child).

His temple precinct in Alexandria, called the Serapeum, was erected in Rhakotis, situated in the southwestern part of the city. The earliest building phase of the sanctuary dates back to the first Ptolemies, who reigned in the third century BC, while Ptolemy IV Philopator (r. 221–205 BC) added a small shrine dedicated to Serapis' son, the child-god Harpokrates. Statues of Ptolemy IV and his wife Arsinoe III have been discovered among the ruins of the temple, and their images on coins document the close association of the king and his wife with Serapis and Isis. The cult of these two deities continued to enjoy enormous popularity during Roman times, rapidly spreading throughout the whole empire.

Following the introduction of Christianity during the late Roman period, the Serapeum became a symbol of pagan religion and it was subsequently destroyed by the Christians in AD 391. On its ruins were built a monastery and the church of St John the Baptist, which remained active until the tenth century AD. [MSD]

Greek text
'King Ptolemy, Son of King Ptolemy, with the Queen Berenike, the Beneficent Gods, to Harpokrates by order of Serapis and Isis'.

Hieroglyphic text
'King Ptolemy beloved of Isis, Son of King Ptolemy, with the Queen Berenike, to Horus-the-child by order of Osiris-Apis and Isis'.[109]

Foundation plaque from the Serapeum in Alexandria
221–204 BC
Gold
L. 12 cm
Graeco-Roman Museum,
Alexandria P.10035

Foundation deposits

Foundation deposits and associated ceremonies are an old pharaonic tradition, dating back to at least the Old Kingdom (2686–2182 BC). A series of rites were performed at the beginning and end of the building process, purifying and establishing the boundaries of the site of each new sacred construction.[110] The most detailed accounts date to the Ptolemaic period,[111] indicative of the Ptolemies' willingness to adopt this age-old tradition. Dedicatory plaques emphasizing the commemorative aspect of the ritual were a novelty that they introduced. These plaques exist in hieroglyphic,[112] Greek[113] and bilingual versions.[114] In the case of this foundation deposit, the hieroglyphic text is nearly a literal transcription of the Greek inscription, using a sophisticated system of alphabetical ideograms. The god Serapis is also rendered

as Osiris-Apis in the hieroglyphic script, further showing the assimilation between the two gods.

The thin gold plaque illustrated here bears a finely dotted bilingual inscription. It records, in both Greek and hieroglyphs, the consecration of a shrine to Harpokrates (Horus-the-child), the son of Serapis and Isis in Ptolemaic belief. Ptolemy IV Philopator (r. 221–205 BC) erected the shrine within the religious complex of the Serapeum at Alexandria. Not much of the original monument remains at the site (it was rebuilt in the Roman period), but the foundation deposits placed below the four corners of the building are evidence of its existence. Intact deposits include a mudbrick model as well as nine bilingual plaques[115] in gold (such as this one), silver, copper, opaque glass and green faience.

[AMB]

Monumental Serapis

This colossal male head in white marble is broken at the base of the neck and has a sea-damaged face. It has an abundant beard of tightly wound curls, with hair falling in long wavy locks marked by deep grooves on both sides of the head. This, and the head's impressive size, prove that it is a divine image. The powerful face, with its luxuriant beard and hair, is characteristic of representations of Serapis. The top of the head is surmounted by a circular horizontal surface, in the middle of which is a square hole, designed for additional attachment. This was for a grain measure, known as the *kalathos*, which the god routinely wore in representations. Like the head, it was also made of white marble and it is cylindrical in form, flaring out slightly towards the top. The *kalathos* is decorated with a stylized depiction of olive trees. From the style of the hair and the empty eyes, which would have been inlaid originally, a date in the second half of the second century BC can be suggested for the head. The *kalathos* appears to have been a later addition or replacement from the Roman period.

The size of the sculpture (83 centimetres when joined) would suggest that it comes from a monumental piece, most likely a statue of an enthroned god between 4 and 4.5 metres in height. This may well have been the main cult statue from the healing shrine of Serapis, celebrated in antiquity for its effectiveness.[116] The IEASM has discovered the substantial remains of this sanctuary, the wall of which measured 101 by 78 metres, making it one of the largest temples in the region. This monumental building may have been founded in the pre-Ptolemaic period, and it is likely that it was originally the temple of Osiris, who later became assimilated with the Greek divine figure of Serapis. The celebrations in honour of the god in the month of Khoiak would have taken place here in the Serapeum.

The head of Serapis and its *kalathos* were excavated separately, in an area where statues and architectural fragments had been dumped in the Byzantine period when a Christian shrine was built next to the Serapeum.[117]   [DJR, from ZK]

Head of Serapis
Head:
2nd century BC
Canopus
Marble
H. 59 cm | W. 34 cm | D. 34 cm
Bibliotheca Alexandrina Antiquities Museum SCA 169

Kalathos:
Roman (?)
Canopus
Marble
H. 24 cm | Upper diam. 26.5 cm | Lower diam. 18.5 cm
Bibliotheca Alexandrina Antiquities Museum SCA 206

Osiris-Canopus jar

This marble jar represents a form of the god Osiris particular to Canopus, known as Osiris-*hydreios*, who assumed a crucial position in the Egyptian cults during Roman times. Similar vessels have been discovered in a small Isis temple at Ras el-Soda (see p. 236).

Abandoning his usual mummy shape, Osiris is depicted as a jar topped by a human head with a three-part wig. He probably once wore an artificial beard, which has broken off. The front side of the vase-like body is decorated with a religious scene: a winged scarab, surrounded by dog-headed figures, is holding the sun disc flanked by two *uraei* (cobras) and surmounted by a naos (shrine) crowned with two falcons. On either side two representations of Harpokrates (Horus-the-child) are visible, with the goddesses Isis and Nephthys behind.

The jar once probably contained the life-bringing waters of the river Nile's flood, which, according to texts inscribed on the walls of the Osiris chapels in the Upper Egyptian temple of Dendera, were associated with the 'humours' (the four bodily fluids) of the god. In Plutarch's famous book *Isis and Osiris* the god is even synonymous with the river itself:

And thus among the Egyptians such men say that Osiris is the Nile consorting with the Earth, which is Isis, and that the sea is Typhon into which the Nile discharges its waters and is lost to view and dissipated, save for that part which the earth takes up and absorbs and thereby becomes fertilized.[118]

This type of object is also known as Osiris-Canopus, because this specific shape of Osiris was originally exclusively connected to the Canopic region where he was probably venerated in the temple dedicated to Isis and Anubis, the jackal-headed god associated with mummification and the afterlife.[119] However, their name has often been confused with 'Canopic jars', a term used since the eighteenth century to refer to human- or animal-headed vessels found in Egyptian tombs, which held the mummified organs of the tomb owners.   [DR]

Head of Nectanebo II

This superb portrait was found underwater in a statue dump near the Serapeum at Canopus, together with a sculpture of Queen Arsinoe (p. 93).

The head represents Nectanebo II (r. 360–342 BC), the last native Egyptian king of the 30th dynasty. It is made of granodiorite with two clearly visible veins of rose quartz running through the king's crown and face. His small mouth has slightly raised corners that give the hint of a smile, while the eyebrow arches are only faintly visible above his almond-shaped eyes. His rather full, oval face is topped by the helmet-shaped blue crown or *khepresh*, and the *uraeus* (sacred cobra) on the forehead coils into four loops, before finally rearing up. The sculpture is not inscribed but the four-looped cobra seems to have been uniquely characteristic of sculpture of Nectanebo II.

Nectanebo's reign was defined by a constant struggle to retain Egypt's political independence and he succeeded in keeping the Persians at bay for several years. However, he was eventually defeated and the country, for a second time within two centuries, had to accept Persian rule. Despite the Persian threat that loomed over his entire reign, Nectanebo II initiated a large-scale country-wide building programme, and the Ptolemies finished many of his temples.

According to the *Alexander Romance* (a late, idealized account of the life of Alexander the Great, the earliest version of which dates to the third century AD), Nectanebo II seduced the Macedonian queen Olympias and fathered Alexander, the future king and liberator of Egypt. Alexander continued the Egyptian tradition of the royal cult, thus legitimizing his reign.   [DR]

Head of Nectanebo II
360–342 BC
Canopus
Granodiorite
H. 37 cm | W. 17 cm | D. 14 cm
Bibliotheca Alexandrina Antiquities Museum SCA 168

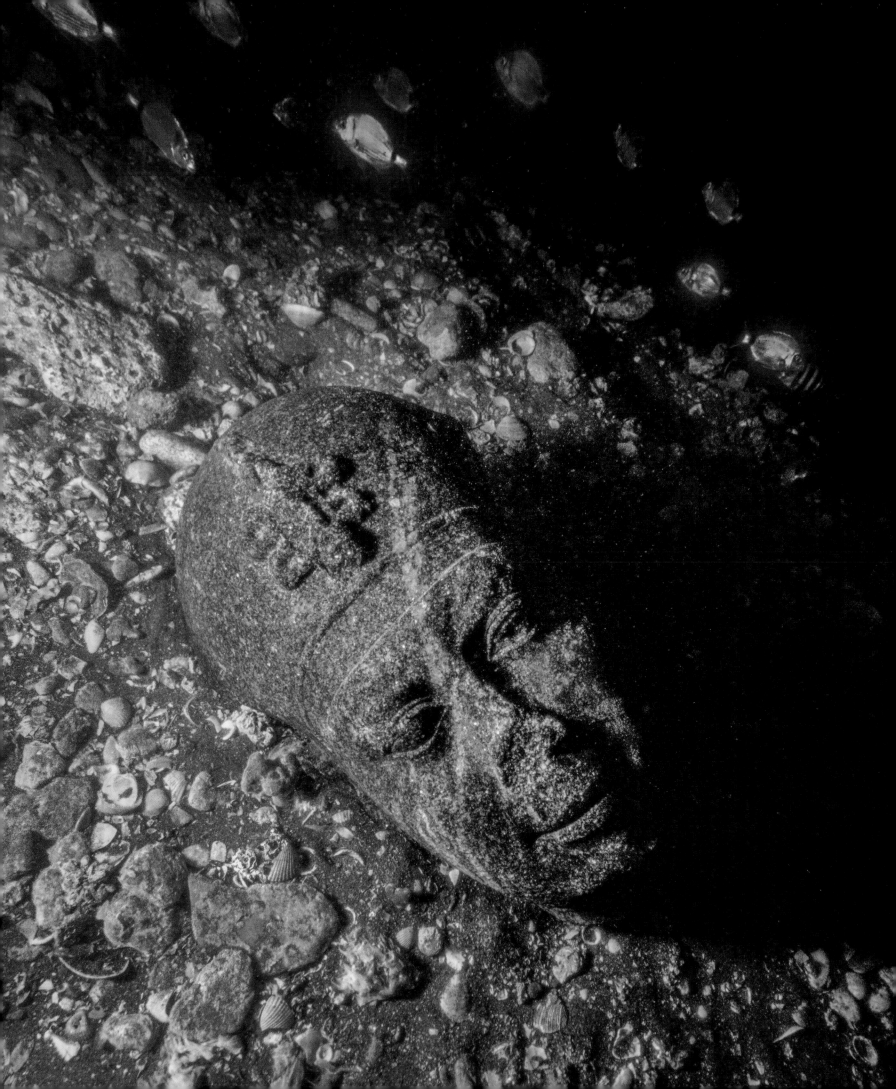

Naos of the Decades

This outstanding monument was hewn from one single block of dark granite. Its walls are meticulously decorated with hieroglyphic texts and figures that help us to reconstruct the history and development of ancient Egyptian astrology, proving its foundation in astronomical observations.

The naos (shrine) was commissioned by Nectanebo I, the founder of the 30th and last native Egyptian dynasty, and originally stood in the temple of the god Shu at the site of Saft el-Hennah in the eastern Nile Delta. At an unknown point in history it was transferred westwards to the Canopic region, where it was smashed and its pieces dispersed. Its roof was rediscovered at the end of the eighteenth century, somewhere near Canopus, and entered the collection of the Louvre in 1817 (D 37). Two more fragments, belonging to the base and the rear wall of the shrine, came to light more than a hundred years later during investigations of an area of ruins underwater in the Abukir Bay, undertaken by Prince Omar Toussoun in 1933 (see p. 17).

These pieces were donated to the Graeco-Roman Museum in Alexandria (JE 25774). Finally, in 1999, the mission of the IEASM discovered four additional pieces in east Canopus while exploring the Abukir Bay. It is only now, more than 1,000 years after its destruction, that the pieces of this unique monument are virtually re-joined.

The inner rear wall of the naos shows the cult statue of Shu in the form of a seated lion. The associated inscription informs us that the real-life image of the god was made of silver covered with fine gold and was four palms (approximately 30 centimetres) high. The external surfaces of the shrine depict a calendar that divides the Egyptian year into sections of ten days or *decades*, which are connected to the successive rising of particular stars, the so-called *decans*. Altogether thirty-seven panels each show five images of deities that are related to different moments of the annual cycle of the *decan* stars: a bird with a human head, a hawk-headed sphinx, a lion-headed ram, a standing mummy and a mummy lying on a

funerary bed. The inscriptions specify the influence the *decans* and the god Shu were supposed to have on life on Earth – especially in connection to wars, massacres and epidemics – and the decor of the naos mainly focuses on the protection of the pharaoh and all of Egypt against evil forces and the defence of the country against rebels.

The Naos of the Decades is one of a large number of monolithic shrines that survive from the Egyptian Late Period (664–332 BC). Some of them show additional inscriptions and depictions that seem to hint at an extended function of this group of monuments on top of their main purpose of housing a god's cult image: they provide detailed cultic, mythological, theological, topographical or – as in this case – astronomical information. This kind of knowledge would usually have been written down on perishable papyrus rolls and stored in temple libraries, but the Late Period clearly saw an increased need to protect Egypt's sacred knowledge by preserving it in a more durable form: carved onto temple and shrine walls made of hard stone.   [DR]

Naos of the Decades
380–362 BC (reign of Nectanebo I)
Canopus
Black granite
H. 1.30 m (reconstructed total height
1.78 m) | W. 0.87 m
Graeco-Roman Museum, Alexandria SCA
161, 163, 162, 164 & JE 25774

4 From myth to festivals

Franck Goddio and Aurélia Masson-Berghoff

The myth of Osiris

Osiris, benevolent god and mythical king, taught men agriculture, gave them laws, educated them in the worship of the gods, and brought them civilization, before his treacherous brother Seth conspired to have him killed. Seth lured Osiris into a chest that he had especially made for him, locked him in and threw the chest into the Nile, causing Osiris to drown. After a long journey that took it to Byblos, Isis, sister and wife of Osiris, recovered the chest containing her dead husband and hid it in the marshes; but Seth discovered it, cut Osiris' body into fourteen pieces, and scattered them throughout Egypt. Isis went in search of each part of the corpse, found one after another, and reassembled her deceased husband. Isis and her sister Nephthys watched over Osiris in the form of kites and beat their wings to instil in him a new breath of life. As a great magician, the goddess boosted her dead husband's virility for long enough to conceive their son and heir Horus. This scene of their union is known from a hymn from the New Kingdom, and is reproduced in the bas-reliefs of temples and tombs from the reign of Seti I (1291–1278 BC) onwards, and later also on coffins.[1] It is illustrated by a unique monument (p. 155) dating from the 13th dynasty (reign of king Khendjer, *c.* 1747 BC). It shows the god stretched out on his nuptial/funerary bed, with Isis on his body in the very act of begetting their son Horus, and watched over by the quadruple falcon effigy of Horus, the heir-to-be. The presence of the image of the Horus falcons on the four cardinal points safeguarding Osiris accentuates the two major functions expected of Horus, and through and after him of all the kings of Egypt: first to avenge his father, and second to take care of his father.

For Horus, 'to avenge his father' meant to check Seth, and to eliminate the evil and disorder he represents; for the pharaohs, 'to avenge his father' was to guarantee the reign of order and justice throughout the country. 'To take care of his father' Horus would, with the help of Isis and Anubis the Embalmer, complete the funerary rites assuring the survival of Osiris in the netherworld, and the perpetual maintenance of his name over the millennia. For the succeeding kings of Egypt, 'to take care of his father' was to guarantee the funerary cults for the preceding sovereigns, and the perpetuation of their names. Kings built mortuary temples to maintain the cult of the dead pharaohs over the centuries.

In this way, the myth of Osiris constitutes the very core and backbone of the ideology of Egyptian kingship: each new pharaoh is a 'Horus' whose task

51   A statuette of Osiris and a model of a processional barge for this god, shown in their place of excavation in Thonis-Heracleion

52 False door
Late Period (664–332 BC)
Sais, Egypt
Limestone
H 37.0 cm
Bibliotheca Alexandrina Antiquities
Museum 587, CG 42879

The 'false door' was an imitation doorway placed in the tomb, facing west, and seen as linking the living and the dead. Here, it reproduced the facade of an Egyptian temple which was supposedly dedicated to Osiris. He appears between the jambs of the door (central figure), flanked by the goddesses Isis and Nephthys.

is to defend Egypt against all enemies, who were equated with Seth and with evil, and to maintain the cult of his predecessors. Ever since the time of the Pyramid Texts (funerary spells inscribed on the walls inside pyramids of the 5th and 6th dynasties), any deceased pharaoh becomes an Osiris, and the new king, his divine heir, is a Horus.

Once the son of Osiris was born, Isis hid the child Horus in the marshes of the Delta to protect him from Seth's murderous intent. Her great magic powers and spells allowed her to save Horus from a venomous animal's mortal bite. Her spells are reproduced on papyri, and on stone. So-called 'healing stelae', with engravings of the incantations Isis had pronounced to save her son, show the child Horus standing on crocodiles, brandishing in his hands dangerous animals such as snakes and scorpions, which he has vanquished and holds fast to control their noxiousness. The water running down over the saving formulae of Isis captures their magic power and is collected in a basin to be used for its healing virtues (p. 159).

Above all, Isis is the goddess who, in her name of 'Great-in-magic', reinstils life. With this epithet she can be found, together with Osiris, in a set of beautiful statues from a tomb of the Saite period (26th dynasty). The inscriptions indicate that she offers life to a deceased high dignitary called Psamtik, a contemporary of the pharaoh Amasis (r. 570–526 BC), while Osiris grants him a beautiful burial and the offerings that assure him eternal life (p. 153).

The Mysteries of Osiris

From at least as early as the Middle Kingdom (c. 2055–1650 BC), the Mysteries of Osiris were the most important ritual celebrations to take place in Egypt each year. The greatest part of the sequences of the ceremonies and the details of the rituals remained secret; however, stelae from the Middle and New Kingdoms found in Abydos, the sacred town of Osiris since predynastic times, indicate that an effigy of the god, probably made during the Mysteries, emerged from the temple for a public procession in its golden barque (sailing boat), called *Neshemet*. After that, only the initiated accompanied the divine cortège to the tomb of the god. In the course of this mystery in the 'House of Gold' in Abydos, it seems that other secret ceremonies took place to commemorate the reconstitution of Osiris' dismembered body and its return to life.[2]

According to the bas-reliefs in the Osirian chapels on the roof of the temple at Dendera,[3] ritual practices of transformation recreated life from earth and water by fabricating two Osirian figures: Osiris *vegetans* and Osiris-Sokar. On the 12th day of Khoiak, the last month of the Nile Inundation when the floodwaters receded to free the fields for cultivation, the priests began the process of creating the Osiris *vegetans* statuette. They placed earth, barley and floodwater in two halves of a special golden mould and watered it using a golden pail (*situla*) until the plants sprouted (see p. 168). The germination of plants from the 'corpse' of this 'Osiris *vegetans*' symbolized eternally renewed life. It also prefigured the awakening of nature in the season of germination, which began

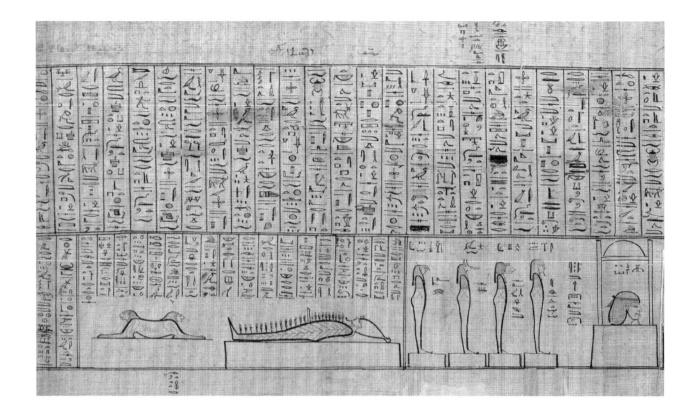

as the month of Khoiak ended. On the 22nd of Khoiak, the completed Osiris *vegetans* took part in a nautical event on the sacred lake of the temple. Thirty-four papyrus barques (one cubit and two palms, i.e. 67.5 cm, long), each carrying a divinity (the Osiris *vegetans* figure, and thirty-three other figures each representing an Egyptian god sitting on a throne), were illuminated by 365 small lamps symbolizing the number of days in a year.

The material for a second statuette called 'Osiris-Sokar' was prepared in parallel on the 12th day of Khoiak: all the required substances (earth, spices, resins, crushed precious stones and minerals) were carefully measured into fourteen vessels, each described in the ritual and made in a particular shape and material. Into each of these fourteen receptacles, which recalled the severed pieces of Osiris' body, was poured earth soaked in water from the sacred lake with a long ladle called a *simpulum*, its Egyptian name being 'the great Assembleress', or 'she-who-reunites'.[4] Once all these substances were mixed together, the resulting paste was modelled into the shape of an egg and put into a silver vase covered with sycamore branches to maintain its softness. On the 16th of Khoiak, this paste was poured into the two halves of a golden mould of the same size (one cubit) as that of the Osiris *vegetans* (pp. 168–69). For four days, from the 16th to the 19th of Khoiak, the mould of the Osiris-Sokar was put to rest on a golden bed turned to the north. On the 19th of Khoiak the two halves were assembled and the statuette set on a golden pedestal and left in the sun to dry. It was then anointed, wrapped in linen bandages and finally painted on the 23rd or 24th of Khoiak. It was first painted with a blackish unguent, which is described in reliefs at the temple of Edfu (see pp. 174–75), and then colours were applied – yellow for

53 Jumilhac papyrus. This papyrus details various myths from a region in southern Egypt (XVIIIth nome of Upper Egypt), and features a representation of Osiris *vegetans*, seeds germinating from his body
Late Ptolemaic period.
Louvre Museum, Paris E 17110

54 Decree of Canopus
238 BC
Kom el-Hisn
Limestone
H. 2.02 m
Egyptian Museum, Cairo CG 22186

the face (gold to represent the skin of the gods) and blue for the wig, as well as the eyes, as if they were inlaid.[5] As it was only completed on the 24th, the Osiris-Sokar statuette could not participate in the navigation on the 22nd.[6]

At the end of the Mysteries, both the Osiris *vegetans* and the Osiris-Sokar made during the ceremonies that year were put into sycamore coffins and placed in an 'upper' tomb. They remained there for the next year, replacing the previous ones, which were removed and buried in 'lower' tombs, cemeteries reserved for these figures.

The Mysteries in Thonis-Heracleion and Canopus

The excavations carried out in the towns of Thonis-Heracleion and Canopus by the European Institute for Underwater Archaeology, brought to light ritual deposits and instruments linked to the Mysteries of the month of Khoiak. These objects demonstrate the sacred character of the Grand Canal, the waterway that flowed along the north side of the temple of Amun-Gereb. Almost all of the long ladles called *simpula* (p. 189) were found in this canal, and in the basins and waterways around it. All of them were ritually deposited in the water, some deliberately twisted or damaged. The practice of dropping objects into water, and sometimes even damaging them, is known from elsewhere: such objects were not intended to serve again after their sacred function, so they were deliberately rendered unusable (by mutilating them) and inaccessible (by their immersion in the canal).[7]

The Grand Canal also served as the sacred lake for the navigation of the 22nd of Khoiak: leaden votive barques have been found at its bottom, their size and decoration imitating the papyrus boats that were used in the nautical event described in the ritual at Dendera.

A large 'garden tank' of pink granite was discovered within the grounds of the temple of Amun-Gereb (pp. 170–71). Its presence close to the naos (shrine) of the god, to whom a dynastic function was attributed, strongly suggests that Osirian rites may have played a role in the rituals of the transmission of royal power in Thonis-Heracleion (see Chapter 3, p. 79). This accords with the growing development of the Osiris cult in the first millennium BC, when the temples were increasingly seats of Osirian rites.[8] The link between Amun-Gereb's granting of sovereignty and the rites of Khoiak is further supported by a monumental stele found at Thonis-Heracleion (p. 96) of Ptolemy VIII Euergetes II (170–163, 145–116 BC), found north of the North Canal, which mentions the goddesses Shentayt, Isis and Nephthys (the goddesses who participate in the Mysteries) among the deities of the temple.[9]

Numerous discoveries in the Canopic region echo the terms of the Decree of Canopus (238 BC) (fig. 54), which mentions a ritual navigation of Osiris from Thonis-Heracleion to Canopus on the 29th of Khoiak, on a special ceremonial barque. The canal linking Thonis-Heracleion to Canopus has been rediscovered by the IEASM and its route well defined.[10] The existence of this waterway, which flowed into the great western lake and on into the canal linking

55 Head of Berenike II
3rd century BC
Canopus
Diorite
H. 13.7 cm
Bibliotheca Alexandrina Antiquities Museum
SCA 204

Berenike was the daughter of Magas
of Cyrene and the wife of Ptolemy III
Euergetes I. She was also the mother
of Princess Berenike, who, according to
the Decree of Canopus, died as a virgin
and was celebrated alongside Osiris
during the sacred navigation of the 29th
of Khoiak.

Thonis-Heracleion with Canopus, demonstrates that the procession from the temple of Amun-Gereb in Thonis-Heracleion to Canopus could have been carried out on the water. The navigation of the 29th of Khoiak is distinct from that on the 22nd, suggesting two different nautical processions. The later navigation covered a distance of 3.5 km between the two towns, meaning that the barque carrying Osiris must have been a much larger and more robust vessel than the small papyrus barques (67.5 cm long) used during the navigation of the 22nd. On the now submerged banks of the Grand Canal (that is, the waterway that flowed into the canal linking Thonis-Heracleion with Canopus), excavations have revealed groups of plates with offerings, together with many votive deposits which were placed into the waters at successive points along the course of the procession. Such findings are evidence of the acts of devotion which punctuated this sacred journey.[11]

Between two such places of worship, facing each other on opposite sides of the Grand Canal, an 11-metre-long sycamore barque was carefully scuttled with its keel exactly in line with these two offering places. Among sixty-nine

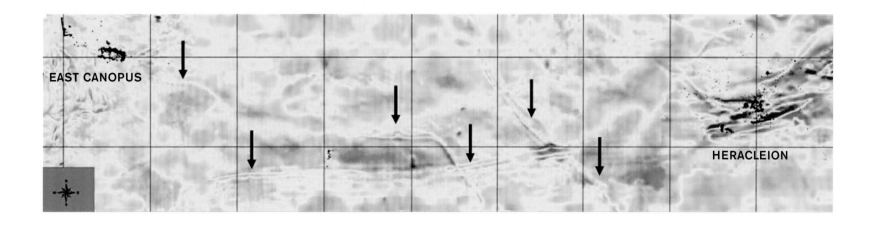

EAST CANOPUS

HERACLEION

56 A detailed map, created by the magnetometer survey, illustrating the line of the canals in the region between Thonis-Heracleion and Canopus. The arrows mark the locations of small test excavations that confirmed their existence

ships and boats so far discovered in the waters of Thonis-Heracleion, this is the only one built of sycamore, a wood which is linked to the rebirth of Osiris. Its position in the sacred way, specifically aligned and surrounded by *simpula* and votive items, clearly suggests that this is most probably a ritual (Osirian?) boat. After it had served its purpose in the Mysteries, it might have been ritually sunk in the sacred canal, protected from any possible dismantling or sacrilege.[12]

In addition to the Egyptian items connected with the Mysteries of Osiris, a number of objects linked to Dionysian rituals have also been found, such as a skyphoid pyxis (a small lidded ceramic pot) which displays a maenad, a female follower of Dionysos, dancing to the sound of her tambourine, as one of the typical participants in Dionysian processions.[13] Theological connections between Osiris and Dionysos do indeed go back to the very early presence of the Greeks in Egypt, particularly in the Canopic region.

'Osiris, he who is called Dionysos in the Greek tongue'[14]

Dionysos, Greek god of wine and vegetation, ecstasy and transformation, was equated with the Egyptian god Osiris, with whom he shared similar aspects and roles.[15] The fifth-century BC Greek historian Herodotus states that he learnt about this identification from Egyptian priests. Later Greek authors, Diodorus Siculus (first century BC) and Plutarch (*c.* AD 46–125), also note many similarities between the myths and the nature of the two deities. Dionysos was the god who brought civilization to humanity; he was dismembered by the Titans and revived by Rhea who reassembled his limbs; Plutarch called him 'the lord and master not only of wine, but of the nature of every sort of moisture'.[16] Like Osiris, Dionysos sustained the cyclic regeneration of nature and life itself. The equation of the two gods probably goes back to the first Greek settlers in Egypt, who, in the seventh century BC, sought to find common ground with an otherwise alien culture. Participating in the Osirian cult and enticed by its promise of revival, and engaging with Egyptians and their priests,[17] they recognized in Osiris one of their own gods. This Greek 'translation' (*interpretatio graeca*)[18] was also applied to other deities in the Osirian myths: Egyptian Horus found his counterpart in the Greek Apollo, Seth in the Titan Typhon (p. 214) and Thoth in Hermes (p. 216).

In later art Dionysos typically appears as a youthful god surrounded by ivy and vine leaves (p. 218), holding a *thyrsos*, a fennel stalk topped by a pine cone. Earlier representations show him mature and bearded, as on a colossal limestone mask from Cyprus (p. 146).[19] It was once fixed atop a pillar, probably in a theatre or another public building. As we can see on a series of fifth-century BC wine

**57 Colossal mask of a bearded
and ivy-crowned Dionysos**
100 BC– AD 100 (?)
From Soloi (Cyprus)
Limestone
H. 89 cm | W. 61 cm | D. 25 cm
British Museum 1910,1014.1

jars from Attica in Greece, such pillars were the centre of rituals performed by women, priestesses or maenads, the mythical unruly female followers of Dionysos.[20] On the wine jar in fig. 58, the bearded and wreathed mask is mounted on a column adorned with ivy and draped in a long garment to form a kind of effigy of the god. In front of it, wine jars stand on a low table and women transfer wine into smaller cups using a long-handled ladle.

Ladles featuring the graceful head of a duck at the end of their long handle initially appeared in Egypt by around 1000 BC. The earliest known example was discovered in the tomb of Psusennes (r. 1047–1001 BC) in Tanis. They later became familiar instruments throughout the Mediterranean world (termed *kyathos* in Greek and *simpulum* in Latin), prominently connected with the consumption of wine in Dionysian rituals and festivals in pouring libations – offerings of drink to the gods.[21] In Thonis-Heracleion, they form the most common ritual instruments discovered in the Grand Canal along the north side of the temple of Amun-Gereb, the canal which was used in sacred navigations during the festival of Khoiak. A passage from the Roman geographer Strabo (*c.* 64 BC–AD 24) echoes the Dionysian atmosphere of the Khoiak festivals in the Canopic region:

> *But remarkable above everything else is the multitude of persons who resort to the public festivals, and come from Alexandria by the canal. For day and night there are crowds of men and women in boats, singing and dancing, without restraint, and with the utmost licentiousness. Others, at Canopus itself, keep hostelries situated on the banks of the canal, which are well adapted for such kind of diversion and revelry.*[22]

A further analogy between Osiris and Dionysos is the phallic aspect of celebrations held in their honour. Both Herodotus and Plutarch describe a statue of Osiris with a large movable phallus carried in procession during the Pamylia, a Theban festival associated with the annual Nile flood. To Herodotus this recalled the Greek *phallophoria*, a Dionysian procession that also featured a gigantic phallus.[23] A lavish and colourful procession in Alexandria initiated by the Greco-Macedonian king Ptolemy II Philadelphos (r. 285–246 BC) involved the parading of statues of Alexander the Great and Ptolemy I Soter I (both wearing a golden crown of ivy) alongside those of Dionysos and a gigantic golden phallus 180 Roman feet (about 53 metres) long.[24] Since the sixth century BC, figures representing youths with disproportionately large phalluses, sometimes carried in procession, were very common in Lower Egypt, including in the international harbour towns of Thonis-Heracleion (p. 211) and Naukratis. Such fertility figures were not necessarily directly associated with Osiris but with his son Harpokrates (another name for Horus-the-child), and were used in Egyptian domestic rituals and religious festivities celebrating the Inundation and the renewed fertility it brought to the fields.[25] The celebrations were, nonetheless, deeply connected with Osirian rites.

Claiming to descend from Dionysos on the maternal side, the Ptolemies promoted the Osirian and Dionysian cults, together with the royal and Serapis cults.[26] They all contributed differently and yet coherently to the message of royal legitimacy that the Ptolemaic dynasty was intent on telling. The recent discoveries by the IEASM in the Canopic region demonstrate the extent to which Thonis-Heracleion and Canopus participated in this powerful propaganda and benefited from royal favour and interest.

58 Greek wine jar (*stamnos*)
470–450 BC
Vulci (Italy)
Pottery
H. 34.3 cm
British Museum 1856,0512.14

This red-figured vase shows rituals performed in front of an image of Dionysos.

59 Moulded vase
End of Ptolemaic period
(late 1st century BC)
Alexandria east harbour
Pottery
H. 16 cm
Maritime Museum, Alexandria SCA 1608

The vase is decorated with a scene set in a
vineyard, referring to Dionysos as a god of wine.

Words pronounced (by Nitokris):

'Greetings to you, Osiris who presides over the west, Unnefer, Lord of Life, sovereign in the underworld (duat), master of the fear towards his enemies, appearing with the White Crown, master of the Ureret Crown, venerable image, Lord of Memphis, great in Busiris, God, prince in Opet, master of the prestige in the temple of the Phoenix, Osiris who presides over the West, bull in Heliopolis, he who favours the one he loves, Nitokris, beloved by Mut, proclaimed just.'

Osiris, Lord of Life

In this statue the god Osiris wears the white crown of Upper Egypt adorned by a rearing cobra (*uraeus*) and holds his regalia, the crook and flail.[27] The figure makes a majestic impression; the god's face is grave, and his eyes are emphasized by pronounced cosmetic lines and prominent eyebrows, which are characteristic of the sculptural style of the previous 25th dynasty (760–656 BC).[28] The high crown accentuates the shape of his slender body, the muscular form of which is revealed through the fine and supple clothing carefully rendered by the artist.

The statue was dedicated to Osiris by the 'God's Wife of Amun' (the highest-ranking priestess of the Amun cult) called Nitokris, daughter of Psamtik I (r. 664–610 BC). Nitokris' request for the gift of life and power is expressed in an inscription on the pedestal. Cartouches (ovals containing royal names) of Nitokris (right) and her father (left) frame the cartouche of the god, which is adorned by two tall feathers. On the back pillar, which simulates an obelisk, she glorifies the epithets of Osiris, notably 'Osiris who presides over the west', and 'Lord of Life'.[29] [ASvB]

Standing statue of Osiris
26th dynasty (664–525 BC)
Medinet Habu
Greywacke
H. 1.5 m
Egyptian Museum, Cairo CG 38231

Isis and Osiris

These seated statues of the divine Isis and her husband Osiris were found together in the tomb of an official titled 'Superior of the Seal', 'Superior of the Palace', a contemporary to king Amasis.[30] Isis, slender in form, wears a sheath dress and a crown in the form of the emblem of Hathor, which consists of a solar disc set between cow's horns. In her right hand she holds the *ankh*, the sign of life. Her face is modelled with wide-open eyes and a slight smile. Osiris, carved in the same beautiful style of the 26th dynasty, is wrapped in fine cloth, from which his hands emerge holding the flail and the *heqa* sceptre (or crook), symbols of sovereignty. On his head Osiris wears his usual *atef* crown, consisting of the white crown of Upper Egypt with two ostrich feathers at the side and a sacred rearing cobra at the front (the *uraeus*). He also has a finely braided divine false beard. The inscriptions around the bases of the statues were intended to invoke 'Isis, mother of the god, great in magic, mistress of the Two Lands', and 'Osiris who presides in the west, great god, lord of Ro-Setaou'. Following his judgement of the deceased, Osiris could grant wishes for a peaceful arrival in the netherworld, while Isis gives life, her epithets and the carved life symbol revealing her to be a magician stronger than death.[31] This divine couple, together with a third statue of Hathor 'protectress of the deceased', belonged to a sumptuous burial and would have ensured perpetual protection for the person with whom they were interred.[32]   [JB-K]

Isis and Osiris seated
26th dynasty (reign of Amasis, 570–526 BC)
Saqqara
Greywacke, with a satin polish
H. 90 cm and 89 cm
Egyptian Museum, Cairo CG 38354 and CG 38358

Isis, as guardian of Osiris

This is an unusual sculpture, which was found in a tomb. It represents a kneeling Isis, holding a statuette of a mummified Osiris across her knees, the edges of her hands resting on her thighs.[33] Isis is smiling and her slender body is emphasized by the large volume of her head with its 'bag wig' and hair band. She kneels upon a thick pedestal with her back against an arched stele, both of which are engraved with hieroglyphs, although their magical meaning remains obscure.

Isis is commonly portrayed in her maternal role from the Third Intermediate Period (c. 1069–664 BC) onwards, with countless representations of her suckling the child Horus/Harpokrates. In this statuette, however, she is portrayed in her role as the 'guardian of the heavenly flesh'. After she has succeeded in reassembling the dismembered Osiris, she has to save her beloved brother/husband from death and perform the rituals necessary for his rebirth. In this form the statuette is a visual metaphor of the 'Mansion of Gold', the room reserved in the temple for divine embalming.[34] At Dendera, a similar iconography shows a figure in the same position, called 'Hathor-Nebethetepet'; the feet of the Osiris figurine she holds are set upon a support shaped like the face of Hathor, and she presides over the mysteries of the 'garden tank' (see p. 171). In this vat a mould in the shape of a mummy with the white crown was used to create the figure of Osiris *vegetans* during the celebration of the Mysteries,[35] in the festival of Khoiak (p. 182). The statuette here illustrates one of the key points of the mysteries represented in the decoration of the six chapels on the roof of the temple of Hathor at Dendera.[36]

The presence of this goddess in a tomb is very significant: like some other statuettes from the Late Period, it upholds the promise of rebirth for the owner of the tomb, with the goddess at the heart of this magical transformation.[37]   [From JB-K]

Statuette of Isis holding Osiris
25th dynasty (760–656 BC)
Northern necropolis of Abydos (Upper Egypt)
Limestone
H: 19.5 cm
Egyptian Museum, Cairo CG 38867

Cult statue of Osiris lying on a leonine bed with Isis, in the form of a kite
Probably 13th dynasty (reign of Khendjer)
Tomb of king Djer (1st dynasty),
at Umm el-Qa'ab (Abydos;
8th nome *Ta-our* of Upper Egypt)
Basalt
L. 1.78 m
Egyptian Museum, Cairo JE 32090

Isis revivifies Osiris

This unique cult statue represents a key moment in the myth of Osiris, when the magician Isis appears as a kite and revivifies her murdered husband, mating with him to beget Horus, their son and heir.[38] This form of the divine union, which was first described in the texts in the pyramid of Unas (*c.* 2360 BC), is clearly expressed during the 18th dynasty (1570–1293 BC), when Isis was celebrated for her power of bringing Osiris back to life with the shadow and the breath of her wings.[39]

Here, Osiris wears the white crown of Upper Egypt and the divine beard and carries the sceptres of sovereignty – the flail (*nekhakha*) and the cane (in place of the classic crook). He lies in the middle of a funerary bed, which is in the form

of two lions standing side by side.[40] At each end of the lion bed, a pair of standing hawks embrace the head and feet of the god with their long wings.

This monumental sculpture in the round was discovered in the tomb of the king Djer (*c.* 3000 BC) in the royal necropolis at Abydos – which was reinterpreted later as the 'Tomb of Osiris'. There has been much controversy over the statue's date, because of the difficulty of deciphering its lightly engraved inscriptions, the carefully erased titulary (the set of names by which a king is designated) and the deliberate damage (particularly to the face, apart from the eyes). It is likely that the piece should actually be attributed to king Khendjer of the 13th dynasty (towards 1747 BC), designated on the monument

as 'Beloved of Osiris Lord of Abydos, and of Wepwawet (Opener of the Way) Lord of the Sacred Land'.[41]

This imagery endures over the centuries, as it can be found in duplicate in the temples of Abydos (Seti I, r. 1290–1279 BC) and Dendera (Late Ptolemaic, *c.* 54–30 BC).[42] It places Osiris, the mythical king, at the beginning of the line of his historical descendants ruling Earth. He is Unnefer – the 'Perfect Being' – who overcomes death to impregnate his sister-wife Isis and create his heir Horus. Osiris is the model of the terrestrial king, whose dynastic successions he legitimizes, and he gives hope to the devoted believer that he or she will reach the state of being a blessed soul – *akh* – near the god after death. [JB-K]

Osiris awakened

This statue portrays the newly awakened Osiris. The god is covered with a pale sheath garment and is stretched out on his stomach. His smiling head with a beard – a symbol of divine kingship – lifts up in its awakening. Its majesty is emphasized by the *tcheni* crown, a symbol of the (re)born Osiris, with its ostrich feathers and twisted ram's horns with a sun disc.[43] The refined style of the sculpture is typical of the Saite period (26th dynasty, 664–525 BC) and is perhaps reminiscent of a 'portrait' of the pharaoh Apries.[44]

This image of the revived Osiris appears in temples, shrines,[45] tombs and coffins.[46] Seti I (r. 1290–1279 BC) chose it for the ceiling of his 'Osireion' temple at Abydos, as did Apries at Hermopolis Parva. In both cases, the iconography of the awakening remains the same as that later recorded in the upper chapels of Ptolemaic Dendera.

Enhanced by the precious metals of the crown, this unique cult object would have belonged to a sacred space.[47] The use of gneiss for its manufacture is interesting, as this rare, hard metamorphic rock was not commonly used in the Saite period when the statue was made. It would consequently appear that this piece was carved in a workshop in the north of the country by craftsmen who deliberately chose gneiss to recall earlier sacred statuary, to emphasize the importance of this particular incarnation of Osiris.

At a length of close to one cubit, this statue is the same size as the corn-mummy and the Osiris-Sokar described in the rituals of the festival of Khoiak. This similarity in size is not coincidental, as all three emphasize the awakening of the god. [JB–K]

Statue of Osiris awakened
26th dynasty (664–525 BC) perhaps reign of Apries (580–570 BC)
Horbeit (*Chedenou*/Pharbaïtos)
Gneiss, gold/electrum, bronze
L. 55.5 cm
Egyptian Museum, Cairo CG 38424

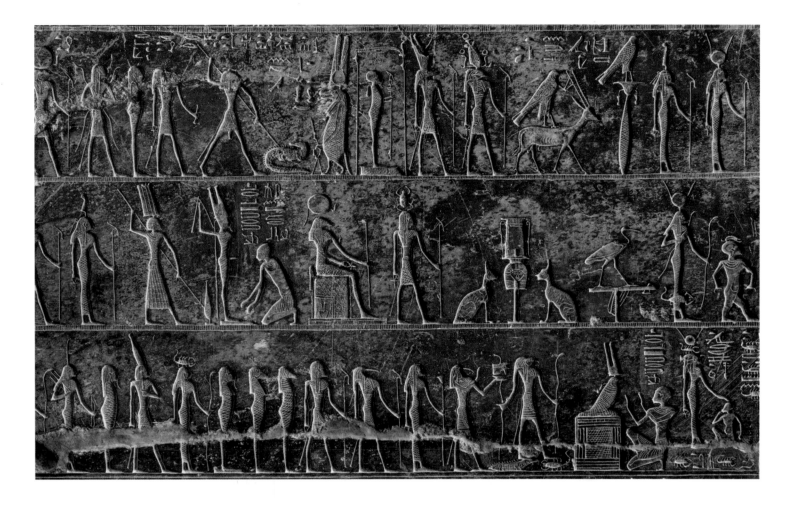

Magical stele of Horus

Stele of Horus
30th dynasty (380–342 BC)
Tell el-Qalâh (Lower Egypt)
Greywacke (stele), limestone (base)
Total H. 93 cm | H. of stele 61 cm
Egyptian Museum, Cairo CG 9402 = JE 33
264 and 34 081.

This small stele had healing and protective powers. Set upon a limestone base[48] on which a Phoenician inscription names the dedicant – Pâl-Astarte, son of Chemrebi[49] – the monument is full of the magical knowledge of its time. Carved half in the round, Horus stands naked on the upturned heads of crocodiles. He wears a thick side-lock of hair, a large necklace, bracelets and a heart-shaped pendant. In his fists he grasps bunches of evil animals, absorbing their power for his own benefit: arched scorpions, twin snakes, a chained oryx with sharpened horns (right) and a lion (left). Horus is flanked on his right by the falcon-headed Ra-Horakhty-Sokar-Osiris, set on a coiled snake, and on his left by the lotus-shaped emblem of Nefertum. Further divine protection would have been provided by a mask of Bes, protector of births, which would have been inserted at the top of the stele.

The engraved images and inscriptions were intended to counter any deadly attack from the enemy, particularly bites and stings. They draw upon the vast textual corpus of incantations and rituals of divine origin.[50] Through speech, *heka* (magic) comes into being,[51] when performed by the magician summoning the gods Thoth, Horus-the-Saviour and Osiris. Water poured over the inscriptions absorbed the magical power of the words. This transformed precious fluid was collected in the hollow of the limestone base and used for healing – by either drinking or applying to the body.

Horus also offered divine protection during the celebration of the resurrection of Osiris during the festival of Khoiak. He is depicted at the entrance of the penultimate upper chapel of the temple at Dendera, where representations of each of Egypt's provinces (nomes) bring their Canopic jars filled with purifying water.[52] Here he proclaims 'I am Horus the Saviour!' and safeguards Osiris 'awakened' by his celebrations, spreading joy throughout all Egypt.

[JB-K]

Votive Horus falcon
26th–30th dynasty (664–342 BC)
Probably from Buto[53]
Bronze
H. 15 cm
Graeco-Roman Museum, Alexandria 247

Votive falcon

Votive donations were offered to a god to request long life in this world and the next. This bronze was dedicated to a form of the god Horus revered in the town of Buto in the western Delta, and to Wadjit, its patron goddess. Many similar objects of various sizes are known: their bases were reliquaries and may have contained a falcon's bone, a feather or an entire mummified animal.[54] Here, the falcon wears the crown of Upper and Lower Egypt, once adorned with a *uraeus* (the sacred rearing cobra), which is now lost. Such statuettes were very common during the Late Period and are usually dated to between the 26th and 30th dynasties (664–342 BC).

Three lines of text are engraved on the base below the bird's powerful claws:

May Horus of Pe [Buto] and
Wadjit offer life to Queref,
son of Padiusir, who was brought
into life by the mistress of the
house Tasenekhet …

We know that one of pharaoh Psamtik I's (r. 664–610 BC) generals bore the rare name of Queref, which was of Libyan origin. However, the names of the father and mother of the donor of this statuette are different, and it is probable that this Queref was one of the general's descendants.   [ASvB]

Eye of Horus

This tiny bead representing the eye of Horus, the *wedjat*-eye, is finely decorated with delicate gold wire and a gold sphere for the pupil.[55] The *wedjat*-eye is half human (the eye and brow), and half falcon (the vertical and spiral elements underneath).[56] Horus eye amulets and jewellery were very popular in ancient Egypt from the Old Kingdom to Roman times. The eye had great symbolic significance,[57] representing integrity, health, the full moon and sometimes also the sun (Ra) or Egypt itself.   [ASvB]

Bead representing the eye of Horus
26th–30th dynasty (664–342 BC)[58]
Thonis-Heracleion
Gold
L. 0.82 cm | H. 0.68 cm | D. 0.18 cm
Graeco-Roman Museum, Alexandria SCA 1123

'Beloved of Osiris': golden objects from a royal tomb

The amulet depicting the god Osiris (opposite) and the ewer (right), both made of gold, were discovered in 1939 and 1940 in the royal burial complex at Tanis, where several kings of the 21st and 22nd dynasties found their final resting place. The tombs contained a great number of objects made of gold, silver, lapis lazuli and other precious stones. It was only because their discovery coincided with the beginning of the Second World War that the royal tombs of Tanis did not gain the same public attention as Tutankhamun's burial, found seventeen years earlier.

The Osiris amulet originally belonged to Prince Hornakht, the son of pharaoh Osorkon II, who ruled Egypt during the 22nd dynasty. Hornakht was appointed by his father to the office of Chief Priest of the god Amun at Tanis – a town in the northeastern Nile Delta and at that time capital of the country – in the hope of strengthening the king's authority in Lower Egypt. When the prince died at a young age, Osorkon II made provisions to ensure that his son would be buried in his own tomb at Tanis.

During the excavations of his burial, a series of gold amulets that covered parts of the prince's mummy were found. They are small in size but are finished to a high quality, and represent various mythical symbols intended to safeguard the sanctity of Hornakht's mummified body. The god

Osiris was undoubtedly one of the most popular deities in ancient Egypt; his role as lord of the underworld meant that he was strongly connected to the idea of life after death. His myth tells us that the god, who ruled Egypt as a primeval king, was killed by his jealous brother Seth, then brought back to life for a short period of time with the help of his sister-wife Isis, before finally becoming the lord of the dead. Initially it was only the king and his family and closest entourage who could hope for the same fate as Osiris – being reborn after death – but during the course of the first millennium BC this privilege also became available to common people, and by the end of this millennium anyone could hope to defeat death in the afterlife.

The golden ewer (right) once belonged to Amenemope, a pharaoh of the 21st dynasty. The king is mentioned in the engraved inscription and referred to as 'beloved of Osiris, lord of Abydos'. Although Osiris was extensively worshipped in the Canopic region during the Late and Ptolemaic periods (664–31 BC), it was the Upper Egyptian town of Abydos that, since early dynastic times, was regarded as his main cult centre, and this was also where the god was believed to be buried. The ewer was probably used to serve a libation, a ritual pouring of a liquid, as an offering to Osiris in the hope of ensuring eternal life after death. [DR]

Libation ewer
21st dynasty (reign of Amenemope, 993–984 BC)
Tanis
Gold
H. 20 cm
Egyptian Museum, Cairo JE 86098

Osiris amulet
22nd dynasty (reign of Osorkon II, 874–850 BC)
Tanis
Gold
H. 8.2 cm
Egyptian Museum, Cairo JE 87146

The name of Osiris

To date, this stele is unique, but it echoes an image engraved during the reign of Ptolemy IV Philopator (r. 221–205 BC) on the outer northeastern wall of the Amun temple at Karnak. The lower half of the stele displays a wide, low domed structure with the name of Osiris in hieroglyphs inside: a combination of the eye, the seated god with the *ankh* symbol of life and the throne. From the top of the dome, a network of lush vegetation spreads out in five branches, with leaves shaped like arrowheads. The entire shape of the engraved dome is a representation of the hieroglyph for 'mound', which depicts a mound of earth with shrubs:

The image on the Karnak temple wall shows a similar mound in front of the silhouette of Osiris-Unnefer ('Osiris the Perfect Being'), termed here 'Osiris-in-the-Great-Place'.[59] Clearly, the decoration of the stele is a two-dimensional representation of the actual Osirian mound, the 'Great Place' in Karnak. This real mound incorporated the tombs in which the Osirian figures created during the Mysteries (p. 168) were buried each year, accumulating year after year in underground niches. In Karnak, excavations revealed a few niches from the New Kingdom, without any real organization, that were later developed into domed catacombs, and further extended during the reign of Ptolemy IV. The Osirian mound depicted on the wall of the temple of Amun and on this stele is specifically linked to the 'Great Place', since the Osiris facing the mound in the temple relief is said to be 'in the Great Place'.[60]

The tree is most likely an *iched* tree,[61] indicated by the alternating leaves shaped like arrowheads, resembling those of the desert date tree (*Balanites aegyptiaca*). This was a common tree in Upper Egypt and was linked to vigour and the transmission of royal power. Thus, the carving of arrowhead leaves on the stele is a clear link to Osiris' dynastic role. [DJR, from SA]

Osiris stele
30th dynasty–Ptolemaic period (380–31 BC)
Karnak
Sandstone
H. 60 cm
Egyptian Museum, Cairo PV.2014.18

An Egyptian priest

This head of a priest was discovered during the IEASM's underwater excavations in the eastern harbour of Alexandria. In accordance with ancient Egyptian customs, the priest is shown with a fully shaven head; his facial features are rather worn.

Ancient Egyptians believed that the gods lived in the temples erected for their worship. Only the priests were allowed to enter the sacred area of a temple and approach the statue of the deity during the daily rituals. These included saying prayers, burning incense, placing food offerings in front of the cult image of the god housed in a shrine and singing hymns of praise. As ordinary people were not allowed to enter the temple building, priests played a vital role in ancient Egyptian society.

Alexander the Great and his successors, the Ptolemies, respected Egyptian religion and customs and some of the Greeks living in Egypt during the Ptolemaic period even became members of the clergy in the service of Egyptian gods. In return, the priesthood supported the development of the royal cult and made it acceptable to the Greek and Egyptian communities alike.

Under certain circumstances priests from all over Egypt gathered together during so-called synods that were held to celebrate a king's birthday or coronation, or to commemorate a special event. These synods provided an opportunity for a practical dialogue between the royal court in Alexandria and the intellectual Greek elite of Egypt. Decrees passed by the council of priests were written down on stone stelae, and several copies of each were erected in various temples throughout the country – the most famous one undoubtedly being the Rosetta Stone. [DR]

Head of a priest
Ptolemaic period (332–31 BC)
Alexandria
Granodiorite
H. 21.8 cm | W. 13.6 cm | D. 17 cm
Maritime Museum, Alexandria SCA 1398

Making the figures of Osiris *vegetans*

Inscription on Osiris *vegetans* figure:

'Words to speak by Osiris who presides over the west, the great god, lord of Bekh,[63] *by Osiris master of Mer-nefer, the great god, lord of Ro-Setaou'*[64]

Osiris *vegetans* figures are sometimes also known as corn-mummies or pseudo-mummies. Temple reliefs at Dendera describe in detail the method of their making. Their creation began each year on the 12th day of the month of Khoiak, the last month of the season of the Inundation. The priests took silt, barley seeds, and water from the flood and poured the mixture into two halves of a golden mould. This was one cubit long (*c*. 50 cm) and shaped like a mummy, with a human face, wearing the white crown.[62] The halves were placed between layers of rushes in a stone vessel called the 'garden tank' and sprayed with water from the sacred lake, using a *situla* – a small ceremonial pail – made of gold. The liquid flowing out from the garden tank, considered as the 'humours of Osiris', was collected in a lower basin.

After nine days, both halves of the figure were covered with fresh cereal shoots. On the 21st of Khoiak, the two halves of Osiris *vegetans* were removed from the mould and assembled, glued together and bound by four papyrus bands. The now-complete figure was dried in the sun throughout that day, and then wrapped in linen bands. On the following day, it was carried in procession on a papyrus barque (boat) during the ritual navigation of the 22nd of Khoiak. Later, funerary rituals were performed for it and it was placed inside a sycamore coffin in an 'upper' tomb. It remained there for a year. The previous year's Osiris *vegetans* figure, which it replaced, was reburied on the 30th of Khoiak in a 'lower' tomb in a special cemetery devoted to these figures. [FG]

**Osiris *vegetans* figure in a
falcon-headed coffin**
8th–7th century BC
Tihna el-Gebel (Akoris in Middle Egypt)
Coffin: sycamore wood, L. 61.5 cm;
mummy: earth and grain, L. 50 cm
Egyptian Museum, Cairo JE 36539

This Osiris *vegetans* figure or corn-mummy, with erect phallus and swaddled in linen, is impregnated with a bituminous resin. Its length (one cubit = *c.* 50 cm) conforms to the ritual descriptions of such objects in the temple at Dendera. A smiling face is modelled from blackish-green wax. The head is topped by an *atef* crown, the white crown of Upper Egypt with ostrich feathers that are set on (partly preserved) twisted horizontal ram's horns. The crown also has a long axial *uraeus*, the rearing cobra that was the symbol of divine sovereignty. The *uraeus* and the crown feathers are of gilded wax. The twin insignia of the flail and the cross, clasped in the right fist in dark wax, clearly stand out from the funerary cloth. A wax scarab was set near the head of the mummy, and four linen packages containing the classical children of Horus with wax masks were placed in twos at his head and feet. The sons of Horus – the jackal-headed Duamutef, baboon-headed Hapy, human-headed Imsety and falcon-headed Qebehsenuef – were traditional guardians of the four Canopic jars containing mummified organs.

The mummy-shaped coffin shows the golden head of a hawk shining between the two parts of the great blue lapis lazuli wig. The materials emphasized divinity: the flesh of the gods was believed to be of gold and their hair of the blue semi-precious stone. The head of the coffin, in the form of a falcon, is coated with a black substance called 'divine stone' that recalls the precious unguent used in the Osirian rituals of rebirth as recorded at Dendera (p. 174). The colour of the coffin suggests black fertile earth and the green wax of the mummy, vegetal growth: black and green were the two colours of life for the Egyptians. The coffin was made from sycamore wood, which was used in the rituals surrounding the rebirth of Osiris.

On the coffin, a lengthwise column of white hieroglyphs extends the meaning of the three symbols (sun, head of a hawk, heart) depicted at its top. During the Late Period, necropoleis of these corn-mummies were common throughout Egypt, such as the one near Thebes in Wadi Qubbanet al-Quirud, or that of Oxyrhynchos/El-Bahnasah north of Tuna el-Gebel. In the temple of Karnak in Thebes, a graveyard of Osirian corn-mummies was found at the end of the twentieth century, and more probably still remain to be discovered.[65]   [ASvB]

An Osirian 'plant pot'

Made from terracotta, this object is shaped and sized like a fired red brick. Cut out of its upper face is an image of Osiris, with a shallow recess all around, suggesting it may once have had a lid.[66] The mummiform god, facing right, wears the *atef* crown, the white crown with ostrich feathers, and has the long beard that signifies divinity. He holds the flail and the crook, his traditional attributes. Several similar finds were discovered in the Theban area and are likely to come from the Valley of the Monkeys, near the Valley of the Kings, where numerous mummiform figures placed in pottery coffins and corn-mummies of Osiris were deposited. A couple of bricks still retained soil, ungerminated cereal grains and linen in the hollow profile silhouette of the god. These Osiris bricks are seen as plant pots containing all the ingredients necessary for the fabrication of an Osiris *vegetans* figure (see p. 168). They could represent a local, Theban variation of the Osiris relics produced during the festival of Khoiak. [AMB]

Osiris brick
c. 950–350 BC
Said to be from Thebes (Egypt)
Terracotta
L. 24.9 cm | W. 12.4 cm | H. 6.1 cm
Ashmolean Museum, Oxford 1991.18

The garden of Shentayt

So-called 'garden tanks' were known as 'the garden of Shentayt', a goddess connected with the celebrations of Osirian mysteries.[67] The moulds of the Osiris *vegetans* figures, filled with silt from the Nile mixed with barley seeds, were placed in these tanks between layers of rushes and the contents were watered until germination (p. 168).[68]

This example was discovered in the temple of Amun-Gereb in Thonis-Heracleion. It is rectangular, with one straight and one rounded extremity, and its highly eroded surface shows no trace of inscriptions. One of its two holes was used in its sacred function as a garden tank; the other was added later.[69]

The garden tank's material (granite), rectangular shape and dimensions differ from the one described in the ritual at Dendera (shale, square, 67.5 by 67.5 cm, and 28.2 cm high, in modern measurements). Garden tanks, however, existed in different sizes and shapes in different places: a rectangular granite one from Koptos (JE 37516) (154 by 88 by 60 cm) shows engraved hymns to Shentayt, and incantations to be recited during the Mysteries.[70]

In Thonis-Heracleion, this garden tank was found close to the naos (shrine) of Amun-Gereb. This god fulfilled a dynastic function, granting to the future king the *gereb*, a deed of property conferring the sovereignty of Egypt and the world. Furthermore, the text of the Decree of Canopus (238 BC) (p. 143) relates this sanctuary to the celebration of the Mysteries. All this strongly suggests that, in Thonis-Heracleion, Osirian rites were linked to the transmission of royal power. [FG]

'Garden tank' under excavation
4th–2nd century BC
Thonis-Heracleion
Pink granite
L. 2.05 m | W. 90 cm | H. 63 cm
Maritime Museum, Alexandria SCA 459

Shallow dish (phiale)
6th–2nd century BC (probably 4th–2nd century BC)
Thonis-Heracleion
Gold
H. 1.5 cm | Diam. 18.9 cm | Th. 0.1 cm | Wt 172 g
National Museum of Alexandria 313, SCA 296

Libation vessel (*phiale*)

Phialai were shallow dishes used throughout the Greek world for drinking and especially pouring sacrifices of wine, but they were rare in Egypt. This example has a flat bottom and vertical sides that meet the base at a ninety-degree angle. The sides flare slightly at the rim before the gold is turned sharply back on itself to create a lip. The central boss projects up a couple of millimetres from the base and has a flattened top surface. The *phiale* is made from a sheet of gold, most probably hammered into shape and then finished with a lathe.[71] It was found trapped beneath collapsed blocks in the temple of Amun-Gereb in Thonis-Heracleion. The thinness of the gold used for the vessel means that it could be easily bent, suggesting that it was for display and not ritual use; perhaps it was a dedication in a temple treasury.   [DJR, from ZK]

Ritual pail (*situla*)

Situla is Latin for a type of pail, often used as a ceremonial vessel in temples or in the private mortuary cult to sprinkle milk or water, but also to offer drink to the gods or to the deceased. In Egyptian, it is named *usheb*. Known from as early as the Middle Kingdom (early second millennium BC),[72] it appears in the New Kingdom (1550–1077 BC) in a great variety of shapes and materials, both as physical objects and in pictorial representations.

This *situla* was found on the Central Island of Thonis-Heracleion in the area of the main temple.[73] It possesses the cylindrical shape common in the Late Period (664–332 BC), widening slightly towards the bottom, which is rounded and ends in a central knob. The short neck holds two rings attached on opposite sides of its rim, through which protrude the tips of the large swinging handle shaped like the Greek letter *omega*: Ω.

During the Mysteries of Khoiak, the Osiris *vegetans* figure set into the 'garden tank' was watered daily by water poured from a *situla* made of gold.[74] *Situlae* were pre-eminent in the iconography of the cult of Isis, and as her cult subsequently spread throughout the Greco-Roman world, the goddess was often depicted carrying one. This popular cult promoted the same ideas of revitalization, sustenance and purification that Isis performed for her husband Osiris.   [ASvB]

Pail (*situla*)
4th–2nd century BC
Thonis-Heracleion
Bronze
H. 15.6 cm | D. 5.6 cm |
Th. 0.3 cm
Maritime Museum, Alexandria
SCA 1604

Strainers and ladle
4th–2nd century BC
Thonis-Heracleion
Bronze
L. 17.6–26.5 cm
Maritime Museum, Alexandria SCA 1062, 1063, 1064

Strainers were used in the serving of wine to remove any sediment before drinking. One of the two examples shown here has two curved cylindrical handles terminating in swans' heads and a depression that leads to a central hole which would have held a filter. Strainers were parts of dining sets and are often depicted with kraters, large bowls used for mixing wine with water and with ladles for serving it.   [DJR, from ZK]

The Osiris-Sokar figure: sacred recipes

A key component of the celebration of the Mysteries of Osiris during the month of Khoiak was the preparation of the Osiris-Sokar figure.[75] The process had numerous stages, but can be separated into two main events: the preparation of the figure and its coating with an unguent. As might be expected, all the ingredients used for creating both figure and unguent were carefully chosen, and Papyrus Salt 825 provides a mythological explanation for each of the substances used.[76]

The substances from which the figure was created were assembled in a series of steps, during which the ladle 'she who reunites' was used. Herbs, twelve aromatic substances, cereals, dates and perfumed resins were placed into a container, known as the 'precious recipient', to which twenty-four finely crushed precious minerals[77] were added and blended with soil and water from the sacred lake. This mixture of ingredients was then used to fill the two sides of a human-shaped mould.

The recipe for the 'precious unguent', as carved on the wall of a chamber of the temple of Edfu – a location where the recipes for various unguents and perfumes used in temple ritual were precisely described – was common to all places supposed to have held one of the pieces of Osiris' body.[78] This recipe contains moulded and sifted bitumen, vegetal tar (a by-product from fir trees), fine lotus essence, frankincense, fine oil, wax, fresh and dry turpentine resin, an extract of carob bean, and herbs and spices diluted in wine, as well as precious metals and minerals crushed into a very fine powder and spread over honey mixed with dry frankincense. The mixture was cooked and formed a blackish liquid with a predominant odour of bitumen.[79]

The unguent was manufactured in several stages between the 15th and 22nd of Khoiak. Once completed, it was applied with a spatula to the figure of Osiris-Sokar on the 24th. This blackish substance, made from the most refined products in the universe, was destined for the unique use of gods and deified beings. Adding the unguent to the figure was a key moment in its 'life-cycle', transforming it from a predominantly organic object, susceptible to decay and death, into one that could have everlasting life. [DJR, from SA]

Ladle (*simpulum*) with *wedjat*-eye
5th–2nd century BC
Thonis-Heracleion
Bronze
L. 50.4 cm
Maritime Museum, Alexandria SCA 220

To date, 111 long ceremonial ladles – called *simpula* – of various capacities have been discovered in Thonis-Heracleion, mostly in the canals, where they had been deposited as votive objects.[80] During the rituals of Khoiak they were used in the creation of the Osiris-Sokar figure, to measure the earth soaked in floodwater that was added to the fourteen special vessels containing various spices and crushed precious stones (see p. 142).[81] Two ladles from Thonis-Heracleion are marked with a *wedjat*-eye at the back of the bowl, just below the handle; this characteristic is rare, but is known elsewhere.[82]

The *wedjat*-eye, the image of the eye of Horus wounded by Seth then healed, symbolizes the reconstitution of Osiris' body. The *simpulum's* Egyptian name means 'she who reunites', illustrating its role in assembling the substances that will 'rebuild' the god's 'body'. In the Dendera texts, the word is accompanied by a special hieroglyph indicating meaning (called a determinative) that depicts the utensil.[83] 'She who reunites' is also a name or title of the sky goddess Nut, in whose womb Osiris was believed to be reconstituted and regenerated. [ASvB]

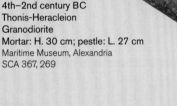

Mortar and pestle
4th–2nd century BC
Thonis-Heracleion
Granodiorite
Mortar: H. 30 cm; pestle: L. 27 cm
Maritime Museum, Alexandria
SCA 367, 269

Bowl
4th century BC
Thonis-Heracleion
Silver
H. 6.4 cm | Diam. 11 cm
Maritime Museum, Alexandria
SCA 951

Incense burners

In ancient Egypt and the Hellenistic world, incense was believed to possess sacred qualities. Temple ceremonies would begin with the burning of incense, which purified the air of evil and brought those attending the ceremony into the sacred realm. Incense burners were thus important pieces of the ritual furniture of the temple of Thonis-Heracleion, where these two were found.

One of the incense burners (below) is accompanied by a small shovel that may have been used to place burning charcoal into the body of the censer, or perhaps to add pieces of resin to the hot plate. The shovel has a rectangular scoop attached to a handle that ends in a duck's head finial. The incense burner is composed of a round bowl resting on three legs, shaped to resemble those of cows. It contains two bronze inserts fitting one inside the other.[84] [DJR, from ZK]

Brazier and spoon
4th–2nd century BC
Thonis-Heracleion
Bronze

Brazier:
H. 9.6 cm | Diam. 9.9 cm
Maritime Museum, Alexandria SCA 1073

Spoon:
L. 20.3 cm | Diam. (scoop) 10.2 cm
Maritime Museum, Alexandria SCA 1057

Incense burner and shovel
4th–2nd century BC
Thonis-Heracleion
Bronze

Incense burner:
H. 7.9 cm | Diam. 10.4 cm |
Inner diam. 10.1 cm | Wt 668 g
Maritime Museum, Alexandria SCA 392

Shovel:
L. (handle) 22.6 cm | L. (scoop) 5.2 cm |
W. (scoop) 3.8 cm | Wt 36 g
Maritime Museum, Alexandria SCA 580

Incense burner fragment

This hollow-cast object made of bronze forms part of an incense burner, an instrument used during various cultic rituals. Its tubular double shaft ends in handles that depict the heads of two falcons, each wearing a tripartite wig and still displaying fine facial features. This specific shape of incense burner appears from the beginning of the New Kingdom, although more commonly only one falcon head is attached to a single shaft.

The necks of the falcons slotted on to the shaft, which would have held an interior wooden shaft pole. Similar, completely preserved incense burners have been discovered in various tombs and temples (for a parallel see below). They confirm that the shafts terminated in a bound papyrus flower and an outstretched human hand with a cup resting on the palm which was used for burning the incense pellets. Cast onto the shaft was a cartouche-shaped receptacle for the incense. In many cases this receptacle was held by a small figure of a kneeling king wearing the blue crown and a kilt.

The incense burner discovered in Thonis-Heracleion was most likely used in rituals connected to the Mysteries of Osiris or in the daily cult celebrated at the temples of Amun-Gereb and Khonsu-the-child. Thanks to depictions on temple walls, for example in Abydos, we know that incense was burnt either by priests or the pharaoh himself in front of cult statues of the gods. [DR]

Fragment of an incense burner
5th–2nd century BC
Thonis-Heracleion
Bronze
H. 4 cm | L. 4.3 cm | D. 2.5 cm
Maritime Museum, Alexandria SCA 1569

60 Incense burner
4th–2nd century BC
Saqqara
Bronze
H. 9.15 cm | L. 50.4 cm | W. 3.8 cm
British Museum, EA 67189

Votive box

This object is a small casket on four feet with a lid connected by two hinges with a central axis running along its length. Two buttons near the top of the front jambs probably served to fix closing strings. A horizontal band framed by parallel, incised lines decorates each side. No inscriptions are visible. The object was found on the Central Island of Thonis-Heracleion, a few metres away from the foundation deposit (pp. 118–19) discovered at the northeastern corner of the temple of Khonsu. As a miniature reproduction of a strongbox for offerings, it is very likely a votive gift to Khonsu/Herakles.   [ASvB]

Bronze box
4th–2nd century BC
Thonis-Heracleion
Bronze
L. 6.9 cm | H. 3.6 cm | W. 5.1 cm
Maritime Museum, Alexandria SCA 1605

Duck's head lamp

This is an unusual lamp.[85] It has an elongated egg-shaped body with a wide opening at the narrower end, supported on three hoofed feet. The lamp would originally have been lidded, although the lid is now lost. The Vatican Museum owns a similar example with a detachable lid fitted in place by grooves on the body of the receptacle.[86] On the lamp from Thonis-Heracleion, a long suspension bar rises almost vertically from the centre of the widest part of the body. The handle ends in a hook in the shape of a duck's head. Similar lamps are dated to between the second century BC and the second century AD. The presence of this one in Thonis-Heracleion allows it to be dated to the second century BC at the latest, because few artefacts are found from that time onwards.

The lamp was discovered in the central port basin, and another example of this rare type, highly eroded and in bad condition, was recovered from the waters of the Grand Canal.[87] These elaborate lamps were probably part of the temple furnishings.   [DJR, from DF and ZK]

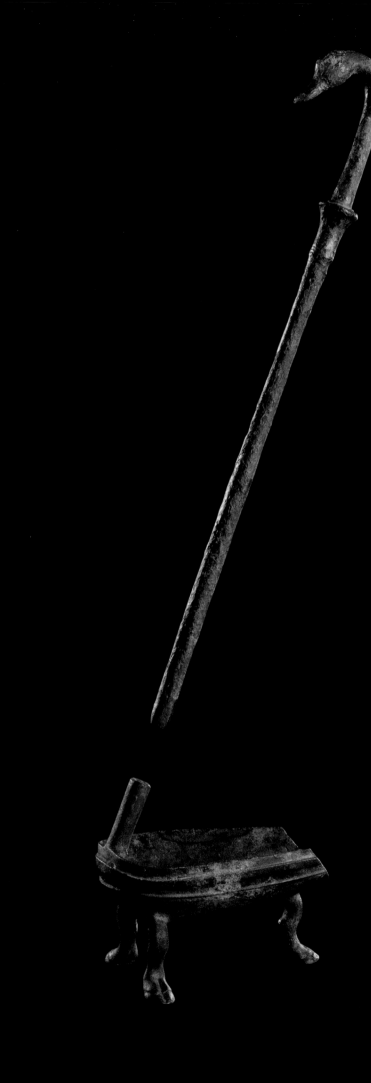

Lamp
4th–2nd century BC
Thonis-Heracleion
Bronze
Body: H. 11.0 cm | L. 13.2 cm | W. 7.6 cm | Wt 361 g
Handle: D. 1.1 cm | L. 36.4 cm | W. widest point 2.3 cm
| Wt 357 g
Maritime Museum, Alexandria SCA 1024, 1028

Sailing on the primeval waters

This pectoral (ornament worn on the chest) is made of gold and inlaid with lapis lazuli and red- and green-coloured glass paste, a material often used to imitate semi-precious stones. It was discovered by Pierre Montet in the grave of king Sheshonq II (r. 887–885 BC) at the royal necropolis at Tanis. There it was probably stored as an heirloom, as the inscriptions carved into the two gold plaques give the name of 'Sheshonq, son of Nimlot and Great Chief of the Meshwesh', who later became pharaoh Sheshonq I (r. 943–922 BC), founder of the 22nd dynasty.

This extraordinary piece of jewellery shows the solar barque (boat) under a star-filled sky, sailing on the primeval waters. It is flanked by the heraldic plants of Egypt, lotus and papyrus. The pectoral is crowned by two golden falcons wearing the double crown of Upper and Lower Egypt. On top

of the barge, an image of the sun as the seated god Amun-Ra-Horakhty is depicted: he is holding an *ankh*-sign (life) and a *was*-sceptre (power) while the goddess of truth and justice, Maat, is standing in front of him. The protective deities Isis and Nephthys spread their wings around the sun in order to shelter it from any danger that might be encountered during its voyage across the sky.

Most sacred festivals in ancient Egypt involved one or more divine statues being carried in procession on a sacred barque. Egyptians believed that the gods travelled through the starry sky by boat, and during festivals barque processions evoked this divine journey. The discoveries of numerous models of sacred barques, as well as a real one, at Thonis-Heracleion provide extraordinary archaeological evidence of something that is otherwise known only through texts and images. [DR]

Pectoral
22nd dynasty (reign of Sheshonq I, 943–922 BC)
Tanis
Gold, lapis lazuli, glass paste
H. 37.5 cm | W. 19 cm | Th. 1.2 cm
Egyptian Museum, Cairo JE 72171

The navigation of Osiris *vegetans* of the 22nd of Khoiak

The lead votive barques found at Thonis-Heracleion are associated with the celebration of the Mysteries.[88] Texts engraved on the walls of the Osirian chapel in the temple of Dendera describe the ritual. On the 22nd Khoiak, at the time of the eighth hour (2 pm), a fleet of thirty-four boats, each a cubit and two palms long (67.5 cm), sailed on the sacred lake of the temple of Osiris. Each of the papyrus barques transported a deity on a throne, accompanying Osiris *vegetans* and the 'divine member' (an item that is not explained in the Dendera ritual texts, but which may symbolize part of the body of Osiris). The thirty-four boats carried 365 lamps.[89]

The votive boats are identical to the barques, with a throne as described in the texts, and the models are carefully made with shallow incisions to replicate the bundles of papyrus of which the vessels and thrones of the real cultic fleet were made.[90] Even the choice of material of their manufacture may have been significant, as lead is the metal most often associated with Osiris. The model barques vary in size from 9 cm to 62 cm in length or more. Most of them still have their throne, but the gods that they carried have not survived. Perhaps they, like the figure of Osiris *vegetans* itself, were made of materials that have not been preserved in the archaeological record. It is also possible that the model boats never carried divinities, the thrones alone being sufficient to suggest their presence.

The location of the boat models is particularly noteworthy: the majority were deposited in the canals around the temple of Amun-Gereb, mostly in the Grand Canal, which fulfilled the role of the sacred temple lake in Thonis-Heracleion. Their positions suggest that they were probably placed along the route that the papyrus barques followed on the 22nd of Khoiak, as if a 'votive' procession at the bottom of the canal replicated that of the real papyrus boats gliding along the surface.

Other barque models found deposited under flagstones were votive or foundation deposits. One was carefully disassembled into three parts (the hull, the throne and the steering oars); the parts were found close to each other, but under separate slabs of a mole alongside a canal.[91] In addition to this, fifteen lead oil lamps have also been recovered from the harbour basins and canals. They, too, were often found near the lead votive barques and could recall the 365 lamps mentioned in the ritual.

[FG]

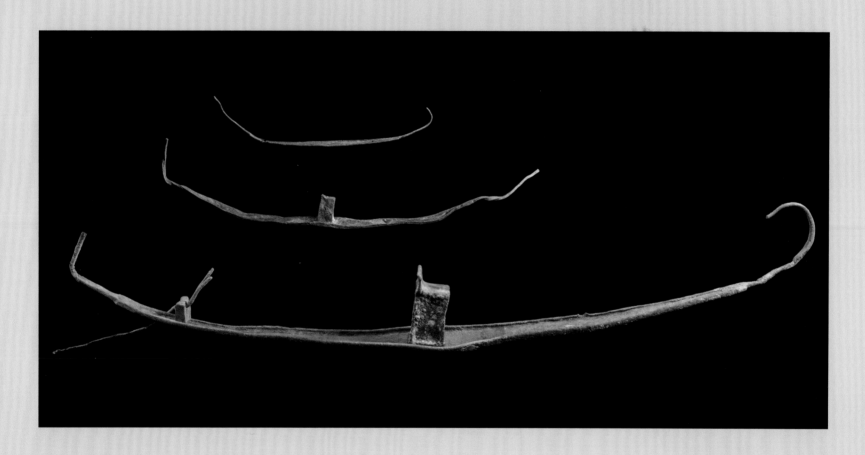

A number of votive model boats (most of them made of lead) were excavated in Thonis-Heracleion, and they are without precise parallel elsewhere in Late Period and Ptolemaic Egypt. Their presence is easily interpreted in the context of the ritual of the navigation of Osiris *vegetans* on the 22nd of Khoiak.   [FG]

Lead votive barques
4th–2nd century BC
Thonis-Heracleion
Lead
From top to bottom:
L. 61.5 cm (SCA 1607)
L. 59 cm (SCA 1591)
L. 62 cm (SCA 1606 [with SCA 1617])
Maritime Museum, Alexandria

Waterfowl figurehead

This rare head of a waterfowl on a bronze plate was found in the Grand Canal at Thonis-Heracleion.[92] The angle of the beak to the plate and the presence of bronze nails suggest that it was fastened to the inclined stem of a barque, as a figurehead.

The waterfowl could be a swan, possibly of the species *Cygnus olor* whose males have a bump on the upper beak, as this fowl does. These birds must have possessed some religious significance, since some tombs of the Middle and New Kingdom contained a life-size wooden statue of a swan. The waterfowl may have played a role in the regeneration of the deceased during funerary and Osirian cults.[93]

Swans are visitors to Egypt, flying in from the north. The Egyptians might have considered these birds, passing in the course of their north–south migration, as piloting the sun (and the deceased) across the waters of the underworld.[94] Consequently, the swan would be an appropriate figurehead for a sacred barque, perhaps even one of those involved in the navigation of Osiris *vegetans*, piloting the vessel across the sacred temple waters of Thonis-Heracleion.

Another possibility for the waterfowl would be the goose (*ngg*), which is also associated with ascending to heaven, or the geese related to the procession of the 26th of Khoiak, during the feast of Sokar.[95]   [ASvB]

Figurehead
4th century BC
Thonis-Heracleion
Bronze
H. 17 cm
Maritime Museum, Alexandria SCA 1592

Greek-style lamps from Athens and Alexandria
c. 350–200 BC
Thonis-Heracleion
Pottery
L. 5.7–9 cm
Maritime Museum, Alexandria
SCA 1584, 1587, 856, 1589, 1324, 1594

Lamps

Lamps were mass-produced in moulds or on the pottery wheel, yet these utilitarian objects also held important religious and ritual meaning in certain contexts. Lamps may have been used, by Egyptians and Greeks alike, in a temple or shrine where they were integral to a variety of rituals, such as sacrifices, oath-taking, ritual meals and nocturnal feasts. An Egyptian religious festival at the city of Sais is described by Herodotus:

> On a certain night they all kindle lamps
> many in number in the open air round
> about the houses … and this burns
> during the whole night; and to the festival
> is given the name Lychnokaia [the
> lighting of lamps] … not in Sais alone
> are they lighted, but over all Egypt.[96]

These lamps may have been used during the sacred navigation of the 22nd of Khoiak, when a procession of thirty-four papyrus barges was illuminated by 365 lamps. A number of them were discovered in canals and basins at Thonis-Heracleion. The fine examples with a black slip were brought from Athens, while others are of Egyptian production, but in a Greek style introduced to Egypt under Greco-Macedonian rule. These are distinct from and of finer quality than the traditional Egyptian lamps of the period.   [RT]

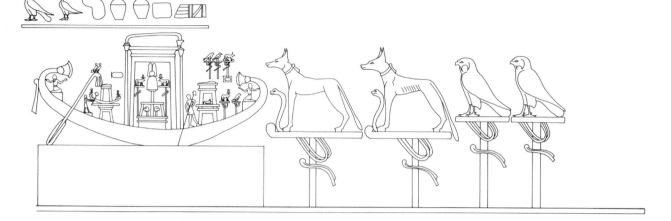

Divine emblems

Anubis and Horus emblems
4th century BC
Thonis-Heracleion
Bronze
Anubis/Wepwawet: H. 18 cm (SCA 975) | H. 8.6 cm
(SCA 981) | *Horus falcon*: H. 6.9 cm (SCA 997)
Maritime Museum, Alexandria

opposite
**A votive lead model barque
as discovered underwater**

In artistic representations of their journeys, gods and kings were frequently accompanied by emblems, particularly of the god Anubis/Wepwawet, whose name means 'He-who-opens-the-way'. This can be seen in the relief of a boat on an Osirian chapel from Dendera, which carries the symbol of Abydos and is depicted alongside emblems of Anubis and Horus the falcon (fig. 61). These objects have been found at Thonis-Heracleion, where excavations have revealed both large emblems that would have been carried on poles as standards (e.g. SCA 975), and smaller examples, perhaps models (e.g. SCA 981, SCA 997). The large emblem was found in the North Canal and probably dates from the Saite period (the 26th dynasty, 664–525 BC). The bronze models were found on the (now submerged) land, one (SCA 981) on the great mole of the Central Island, the other (SCA 997) beyond the North Canal.

Emblems of Anubis and of falcons are found from as early as 3100 BC[97] and are often depicted together on temple walls from all periods of Egyptian history. Their duality is linked to the ideal of the Two Lands – Upper and Lower Egypt – and they glorify royal supremacy, the king being the earthly incarnation of both Horus the falcon and Anubis, who assists Horus in his funerary role guiding Osiris on his road westward to the netherworld.   [ASvB]

The great nautical procession

The jackal-headed god Anubis played an important role in the festivities of Khoiak in the Middle Kingdom (2055–1650 BC). At Abydos, the sacred town of Osiris, it seems that the scene of Osiris' murder was re-enacted, and in order to help Osiris, the god Wepwawet makes a 'sortie' called 'the Wepwawet sortie' (*peret Wepwawet*) to repel the enemies of Osiris from the god's barque.[98] He also accompanied Osiris at the end of the Mysteries on his journey to his tomb.[99] At Thonis-Heracleion, the text of the Decree of Canopus (238 BC) indicates that on the 29th of Khoiak (that is, on the last day but one of the celebrations of the Mysteries) the god navigated on his sacred boat from the temple of Amun-Gereb in Thonis-Heracleion to the

Osiris temple at Canopus. The voyage probably went along the canal linking the two towns.[100] The date of this ritual navigation at the end of the month of Khoiak recalls the last navigation at Abydos taking Osiris to his final tomb.[101] The nautical events of the 22nd and the 24th–25th Khoiak[102] related in the texts at Dendera temple were celebrated throughout Egypt during the Mysteries. We know that they took place at Thonis-Heracleion, because of the presence in the canals of votive boats imitating the papyrus barques described in the Dendera ritual (pp. 182–83). However, a later navigation at the end of the month seems – on current evidence – to have happened only at Abydos and Thonis-Heracleion. [ASvB]

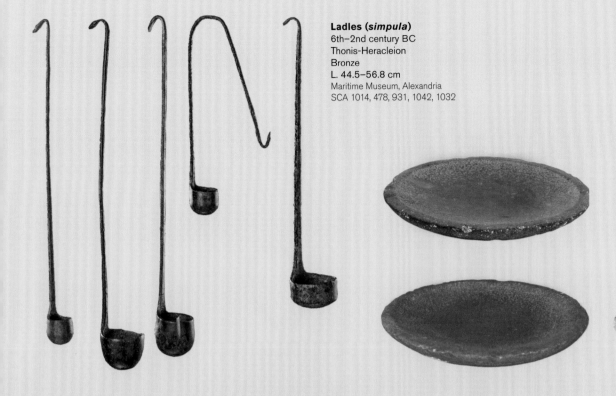

Ladles (*simpula*)
6th–2nd century BC
Thonis-Heracleion
Bronze
L. 44.5–56.8 cm
Maritime Museum, Alexandria
SCA 1014, 478, 931, 1042, 1032

Offering dishes
6th–2nd century BC
Thonis-Heracleion

Granodiorite: D. 30.5 cm (SCA 1091);
D. 33 cm (SCA 1280); D. 46 cm (SCA 265)

Quartzite: D. 46 cm (SCA 374)
Maritime Museum, Alexandria

Stone dishes of comparable shape and size have been found throughout Egypt from the Old Kingdom onwards (beginning *c.* 2686 BC).[103] With a pedestal, they became the prototype for offering tables.

These dishes were found at Thonis-Heracleion in the Grand Canal, or along its banks, and were often excavated together with votive objects, demonstrating their use as offering dishes. The majority of dateable artefacts associated with the dishes are from the fourth and third centuries BC. Clusters of dishes were found at specific locations, for example around the ritually deposited boat, suggesting the presence of open sites for devotion and offerings from which people could place their sacrifices into the sacred waterway. It is possible that these sites could be way stations on a processional route.

More than a hundred ceremonial ladles have been found at Thonis-Heracleion, almost always in waterways, where they had been dropped to render them inaccessible after their use in rituals. [ASvB]

**The excavated sycamore barge,
discovered in the Grand Canal**

Appeasing the goddess

This elegant object is a *sistrum*, a rattle-like musical instrument used in sacred rites and festivals, particularly for the cult of the Egyptian goddesses Hathor and Isis. In the Ptolemaic period, the two deities often merged, sharing attributes and roles. The head of Hathor shown frontally, with cow ears and her distinctive wig with curled-out ends, adorns the join between the *sistrum*'s handle and a shrine-shaped frame. Rods, fitted with small discs, run through holes made in the sides of the frame. When shaken, the clattering of the discs emits a sound that was believed to propitiate goddesses, and according to the Greek author Plutarch, the movement itself could 'avert and repel Typhon'.[104] Considering its small size, this *sistrum* could have been a model deposited as a votive offering. [AMB]

Sistrum (rattle)
Ptolemaic period (332–31 BC)
Unknown provenance
Gold
H. 16 cm | W. 4.5 cm
Egyptian Museum, Cairo JE 67887

Bells
6th–2nd century BC
Thonis-Heracleion
Bronze
H. 7.4–9.4 cm
Maritime Museum, Alexandria SCA 388, 385, 1381

Sistrum (rattle)
4th–2nd century BC
Thonis-Heracleion
Bronze
L. 14.4 cm
Maritime Museum, Alexandria SCA 1619

Elements of a sistrum
6th–2nd century BC
Thonis-Heracleion
Bronze
L. 26 cm
Maritime Museum, Alexandria SCA 906, 581

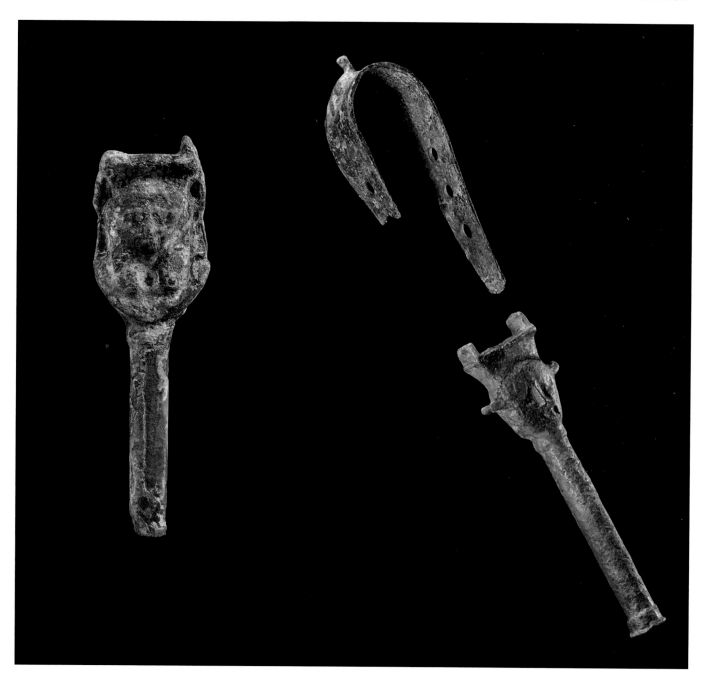

Osiris statuettes

Osiris and the celebration of the Osirian Mysteries were central to the religious identity of Thonis-Heracleion[105] and statuettes of the deity are a common find in the archaeology of the port-city.[106] Osiris was represented standing and fully draped in a shroud-like garment from which his head and hands emerge. He holds the crook and flail, two symbols related to kingship, and wears a divine beard. Both of the examples shown right wear Osiris' usual *atef* crown, which is a composite consisting of the white crown flanked by two feathers. More elaborate versions with horizontal twisted ram horns and further *uraei* are also found in the assemblage (e.g. SCA 1267, below right and opposite).

Osiris statuettes are found throughout the port-city, both in the northern areas that were the first to be settled (SCA 1081, 1266) and in the south, suggesting that the artefact type maintained its importance throughout the life of Thonis-Heracleion.[107] They were also found predominantly on land, suggesting that they were not deposited into the waterways as part of the same Osirian rituals as *simpula* and lead barques during the festival of Khoiak (p. 182),[108] but donated to the god (e.g. SCA 1081, inscribed with customary wishes for a long life). A concentration of statuettes was found in excavations on an island in the southeast port, near to an offering table and other votive material, which could suggest the presence of a sanctuary or temple at this location.[109]   [SH]

Statuettes of Osiris
6th–2nd century BC
Thonis-Heracleion
Bronze
H. 21.0 cm | W. 4.3 cm | D. 2.2 cm (SCA 1081);
H. 30.5 cm | W. 7.6 cm | D. 6.0 cm | Wt 2,012 g (SCA 1266)
Maritime Museum, Alexandria

right, opposite and overleaf
Statuette of Osiris with golden eyes
Late Period (664–332 BC)
Thonis-Heracleion
Bronze and gold
H. 26.5 cm | W. 7.2 cm | D. 4.3 cm
Maritime Museum, Alexandria SCA 1267

Head of Osiris
Late Period (664–332 BC)
Thonis-Heracleion
Bronze
H. 5.5 cm
Maritime Museum, Alexandria SCA 926

Divine beard from a statue
Late 7th–4th century BC
Thonis-Heracleion
Bronze
H. 16.6 cm
Maritime Museum, Alexandria SCA 1079

Divine false beards

Divine false beards were a common attribute for male Egyptian gods and the deceased pharaoh. This hollow-cast, long, tapering beard in bronze features at the upper end a small tang,[110] by which it would once have been fixed to a statue. Bronze fittings were sometimes the only elements that survived from large statues that were otherwise made out of perishable material. Examples of such were preserved in a votive cache in North Saqqara[111] and in the temple of Osiris-iu in 'Ayn Manawir (Oasis of Kharga).[112] In both cases, a large wooden cult statue of Osiris was surrounded by numerous small bronze figures, often representing Osiris himself or the other members of the Osirian triad, Isis and Horus-the-child. Considering the importance of Osiris' cult and the number of bronzes representing the Osirian triad in Thonis-Heracleion, it is likely that this beard was once attached to a large statue of Osiris.   [AMB]

Amulet of Osiris-Sokar
4th–2nd century BC
Thonis-Heracleion
Bronze
H. 6.6 cm
Maritime Museum, Alexandria SCA 1616

Statuettes of Isis

Two bronze statuettes depict Isis sitting on a throne, dressed in a long form-fitting dress and holding her child Horus in her left arm, to whom she is offering her breast with the right hand.[113] Isis wears the three-part wig and the Hathor crown composed of a sun disc between cow's horns on a circular base, which is decorated with small squares on SCA 972. Her feet rest on a base with a tenon to fix the statuette on its support. The child is naked, with a *uraeus* (sacred rearing cobra) on its forehead on SCA 972.

Only the upper part of the faience statuette remains (SCA 522). Isis wears the hieroglyphic sign of a throne on her head, which continued downward into a dorsal pillar. Her three-part wig is adorned by a *uraeus*, and she wears a necklace of three rounds of beads. The fine style of the statuette is very similar to the faience amulets of a foundation deposit found in the northeast corner of the temple of Khonsu. As it was found on the opposite northwest corner of the same temple, it might have been part of a foundation deposit contemporary to that found at the northeast corner (see pp. 118–19).[114]   [ASvB]

Statuettes of Isis
6th–2nd century BC
Thonis-Heracleion
Bronze: 12.3 cm (SCA 972);
faience: 7 cm (SCA 522)
Maritime Museum, Alexandria

Child deities

Numerous bronze figures of child deities were found at Thonis-Heracleion. They are the most common type of statuette at the site, and are found in both traditional Egyptian and Ptolemaic styles.[115] In the Egyptian style, the god wears the juvenile side-lock of hair, and can be depicted in various positions, with bent or straight knees, finger at the mouth or both arms alongside the body.[116] As the principal deity of the town, Harpokrates fulfils different functions of kingship and strength, which are characterized by different crowns: the *uraeus*, the double crown, the blue crown and the *hem-hem* crown (see p. 120).

Other statuettes of child deities made in lead are Ptolemaic in style: plump, seated figures that hold a pot, as a symbol of abundant food, under one arm.[117] The fact that they are found at Thonis-Heracleion proves that this type goes back at least to the second century BC. The differences in the distribution patterns of these two types are striking. Egyptian-style examples are located mainly in the north of the port-city and the sanctuary of Khonsu.[118] Ptolemaic examples have come to light predominantly around the southern shores of the Central Island.[119] This undoubtedly reflects the fact that the northern part of the city was the cult centre during the earlier period of the town's history. The area was subsequently abandoned and the centre of the settlement moved to the south,[120] where eventually both types of statuettes were deposited during the Ptolemaic period.   [ASvB]

Statuettes of Harpokrates
6th–2nd century BC
Thonis-Heracleion
Bronze: H. 9.5 cm (SCA 995) | 3.3 cm (SCA 423);
lead: H. 4 cm (SCA 925)
Maritime Museum, Alexandria

Child deity statuette from a foundation deposit at the sanctuary of Khonsu-the-child
30th dynasty (380–342 BC)
Thonis-Heracleion
Faience
H. 7.9 cm | W. 2.2 cm | D. 1.8 cm
National Museum of Alexandria SCA 562

Small container with offering
6th–2nd century BC
Thonis-Heracleion
Lead
H. 2.8 cm | D. 7 cm
Maritime Museum, Alexandria SCA 1077

Votive deposit
4th–2nd century BC
Thonis-Heracleion
Limestone, lead
H. 4–11.5 cm
Maritime Museum, Alexandria SCA 1050 (figure of owl?); 1052 and
952 (child deities); 1053 (miniature bowl); 1051 (miniature vessel)

Votive boxes
6th–2nd century BC
Thonis-Heracleion
Lead
H. 2.5–7.3 cm
Maritime Museum, Alexandria SCA 938,
939, 923, 1009

Ritual deposit

Numerous ritual deposits of small lead containers with faunal or floral residues were found at Thonis-Heracleion, most frequently in the Grand Canal and the harbour basins.[121] They were usually sealed by pressing the opening by hand to trap the contents, before they were thrown into the water. Sometimes a lead cover was added before crushing to ensure a perfect seal, as with the small vessel above. It was left intact after its discovery, and its contents are unknown.[122] The practice of throwing food offerings into water is reported in the Book of the Temple, a manual that describes in detail how the ideal temple should be built and operated. The section dedicated to Osiris states that offerings to Osiris were not destined for human consumption but should be destroyed by fire or by throwing them into the sacred lake.[123] At Thonis-Heracleion the Grand Canal assumed the function of the sacred lake. The ritual navigations during the Mysteries of Khoiak took place there, and numerous votive gifts, such as bronze ceremonial ladles, lead votive barques (model boats) and other votive objects were discovered there.   [ASvB]

Offering table

Offering tables were integral to the architecture and equipment of temples to Egyptian deities. They provided both a symbolic and a physical location for commodities intended for the god's consumption.[124] They are sometimes sumptuously decorated.[125] The shape of the offering table can be compared with its hieroglyphic sign *htp* (meaning 'satisfied'), which shows a loaf of bread on a reed mat. The upper surface of this offering table has a drain around its edges and part of the way up the centre of the table, from which liquids exited via a central spout. Two cartouche-shaped troughs, one on either side of the central dividing drain, provided places to hold physical offerings. The table is also engraved with two *hes*-vases, vessels that were used for the pouring of libations (drink offerings).

This offering table was discovered on an island southeast of the harbour basins. Excavations on the island revealed that the offering table was found alongside bronze statuettes of Harpokrates and Osiris[126] (p. 200), as well as other votive material such as a small bronze model of an offering table (right).[127] In combination, these objects help to suggest the presence of a sanctuary, perhaps to Osiris, at this location.[128]   [DJR, from EL]

Offering table
4th–2nd century BC
Thonis-Heracleion
Granodiorite
H. 64 cm | W. 63 cm | D. 19 cm
Maritime Museum, Alexandria SCA 1257

Model of an offering table
6th–2nd century BC
Thonis-Heracleion
Bronze
H. 5.1 cm
Maritime Museum, Alexandria SCA 1250

Model offering table

This tiny model reproduces the form and decoration of a real offering table.[129] It is rectangular in shape, with a central projecting channel in front and two loops opposite the spout. Other miniatures of offering tables still have a chain attached to these suspension loops. The upper surface of this model is adorned with two libation vases framing bread loaves in low relief. More elaborate, or perhaps better-preserved, examples display small figures, such as a priest kneeling at the back and pouring a libation over the table, a pair of reclining jackals at the front edges of the table, or a frog sitting astride the spout. Models of cult equipment are often found among offerings in votive caches, themselves originating from a temple or a shrine. This model was discovered alongside a real offering table and numerous bronze figures representing Osiris and Harpokrates.[130] Such objects are often dated between the fourth and second century BC, but recent discoveries now show they go back as early as the late seventh century BC.[131]   [AMB]

Bes vase
Late 5th–mid-4th century BC
Thonis-Heracleion
Lead
H. 7.5 cm | W. 2.8 cm
Maritime Museum, Alexandria SCA 1234

Figure of Bes as a warrior
3rd–2nd century BC
Thonis-Heracleion
Terracotta
H. 25 cm | W. 15 cm
Maritime Museum, Alexandria SCA 1586

The god Bes

This representation of the Egyptian dwarf-god Bes is actually a small vase, possibly used for storing perfume. It is made of lead, a material associated with Osiris, which may imply a connection to the Khoiak celebrations.

Bes is depicted as a sitting dwarf with his fists resting on his knees. His huge belly is topped by two circular features that might be interpreted as female breasts, hinting at a certain androgynous aspect of the god. His face shows large eyes under strongly marked eyebrows and he has a knob-like nose. The vase is hollow and the god's headdress forms its funnel-shaped neck.

The cult of Bes emerged in the Middle Kingdom (2055–1650 BC) but clearly enjoyed its greatest popularity from the New Kingdom (1550–1077 BC) onwards. Bes was a rather atypical addition to the Egyptian pantheon, lacking an elegant appearance. He was usually shown in the form of a squatting dwarf with a rather peculiar facial expression. He was extremely popular among all sections of society, because he was connected to fertility and responsible for the protection of pregnant women and small children. He is very frequently depicted on household objects, which might have been used in domestic cult activities, and his cult spread rapidly during the Ptolemaic period throughout the whole eastern Mediterranean.   [DR]

Bes as a warrior

This upper part of a small figure made of clay shows the face, right arm and crown of the god Bes, who has a very specific iconography. His facial features are moulded in an immense degree of detail: his huge eyes are clearly visible under his bushy eyebrows, while the strands of his beard are formed by vertical curls. His head is adorned by his usual headdress consisting of ostrich feathers; however, its upper section shows a bull crowned by a sun disc between his horns. The bull deity can most likely be interpreted as the god Apis, who was one of the most popular gods in Egypt in the first millennium BC. With his right hand Bes is holding a long sword, resembling a Macedonian type, over his head. His left hand would have held an object as well; this is now lost, but according to parallels might have been a shield or snake.

Bes was primarily associated with the sphere of fertility, pregnancy, birth and childhood, and this specific representation of him as a warrior clearly underlines his protective role in driving away demons. Thus he was often depicted with the young Horus (Horus-the-child or Harpokrates), protecting him during his childhood when his mother Isis hid him from his evil uncle Seth in the marshes of the Delta. The fact that Bes is associated here with a Macedonian sword illustrates the amalgamation of Greek and Egyptian culture.   [DR]

Bes vase

This high-necked vessel has a rounded base and two lug-handles. Its globular body is decorated with a horizontal external bulge. Below it the face of the god Bes is depicted, with his arms bent upwards at the elbows. Bes' face shows his typical grotesque features with an outstretched tongue, bushy moustache and leonine mane.

The god Bes appears commonly on Late and Ptolemaic period vases in ceramic or faience; similar vases made of metal are often seen as prototypes. This vase is made of bronze, a valuable material prone to being melted down and reused. However, the fate of Thonis-Heracleion, a city submerged by the sea for more than a thousand years, guaranteed that this object survived. Bes vases are usually decorated – sometimes rather crudely – with incised or applied elements that depict not only the face of the god but also his entire body including his belly, legs and feathered crown. Although Bes vases have been discovered in settlement and funerary contexts at many sites in Egypt, little is known about their role and whether they were always used in the same way throughout history. As Bes is strongly associated with aspects of fertility, motherhood and childbirth these vases might have been deployed in domestic rites, and contained milk. [DR]

Bes vase
5th–4th century BC
Thonis-Heracleion
Bronze
H. 9.5 cm | W. 11.9 cm
Maritime Museum, Alexandria SCA 1235

Bes, Serapis and Isis

This small fragment of a vase shows moulded depictions of the gods Bes, Serapis and Isis in frontal view. While only the faces and upper parts of the bodies of Serapis and Isis are preserved, Bes is depicted full-length. The central figure, Serapis, is shown as a bearded, majestic man, wearing the *atef* crown, which is normally associated with the god Osiris. His right hand holds a pilaster, an architectural element. To his right, Bes is represented in his usual form as a squatting dwarf and wearing his tall feathered crown. Isis is shown to the left of Serapis.

Although Isis was regarded as the consort of Osiris, to whom she had been firmly tied throughout the entire pharaonic period, she became associated with Serapis in Greek and Roman times. After all, Serapis was a syncretistic deity combining attributes of the Egyptian gods Osiris and Apis. That these three gods are shown here together can probably be explained by their common sphere of influence on family matters. Isis and Serapis are more commonly depicted together with their child Harpokrates, with whom they form the divine triad of Alexandria. However, on this vase Harpokrates has been replaced by Bes who, being a protector of pregnant women and children, seems to have been regarded as a suitable companion to Serapis and Isis. [DR]

Vase fragment depicting Bes, Serapis and Isis
3rd–2nd century BC
Thonis-Heracleion
Pottery
H. 6 cm
Maritime Museum, Alexandria SCA 1588

Taweret, 'the Great One'

This splendid sculpture represents the goddess Taweret, 'the Great One'. Her head and body is that of a hippopotamus, with the limbs of a lion and the tail of a crocodile – all dangerous creatures. The prominent belly and hanging breasts give her a motherly appearance and relate her to the god of the Inundation and bringer of fertility, Hapy. The finely grooved tripartite wig was perhaps once topped by a Hathoric crown, with cow horns framing a sun disc. Taweret is standing on her hind legs, and her forepaws rest above large hieroglyphic s3-signs, meaning protection. Here, she only bares her teeth and sticks out a tongue, but she is often shown holding a knife in each hand ready to strike down any threat. With her frightening appearance, she wards off evil and protects women in labour and children. As such, she is often associated with another guardian of pregnancy and childhood, the leonine dwarf-god Bes. The incongruous figures of these popular deities were reproduced on countless amulets, usually sported by women and children.

In the Osirian myth, Taweret protected Isis and the newly born Horus against the murderous intent of Seth. Her association with Osiris himself is particularly enhanced in the Theban region (modern Luxor) where this statue originates. There, Taweret was assimilated with another hippopotamus goddess, Ipet, herself assimilated with the sky goddess Nut, as the mother of Osiris. Ipet was worshipped in a temple at Karnak – to the south of the temple of Amun – which was seen as the birthplace of Osiris.

This sculpture was, however, discovered to the north of the temple of Amun, in an area where multiple aspects of Osiris were revered in chapels. The dark greywacke cult statue was found still in its limestone shrine, near the chapel of Osiris Padedankh ('Who gives life'). This chapel, restored in the Saite period (26th dynasty, 664–525 BC), possibly celebrated the birth of Osiris. The inscription on the back pillar is a plea from Psamtik I (664–610 BC), the founder of the Saite dynasty, to Taweret to protect his daughter Nitokris. The smooth polished surface of the dark green stone marks this sculpture as a majestic example of Saite art.   [AMB]

Statue of Taweret
Reign of Psamtik I (664–610 BC)
Luxor (North Karnak)
Greywacke
H. 96 cm
Egyptian Museum, Cairo CG 39145

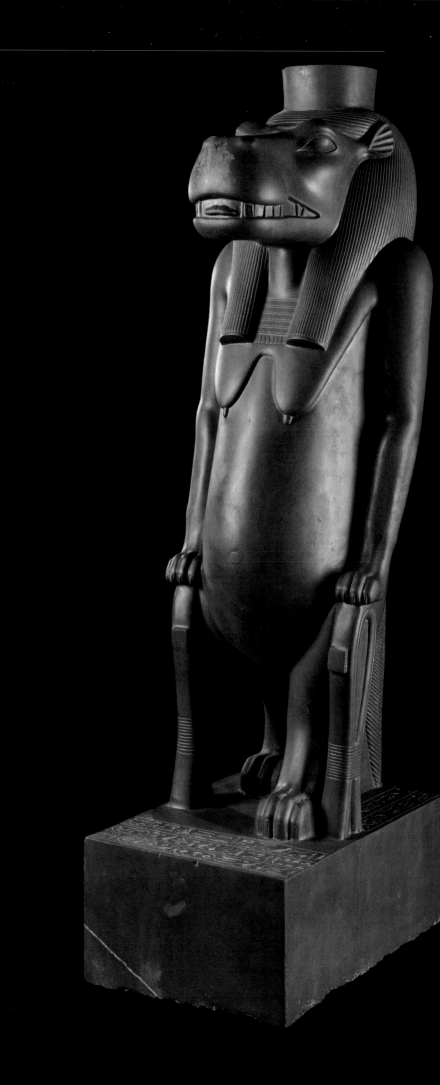

Neilos, god of the Nile

This finely polished bust depicts the Nile river god, Neilos, as a mature, bearded man, dressed in a so-called *himation*, a mantle or wrap worn by Greeks. His hair is parted in the centre and its wavy strands are held back from his face in a bun. He is carrying the cornucopia, a symbol of nourishment and abundance visible on his upper left shoulder. The back of the bust is flat and displays a wide-gauge dowel hole, indicating that it was once mounted into a shield frame that might have adorned a temple or public space in Canopus. It is made of greywacke, a hard stone characterized by its dark, green-greyish colour, and thus considered suitable for a statue representing a river god.

The bust is executed in classical Greek style and was probably produced in a specialist workshop in Alexandria, where purely Egyptian-style, purely classical Greek-style and mixed Greek–Egyptian-style sculptures were manufactured for potential clients from the Egyptian Delta region or Central Italy.

Neilos was appealing to Egyptians and Greeks alike: he was considered the Greek version of Hapy, whom the Egyptians did not worship in an abstract form but as the deification of the annual flooding that brought prosperity and fertility to the country. Through the *interpretatio graeca* (the Greek interpretation of Egyptian gods), the Greeks saw him as a son of the Titan Oceanus, the divine personification of the sea, and the Titaness Tethys.[132] Neilos also played a major role in one of the most important festivals in Egypt, as the beginning of the annual flood also marked the Egyptian New Year.   [DR]

Bust of Neilos, god of the Nile
2nd century AD
Canopus
Greywacke
H. 67 cm | W. 56 cm | D. 30 cm
Maritime Museum, Alexandria SCA 842

The Inundation season and the New Year's festival

The Inundation season (called Akhet in Ancient Egyptian), a four-month period from mid-July to mid-November, was crucially significant in Egyptian liturgy. The Khoiak festival marked the end of the season, but the New Year's festival took place at its beginning, during the month of Thoth. Lasting fourteen days, the New Year's festival was celebrated across all Egypt to welcome the arrival of the Nile flood and the fertility it brought. This popular festival was also associated with the rebirth of Osiris as well as with the renewal and confirmation of royal power.[133] The beginning of this season coincided, furthermore, with the heliacal rise of Sirius (the first time each year that the star becomes visible in the sky just before dawn). Known as Sothis to the ancient Egyptians, this star was associated with the goddess Isis.

The Egyptians believed the Nile to be the efflux (humours of the body) of Osiris, and the earth was fertilized by the flood as Isis was by her husband. Thus the Nile's annual life-bringing flood was seen as the union of Osiris and Isis, when they conceived Horus. Mass-produced male and female fertility figurines seem to have played an important role in the festivals of the Inundation season. They were deeply connected with the sacred Osirian family.   [AMB]

'O Osiris! The inundation is coming; abundance surges in.
The flood-season is coming, arising from the torrent issuing from Osiris …'

Egyptian representations of Egyptian child gods with oversized phalli played an important role in rituals related to the Inundation. The first of the two figures here shows a plump baby with shaved head and side-lock, holding a drum or tambour above his exaggerated phallus. This is a representation of a child god, probably Harpokrates (Horus-the-child), made in Saqqara and associated with the cult of the Osirian triad worshipped in Memphis. These religious figures symbolized the fertility of the Nile flood, which was associated with the conception and birth of Horus. The god's creative and fertile power is emphasized by his exaggerated phallus. Festivals celebrating the Nile Inundation were colourful events involving music, represented here by the drum held by Horus. Other examples show Horus carrying wine amphorae or libation bowls, playing a harp or flute, or holding a frog (another symbol of the Nile Inundation and its fertility).

The second figure here shows an Egyptian priest with a shaved head, carrying a statue of the phallic child-god Harpokrates during a procession, perhaps during one of these festivals. The '*phallophoria*' or 'Pamylia' of Osiris (the father of Horus) are vividly described by Herodotus and Plutarch.

Phallic Horus-the-child figures are occasionally found outside Egypt, within overseas Ptolemaic settlements in Greece, but are common in Lower Egypt, the Nile Delta, and especially at Saqqara, near Memphis, where they were made and sold to pilgrims. Large quantities of these figures were found at Naukratis, where they were also made in terracotta and possibly faience; they have also been found along the length of the Canopic branch of the Nile from Memphis to Thonis-Heracleion.   [RT]

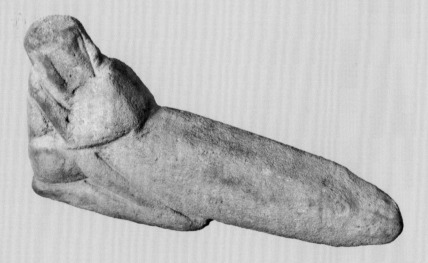

**Phallic representations of
Horus-the-child (Harpokrates)**
Holding a drum:
4th–2nd century BC
Thonis-Heracleion
Limestone
L. 8.6 cm
Maritime Museum, Alexandria SCA 1590

Carried by a priest:
4th–2nd century BC
Thonis-Heracleion
Limestone
H. 14 cm
Maritime Museum, Alexandria SCA 383

**Gilded and painted figure of
Egyptian goddess, probably Hathor**
c. 400–200 BC
Sanctuary of Amun-Ra, Naukratis
Limestone
H. 13.1 cm | W. 5.1 cm
British Museum EA 68814

Egyptian goddess

This exceptional gilded limestone figure is probably
a representation of the goddess Hathor, who is
commonly depicted standing nude, with her arms
held beside her body.[134] Here she wears only a
collar in gilded relief and a girdle that decorates
her back with the sacred eye of Horus, and ties in
front, with the loose ends decorated with lotus-
flowers hanging onto each thigh. The fingers
have rings painted on them in red. Nude female
figures, in various materials, were made in Egypt for
millennia. They were used in a variety of ways by
communities and individuals in domestic, funerary,
private and public religion, in spells and medicine,
for protection and for fertility (both safe childbirth
and a successful Nile Inundation). This example
was found within the storehouse of the sanctuary
of Amun-Ra at Naukratis. The fine work and gilding
means this must have been an expensive dedication
by a wealthy follower of the local Egyptian cults. [RT]

Isis-Bubastis

By the Ptolemaic period, Isis was known by a
variety of names and had absorbed aspects of
other Egyptian and Greek goddesses, including
the cat-headed Egyptian goddess and protector
of children Bastet, known to the Greeks as
Bubastis. This terracotta figure shows the
goddess wearing festival dress; she is holding
up the front of her tunic to show her pubic area.
This practice was recorded by Herodotus, who
experienced the river festival of Bubastis:

> *They sail, men and women together, and
> many of each in every river barge. Some
> women have clappers and rattle them,
> some men play pipes throughout the
> journey, while the other women and men
> sing and clap their hands. And when,
> as they sail, they pass any city [...] some
> of the women [...] jeeringly shout at the
> women in that city, some dance, and some
> stand up and pull up their clothes.[135]*

This example is still brightly painted, as all such
figures would have been in antiquity. The figure's
large headdress (*kalathos*) with wreaths and
garlands over her long 'Isis-locks' give some
impression of the colour and vibrancy of the
Egyptian festivals surrounding the cult of Isis
and the Nile Inundation. The figure was made
in Naukratis, where a workshop produced such
items for the local Egyptian population, but in a
style and of a type found throughout Egypt. [RT]

Figure of Isis-Bubastis wearing festival dress
c. 300–100 BC
Found and made in a figure workshop at Naukratis
Terracotta
H. 24.5 cm | W. 8.2 cm
British Museum 1886,0401.1451

Plaque of Isis-Hathor standing within a shrine
c. 400–300 BC
Made in Naukratis, probably acquired in Naukratis
Terracotta
H. 9.5 cm | W. 8.4 cm
British Museum 1885,1010.28

Isis-Hathor

This terracotta figure-plaque depicts a naked goddess wearing an Egyptian wig, probably Isis-Hathor.[136] She stands in a shrine with a triangular pediment supported by columns in the form of two standing Bes figures above two recumbent lions. Bes, protector of Horus-the-child, babies and pregnant women, is represented with a tall feathered crown. Plaques such as this often depict important people, objects or events relating to the 'festival of drunkenness'. This festival celebrated the return of Isis-Hathor from the south to her husband Osiris, which resulted in the conception of Horus-the-child. This religious event was important symbolically both for the renewal of the dynasty and the renewal of the land, as it immediately preceded the Nile Inundation.

Isis-Hathor figure-plaques are common in Lower Egypt and Memphis. 'Hathoric figures' were also thrown into the Nile to arouse the desire of the river god Hapy during Inundation rituals from the New Kingdom onwards. Examples found within the Nile river channels at Naukratis and Mendes (in the eastern Delta) give possible evidence of the continuation of this ritual during festivals on the river. This example was produced at Naukratis, where many similar plaques were made for the town's Egyptian inhabitants. Some had been placed outside the walls of the Egyptian sanctuary precinct of Amun-Ra, which was not open to ordinary Egyptians. Isis-Hathor figures were even found within the Greek sanctuaries of the Hellenion; perhaps Hathor was reinterpreted as Aphrodite by the Greeks. [RT]

East Greek *situla* with struggle between Apollo/Horus and Typhon/Seth
600–570 BC
Made on Rhodes, Greece.
Excavated in 1886 at Daphnae/Tell Dafana
Pottery
H. 53.6 cm | D. 26.7 cm
British Museum 1888,0208.1

Greek depiction of an Egyptian myth

This large East Greek pottery jar[137] was found in the Egyptian temple complex at Daphnae (Tell Dafana) in the eastern Nile Delta.[138] Its unique Greek rendering of an Egyptian myth shows how Greeks tried to make sense of other cultures by 'translating' foreign gods and myths.

The two sides of the *situla* represent a single myth. Monstrous, earth-born Typhon, part-snake and part-human, is pursued by the youthful god Apollo; both are winged, denoting their superhuman nature. While the battle between Zeus and Typhon is a well-known Greek myth, it is unusual to find Apollo as monster-slayer instead. The reason behind the vase-painter's choice is that he used the Greek visual language to depict a famous Egyptian story: the overthrowing of Seth by Horus, in revenge for the death of Osiris.

The battle between Horus and Seth formed part of the most important religious mythical cycle of Late Period Egypt, that of Osiris. It was carved on temple walls and dramatically re-enacted at religious festivals such as the Apis bull ritual at Memphis and mystery rites at the sanctuary of Neith at Sais, but also perhaps during the Khoiak festival at Thonis-Heracleion (pp. 182, 188).[139] It is here that resident foreigners recognized similarities between Egyptian gods and myths and their own. We know from Herodotus that this also happened with Horus and Apollo:

The last of these divine beings to rule Egypt was Horus, the son of Osiris, whom the Greeks call Apollo. He, they say, deposed Typhon [i.e. Seth] and became the last god to rule Egypt.[140]

Apollo slaying Typhon provided a good match for the story of Horus and Seth: just like the hunter-god Apollo, young Horus commands and defeats the destructive forces of nature (birds, locusts); and just like the slaying of Typhon, Horus' victory over Seth, god of desert and disorder,[141] restores order and civilization.

Horus' slaying of Seth was associated especially with the area around and east of Daphnae. Along with several other jars bearing Egyptian-inspired scenes, the Typhon jar was probably commissioned and imported by Greeks specifically as gifts for the Egyptian temple, perhaps filled with offerings of Greek wine. Even their shape was probably modelled on Egyptian vessels. [AV]

A Dionysiac ritual pail

The bucket[142] (*kados* in Ancient Greek) shown here displays a wide, slightly flaring neck and a swinging handle ending in stylized buds. It combines the shape of a Greek wine-mixing bowl (*krater*), used for drinking parties or Dionysiac rituals, with the Egyptian *situla* that was particularly common in rituals related to Isis. Some parallels have been found in Greek contexts of the late Archaic and Classical periods (late 6th–5th centuries BC) and also in Egyptian Late Ptolemaic or early Roman contexts.[143] More elaborate specimens have supports for the handle in the shape of a Dionysiac/Bacchic mask (fig. 62),[144] a variant that possibly originated in Hellenistic Egypt and may have been produced in an Alexandrian workshop.[145] One such vessel was discovered far to the south in the pyramid of queen Amanishaketo (r. 10 BC–1 AD) in Meroë in Sudan.[146] Although the Thonis-Heracleion example does not feature such an attachment, the association of this vessel shape with Dionysos might be implied by the Greek inscription crudely incised on the handle. Specialists tentatively read the beginning as a mention of Bacchus-Dionysos, *BAKOI.*[147]   [AMB]

Ritual bucket with Greek inscription on handle
c. 4th–2nd century BC
Thonis-Heracleion
Bronze
H. 25 cm
National Museum of Alexandria 310, SCA 223

62   *Situla*-fitting representing a mask of a horned and full-bearded Dionysos
200 BC–AD 100
(probably late Ptolemaic period)
Greece
Bronze with silver and copper inlays
H. 21.4 cm
British Museum 1989,0130.1

Hermes, a divine guide to the Underworld

This relief was discovered in the non-submerged part of Canopus around 1825 and brought to Alexandria, where it was almost reused in a baker's oven. The Admiral William Henry Smyth, an officer of the British Royal Navy, noticed the beautiful piece and acquired it, later donating it to the Duke of Buckingham.

A representation of the Greek god Hermes occupies almost the entire slab. Being the swift-footed messenger of the gods, Hermes is shown striding to the left, with his usual attributes, wearing a *petasos* – a large traveller's hat – and carrying a winged staff, the *caduceus*. In his left hand he holds a tortoiseshell lyre, the musical instrument he is said to have invented. Apart from a narrow short mantle, casually thrown across his left shoulder, he is naked. The muscles of his athletic body are rendered with precision and energy. His face, slightly damaged, is framed by detailed short curls and longer locks are visible behind his neck.

The relief was made in an Alexandrian workshop in the first century BC, but in a deliberately archaizing style based on Attic art of the late sixth to early fifth century BC. We can see this especially in the stiff, stylized folds of Hermes' mantle. The revival of past styles is a prominent feature of late Hellenistic art. The combination of the Greek-style figure with a dark local stone – a common material in Egyptian temples – is especially striking.

Hermes was the god of transitions and boundaries, but also of cunning and trickery, inventions and trade. As a mediator between the mortal and divine worlds, he conducted the souls of the dead into the afterlife. Greeks saw in him the equivalent to the ibis-headed Egyptian god Thoth, who played an essential role in the Osirian myth. Thoth helped Isis resurrect Osiris and, as an arbitrator, he settled the dispute between the god of chaos Seth and the rightful heir to the terrestrial throne, Horus. As the god of sacred scripture, sciences and magic, Thoth was the clerk in the divine tribunal of the underworld, writing down the judgement following the weighing of the heart, when a deceased person's good or bad deeds were judged. According to a legend recounted by Plutarch, Hermes cut out the sinews of Typhon, the Greek counterpart of Seth, and used them as the strings of his lyre, 'thereby instructing us that Reason adjusts the Universe and creates concord out of discordant elements, and that it does not destroy but only cripples the destructive force'.[148] The lyre displayed on the relief here acts as a reminder of that wisdom. [AMB]

Hermes relief
Early 1st century BC
Canopus
Granite or basalt
H. 1.21 m | W. 79 cm
British Museum 1848,1014.1

2205

HERMES

CANOPUS, EGYPT.   *Stowe Coll.*

Dionysos, a youthful god

This gilded silver goblet was probably cast in a mould, and is decorated in raised relief with figures of Dionysos, satyrs, maenads (female followers of the god) and cupids in a vineyard. The vessel is an outstanding example of Egyptian silverware, testifying to the mastery of the metalworker's craft in Roman Egypt. It probably belonged with a pair of silver plates (now in the Graeco-Roman Museum, Alexandria) that formed part of a silver treasure discovered in Hermopolis Magna (now in Berlin).

The scene is set in a vineyard where, surrounded by birds and plant tendrils, cupids are harvesting the grapes and preparing the wine by trampling the fruits in a vat. On the opposite side Dionysos is depicted reclining and covered in a mantle (*himation*), with his *thyrsos* staff in one hand and a *rhyton* (drinking horn) in the other. A satyr and a maenad are pictured next to him, entertaining the god by playing the double pipe and the lyre. All the figures appear in the midst of foliage, with heavy clusters of grapes hanging from the vine branches. A variety of birds, tendrils and acanthus leaves are delicately rendered with great care.

In Ptolemaic Egypt festivals were held for Dionysos, the god of wine, vegetation, pleasure and festivity and one of the most popular gods in Ptolemaic and Roman Alexandria. Named Dionysia after the god, these festivals featured theatrical performances, and reflected the wealth and luxurious lifestyle of Alexandrian society. Drinking was considered a social event and *symposia*, drinking parties, were not imaginable without a significant amount of wine. Often referred to by ancient historians, Egyptian wine was famous for its unusually high quality thanks to the country's fertile soil and ideal climate. [MSD]

Silver goblet
1st / 2nd century AD
Hermopolis Magna (El Ashmunein)
Gilded silver
H. 13 cm | D. 10.3 cm
Graeco-Roman Museum, Alexandria 24201

5 Egypt and Rome

Ross Thomas and Damian Robinson

Cleopatra, Mark Antony and Augustus

The kingdom inherited in 51 BC by Cleopatra VII (r. 51–30 BC), together with her brother and husband Ptolemy XIII, was a shadow of the former Ptolemaic empire. Egypt had already lost its overseas provinces to Rome, and a substantial Roman loan used by Cleopatra's father, Ptolemy XII (r. 80–58, 55–51 BC), to reinstall himself on the throne had left Cleopatra with a difficult state to rule.[1] She would need to exercise great diplomatic skill in order to navigate between the interests of the Roman Senate (and other influential power brokers), an Alexandrian population prone to mob violence, and ambitious Egyptian courtiers and elites. Cleopatra was drawn into the Roman civil war, at first supplying Pompey's (106–48 BC) army in his war against Julius Caesar (100–44 BC) before being exiled by her own court, after which she formed her famous political alliance with Caesar. She was reinstalled by Caesar in 48 BC and subsequently protected by three Roman legions, which Caesar left in Egypt as an occupying force.

Together with their son Caesarion ('Little Caesar'), Cleopatra followed Caesar to Rome. There they were hosted by Caesar, who placed a gilded statue of the young queen in the temple of Venus Genetrix (Venus 'the Mother', the Roman equivalent of the Greek Aphrodite), the goddess from whom his family, and later the Julio-Claudian dynasty, claimed to be descended. Cleopatra's visit, and Caesar's approval, introduced and promoted the culture, customs and cults of Ptolemaic Egypt, particularly the cult of Isis and Serapis, to some members of the Roman elite. Others, however, reacted to her presence with suspicion and envy. After Caesar was murdered in 44 BC, Cleopatra returned to Egypt, elevating their son Caesarion to the throne as Ptolemy XV after she had despatched her second husband (and brother) Ptolemy XIV (r. 47–44 BC).

Cleopatra now allied herself with the Roman general Mark Antony (fig. 64), who avenged Caesar's death by defeating the armies of his assassins, which had gathered in the east. Her subsequent relationship with Mark Antony resulted in the birth of their twins, Cleopatra and Alexander, and youngest son Ptolemy. Cleopatra's diplomacy and her relationships, first with Caesar and then with Mark Antony, re-established her dynasty, allowing her to add provinces to her domain in Gaza, Lebanon, Syria and Cyprus. At this time Cleopatra and Mark Antony presented themselves as the living gods Isis-Aphrodite and Osiris-Dionysos, in the same fashion as previous Ptolemaic rulers.

63 Priest holding an Osiris-Canopus jar in veiled hands, framed by sphinxes. See pp. 228–29

64 Cleopatra seated on a barge, admired from an adjacent boat by Mark Antony
Engraving after the painting of 1883
by Sir Lawrence Alma-Tadema,
The Meeting of Antony and Cleopatra.
30 x 41.5 cm
British Museum 2010,7033.4

Mark Antony's relationship with Cleopatra destabilized his alliance with Octavian, the future Roman emperor Augustus and Caesar's heir – in part because Mark Antony was married to Octavian's sister, Octavia. Their estrangement ultimately led to a civil war into which Egypt was drawn and cast as the real enemy in Octavian's propaganda. Inflammatory reports of Cleopatra and Mark Antony's 'degenerate lifestyle' and self-depiction as living gods were supported by the reading of Antony's will in the Senate.[2] The representation of Cleopatra as the queen of a threatening foreign tyranny, and Mark Antony as entirely enthralled by her power, was an image cemented over many years after Octavian's victory. Cruel and crude propaganda representing Cleopatra and Mark Antony as morally and sexually corrupt apparently continued to be produced long after their deaths (p. 227).[3]

In 31 BC Cleopatra and Mark Antony's forces were held in the bay of Actium, Greece, by Octavian's naval blockade. Following their breakout and flight, all was lost. In 30 BC, Mark Antony and Cleopatra committed suicide. Her son Caesarion was executed by Octavian, but her three children with Mark Antony lived on.[4] After the war, Roman interest in Egypt grew, and Egyptian cults as well as imported objects, sculpture and monuments became fashionable.

After Octavian entered Alexandria, Egypt became one of many Roman provinces ruled by prefects appointed by the emperor. Compared with the earlier Ptolemaic rulers, the Roman government seems to have invested less in the temples.[5] There were, nevertheless, Egyptian temples built and refurbished, especially in the first and second centuries AD.[6] At this time, new influences from across the Roman empire inspired changes to the representation of Egyptian gods and the construction of their temples in Egypt.[7]

For 300 years Alexandria had been a hub of Mediterranean trade, where Egyptians, Greeks, Romans and others mingled, each learning of the others' beliefs. Visitors sailing into Alexandria would have passed the temple of Isis within the grounds of the royal palaces in the east harbour, before seeing the magnificent Caesareum,[8] a temple deliberately located so as to be visible from approaching ships. The Caesareum was founded by Cleopatra, but completed by Augustus and dedicated to the worship of the divine Caesar. The temple of Isis was also founded during, or just before, the reign of Cleopatra, and remained a place of worship throughout the Roman period. Discovered underwater, this temple was decorated with beautiful sculptures including a priest bearing an Osiris-Canopus jar and two sphinxes (pp. 228, 232–33).[9]

The spread of Egyptian cult in the Roman empire

The number of gods worshipped in Roman Egypt had swelled as people of many religious faiths arrived from across the empire and beyond. Some Egyptian gods absorbed the qualities and features of deities from other cultures (p. 234), and were understood by their believers as different manifestations of the same being. This was particularly the case for Isis and Serapis, universalized deities, whose worshippers believed them to be the foremost among gods,[10] as described in Apuleius' popular second-century AD novel *Metamorphoses*:

> *I am she that is the natural mother of all things ... my divinity is adored throughout all the world ... the Athenians [call me] Minerva; the Cyprians, Venus; the Cretans, Diana; the Sicilians, Proserpina; the Eleusians, Ceres; some Juno, others Bellona, others Hecate ... the Egyptians which are excellent in all kind of ancient doctrine, and by their proper ceremonies ... do call me by my true name, Queen Isis.*[11]

Just as visiting foreigners influenced belief and ritual practice in Egypt, so travellers took Egyptian cults to other lands. The Ptolemaic empire brought Egyptian cults to its occupied territories and allies through political, military and economic influence, as well as dynastic building projects, but also through the influence of private individuals. In this way Egyptian cults reached across the eastern Mediterranean, Rome, Greece and North Africa (p. 235). After the first century AD, Egyptian cults were spread further across the western empire by Roman merchants, soldiers and officials,[12] and reached Roman settlements as far away as Faversham and London in Britain (p. 239).

The Isis cult, despite being prohibited in Rome on several occasions,[13] was favoured among the Roman elite, who regarded Isis as a member of the Roman pantheon. It was adopted alongside other oriental influences that Roman subjects experienced as the Roman empire grew. Originally popular in elite urban settings, Egyptian gods even became popular in rural areas across the empire.[14] Indeed, one contemporary commentator stated that the gods and 'rituals that were once Egyptian are now Roman'.[15]

The worship and display of Egyptian cults in Egypt was in turn transformed by these external influences. The podium (raised platform) temple at Ras el-Soda (p. 236) was dedicated to Egyptian Isis, Osiris and Horus (the Osirian triad). However, the temple itself was built in a Roman style that was common across the eastern Mediterranean. The temple was decorated with votive statues of Egyptian deities made of imported marble in the style and form of the Roman period (such as the Osiris-Canopus jar, see p. 237).[16] The temple may have been built by the same man who dedicated a Greek inscription and a votive foot (p. 238) to Isis, Serapis or both at the temple. He was named Isidoros ('Gift of Isis') and was a Greek-speaking Roman subject. This temple illustrates clearly some of the multidirectional international influences on the subjects, styles and materials used by followers of the cult of the Osirian triad, within the multicultural society of the ancient port of Alexandria.

Hadrian and Osiris-Antinous

'He [Antinous] had been a favourite of the emperor and had died in Egypt, either by falling into the Nile, as Hadrian writes, or, as the truth is, by being offered as a sacrifice' wrote Cassius Dio, perhaps half a century after the events on the banks of the river in AD 130.[17] By that time, the cult of the deified Antinous had reached the very edges of the empire, spreading outwards from Egypt and Antinopolis, the city founded in Middle Egypt by the Roman emperor Hadrian at the site of his young favourite's death. At Lanuvium, southeast of Rome, a group of men, including slaves, formed a club in which they publicly worshipped Antinous as a god of salvation. They inscribed the rules of their association on his new temple in the town in August AD 132, only twenty months after his death.[18] In Aquileia, at the northern end of the Adriatic Sea, terracotta plaques bearing his images were nailed to sarcophagi, while back in Egypt, his name was written on wooden tablets and fixed to mummy-cases in Luxor.[19] In all these locations the purpose was the same: redemption. This was part of an empire-wide, and at least initially imperially supported, outpouring of religious sentiment that produced a wealth of archaeological evidence in sculpture (p. 241), busts, cameos and coins. The intensity of the cult's popularity, even after the death of Hadrian in AD 138, was clearly due to something in the religious atmosphere of the second century AD. At this time elective cults (those which any individual could choose to join), like that at Lanuvium, developed special initiatory rituals, such as those associated with the closely related cult of Isis.[20] The appeal of these Egyptian cults, alongside Christianity and the cult of Mithras, was both the community they offered during life, and their promise of a 'transformation' that secured the fate of the initiate after death.[21]

Why, though, did Antinous progress from being just another 'imperial pretty boy'[22] to a saviour god, revered across the empire for his powers of healing?[23] To understand this we need to return to the waters of the Nile and the events of late October AD 130. While Hadrian's account of Antinous' death is somewhat vague, Cassius Dio and later ancient authors suspected that there was more to it than a simple accident: that this was a 'sacrifice of substitution', with the young man dying voluntarily to 'save' Hadrian.[24] Here then was the origin of the 'medicinal' aspect of his divinity. Yet, as seen in Aquileia and Luxor and elsewhere, Antinous' real power lay in his role as Osiris-Antinous and its connection with believers facing their own deaths. For the Egyptians, a death in the river conferred sanctity upon the drowned person – especially during the Khoiak festival. It marked the deceased as somewhat 'more than human' through their association with the god Osiris, who (prior to his dismemberment) also drowned in the Nile, but was revived to eternal life.[25] Antinous was immediately identified with this god, and his body was treated in accordance with 'all of the customs of the ritual of Osiris together with all his secret rites', according to the text on an obelisk raised in his honour.[26] Hadrian built

65 *left* **Marble bust of the emperor Hadrian wearing military dress**
From Hadrian's Villa, Tivoli, Italy
AD 125–30. H. 84 cm
British Museum 1805,0703.95.

right **Marble portrait head from a statue of Antinous, as Dionysos, wearing a wreath of ivy**
From Janiculine Hill, Rome
c. AD 130–40 (the bust is modern)
British Museum 1805,0703.97

upon these Egyptian traditions, either through grief or a desire to promote a new Greek deity throughout the empire, and quickly declared Antinous a god, establishing a cult with its own iconography, priests, temples and altars. But this was not a simple offshoot of the Imperial cult (the worship of the Roman emperor); it developed its own religious vitality through the message that it offered. Osiris-Antinous – or Dionysos-Antinous in the Greek world – promised well-being to his believers during life, and a guarantee of eternity thereafter. While never rivalling the great cults of Isis or Serapis, that of Antinous played an important role in the changing religious worldview of the second century AD and in the rise of faith in saviour gods far beyond the shores of Egypt.

66 South-facing view of the Canopus at Hadrian's villa at Tivoli, with a scenic triclinium, or outdoor dining room, known as the 'Serapeum' under a semi-dome

Afterward

The cult of Osiris-Antinous was one of many popular elective cults of saviour deities in the second century AD that were a product of the Roman Imperial religious world, such as Mithraism and Christianity. The eventual dominance of Christianity in this region was neither inevitable nor achieved without significant borrowing from other older ritual practices and beliefs in Roman Egypt. For example, the famous healing shrine of Saints Cyrus and John at Menouthis[27] was established by moving the martyrs' remains from Alexandria in the fifth century AD. It competed with, and then replaced, a famous pilgrimage shrine for the cult of Isis that had long performed healing and oracular services for pilgrims until it was attacked in *c.* AD 489 by Christians. At both shrines miraculous cures were revealed to those sleeping within the sanctuary (known as incubation), a striking continuum of ritual practice at this sacred place on the Canopic mouth.[28] With the submergence of the region in the eighth century AD, the saints' shrine disappeared, as much of the city slipped beneath the sea.[29] It still lies undiscovered somewhere out in Abukir Bay, another lost world beneath Egypt's 'Sea of the Greeks'.

**Roman relief of a Nile scene
with two lovers, possibly
Cleopatra VII and Mark Antony**
c. 30 BC–AD 100
Probably from Italy
Marble
H. 35 cm | W. 40 cm | D. 5.5 cm
British Museum 1865,1118.252

Roman propaganda

This marble relief depicts a Nile scene with two lovers on a boat. The boatman standing at the bow wears a distinctive pointed hat identifying him as a marsh-dweller of the Nile Delta. The boat approaches land to the left, represented by a building, a flower and the rear of a hippopotamus. Two dolphins are depicted either decorating or swimming alongside the boat. The iconography may represent the meeting of the Mediterranean (dolphin) and the Nile (hippopotamus), placing this scene in the Canopic region. The lovers may have been intended as an obscene caricature of Cleopatra VII and Mark Antony, as the hairstyle of the woman resembles that favoured by Cleopatra, which became unpopular after her death. The criticism levelled against Cleopatra and Mark Antony by Octavian's supporters was reinforced by such depictions. [RT]

Reverent priest

This life-sized statue represents a young man dressed in a cloak that closely envelops the upper part of the body, including his arms, over a long tunic with folds. The head of the figure appears to be carefully shaved, indicating that he is a priest. In his hands, hidden under the folds of his cloak, the young priest carries at shoulder height, and pressed against his cheek, a vase with a round body and a human head on top. On the front surface of the body of the vase were once ornaments in relief, now eroded. The male head with a beard and the *nemes* headdress identifies the object as an Osiris-Canopus jar. Although statues of priests with these jars are known, they are usually from outside Egypt, and as such this Alexandrian discovery is exceptional, particularly because the statue is so well preserved.

The young priest bearing the divine jar was most likely represented taking part in a procession or cult ritual, such as that depicted in a wall painting from Herculaneum, Italy (fig. 67). Here the priest at the top of the stairs holds the jar in exactly the same manner as the statue from Alexandria. Like the scene that the painting depicts, the statue itself was excavated from the site of a small Iseum – a temple to Isis – on the royal island of Antirhodos in the Portus Magnus, the great eastern harbour of Alexandria.

Two examples of these Osiris-Canopus jars have been discovered in the underwater excavations in Abukir Bay (p. 133), during the investigation of a dumping area for statues that had been gathered together, possibly in a workshop where hard stone was cut for reuse.[30] This dump was most likely created during the Christian Byzantine period, with material coming from the adjacent pagan Serapeum of Canopus. The jars may have stood together and been used as a pair in the temple's ritual life in the Roman period.[31]

The varied uses of these types of jars have been described in Greco-Roman literature.[32] Links have been made between 'Canopic jars', intended to contain the mummified internal organs of the deceased in a burial, and the type of jar held by the priest. Indeed, the reliefs of one of the Osirian temples from Dendera depicts a procession of nome (province) gods bearing jars of the Canopic type containing pieces of the body of Osiris. Yet while the form of the jars and the processional ceremony may have been consistent with Egyptian cult practices, it was in the Roman period in Egypt and beyond that the imagery of the jar itself became popularized. In the first century AD the Osiris-Canopus jar motif appears on Alexandrian coins, becoming common from year four of the reign of the emperor Vespasian in AD 73, and remaining so until around AD 267. A 'theology' of the Canopic jar thus appears to develop in the Imperial Roman period in Egypt and abroad, with the complex decoration of the jars referring to water as a source of life, specifically the water that Osiris bestows on the deceased for their regeneration.

[DJR, from DF]

Priest with Osiris-Canopus jar
1st century BC–2nd century AD
Alexandria
Granodiorite
H. 122 cm
National Museum of Alexandria SCA 449

67 Wall painting from Herculaneum representing a ceremony of Isis with her priest holding a jar. National Archaeological Museum, Naples

68 Diver facing a sphinx discovered in a temple to Isis on the Royal island of Antirhodos in the Portus Magnus of Alexandria (see overleaf)

Royal guardians

Pair of sphinxes
1st century BC
Alexandria
Granodiorite
H. 75 cm | L. 1.4 m
National Museum of Alexandria 284, SCA 451

H. 70 cm | L. 1.5 m
National Museum of Alexandria 283, SCA 450

This pair of sphinxes was discovered during the excavation of what was most likely a small Iseum – a temple of Isis – on the island of Antirhodos in the Portus Magnus, the great eastern harbour of Alexandria. They were found alongside the statue of a priest holding an Osiris-Canopus jar (p. 228).[33] Sphinxes were traditionally used to line a processional way to the doorways of temples,

and this pair may have been similarly used for the Iseum (p. 230). Antirhodos was part of the Royal Quarters, indicating that the temple was likely to have been used by members of the royal household: it continued to be used well into the Roman period.

Both of the sphinxes are represented in the traditional pose: the front feet stretched forwards,

the back legs tucked up underneath the body and the tail running up along the left thigh. In the majority of cases the head of the sphinx represents the sovereign, as indicated by the *nemes* headcloth worn by pharaohs, with the royal *uraeus* (sacred rearing cobra) decorating its front. It is possible to identify the king represented from the treatment of the face, which begins to blend pharaonic traditions with styles of Greek portraiture from the period of Ptolemy VI (r. 180–145 BC) onwards. It seems that the treatment of the hair on one of the sphinxes is characteristic of coin portraits of Ptolemy XII Auletes, who ruled between 80–58 BC and 55–51 BC and was the father of Cleopatra VII, the last active pharaoh of Ptolemaic Egypt.

[DJR, from ZK]

Symbols of power

This sumptuous ring was discovered in a shipwreck in Alexandria's Portus Magnus near the island of Antirhodos, close to the royal palaces and an Iseum (temple of Isis). The ring and its carved stone (intaglio) are perfectly preserved. The ring is composed of three thick intertwined golden threads. The gem carver used the various colours of the chalcedony stone when crafting the intaglio. The silhouette of an eagle[34] is engraved in night blue over a lighter background, silhouette turned left, wings half opened, raised head turned right and the beak holding the attachment of a vegetal crown (perhaps laurel or olive leaf) with two small blades pointing symmetrically either side of the clasped piece.

The motif of the eagle of Zeus holding a lightning bolt had become the mark of the Ptolemaic dynasty and was used on their coins as a symbol of the celestial forces and of universal domination. During the Roman period the eagle was associated with Jupiter. The crown here introduces notions of glory and victory, and adorns many of the Greco-Roman gems.   [ASvB]

Bust of Serapis
c. AD 1–100
Unknown provenance,
acquired in Egypt
Calcite (?)
H. 27 cm
Graeco-Roman Museum,
Alexandria 23925

Intaglio ring
End of 1st century BC–1st century AD
Alexandria
Gold and chalcedony
Ring Diam. 2.95 cm | Setting Diam. 1.8 cm
Bibliotheca Alexandrina Antiquities Museum SCA 84

'Hybrid' portraiture

This alabaster or calcite bust of Serapis, with its thick curly hair and beard, resembles images of senior Olympian Greek deities, such as Zeus. Small wings are also depicted within the curls of the hair, an aspect associated with another Egyptian deity, Hermanubis, whose attributes are here absorbed by Serapis.[35] While this example was acquired in Egypt, depictions of Serapis have been found on various media across the Roman empire, reaching Rome itself before the reign of Augustus. Similar alabaster Serapis busts have been found in the capital. Egyptian cults were spread by sailors and travellers. In Alexandria, Serapis was worshipped at the Serapeum, a magnificent temple dedicated to Serapis and his family (Isis and Horus-the-child). This structure was enlarged in AD 181, and used until its destruction in AD 391–392, after which it was converted into a church.   [RT]

Isis abroad

Isis was worshipped outside Egypt, where she was sometimes associated with other deities. This representation of the goddess was found within the sanctuary of Aphrodite in Cyrene (Libya). Although the bust is possibly not of Egyptian manufacture, Isis is readily identifiable from her hairstyle and dress, with the typical twisted 'Isis locks' falling onto her shoulders and fringed shawl knotted between her breasts. However, her hair fringe is more in keeping with Roman fashions of the period; close parallels are known from Italy.[36]   [RT]

Bust of Isis in Roman style
AD 150–200
Temple of Aphrodite, Cyrene,
Cyrenaica (Libya)
Calcite
H. 30 cm
British Museum 1861,1127.83

The temple of Ras el-Soda

The modest temple at Ras el-Soda was built on the road from Alexandria to Canopus in the late second century AD. The small (5 by 7.5 metres) temple comprised a staircase leading to a raised platform on which stood four Ionic columns, behind which were three rooms, including living quarters and a bench which functioned as a bed for the resident priest. In the middle of the platform stood a marble foot on a column recording the dedication of the charioteer Isidoros (p. 238). The temple was richly endowed with statues of imported marble representing the Osirian triad of Osiris, his sister-wife Isis and their son Harpokrates (Horus-the-child). The largest and most significant statues are of Isis, to whom Isidoros probably made his dedication, as thanks for his survival and recovery from a chariot accident in which he injured his feet.

The podium temple is not an Egyptian form of temple architecture, but a Roman one. Contemporary temples of Isis or Serapis in this style are known from Egypt, Greece, Libya and Italy and the podium temple was an architectural style used widely across the eastern Mediterranean during the Roman period. It is not typical of Isis, or of Egyptian cults, but was adapted here for local use by a member of the Roman elite.

The marble vases opposite depict Osiris in the form of a water jar, or Osiris-*hydreios*, more commonly known as Osiris-Canopus. This form of Osiris was worshipped in Canopus, where similar examples have been found (p. 133). Produced only after the reign of Augustus (27 BC–AD 14), such vases are a distinctively Roman-period interpretation and representation of the Egyptian god. How these vessels may have been used can be deduced from sculptures depicting priests carrying them (p. 228).

On the first jar, Osiris wears a wig and beard, and a tall *atef* crown with rams' horns and protective *uraei* (rearing cobras). The body of the vase is decorated with a depiction of a shrine above a winged scarab beetle, itself below a sun disc, flanked by representations of Harpokrates (Horus-the-child) and Isis. Two Horus falcons, wearing the double crown of Egypt, sit on the shrine. The second jar is less elaborately decorated, with the bearded Osiris simply wearing a crown and dressed in stylized mummy wrappings. A sun disc flanked by two *uraei* adorns the front of the jar.

These two jars were found in the Roman temple at Ras el-Soda, placed on a marble bench alongside statues of Isis and Harpokrates. Representations of Osiris-Canopus are also known from Rome, Pompeii and Soli (Cyprus). Osiris-Canopus jars are the source of the modern term 'Canopic jar', though this is now commonly associated with Egyptian jars used for a very different purpose: containing the human organs removed during the mummification process.   [RT]

Osiris-Canopus jars
AD 150–200
Found in the temple of
Ras el-Soda, Alexandria
Marble
H. 1.07 m (left) | H. 95 cm (right)
Graeco-Roman Museum, Alexandria
25787 (left) and 25786 (right)

Personal dedications

This marble foot was dedicated by Isidoros, whose name means 'Gift of Isis', after he recovered from foot injuries, thought to have been sustained during a chariot-race crash.[37] The Greek inscription reads: 'Flung from his carriage by his horses at the spot, Isidoros, restored to health by divine intervention, in exchange for his feet, dedicated this image of a foot to the "Blessed"'.[38] The epithet 'The Blessed' was frequently used to describe Isis or her partner Serapis.

The foot is similar to a number of marble and porphyry feet known from Roman Egypt and associated with Serapis. They are usually sandalled right feet like this one. Most depict the bust, or a full enthroned figure, of Serapis above the ankle. One example, said to come from the Caesareum in Alexandria, is part of the British Museum's collection.[39] Although most were found in Egypt, examples are known from Rome, Istanbul, Athens and Turin, and the device is found on contemporary Alexandrian coinage.[40]

Since this dedication was placed in the centre of the podium (temple platform), in front of the altar, the grateful Isidoros probably built the temple of the Osirian triad. The temple was built on the road from Alexandria to Canopus, at Ras el-Soda, and may have been located at the spot where he was 'flung from his carriage'.   [RT]

Marble votive foot dedicated by Isidoros to Isis or Serapis
AD 150–200
From Ras el-Soda
Marble
H. (stand) 1.02 m | H. (foot) 28 cm
Graeco-Roman Museum, Alexandria 25788, 25789

Egyptian religion abroad

This Egyptian terracotta mould-made lamp handle is decorated with a representation of Isis sitting on a throne nursing Horus-the-child. The Osirian triad (Osiris, Isis and Horus-the-child) was represented on a range of media, including everyday items such as these mass-produced lamps. Lamps were not only mundane objects, but were also used in a variety of religious, magical and funerary practices in Egypt. Specially made lamps depicting Egyptian deities spread across the Roman empire as far as Britain. Roman officials, soldiers and traders carried with them not only Roman religion, but also aspects of Egyptian religion that had been adopted by the Roman elite. This lamp was found in Faversham, Kent, near the Roman town of Durolevum, which had a Romano-British temple and a Roman theatre.

A temple of Isis was active in London during the second and third centuries AD, as evidenced by an inscribed altar stone dedicated to the goddess. The inscription reads: 'In tribute, a gift donated by Marcus Martiannius Pulcher, most honourable of men, pro-praetorian legate of the emperors, who restored this temple to Isis, which had collapsed through old age and lay in ruins'.[41]

[RT]

Roman lamp handle with Isis nursing Harpokrates (Horus-the-child)
c. AD 100–200
Found in Faversham, UK
(the Roman town of Durolevum)
Pottery
H. 7.7 cm
British Museum 1984.1004.3

Emulating the emperor

This bronze head depicts a private individual copying the style of the Roman emperor Hadrian (r. AD 117–138). Hadrian travelled widely around his empire, particularly in the eastern Greek provinces. His visit to Egypt in AD 130 had a profound impact upon him. In Alexandria, at that time the largest Greek city in the world, he established a chapel to himself as a god in the Serapeum – the temple to Serapis – to which he also dedicated a statue of the Apis bull (p. 127). Thereafter he began to promote Serapis (pp. 80–85) as one of the great gods of the empire alongside Zeus and Jupiter.

This particular bronze head was discovered at Qena in Upper Egypt,[42] a port-settlement on the eastern bank of the Nile. Here the river met the road leading to the quarry at Mons Claudianus, which provided granodiorite stone for some of Hadrian's most lavish building projects,[43] including his villa at Tivoli. There, just outside Rome, the Nile and Egypt were central to the architecture of several of the buildings, which included both a 'Canopus', a man-made water feature (p. 226), and a Serapeum. The latter was decorated with statues that portrayed the cult of Osiris, who was identified with the deified Antinous (p. 241) following his death in the Nile.[44]   [DJR]

Bronze head of a private individual
2nd century AD
Qena, Upper Egypt
Bronze
H. 38 cm
Graeco-Roman Museum, Alexandria 22902

A deified lover

Antinous, the favourite of the Roman emperor
Hadrian, drowned in the Nile on 24 October
AD 130. This was an auspicious date in the
Egyptian calendar as it commemorated the death
by drowning of Osiris, with whom Antinous was
thus compared; subsequently a cult to the deified
youth was rapidly established. We know of more
representations of Antinous than of any other figure
in classical antiquity, with the exceptions of the
emperors Augustus and Hadrian. The majority of
such Antinous figures are classical in style and are
found outside Egypt, where such images are
surprisingly rare. This statue, found during
excavations of a Roman-period cemetery close to
Canopus, is therefore unusual, as it depicts
Antinous in a purely Egyptian tradition.[45] Here he is
modelled with an Egyptian-style back pillar; his left
foot is set slightly forwards to give the impression
of movement, with his arms straight down by his
sides. He is shown in Egyptian royal attire, bare-
chested and wearing the pharaoh's pleated *shendyt*
kilt and striped *nemes* headdress with a *uraeus*
(rearing cobra).   [DJR]

Statue of Antinous
2nd–4th century AD?[46]
Canopus
Limestone
H. 45 cm
Graeco-Roman Museum, Alexandria 22829

Key of gods

Egyptian

Amun

Mut

Khonsu
(as a child
and adult)

Osiris

Isis/Hathor

Horus
(as a child
and adult)

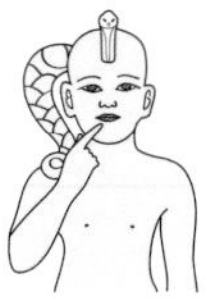

Seth

Neith

Greek (Roman)

Zeus (Jupiter)

Hera (Juno)

Herakles (Hercules)

Dionysos (Bacchus)

Demeter/Aphrodite
(Ceres/Venus)

Apollo (Bacchus)

Typhon

Athena (Minerva)

Timeline

New Kingdom **1550–1069 BC**
Around 1200 BC, Helen of Troy and Menelaus, king of Sparta, make legendary visit to the Canopic region, followed by the mythical Trojan wars

Third Intermediate Period **1069–664 BC**
Political instability; the state is often divided and ruled by foreigners

Late Period **664–332 BC**

26th dynasty **664–525 BC**
Thonis-Heracleion and Naukratis become the major international trading ports of Egypt

Rise in trade and diplomatic links with the Eastern Mediterranean, notably with Greeks

Major artistic and cultural revival

27th dynasty **525–404 BC**
First Persian domination

525 BC
The Persian king Cambyses conquers Egypt

30th dynasty **380–342 BC**
Last native dynasty of Egypt

380 BC
The Decree of Sais mentions imports from the 'Sea of the Greeks' and trade operations at Thonis and Naukratis

342 BC
Nectanebo II, last native pharaoh, is defeated by the Persians

31st dynasty **342–332 BC**
Second Persian domination

Ptolemaic Period **332–30 BC**

332–331 BC
Alexander the Great conquers Egypt and founds Alexandria, staying in the country for a year

323 BC
Death of Alexander

Ptolemy, Alexander's general and friend, becomes ruler of Egypt

323 BC
Pharaoh Ptolemy I Soter I (323–285 BC) is crowned, founding the Ptolemaic dynasty

c. 275 BC
Ptolemy II Philadelphos (285–246 BC) marries his sister Arsinoe

238 BC
In the Decree of Canopus, during the reign of Ptolemy III Euergetes I (246–222 BC), temples at Thonis-Heracleion and Canopus are mentioned respectively as the start and end of a boat procession celebrating Osiris

196 BC
The Decree of Memphis (the Rosetta Stone) establishes the divine cult of Ptolemy V Epiphanes (205–180 BC)

46 BC
Cleopatra VII (51–30 BC) visits Rome, as Caesar's guest. She introduces and promotes Egyptian culture and cults, particularly those of Isis and Serapis, to members of the Roman elite

44 BC
Assassination of Caesar; Cleopatra co-rules Egypt with their son, Ptolemy XV Caesarion

31 BC
Naval battle at Actium; Marc Antony and Cleopatra are defeated by Octavian (future emperor Augustus)

Roman Period **30 BC–AD 395**

30 BC
Egypt becomes a province of the Roman empire

Suicide of Marc Antony and Cleopatra VII

Ptolemy XV Caesarion is murdered on Octavian's order

AD 130
The emperor Hadrian (AD 117–138) and his lover Antinous visit Egypt. After Antinous drowns in the Nile, he is deified into Osiris-Antinous, a saviour god whose cult spreads across the Roman empire

AD 391
Theodosius I (AD 379–395) declares Christianity the official religion of the empire

Christians destroy the temples of Serapis in Alexandria and Canopus

Pagan religious practices are forbidden

Notes

Chapter 1
Rediscovering Thonis-Heracleion and Canopus

1 For the term Hau-nebut: von Bomhard 2012, 75–76; Fabre 2015, 180–81.
2 Walker 2001.
3 Cf. Cooper 2014; Blouin 2014.
4 Eustathius, *Scholia in Dionysium* 11.
5 Herodotus, *Histories* II.113–14.
6 Strabo, *Geography* 17.1.17.
7 See the Decree of Canopus, Chapter 4, fig. 54.
8 Strabo, *Geography* XVII.17 gives 120 stadia, *c.* 23 km; Ammianus Marcellinus, *History* XXII.14 cites 12 Roman miles, *c.* 18 km. Yoyotte et al. 1997, 107–9; Goddio 2007, 3.
9 Pseudo-Scylax (*Periplus* 107): from Pharos (Alexandria) to Thonis: 150 stadia (*c.* 28.5 km): Zacharias (*Life of Severus*) gives Alexandria to Menouthis – first mentioned in second or third century AD – 14 miles (*c.* 21 km).
10 al-Falaki 1872, 76–87.
11 Breccia 1914; 1926; Faivre 1918. As the names of Thonis and Heracleion appeared separately in the ancient texts, they were believed to be two separate and distinct localities.
12 Daressy 1929.
13 Toussoun 1934, 344.
14 Goddio 1995; Goddio et al. 1998.
15 Goddio 2007, 1–17.
16 Goddio et al. 1998.
17 Goddio 2007, 10–17.
18 Ibid., 24–26.
19 Goddio 2010, 6.
20 Goddio 2009.
21 Yoyotte 1958, 423–30.
22 Maps in Goddio 2007: site of Canopus, 33 fig. 2.8; the Egyptian temple, 54 fig. 2.57.
23 Kiss 2008b.
24 Yoyotte 2008b.
25 Smith 2008; Kiss 2010, 211–13.
26 Kiss 2008a.
27 Habachi and Habachi 1952; Leitz 1995; von Bomhard 2008; 2011; 2012/14; Goddio 2012/14.
28 Tyrannius Rufinus, *Ecclesiastical History* 2.26–27.
29 Goddio 2007, 69–129.
30 Goddio 2011, 123–29.
31 Goddio 2007, 74–75; 2015, 21–22.
32 Goddio 2007, 77; Yoyotte 2008c; von Bomhard 2012; 2015, 101–20.
33 Yoyotte 2008f.
34 Baines 2000, 100–5; Yoyotte 2008d.
35 Goddio 2007, 75–102.
36 Quack 2000–1; Goddio 2015, 31.
37 Goddio 2010, 11–12; 2015, 29–32.
38 Diodorus Siculus, *Library of History* 1–19. On Thonis-Heracleion as an *emporion*, Goddio 2008, 46–48; 2011, 121–29; Fabre 2008, 219–20, 232–33; von Bomhard 2012, 98–102.
39 Fabre 2008, 219–34; Goddio 2011, 125; von Bomhard 2015, 106–7.
40 Fabre 2015, 175–78; Fabre and Belov 2012; Fabre and Goddio 2013.
41 Goddio 2011, 127–29.
42 Herodotus, *Histories* II.113–14.
43 Belov 2015, 195–210.
44 Goddio 2010, 11–12.
45 Meadows 2015; Grataloup 2015, summarized in Robinson and Goddio 2015, 3–4.
46 Goddio 2015, 48.
47 Stanley et al. 2007, 54–57.
48 Ibid., 46–51.
49 Ibid., 51–57.
50 Evidence summarized in Nur 2010, 134–35.
51 Herodotus, *Histories* II.179.
52 Goddio 2015, 45–46.
53 Grataloup 2010; 2015.
54 Goddio 2007, 116 fig. 3.90, 118–20.
55 Yoyotte and Clauss 2008, 140–42.

Chapter 2
Egypt and Greece: early encounters

1 Vasunia 2001; Moyer 2011.
2 *Odyssey* 4.229–31 (author's transl.).
3 *Iliad* 9.381–83 (transl. Murray and Wyatt, Loeb edn).
4 Panagiotopoulos 2005.
5 Kitchen 1995; Jansen-Winkeln 2015.
6 Winnicki 2009, 110–13.
7 Lloyd 1983; Tanner 2003; Vittmann 2003; Agut-Labordère 2013; Fantalkin 2014.
8 Solon fr. 28 (West).
9 Diodorus Siculus, *Library of History* 1.68.8.
10 Höckmann 2008–9, 76; von Bomhard 2015, 105–6, fig. 5.4.
11 von Bomhard 2015, 113; Grataloup 2015, 138–40; Villing 2015, 229–30. Other port towns on the western Delta shoreline also appear to have been frequented by Greek traders, such as Plinthine, where recent fieldwork has revealed late 7th century BC Greek pottery: Boussac et al. 2016.
12 Pennington and Thomas forthcoming.
13 According to the new reading by Jansen-Winkeln 2014, 135.
14 For a likely direct connection between Thonis-Heracleion without passing through Naukratis, see Höckmann 2008–9, 114.
15 von Bomhard 2015, 109.
16 See Chapter 1, fig. 14.
17 On the discovery of Thonis-Heracleion, see Goddio 2007, 69–130; 2011, 121; 2015, 45–49.
18 Goddio 2007, 102–17; 2011, 127–28 figs 7.5 and 7.6. Most of them are Egyptian boats, made for sailing on the Nile at low water; see Robinson in this catalogue, pp. 58–59.
19 For the most recent research on Naukratis, see Villing et al. 2013–15; on Naukratis as a trading port, see also Möller 2000; Agut-Labordère 2012.
20 Möller 2000, 195–96; Agut-Labordère 2012, 360.
21 Herodotus, *Histories* II.178–80.
22 On the Aramaic tax register found at Elephantine, also known as the Ahiqar scroll, see Briant and Descat 1998.
23 Johnston 2013–2015a; Villing 2013, 77–78; Grataloup 2010.
24 This is the case also at Naukratis, as we now know: Thomas and Villing forthcoming.
25 Meadows 2015.
26 Meadows 2015.
27 Briant and Descat 1998, 77–78; Le Rider 2001, 170–71.
28 Fabre 2008d, 224–25; Masson 2015, 80–84.
29 Van der Wilt 2010.
30 Lead objects are examined in van der Wilt 2014.
31 Natron is the only outgoing shipment that is taxed in the customs register of Elephantine: Villing 2015, 238. Naukratis was situated in an excellent position for the trade in natron, lying close to its source in the Wadi Natrun: Boardman 2013.
32 Bresson 2000; Villing 2013.
33 Masson 2015, 72 fig. 3.1, p. 84.
34 Heinz 2015, 57–62.
35 Both market weights and coin weights were discovered in Thonis-Heracleion: van der Wilt 2010; 2015. The weights from Naukratis are being studied by A. Masson-Berghoff.
36 Muhs 2015, 96.
37 On this type of flat-bottomed boat, see Robinson in this catalogue, pp. 58–59.
38 Herodotus, *Histories* II.179 (author's transl.).
39 Goddio 2007; 2008, 26–48, 'Rediscovered Sites', particularly 46–47; 2011, 129; Grataloup 2015, 140 (for Thonis-Heracleion); Villing et al. 2013–15 (for Naukratis). See also the comparative study of coins found at Naukratis and Thonis-Heracleion during the 5th and first half of the 4th centuries BC: Meadows 2015.
40 As can be deduced from the royal decree of Nectanebo I: von Bomhard 2015, 113.
41 Von Bomhard 2015, esp. 106; Villing 2015, 241.
42 On the Carians, see e.g. Rumscheid 2009.
43 As attested by Greek and Assyrian written sources: Herodotus, *Histories* II.152; Diodorus Siculus, *Library of History* I.66.8–12; Niemeier 2001, 19–20.
44 Many Greek and Carian mercenaries may in fact have been among the troops sent in the mid-650s by Lydian king Gyges to assist Psamtik against the Assyrians, though this is unlikely to have been the sole path of recruitment; cf. Fantalkin 2014.
45 Vittmann 2003, 203–6, fig. 103.
46 Haider 2001; Kaplan 2003; Vittmann 2003, esp. 197–203; Agut-Labordère 2012b; Fantalkin 2014.
47 Agut-Labordère 2013, 990–93; Lloyd 2014, 125–28.
48 Robinson and Goddio 2015, 6.
49 Attested by the finds of a large Ionian bronze shield and greaves: Niemeier 2001, 19–20.
50 According to the new reading by Jansen-Winkeln 2014.
51 Ebbinghaus 2006, 189–90; Agut-Labordère 2012c; Saint-Pierre Hoffmann 2012.
52 Herodotus, *Histories* II.178 (author's transl.).
53 Summaries in Möller 2000; Villing et al. 2013–15.
54 Thomas and Villing 2013 and forthcoming; Villing and Thomas 2013–15.
55 Herodotus, *Histories* II.135; Anakreon fr. 434.
56 Athenaeus, *Banquet of the Learned* 15.675f–76c, quoting Polycharmos.
57 Duplouy 2006.
58 Some of the Greek philosophers' visits to Egypt may have been a cultural *topos* more than a historical reality: Vasunia 2001.
59 Over 2000 inscriptions on pottery make this the largest body of such inscriptions ever found: Johnston 2013–15b. Far less Greek pottery is found at Thonis-Heracleion, where so far the Persian and Ptolemaic periods are better represented than the Saite period: Grataloup 2015.
60 Herodotus, *Histories* IV.152
61 Masson 2013–15a.
62 Thomas 2013–15.
63 Thomas and Villing forthcoming.
64 Yoyotte 1982–83; Guermeur 2005, 126–38; von Recklinghausen 2013–15.
65 British Museum 1886,1005.22.
66 Masson 2013–15b; von Recklinghausen 2013–15.
67 Thomas 2015, 261–62; Masson forthcoming.
68 Goddio 2015, 18–19. For the presence of this triad across Egypt: Guermeur 2005.
69 So far thirty-one animal cemeteries are known in Egypt: Bleiberg 2013, 64.
70 Nicholson 2005.
71 Goddio 2015, 26–28.
72 Yoyotte 2013, 550; Goddio 2015, 26.
73 Such sarcophagi could be used for a variety of animal mummies, see Kessler and Nur el Din 2005. Some bear an elaborate polychrome decoration: Bruno 2013, 130–31 fig. 111 (for a cat mummy).
74 The sarcophagi were looted in antiquity but animal bones found nearby, currently under study, might reveal more on the species ritually buried in them: Goddio 2015, 26–28. Ibises and hawks are often found together in animal necropoleis: Ikram 2012; Bleiberg 2013, 92.
75 Kessler and Nur el Din 2005, 126. In this period, ibises were usually transferred from all over Egypt to be buried in major centres, notably at Hermopolis Magna/Tuna el-Gebel in Middle Egypt, where a vast subterranean complex was used as catacombs for mummified ibises, baboons and other animals: Kessler and Nur el Din 2005, esp. 124–25. In the Ptolemaic period they were buried locally: ibid. 142.
76 Goddio 2015, 26. On Thoth as a god killing evil creatures, see Kessler and Nur el Din 2005, 136.
77 It yielded ceramics and other objects of the 26th dynasty: Goddio 2015, 45.
78 Kessler and Nur el Din 2005, 151.
79 Bleiberg 2013, 100–4.
80 Masson 2015. Votive boxes are attested in Thonis-Heracleion, though rarely: Fabre in Goddio and Fabre 2008, 323, no. 208.
81 See the cache of bronzes, p. 68.
82 Bleiberg 2013, 74–75.
83 Diodorus Siculus, *Library of History* I.86.
84 Pearce 2007, 241–308; cf. Vasunia 2001.
85 Anaxandrides, *Island-Towns* (a fourth-century BC Athenian comedy), quoted in Athenaeus, *Banquet of the Learned* VII.299f (author's transl.).
86 Herodotus, *Histories* II.65 (transl. Godley).
87 Bleiberg 2013, 64.
88 Such as an ibis mummy containing just a few bones and filled with feathers, or a hawk mummy containing a single wing: Bruno 2013, 123 figs 100–2 and 126 fig. 105.
89 Kessler and Nur el Din 2005, 156.
90 Bleiberg 2013, 99.
91 Bruno 2013, 137, no. 119.
92 A violent death (cranial fractures or strangulation) was identified in two-thirds of cases, and a young age of death for three-quarters of cat mummies: Zivie and Lichtenberg 2005, 117–18.
93 Kessler and Nur el Din 2005, 160.
94 See Chapter 3, pp. 121.
95 Kessler and Nur el Din 2005, 155–56.
96 Nicholson 2005, 49–50; Bleiberg 2013, 79–80.

97 Bleiberg 2013, 81–90 suggests that, once mummified, the animals were believed to become the souls (*ba*) of the gods who could intervene on behalf of the dedicant, conveying messages to the god with which the animal was linked. This seems supported by the discovery of 'letters to the gods', containing complaints, requests and/or vows, in animal sanctuaries and necropoleis.

98 See Chapter 4, p. 145.

99 From the 6th century BC onwards: Vittmann 2006, 582–83; Rutherford 2003.

100 Vittmann 2003, 245–46.

101 See for example the bronze depicting the Apis bull, p. 83, fig. 48.

102 Borgeaud and Volokhine 2000, 66–69.

103 Thomas 2013–15; see statuettes p. 211.

104 Vittmann 2003; 2006.

105 Cf. e.g. Haider 2004; Burkert 2004.

106 Cairo, Egyptian Museum JE 34002.

107 Detailed study on both stelae in von Bomhard 2012.

108 The text states more precisely the sea of the Hau-Nebut, a much-disputed term among specialists, but which in that context should be understood as the Mediterranean Sea: von Bomhard 2012, 75–76.

109 Possibly export taxes were also levied in Thonis-Heracleion, though the decree is unclear: von Bomhard 2015, 106.

110 As suggested by a statue of Nekhethorheb, 'governor of the gates of entry into Egypt' (official in charge of Mediterranean customs) appointed by the pharaoh Amasis (r. 570–526 BC): von Bomhard 2012, 74–75; 2015, 104–5. See also Agut-Labordère 2012.

111 Agut-Labordère 2009–10. See, however, how the Persian rulers took noticeable care of the temple of Neith in Sais: von Bomhard 2015, 102–3, esp. note 17.

112 Von Bomhard 2012, 78.

113 Translation after von Bomhard 2012, 54.

114 Weber 2012, 375 no. TD 300; Spencer in Leclère and Spencer 2014, 95, 113, pl. 44. On Klazomenian amphorae, see Bîrzescu 2012, 91–109.

115 Herodotus, *Histories* II.182; Athenaeus, *Banquet of the Learned* XIII.596c; Sappho, fr. 15 (West); Obbink 2014; Strabo, *Geography* 17.1.33.

116 Athenaeus, *Banquet of the Learned* 1.34b; Meeks 1993; Quaegebeur 1990; Poo 1995; Guasch-Jané 2008.

117 Herodotus, *Histories* III.6

118 Panthers are associated with the Dionysiac realm in Classical Greek art and may have been considered an appropriate decoration in connection with the Osirian cult at Thonis-Heracleion: Grataloup, in Goddio and Fabre 2008, 348 no. 298 and fig. 398 on p. 151; Goddio 2015, 33–34, fig. 1.29; Grataloup 2015, 140–43 fig. 7.4.6.

119 See van de Put 2006, 48–49, pl. 204.4–6.

120 Grataloup 2015; Villing 2013. Only Naukratis received a massive number and wider range of high-quality vessels.

121 Petrie 1886, 35–37, pl. 41.

122 Masson forthcoming; Villing 2013. Another faience product related to local cult made at Naukratis were New Year's flasks, see Masson 2013–15.

123 Hölbl 2000.

124 Athenaeus, *Banquet of the Learned* 12.553d–e.

125 Examples from Assyrian palaces such as the Palace of Nineveh in northern Iraq: Searight, Reade and Finkel 2008, 21–30.

126 *Alabastra* are known from Sudan, Egypt, the Levant, Mesopotamia, Eastern Greece, Italy, Spain, Carthage and Malta: Hölbl 1979, 240–53.

127 On this production: Masson 2013–15.

128 Another *alabastron* found in Egypt bears a comparable inscription: Verbanck-Piérard et al. 2008, 434–35 no. V.E.2.

129 Pliny, *Natural History* XIII.2.

130 Piabrm's stele and those of other foreigners are discussed by Vittmann 2003; 2005; 2006; Höckmann 2001; Kammerzell 2001.

131 Herodotus, *Histories* II.61.

132 See essay Chapter 3, pp. 80–83.

133 The inscription reads: píabrm | úśoλś múdonśχi | kbíomś | m[noś (?)]. It is in the Carian script, which is still only partly deciphered. See Adiego 2007; Vittmann 2005.

134 On Carian and Ionian mercenaries, see Vittmann 2006 and Haider 1996; on the Carians in general, see Rumscheid 2009.

135 Herodotus, *Histories* II.154.3.

136 Thompson 2012, 178–92.

137 Diodorus Siculus, *Library of History* 1.19.4.

138 Grataloup 2015.

139 Fabre 2011; 2015; Fabre and Belov 2011; Fabre and Goddio 2013.

140 Robinson, Fabre and Goddio forthcoming; Robinson 2015.

141 See Kapitän 1973; 1984; Haldane 1984.

142 Eiseman and Ridgeway 1987; Trethewey 2001.

143 Rosloff 1991.

144 Galili 1994, 25.

145 Fabre and Belov 2011; Robinson, Fabre and Goddio forthcoming.

146 Herodotus, *Histories* II.96; Fabre 2011; Belov 2015.

147 Belov 2015.

148 Robinson 2015.

149 See Cooper 2014 for the difficulties of navigating on the Nile during the Islamic period.

150 Janssen 2004; Gardiner 1941.

151 Herodotus, *Histories* II.179.

152 Athenaeus of Naucratis. The Deipnosophists, Vol. 7. Trans. Gluick, C.B. 1941. Loeb Classical Library, London.

153 The temple's architecture is discussed in detail by Koenigs 2007, 313–44. We would like to thank Prof. Koenigs for his help and constructive criticism regarding the reconstruction drawing presented here.

154 Herodotus, *Histories* II.178.

155 Cf. Möller 2000, 105–8; Villing and Thomas 2013–15; Thomas and Villing forthcoming.

156 Höckmann and Möller 2006; Malkin 2011, esp. 89–93; cf. also Bowden 1996 and Polinskaya 2010 for a more sceptical view.

157 For the whole group, see Thomas 2013–15; the piece discussed here was first published by C. Gutch in Hogarth et al. 1898–99, 79–80, pl. 11, no.18.

158 First published by Z. Kiss in Goddio and Fabre 2008, 256–57.

159 Hermary 2000, 134–40; Karageorghis 1988, 89–93.

160 See Meadows 2015 for a discussion of the 'Kition' coins discovered at Thonis-Heracleion.

161 The title 'prophet of the snake Shena in Naukratis' appears on the sarcophagus of an Egyptian priest, Panehemise, who lived in Naukratis during the Ptolemaic period: Leitz 2011.

162 Herodotus, *Histories* II.178–82.

163 Possibly a statue of the Egyptian goddess Neith, with whom Athena was equated. Neith was the patron goddess of Sais, the capital of Egypt during the 26th dynasty.

164 Herodotus, *Histories* III.47. The gift to Sparta, however, was intercepted by the Samians.

165 Herodotus, *Histories* II.159.

Chapter 3
Greek kings and Egyptian gods

1 Recent studies on Alexander the Great and his impact in Egypt are compiled in Grieb, Nawotka and Wojciechowska 2014.

2 The historicity of his crowning remains debated; see most recently A. Wojciechowska and K. Nawotka in Grieb, Nawotka and Wojciechowska 2014.

3 Pfeiffer 2011.

4 Arrian, *Anabasis* III.1 and 5. Arrian's account, written in the second century AD, is based on Ptolemy I's own *History of Alexander*.

5 Hölbl 2001, 98–99.

6 Jenkins, Farge and Turner 2015, 232.

7 Romm 2011.

8 Diodorus Siculus, *Library of History* XVIII.3.5 and 26–8; Pausanias, *Description of Egypt* 1.6.3.

9 Ptolemy IV Philopator constructed a collective burial monument with a pyramidal structure for Alexander and the Ptolemaic kings in the palace precinct in Alexandria: Hölbl 2001, 169–70.

10 Stanwick 2002.

11 Brophy 2014, 353.

12 Brophy 2014.

13 His eyebrows with two semicircles indicate a late date in the Ptolemaic period: Stanwick 2002, fig. 199.

14 Goddio and Fabre 2008, 292, no. 2.

15 Smith 1991, 207; Ashton 2001.

16 Parkinson 2005.

17 Hölbl 2001, 165.

18 Vassiliou 2009, 152 and 155.

19 Hölbl 2001, 85.

20 Forgeau 2008.

21 Carney 2013.

22 Guermeur 2005, 1, 3–4.

23 For the cult of Amun-Gereb at Thonis-Heracleion and its surroundings: Guermeur 2005, 143–48.

24 Goddio 2007, 74–75; 2015, 21–22.

25 Thiers 2008, 136; 2009, 20. On the discovery of the colossal stele and the list of surrounding artefacts: Goddio 2007, 118, 129 fig. 3.109; 2009, ix–xvii.

26 Kiss and Yoyotte 2008, 307.

27 Goddio 2008, 46–48; 2015, 48–49.

28 Herodotus, *Histories* II.113.

29 Goddio 2015, 23–28.

30 Plutarch, *Isis and Osiris* 361F–362A; Tacitus, *Histories* IV.82–83.

31 On the formation of Serapis' legend: Borgeaud and Volokhine 2000; Legras 2014.

32 Borgeaud and Volokhine 2000, 62–66.

33 Devauchelle 2010 and 2012.

34 Herodotus, *Histories* III.28: 'he is black, and has on his forehead a three-cornered white spot, and the likeness of an eagle on his back; the hairs of the tail are double, and there is a knot under the tongue'.

35 The succession of the Apis bulls is attested from the 18th dynasty pharaoh Amenhotep III (r. c. 1391–1353 BC) until the fourth century AD: Devauchelle 2010, 51.

36 Borgeaud and Volokhine 2000, 76.

37 Borgeaud and Volokhine 2000, 67–69.

38 Masson 1977, 61–63.

39 Arrian, *The Anabasis of Alexander*, III.1.

40 Herodotus, *Histories* III.27–28. The historicity of this blasphemous act is debated: Briant 2002, 57.

41 Legras 2014, 102.

42 Sources vary between Ptolemy I and III: Borgeaud and Volokhine 2000, 58–59. Serapis is definitely associated with miraculous healing under Ptolemy I: Borgeaud and Volokhine 2000, 50.

43 On the prominent place Serapis and Isis gained in the Roman empire, see studies published in Bricault et al. 2007. See also Chapter 5.

44 According to coins depicting the temple and architectural remains: McKenzie et al. 2004, 86; Sabottka 2008.

45 Yoyotte 2010, 34.

46 Ashton in Walker and Higgs 2001, 73–75.

47 Rowe 1946, 1–10 and 51–52; Weinstein 1973, 379–81, no. 162.

48 Earlier remains of a sacred space with an altar with the name of Ptolemy II and Arsinoe were discovered below Ptolemy III's Serapeum; it is unclear whether they pertained to an earlier Serapeum: Sabottka 2008, 50–66.

49 Ashton in Walker and Higgs 2001, 73.

50 Yoyotte 2010, 34. For cases where Serapis is rendered Osiris and not Osiris-Apis in Egyptian: Devauchelle 2012, 222 and 224. Festivities honouring Serapis and Osiris happened at the same period of the year, in the month of Khoiak (on these festivities, see Chapter 4).

51 Devauchelle 2010.

52 Goddio 2007, 50–57. See p. 130 in this volume.

53 Strabo, *Geography* XVII.1.17: The 'temple of Serapis […] is honoured with great reverence and effects such cures that even the most reputable men believe in it and sleep in it – themselves even on their own behalf or others for them'. Trans. Jones, H. L. 1932. Loeb Classical Library, London.

54 This plaque was discovered in 1818 during the renovation of an ancient canal at Canopus: Bernand 1970, 236–37 and 306–10. See Bricault 2006, 31–33 regarding a silver foundation plaque also written solely in Greek and the dedication of a temple to Serapis by Ptolemy III and Arsinoe, concluding on a possible shrine of Serapis erected within the sacred enclosure of Osiris.

55 On the possible variety of temples and chapels dedicated to Isis in Canopus: Bernand 1970, 309.

56 Borgeaud and Volokhine 2000, 59.

57 Borgeaud and Volokhine 2000, 46–49; Legras 2014, 106–9.

58 As related in Arrian III.3. See chapter 3 in that volume, p. 73.

59 Fulińska 2014.

60 Kroll 2007, 115.

61 Previously published by Fabre in Goddio and Fabre 2008, 241–43; also see pp. 123–25 in the present volume.

62 Illustrated in a letter dated to 258 BC (Papyrus Cairo Zen. I 59021) translated in Meijer and Van Nijf 2015, 65.

63 Kroll 2007, 114.

64 Stanwick 2002, e.g. 166, fig. 36 or 173, fig. 62.

65 On Arsinoe see Carney 2013.

66 Forgeau 2008.

67 Other queens after her gained a divine status, such as Berenike II, wife of Ptolemy III Euergetes, who was also associated with Aphrodite and Isis in the Fayum, though she was far less popular: Hölbl 2001, 105–11, esp. 105.

68 Pliny, Natural History 34.148.

69 Poseidippos 39 A–B, translated in Bing 2002/3, 255.

70 Bing 2002/3, 245.

71 On this statue and the attribution to Arsinoe see Yoyotte in Goddio and Fabre 2008, 124–29.

72 On the association of Arsinoe with Aphrodite and Isis as a patron of the naval empire of the Ptolemies and protectress of sailors and all maritime activities, see Bricault 2006, 22–36.

73 Ptolemaic queens' statues often display such shawls with the so-called 'Isis-knot': Ashton 2001, 45–53.

74 Yoyotte in Goddio and Fabre 2008, 126.

75 Albersmeier 2010, 195.

76 See Thiers 2008 and particularly 2009 for a full discussion of the stele.

77 Thiers 2009, 20, 46–48; Goddio 2015, 19.

78 Goddio 2015, 46–47.

79 Yoyotte 2008e, 309.

80 See Goddio 2015, 22; Fabre 2014, http://www. ieasm.org/downloads/IEASM_religion_Belier_ Amon_df.pdf.

81 See Meadows 2008 on the coin weight SCA 1101.

82 Goddio 2007, 88, 93, 118; Kiss 2008d, 306 (cat. no. 101).

83 Kiss and Yoyotte 2008, 307.

84 The name of the father is intact but seems to be unique with an unclear meaning (Kiss and Yoyotte 2008, 307).

85 Derriks 2001, 6–9, 10–14.

86 Robinson 2008, 171–72, fig. 66; Goddio 2015, 28–34, fig. 1.22.

87 See Moussa and Altermüller 1977, pl. 63 for a depiction of the production of a basin.

88 Goddio 2007, 111; Fabre 2008b, 158; Goddio and Fabre 2008, 171, 326; Robinson 2008, 146, fig. 59.

89 Athenaeus, Banquet of the Learned, 11.477, 478a.

90 Regional variations: Pfrommer 1987, esp. pl. 62.

91 See Fabre 2008, 325–27 and especially Robinson 2008, 95–123 for a discussion and catalogue.

92 Regarding the ancient temple see Goddio 2015, 45.

93 Berlandini-Keller, 2015, 86-87 and forthcoming.

94 See Goddio 2007, 99–100; Goddio 2015, 23–24; Fabre 2008b, 138–39; von Bomhard 2014, 339–55 for more information on the foundation deposit from Thonis-Heracleion, and Andrews 1994, 15 for more detail about amulets inside shrines (naoi); Aufrère 2013b, 15-18, 21–22 for the mastery of the waters; Bianchi 2014, 200–1; Weinstein 1973, 434 for the extreme rarity of divine figures in foundation deposits.

95 Goddio and Fabre 2008, 78 (crown), 76 (naos); Goddio and Fabre 2015, 93; Goddio 2015, 23–25 figs 1.12, 1.13. Heinz 2013, 164.

96 Kiss 2008, 322.

97 For drawn examples of hanging cobras and side-lock: Abubakr 1937, 63–65; on true bronzes: e.g. Bianchi 2014, 200–1.

98 Yoyotte and Chuvin 1988, 171–72.

99 For representations of Herakles-Harpokrates as child-gods bearing the hem-hem crown on the nemes and holding the mace (the emblematic attribute of Herakles) ibid. 176, and note 49.

100 Yoyotte and Lichocka 2008, 351; See Yon 1992, 145–60 for parallels.

101 Meadows 2012, 194–97 and 190 Table 1.

102 Markou 2011, 223–24, cf. 303.

103 Vernier 1927, 163, pl. 33 nos 52492, 52495 ; Bulsink 2015, 70-1 : a similar earring is dated to the 18th and 19th dynasties.

104 Stolz 2008a–b; Williams and Ogden 1994, 198, no. 132, 232 no. 165; Bulsink 2015, 73–74; Goddio and Fabre 2015, 81.

105 Stolz 2008d.

106 Stolz 2008c; Boardman 2001, 300 no. 754.

107 Herodotus, Histories III.28.

108 Pliny, Natural History VIII.186.

109 Translation after Weinstein 1973, 370.

110 On the reconstruction of this complex ritual, see notably Weinstein 1973, 1–22.

111 Scenes depicted in the Temples of Edfu and Dendera: Montet 1964.

112 Foundation deposits dated to Ptolemy IV and discovered in Tanis in the Eastern Delta yielded faience plaques solely written in hieroglyphs: Weinstein 1973, 386–89, no. 168.

113 See the gold foundation plaque of Ptolemy III Euergetes (246–222 BC) discovered in Thonis-Heracleion, mentioning a gymnasium dedicated to Herakles: Goddio and Fabre 2008, 140–43.

114 Similar bilingual plaques are known, notably for the temple and sacred enclosure dedicated to Serapis in the names of Ptolemy III and Berenike II: Rowe 1946, 1–10 and 51–52; Weinstein 1973, 379–81, no. 162.

115 On the sacredness of the number nine for the Egyptians and the presence of nine plaques in a variety of foundation deposits of the Late and Ptolemaic periods: Weinstein 1973, 369.

116 Strabo, Geography 17.1,7.

117 Goddio 2007, 50–57, 53; Kiss 2008b, 174–76.

118 Plutarch, Isis and Osiris 32, translated by F. C. Babbitt.

119 This temple is known from a dedication by Kallikrates of Samos (c. 285–246 BC), a fleet commander of Ptolemy II: Bernand 1970, 232, no. 2.

Chapter 4
From myth to festivals

1 The scene is witnessed centuries earlier in the Pyramid Texts which are inscribed inside the pyramids of the 5th and 6th dynasties. It appears first in that of Unas (2375–2345 BC), comparing the dead kings to Osiris. The passage reads: 'Your sister Isis comes to you rejoicing for love of you. You have placed her on your phallus and your seed issues into her ...'.

2 Lavier 1989, 289–95; 1998, 27–33.

3 Chassinat 1968, 809–23; Cauville 1997b1, 14–28. The decoration of the temple dates from the time of the famous Cleopatra VII, but the origin of the texts is much older.

4 Simpula and Mysteries at Thonis-Heracleion: Goddio 2015, 29–32; Goddio and Fabre 2015, 38–39.

5 Cauville 1997b 1, 26.

6 Chassinat 1966, 24.

7 Quack 2000–1.

8 Coulon 2010, 16; Quack 2006.

9 Thiers 2009, 79–80; Goddio 2015, 35.

10 Goddio 2010, 11–12.

11 Fabre 2008b, 145–46; the C14 dating of the sacred barque indicates a date of the fifth to the beginning of the fourth century BC.

12 Goddio and Fabre 2015, 112–13.

13 Goddio 2015, 33–34.

14 Herodotus, Histories II.144.

15 Burkert 2004, 71–98; Coulon 2013, 177–81; Martín-Hernández 2013.

16 Plutarch, Isis and Osiris 35.

17 Coulon 2013, 181.

18 On religious cultural 'translation', see Assmann 2008.

19 The cult of Dionysos was probably introduced to Cyprus in the Hellenistic period by the Ptolemies who had dominion over the island: Karageorghis 1984.

20 Frontisi-Ducroux 1991.

21 Yoyotte 2010, 38.

22 Strabo, Geography XVII.1, 17, trans. Villing, A.

23 Herodotus, Histories II.48; Plutarch, Isis and Osiris 36; Coulon 2013, 182–84. On early Athenian Dionysian festivals featuring a large phallus see Parker 2005, 318–26.

24 Rice 1983; Thompson 2000.

25 Thomas 2013–15a. A wooden phallus was also recently excavated on the banks of the Canopic branch at Naukratis, possibly having been thrown into the Nile (Thomas and Villing forthcoming).

26 Coulon 2013, 183. See also Chapter 3, p. 85

27 Daressy 1905–6, 66–67, pl. 12; El-Damaty 2002, 169 no. 178.

28 De Meulenaere and Bothmer 1969, 14–16 fig. 12.

29 Complete translation in von Bomhard 2015, 60; for 'Lord of Life' see Cauville 1983, 183–84.

30 Daressy 1905–6, 221 pl. XLIV; 96–97, pl. XIX; Saleh and Sourouzian 1987, nos 250, 252; El-Damaty 2002b, 170, no 79; mer khetem: Yoyotte 1972, 220.

31 Perdu 2013, 93–133: 'Isis of Ptahirdis', in the time of Apries (589–570 BC), compared with this 'Isis of Psamtik' ibid. 118–19; the link with Isis the magician and Ro-nefer, ibid. 112–14; Berlandini 2015, 184.

32 Egyptian Museum, Cairo CG 784.

33 Mariette 1880, 15, no. 79; Daressy 1905–6, 218, pl. 44, no. 38 867; De Meulenaere 2004, 83–84.

34 Labrique 2007, 1061–1070.

35 Cauville 1997a, vol.1, 199–200, 211–12, 218–19, vol. 2 pls 96, 101, 103; 1997b, vol. 2, 96–98; parallel MMA NI 2009.86.

36 Favard-Meeks and Meeks 2010, 39–48.

37 Berlandini 2015, 150–51; and forthcoming.

38 Forgeau 2010, 45–80, pl. 20 (top); act of Isis 'taking man', Desroches-Noblecourt 1953, 19, 41–42 and n. 2; Berlandini-Keller 2015, 48–50.

39 Stele Louvre C 286 (Imenmès). Moret 1931, 743–44, §16; Barucq and Daumas 1980, 91–97.

40 Amelineau 1899, 109–15, pls 3–4; Leahy 1977, 424–34, pls 26–29; U. Effland 2008, 9, fig. 6; 2013, 322, 327–28, fig. 4; A. Effland 2013, 77–79, fig. 7.

41 On the Peret-Wepwawet during the Mysteries, Lavier 1989, 290–92; 1998, 28.

42 O'Connor 2011, 36, fig. 9 (Abydos). Cauville 1997b, Vol. 2, 119–21, fig. 6, 253–54 (Dendera; east high chapel 3).

43 Favard-Meeks 2009, 139–42; Favard-Meeks and Meeks 2010, 42–48 (Andjety's crown-tcheni; Per-qa).

44 Josephson 1992, 93–95, pl. 16–19; Myśliwiec 1988, 45–46, part. 48 (D), pls 58–59.

45 For an awakening Osiris with sphinx-like outstretched hands see Spencer 2006, 10, 80 fig. 8a, pl. 15 (BM EA 1078).

46 Vassilieva 2010, 68–96.

47 Assmann 1977, 91–92, pl. A c, pl. 41; Cauville 1997b, vol. 2, 130, fig. 8; Berlandini-Keller 2002, 23–26, 32–33, fig. 5; 2015, 135–37; Koemoth 2009, 33–36, fig. 2, 42–43.

48 Daressy 1903, 3–11, pls 2–3; Lacau 1922, 195–96, figs 4–6, 200–2, pl. 16, 1–2; Sternberg-El-Hotabi 1999, 108–10, 117, 221 fig. 2, 266, fig. 64; II, 36; Berlandini-Keller 2015, 42–43, 170–71.

49 Ranke 1935, 130, no. 17; Magnanini 1973, 63–64, no. 2; Zivie-Coche 2003, 136–38 (Astarte cult).

50 Gasse 2004, 24–26, 171–73.

51 Most recently Rouffet 2012, 675–89.

52 In front of a snake–legged 'Hathor-Isis'(?), Cauville 1997a, Vol. 1, 218, Vol. 2, 187, pls 185, 215; Cauville 1997b, Vol. 2, 157, 169–70.

53 The object probably comes from Buto; however, similar bronzes were found elsewhere in the western Delta, e.g. the one found by Petrie in Naukratis: Masson 2015, 75, fig. 3.5a.

54 Aubert and Aubert 2001, 234–35.

55 First published by Stolz 2008e, 316.

56 Aufrère 2015a, 45.

57 Müller-Winckler 1985, 824–26.

58 The archaeological context of the discovery of this item in Thonis-Heracleion allows it to be dated to the 5th century BC, in addition to its parallel with an example from Bologna MCA-EGI-Pal_0401 that originates in the region of Alexandria. Similar objects of unknown origin (without an archaeological context) are dated to the Ptolemaic period by Bulsink (2015, 142–43, nos 71, 72), after Vernier 1927, 393.

59 Coulon et al. 1995, pl. 12.

60 Barguet 1962, 33; Leclère and Coulon 1998, 652–55; Aufrère 2005, 307–12; 2015b, 154.

61 Barguet 1962, 34; Aufrère 1999 and 2013 and Leitz 2014 on sacred vegetation.

62 Chassinat 1966, 53–57; Cauville 1997b, vol. 1, 14–17.

63 'Bekh' refers to a raised part of the ancient burial ground of Mer-nefer, now Tihna el-Gebel/Akoris, where almost a hundred small, falcon-headed coffins were discovered at the beginning of the twentieth century.

64 The name of Ro-Setaou is attributed to numerous necropoleis throughout Egypt, in reference to the famous one in the Memphite region.

65 Raven 1982, 22 no. 7; Coulon et al. 1995, 205–52; Centrone 2009, 9 pls 1a–b, 199–215.

66 Inventory and interpretation of Osiris bricks in Tooley 1996.

67 The name of the goddess Shentayt means 'the Widow': Cauville 1981, 21–22.

68 Chassinat 1966, 53–54; Cauville 1997b, vol. 1, 15–16.

69 Yoyotte 2008f, 313.

70 Yoyotte 2013, 385–92, 397–400, 403–6.

71 Goddio 2007, 92–93 figs 3.40–3.41; 2015, 22; Kiss 2008i, 313–14.

72 A situla bearing the prenomen of Amenhemat I (1991–1962 BC).

73 Examples of other situlae from Thonis-Heracleion: Robinson 2008, 139–46.

74 Cauville 1997b, Vol. 1, 16. For examples of variously shaped situlae used during the Mysteries:
Chassinat 1966, inside cover; Goddio 2015, 31 fig. 1.24; Goddio and Fabre 2015, 132–35.

75 Chassinat 1966, 57–58, 271–72; Aufrère 2007, 174–80.

76 Derchain 1965, 137–38.

77 Aufrère 1991, 337–40.

78 Chassinat 1966, 75–90; Vandier 1961, 136–38, 253.

79 Translation and comment on the text of Edfu: Aufrère 1991, 337–40; 2005, 242–43; Aufrère 1998, 29–64.

80 Goddio 2015, 29–33; Goddio and Fabre 2015, 38–39.

81 Chassinat 1966, 59–60; 1968, 775; Cauville 1997b, Vol. 1, 20.

82 Robinson 2008, 60–1, 71; Hayes 1984, 61 no. 9; Benazet 1992, 71.

83 Mariette 1973, pl. 38, col. 118; Chassinat 1966, pl. 7, col. 118.

84 Kiss 2008l, 333; Ragheb 2008, 335.

85 Fabre and Kiss 2008, 332.

86 Grenier 2002, 254 no. 540, pl. 76.

87 HXX–8885; cf. Robinson 2008, 200–2, nos 158 and 159, and 200 fig. 75 for a distribution map.

88 Goddio 2015, 35–36.

89 Chassinat 1966, 64, 71; Chassinat 1968, 614–15; Cauville 1997b Vol. 1, 16, 22.

90 Fabre 2008c, 145–47; Heinz 2013, Vol. II, 185–89, Cat. Map 30.

91 Goddio 2015, 36.

92 Goddio and Fabre 2015, 114. Another similar bird's head (SCA 1561) broken at the neck, found in the southern canal, was perhaps also a figurehead.

93 Vandier d'Abbadie 1973, 36–43; Jequier 1921, 330–1, 343; van de Walle 1984, 756; Germond 2002–3, 84–85.

94 For the yearly journey of the sun from north to south see von Bomhard 2012, 119; 2014a, 116.

95 Abitz 1979, 92–108; Graindorge 1996, 94.

96 Herodotus, Histories II.62. Translation by G. C. Macaulay.

97 Baines 1985, 41–43.

98 Lavier 1989, 290–93.

99 Lavier 1998, 27, 29, 31.

100 Goddio 2010, 11–12.

101 See Goddio 2015, 39 for the comparison between Abydos and Thonis-Heracleion regarding the navigation at the end of the Mysteries celebrations.

102 Barguet 1962, 18.

103 E.g. Lacau and Lauer 1959, 2 no. 12 (alabaster 76 cm), no. 15 (schist 43 cm); 4 no. 26 (limestone 31 cm).

104 Plutarch, Isis and Osiris 63. Translation by Babbitt, F. C., 1936, Loeb Classical Library, London.

105 Fabre 2008, 67, 148, 283; Goddio 2015, 28–39; Goddio and Fabre 2015.

106 Heinz 2013, vol. I 37–42, vol. II 30–43.

107 Goddio 2015, 45–48; Heinz 2013, vol. I 38–42.

108 Goddio 2015, 28–36.

109 Ibid., 37, fig. 1.33.

110 Previously published by Fabre in Goddio and Fabre 2008, no. 211.

111 Davies 2007.

112 Wuttmann, Coulon and Gombert 2008.

113 Goddio and Fabre 2008, 74; Fabre 2008d, 318–319; Heinz 2013, 44–50.

114 Goddio 2015, 39–40; von Bomhard 2014, 343–344.

115 Goddio and Fabre 2008, 75–76; Fabre 2008, 318, 339; Heinz 2013, Vol. I 28–37, Vol. II, 7–22. To date, out of 40 Harpokrates figures, 28 are of the Egyptian type, and 12 of the Greek one.

116 Yoyotte and Chuvin 1988, 176.

117 Malaise 1994, 227–32.

118 von Bomhard 2014.

119 See Heinz 2013, Vol. II, 7 map 3 and 23 map 4.

120 Goddio 2015, 45–46.

121 Goddio 2007, 111; 2015, 33 and note 153.

122 Goddio and Fabre 2008, 193, 341.

123 Quack 2000–1, 12.

124 See Libonati 2008, 164 and 297 for an offering table (SCA 1163) from Canopus, of the same size, engraved with lotus flowers.

125 E.g. BM 1688: Baines 1985, 62 fig. 40.

126 Heinz 2013, Vol. I 28–42, Vol. II 7–43.

127 Goddio and Fabre 2015, 160–61 for images of the offering table and the amulet.

128 Goddio 2015, 37, fig. 1.33.

129 Miniature offering trays studied in detail by Teeter 1994.

130 Goddio and Fabre 2015, 100; the offering table on p. 202 was found alongside this model. Goddio 2015, 37, fig. 1.33 shows the location of this possible temple or shrine – the southern one.

131 For a recent discussion on these objects: Masson 2013–15, 13–14.

132 Hesiod, Theogony 337ff.

133 Goyon 2013.

134 This group is discussed in detail in Thomas 2013–15, 15, 18–20, 34–37, 43, 53–57.

135 Herodotus, Histories II.60,1–2.

136 See note 134 above.

137 Published and discussed in Petrie 1888, 56, 62 pl. 25. 3; Weber 2012, 236–40, 279–80, 360–61 no. TD 238, pl. 49a–b; Villing 2014.

138 Long believed to have been a military fort occupied by Greek mercenaries, Tell Dafana has now conclusively been identified as an Egyptian temple town: Leclère and Spencer 2014.

139 Memphis: Thompson 2012, 185–87. Thompson, D. J., 2012, Memphis under the Ptolemies, 2nd edn, Princeton; Sais: Herodotus, Histories II.171; Khoiak festival: Moyer 2011, 178–79; for the drama, see Fairman 1974.

140 Herodotus, Histories II.144.

141 Emphasized by the dangerous snakes he holds, an image borrowed from Egyptian depictions of Horus-the-child (see Chapter 4, pp. 158–59).

142 See Cox 2008, 328.

143 Such as one from the Theban hoard: Hayes 1984, 56–57, nos 80–81.

144 Jenkins 1994.

145 Perdrizet and Floriani Squarciapino quoted in Jenkins 1994, 282.

146 Jenkins 1994, 279–82.

147 Cox 2008, 328; Robinson 2010, 226–27, fig. 19.7.

148 Plutarch, Isis and Osiris, 55.

Chapter 5
Egypt and Rome

1 Bagnall and Rathbone 2004, 15–16; Meadows 2001, 22–31.

2 Where Antony requested to be buried in Alexandria with Cleopatra, where Caesarion's parentage was declared authentic (threatening the position of Octavian who was only adopted by Caesar) and vast bequests to Antony's children by Cleopatra were promised. See Williams 2001, 192–93.

3 See Walker & Higgs 2001, 336–37.

4 While Alexander Helios, Cleopatra Selene II and Ptolemy Philadelphos were spared by Octavian, only Cleopatra Selene lived until

6 BC; the brothers probably died around 29 BC or shortly after.

5 Bagnall 1993, 262, 315.

6 Klotz 2012, 2.

7 Naerebout 2007, 545–47.

8 McKenzie 2007 177–78.

9 Discovered by the IEASM in collaboration with the Supreme Council of Antiquities. Goddio and Fabre 2008, 38; Goddio and Fabre 2015, 218–21.

10 On the influence of Greek philosophy and the concept of heis theos, or 'one god' henotheism, see O'Connell 2015, p. 44. See Chapter 3 in this volume on the significance of the cult.

11 Apuleius, Metamorphoses or Golden Ass. 11.5.

12 Versluys 2007, 8.

13 Decrees in 58 BC, 53 BC, 48 BC, 28 BC and AD 19 prohibited Egyptian cults from the whole or part of Rome, and ordered the destruction of Egyptian temples and the deportation of their followers (Alfano 2001, 283–86).

14 Versluys 2007, 8.

15 Minucius Felix 23,1. Trans. G. H. Rendall, 1998. Minucius Felix Octavius. The Loeb Classical Library, Bury St Edmonds; Cumont 1911, 84, fn 30.

16 Naerebout 2007, 507; p. 238 GRM 25788, 25789

17 Cassius Dio 69.11.2

18 ILS 7212. Beard et al. 1998, vol. I, 272.

19 Lambert 1984, 188.

20 Cf. Apuleius, Metamorphoses XI.5–6, 23–25.

21 Beard et al. 1998, 287–90.

22 Vout 2005, 83.

23 Origen Contra Celsus III, 36.

24 Cassius Dio 69.11.3; Historia Augusta V. Hadrian 14,5; Grenier 2008, 49–50; Lambert 1984, 128–42.

25 Herodotus, Histories II.90.

26 Lambert 1984, 145 from the text on the western face of Antinous' obelisk.

27 Another city beneath the waters of Abukir bay close to Canopus and Thonis-Heracleion. To date it has not been conclusively located.

28 Montserrat 1998, 257–279.

29 Goddio 2007, 68 and 127; Stanley 2007.

30 Goddio 2007, 50–53; Kiss 1998, 178–81; 2008, 62–63.

31 Libonati 2010a, 204–6, figs 17.1 and 17.2; Libonati 2010b, 73–77.

32 Apuleius, Metamorphosis 11.11; Plutarch, Isis and Osiris 36; Clement of Alexandria, Stromates 6.4.

33 Goddio and Darwish 1998; Kiss 1998, 169, 173-174; 2008, 356-357.

34 The identification of the image as an eagle holding a crown in its beak is thanks to J. Berlandini-Keller, C. Bresson and C. Thiaudière. Personal communication.

35 A statue of Hermanubis was found within a sanctuary dedicated to Serapis and Isis at Ras el-Soda (Adriani 1940, 136–38); see also p. 236.

36 A calcite Isis bust in this style was found at the Roman town of Sentinum, Sasoferrato, Italy (Tiradritti 1997, 489, pl. V.148).

37 Isidoros is often interpreted as a charioteer, although he could have sustained his injuries during a cart crash (Naerebout 2007) on the road.

38 Bernand 1970, 428-30, no.109, pl. 78. See translation in Naerebout 2007, 507, fn 4.

39 British Museum EA 983. Gallery 1 (see also Tiradritti 1997, 224, pl. IV.205).

40 Dow and Upson 1944; Hill 1946, 60–72; Guarducci 1974, 73–74; Petridou 2009, 81–93.

41 Goodburn et al. 1976, 378–79.

42 Cf. Lahusen and Formigli 2001, 209-10.

43 Cf. Bulow-Jacobsen 1996 for a brief overview.

44 Dio Cassius 16.11.2; Historia Augusta XIV.6.

45 This has also led to the statue being identified as a Ptolemy in pharaonic dress, see Savvopoulos et al. 2013, 28, fig. 22.

46 Grenier 2008, 62, fn 17.

Bibliography and references

Bibliographical abbreviations:

ASAE   *Annales du Service des antiquités de l'Égypte*
BdE   *Bibliothèque d'Étude*
BCH   *Bulletin de correspondance hellénique*
CdE   *Chronique d'Égypte*
CEFR   Common European Framework of Reference
CENIM   Les Cahiers Égypte Nilotique et Méditérranéenne
CRIPEL   Cahier de recherches de l'Institut de Papyrologie et Égyptologie de Lille
ENiM   *Égypte Nilotique et Méditerranéenne*
EPRO   *Études préliminaires aux religions orientales dans l'empire romain*
IJNA   *International Journal of Nautical Archaeology*
ILS   H Dessau, *Inscriptiones Latinae Selectae* (1892–1916)
JEA   *Journal of Egyptian Archaeology*
JNES   *Journal of Near Eastern Studies*
JRS   *Journal of Roman Studies*
OLA   Orientalia Lovaniensia Analecta
RdE   *Revue d'Égyptologie*
RDAC   *Report of the Department of Antiquities Cyprus*
SDAIK   Sonderschrift des Deutschen Archäologischen Instituts Abteilung Kairo
ZÄS   *Zeitschrift für Ägyptische Sprache und Altertumskunde*
ZPE   *Zeitschrift für Papyrologie und Epigraphik*

Chapter 1
Rediscovering Thonis-Heracleion and Canopus

Baines, J. (2008) 'Colossal and fertile Hapy, the Inundation of the Nile', in Goddio and Fabre 2008, 100–5

Belov, A. (2015) 'Archaeological evidence for the Egyptian *baris* (Herodotus, *Historiae* 2.96), in D. Robinson and F. Goddio (eds), *Heracleion in Context: The Maritime Economy of the Egyptian Late Period*, Oxford, 195–210

Blouin, K. (2014) *Triangular Landscapes – Environment, Society and the State in the Nile Delta under Roman Rule*, Oxford

von Bomhard, A. S. (2008) *The Naos of the Decades*, Underwater Archaeology in the Canopic Region in Egypt, Oxford Centre for Maritime Archaeology Monograph 3, Oxford

von Bomhard, A. S. (2011) 'Le Naos des Décades, puzzle archéologique et thématique', *ENM* 4, 107–36

von Bomhard, A. S. (2012) *The Decree of Sais*, Underwater Archaeology in the Canopic Region in Egypt, Oxford Centre for Maritime Archaeology Monograph 7, Oxford

von Bomhard, A. S. (2012–14) 'The Naos of the Decades and the Astral Aspects of Divine Judgement', in A.-A. Maravelia (ed.), *Ancient Egyptian Science and Meta-Physics: Quintessence of Religious Allegories, Roots of Scientific Thought. Proceedings of the 1st Egyptological Conference of the Patriarchate of Alexandria, 6 May 2011*, Athens, 180–87

von Bomhard, A. S. (2015) 'The stela of Thonis-Heracleion. Economic, topographic and epigraphic aspects', in D. Robinson and F. Goddio (eds), *Heracleion in Context: The Maritime Economy of the Egyptian Late Period*, Oxford Centre for Maritime Archaeology Monograph 8, Oxford, 101–20

Breccia, E. (1914) *Alexandrea ad Aegyptum: Guide de la Ville Ancienne et Moderne et du Musée Gréco-Romain*, Bergamo

Breccia, E. (1926) *Monuments de l'Égypt gréco-romaine*, I, Bergamo

Cooper, J. P. (2014) *The Medieval Nile – Route, Navigation and Landscape in Islamic Egypt*, Cairo

Daressy, G. (1929) 'Ménélaïs et l'embouchure de la branche Canopique', *Revue de l'Égypte ancienne* 2, 20–51 and pls 1, 2

Fabre, D. (2008a) 'Heracleion-Thonis: Customs station and emporium', in Goddio and Fabre 2008, 219–34

Fabre, D. (2015) 'The ships of Thonis-Heracleion in context' in D. Robinson and F. Goddio (eds), *Heracleion in Context. Oxford Centre for Maritime Archaeology Monograph 8*, Oxford, 175–94

Fabre, D. and Belov, A. (2012) 'The shipwrecks of Heracleion-Thonis (Egypt). An overview' in G. A. Belova (ed.), *Achievements and Problems of Modern Egyptology*, Moscow, 108–20

Fabre, D. and Goddio, F. (2013) 'Thonis-Heracleion, emporion of Egypt. Recent discoveries and research perspectives: The shipwrecks', *Journal of Ancient Egyptian Interconnections* 5 (1), 68–75

Faivre, P. J. (1918) *Canope, Ménoutis, Aboukir, Alexandria*

al-Falaki, M. H. (1872) *Mémoire sur l'antique Alexandrie : Ses faubourgs et environs découverts, par les fouilles, sondages, nivellements et autres recherches.* Copenhagen

Goddio, F. (1995) 'Cartographie des vestiges archéologiques submergés dans le Port Est d'Alexandrie et dans la Rade d'Aboukir', in N. Bonacasa, C. Naro, E. C. Portale and A. Tullio (eds), *Alessandria e il mondo ellenistico-romano, Atti del II Congresso Internazionale Italo-Egiziano*, "L'Erma" di Bretschneider, Rome, 172–77

Goddio, F. (2007) *The Topography and Excavation of Heracleion-Thonis and East Canopus (1996–2006)*, Underwater Archaeology in the Canopic Region in Egypt, Oxford Centre for Maritime Archaeology 1, Oxford

Goddio, F. (2008) 'Rediscovered sites' in Goddio and Fabre 2008, 26–48

Goddio, F. (2009) 'Introduction' in C. Thiers, *La stèle de Ptolémée VIII Évergète II à Héracléion*, Oxford, ix–xvii

Goddio, F. (2010) 'Geophysical survey in the submerged Canopic region', in Robinson and Wilson 2010, 3–13

Goddio, F. (2011) 'Thonis-Heracleion and Alexandria, two ancient emporia of Egypt', in D. Robinson and A. Wilson (eds), *Maritime Archaeology and Ancient Trade in the Mediterranean*, Oxford, 121–37

Goddio, F. (2012–14) 'The Naos of the Decades reconstituted', in A.-A. Maravelia (ed.), *Ancient Egyptian Science and Meta-Physics: Quintessence of Religious Allegories, Roots of Scientific Thought. Proceedings of the 1st Egyptological Conference of the Patriarchate of Alexandria: 6 May 2011*, Athens, 180–87

Goddio, F. (2015) 'The sacred topography of Thonis-Heracleion', in D. Robinson and F. Goddio (eds), *Heracleion in Context: The Maritime Economy of the Egyptian Late Period*, Oxford, 15–54

Goddio, F., Bernand, A., Bernand, É., Darwish, I., Kiss, Z. and Yoyotte, J. (eds) (1998) *Alexandria, The Sunken Royal Quarters*, London

Goddio, F. and Fabre, D. (eds) (2008) *Egypt's Sunken Treasures*, Munich

Grataloup, C. (2010) 'Occupation and trade at Heracleion-Thonis. The evidence from the pottery', in Robinson and Wilson 2010, 151–54

Grataloup, C. (2015) 'Thonis-Heracleion pottery of the Late Period: Traditions and influences', in D. Robinson and F. Goddio (eds), *Thonis-Heracleion in Context*, Oxford Centre for Maritime Archaeology 8, 137–60

Guermeur, I. (2005) *Les cultes d'Amon hors-de-Thèbes*, Turnhout

Habachi, L. and Habachi, B. (1952) 'The naos of the decades (Louvre D 37) and the discovery of another fragment', *JNES* 11, 251–63

Herodotus, *The Persian Wars II*.113–14, Loeb's Classical Library

Kiss, Z. (2008a) 'A jar bringing hope for eternal life, The Osiris-Canopus' in Goddio and Fabre 2008, 62–65

Kiss, Z. (2008b) 'A guarantor for fertility, Serapis and Calathos', in Goddio and Fabre 2008, Munich, 174–76

Kiss, Z. (2010) 'Le dieu Nil Hellénistique – A propos d'une sculpture de Canope' in Robinson and Wilson 2010, 211–18

Klotz, D. and Leblanc, M. (2012) 'An Egyptian priest of the Ptolemaic court: Yale Peabody Museum 264191', in C. Zivie-Coche and I. Guermeur (eds), '*Parcourir l'éternité*', Hommage à Jean Yoyotte 2, Bibliothèque de l'École des Hautes Études, Sciences religieuses 156, Turnhout, 645–98

Leitz, C. (1995) *Altägyptische Sternuhren*, OLA 62, Leuven

Libonati, E. (2010a) 'Hydreios statues from the IEASM excavations in Aboukir Bay', in Robinson and Wilson 2010, 203–10

Maspero, G. (1900) 'La stèle de Naucratis', in M. E. Grébaut (ed.), *Le Musée égyptien. Recueil de monuments et de notices sur les fouilles d'Égypte* 1, Cairo, 40–44, and pl. 45

Meadows, A. (2015) 'Coin circulation and coin production at Thonis-Heracleion and the Delta region in the Late Period', in D. Robinson and F. Goddio (eds), *Thonis-Heracleion in Context*, Oxford Centre for Maritime Archaeology 8, 121–35

Nur, A. (2010) 'Destructive earthquakes in Alexandria and Abukir Bay?' in Robinson and Wilson 2010, 127–37

Quack, J. F. (2000–2001) 'Die rituelle Erneuerung der Osirisfigurinen', *Die Welt des Orients* 31, 5–18

Robinson, D. and Goddio, F. (2015) 'Introduction: Thonis-Heracleion and the "small world" of the northwestern Delta', in D. Robinson and F. Goddio (eds), *Thonis-Heracleion in Context*, Oxford Centre for Maritime Archaeology 8, 1–12

Robinson, D. and Wilson, A. (eds) (2010) *Alexandria and the North-Western Nile Delta*, Oxford Centre for Maritime Archaeology Monograph 5, Oxford

Smith, R. R. R. (2008) 'As grey as the fertile riverbed, Father Nile', in Goddio and Fabre 2008, 80–83

Stanley, J. D., Goddio, F., Jorstad, T. F. and Schnepp, G. (2004) 'Submergence of ancient Greek cities off Egypt's Nile Delta – A cautionary tale', *Geological Society of America Today* 14, 4–10

Stanley, J. D., Goddio, F. and Schnepp, G. (2001) 'Nile flooding sank two ancient cities', *Nature* 412, 293–94

Stanley, J. D., Schnepp, G., and Jorstad T.F., (2007) 'Submergence of archaeological sites in Aboukir Bay, the result of gradual long-term processes plus catastrophic events', in J. D. Stanley (ed.), *Geoarchaeology*, Underwater Archaeology in the Canopic Region in Egypt, Oxford Centre for Maritime Archaeology 2, Oxford, 23–57

Stanley, J. D. and Warne, A. G. (2007) 'Nile Delta geography at the time of Heracleion and East Canopus', in J. D. Stanley (ed.), *Geoarchaeology*, Underwater Archaeology in the Canopic Region in Egypt, Oxford Centre for Maritime Archaeology 2, Oxford, 5–22

Toussoun, O. (1934) 'Les ruines sous-marines de la baie d'Aboukir', *Bulletin de la Société Royale d'Archéologie d'Alexandrie* 29, 342–54, pls 8–9

Walker, S. (2001) 'Nilotic mosaic of Palestrina (photographic reproduction)', in S. Walker and P. Higgs (eds), *Cleopatra of Egypt, from History to Myth*, London, 332–36

Yoyotte, J. (1958) 'Notes de toponymie Égyptienne', *Mitteilungen des Deutschen Archäologischen Instituts Abteilung Kairo* 16, 414–30

Yoyotte, J. (2008a) 'Over life-sized Ptolemaic ruling couple' in Goddio and Fabre 2008, 116–19

Yoyotte, J. (2008b) 'Statue of a queen', in Goddio and Fabre 2008, 124–29

Yoyotte, J. (2008c) 'An extraordinary pair of twins. The steles of the pharaoh Nectanebo I', in Goddio and Fabre 2008, 236–40

Yoyotte, J. (2008d) 'Colossus of a Ptolemaic king, Colossus of a Ptolemaic queen', in Goddio and Fabre 2008, 306–7

Yoyotte, J. (2008e) 'Naos of the temple of Amun-Gereb', in Goddio and Fabre 2008, 309

Yoyotte, J. (2008f) 'Vat' in Goddio and Fabre 2008, 313

Yoyotte, J., Charvet, P. and Gompertz, S. (1997) *Strabon. Le voyage en Égypte*, Paris

Yoyotte, J. and Clauss, P. (2008) 'Gold for the House of the Gods, Ptolemy III foundation plaque', in Goddio and Fabre 2008, 140–43

Chapter 2
Egypt and Greece: early encounters

Agut-Labordère, D. (2012a) 'Le statut égyptien de Naucratis', in C. Feyel, J. Fournier, L. Graslin-Thomé and F. Kirbilher (eds), *Communautés locales et pouvoir central dans l'Orient hellénistique et romain: Actes du colloque organise à Nancy entre le 3 et le 5 juin 2010*, Nancy, 353–73

Agut-Labordère, D. (2012b) 'Plus que des mercenaires! L'intégration des hommes de guerre grecs au service de la monarchie saïte', in L. Martinez-Sève (ed.), *Les diasporas grecques du VIIIe à la fin du IIIe siècle av. J.-C.*, Pallas 89, Lille, 293–306

Agut-Labordère, D. (2012c) 'Approche cartographique des relations des pharaons saïtes (664–526) et indépendants (404–342) avec les cités grecques', in L. Capdretrey and J. Zurbach (eds), *Mobilités grecques: mouvements, réseaux, contacts en Méditerranée de l'époque archaïque à l'époque hellénistique*, Bordeaux, 219–34

Agut-Labordère, D. (2013) 'The Saite period: The emergence of a Mediterranean power', in J. C. M. García (ed.), *Ancient Egyptian Administration*, Leiden, 965–1028

Bleiberg, E. (2013) 'Animal mummies: The souls of the gods', in E. Bleiberg, Y. Barbash and L. Bruno, *Soulful Creatures. Animal Mummies in Ancient Egypt*, London, 63–105

Boardman, J. (1964) *The Greeks Overseas*, Baltimore.

Boardman, J. (2013) 'Why Naukratis?', *Ancient West & East* 12, 265–67

von Bomhard, A. S. (2012) *The Decree of Saïs: The stelae of Thonis-Heracleion and Naukratis, Underwater Archaeology of the Canopic Region in Egypt*, Oxford

von Bomhard, A. S. (2015a) 'Objects from the temple of Khonsu-Thoth', in F. Goddio and D. Fabre (eds), *Osiris. Egypt's Sunken Mysteries*, Paris, 94–95

von Bomhard, A. S. (2015b) 'Small limestone sarcophagi', in F. Goddio and D. Fabre (eds), *Osiris. Egypt's Sunken Mysteries*, Paris, 90–91

von Bomhard, A. S. (2015c) 'The stela of Thonis-Heracleion. Economic, topographic and epigraphic aspects', in Robinson and Goddio 2015, 101–20

Borgeaud, Ph. and Volokhine, Y. (2000) 'La formation de la légende de Sarapis: une approche transculturelle', *Archiv für Religionsgeschichte* 2, 37–76

Bresson, A. (2000) *La cité marchande*, Bordeaux

Briant, P. and Descat, R. (1998) 'Un registre douanier de la satrapie d'Égypte à l'époque achéménide (*TAD* C3,7)', in N. Grimal and B. Menu (eds), *Le commerce en Égypte ancienne*, BdÉ 121, Cairo, 59–104

Bruno, L. (2013) 'The scientific examination of animal mummies', in E. Bleiberg, Y. Barbash, and L. Bruno, *Soulful Creatures. Animal Mummies in Ancient Egypt*, London, 107–37

Boussac, M.-Fr., Dhennin, S. and Redon, B. 2016. 'Plinthine et la Maréotide pharaonique', *Bulletin de l'Institut Français d'Archéologie Orientale* 115, forthcoming

Burkert, W. (2004) *Babylon, Memphis, Persepolis: Eastern Contexts of Greek Culture*, Cambridge, MA

Cooper, J. (2014) *The Medieval Nile – Route, Navigation, and Landscape in Islamic Egypt*, Cairo

Duplouy, A. (2006) *Les prestiges des élites: Recherches sur les modes de reconnaissance sociale en Grèce entre les Xe et Ve siècles avant J.-C.*, Paris

Ebbinghaus, S. (2006) 'Begegnungen mit Ägypten und Vorderasien im archaischen Heraheiligtum von Samos', in A. Naso (ed.), *Stranieri e non cittadini nei santuari Greci: Atti del convegno internazionale, Udine 20 al 22 novembre 2003*, Studi Udinesi sul Mondo Antico 2, Florence, 187–229

Eiseman, C. and Ridgway, B. (1987) *The Porticello Shipwreck. A Mediterranean Merchant Vessel of 415–385 BC*, College Station, TX

Fabre, D. (2008a) 'Heracleion-Thonis: Customs station and emporion', in Goddio and Fabre 2008, 219–34

Fantalkin, A. (2006) 'Identity in the making: Greeks in the Eastern Mediterranean during the Iron Age', in Villing and Schlotzhauer 2006, 199–208

Fantalkin, A. (2014) 'Naukratis as a contact zone: Revealing the Lydian connection', in R. Rollinger and K. Schnegg (eds), *Kulturkontakte in antiken Welten. Vom Denkmodell zur Fallstudie*, Colloquia Antiqua 10, Leuven, 27–51

Galili, E. (1994) 'Three fragments of wooden anchors from the Carmel coast of Israel', *Sefunim*, Bulletin of the Israel National Maritime Museum Haifa 8, 21–28

Gardiner, A. (1941) 'Ramesside texts relating to the taxation and transport of corn', *JEA* 27, 19–73

Goddio, F. (2008) 'Rediscovered sites', in Goddio and Fabre 2008, 26–48

Goddio, F. (2011) 'Thonis-Heracleion and Alexandria, two ancient emporia of Egypt', in D. Robinson and A. Wilson (eds), *Maritime Archaeology and Ancient Trade in the Mediterranean*, Oxford, 121–37

Goddio, F. (2015) 'The sacred topography of Thonis-Heracleion', in Robinson and Goddio 2015, 15–54

Goddio, F. and Fabre, D. (eds) (2008) *Egypt's Sunken Treasures*, Munich

Goddio, F. and Fabre, D. (eds) (2015) *Osiris. Egypt's Sunken Mysteries*, Paris

Grataloup, C. (2010) 'Occupation and trade at Heracleion-Thonis: The evidence from the pottery', in D. Robinson and A. Wilson (eds), *Alexandria and the North-West Delta*, Oxford, 151–59

Grataloup, C. (2015) 'Thonis-Heracleion pottery of the Late Period: Tradition and influences', in Robinson and Goddio 2015, 137–60

Guermeur, I. (2005) *Les cultes d'Amon hors-de-Thèbes*, Turnhout

Haider, P. W. (2001) 'Epigraphische Quellen zur Intergration von Griechen in die ägyptische Gesellschaft der Saïtenzeit', in U. Höckmann and D. Kreikenbom (eds), *Naukratis: Die Beziehungen zu Ostgriechenland, Ägypten und Zypern in archaischer Zeit. Akten der Table Ronde in Mainz, 25.–27. November 1999*, Möhnesee, 197–210

Haider, P. W. (2004) 'Kontakte zwischen Griechen und Ägyptern und ihre Auswirkungen auf die archaisch-griechische Welt', in R. Rollinger and C. Ulf (eds), *Griechische Archaik: Interne Entwicklungen – Externe Impulse*, Berlin, 447–91

Haldane, D. (1984) 'The Wooden Anchor'. Master's thesis, Texas A&M University

Heinz, S. (2015) 'The production and circulation of metal statuettes and amulets at Thonis-Heracleion', in Robinson and Goddio 2015, 55–69

Höckmann, O. (2008–9) 'Griechischer Seeverkehr mit dem archaischen Naukratis in Ägypten', *Talanta* 40–41, 73–135

Ikram, S. (ed.) (2005) *Divine Creatures. Animal Mummies in Ancient Egypt*, Cairo

Ikram, S. (2012) 'An eternal aviary: Bird mummies from ancient Egypt', in R. Bailleul-leSuer (ed.), *Between Heaven and Earth, Birds in Ancient Egypt*, Chicago, 41–48

Jansen-Winkeln, K. (2014) 'The Victory Stele of Amasis', *ZÄS* 12, 132–53

Jansen-Winkeln, K. (2015) 'Egypt and North Africa: Cultural Contacts (1200–750 BC)', in A. Babbi, F. Bubenheimer-Erhart, B. Marin-Aguilera and S. Mühl (eds), *The Mediterranean Mirror. Cultural Contacts in the Mediterranean Sea between 1200 and 750 B.C.*, Mainz, 35–50

Janssen, J. (2004) *Grain Transport in the Ramesside Period. Papyrus Baldwin (BM EA 10061) and Papyrus Amiens. Hieratic Papyri in the British Museum VIII*. London

Johnston, A. W. (2013–15a) 'Greek transport amphorae', in Villing et al. 2013–15 [http://www.britishmuseum.org/research/online_research_catalogues/ng/naukratis_greeks_in_egypt/material_culture_of_naukratis/greek_transport_amphorae.aspx]

Kapitän, G. (1973) 'Greco-Roman anchors and the evidence for the one-armed anchor in antiquity' in D. Blackman (ed.), *Maritime Archaeology. Colston Symposium*, Bristol, 383–95

Kapitän, G. (1984) 'Ancient anchors – technology and classification', *IJNA* 13.1, 33–44

Kaplan, P. (2003) 'Cross-cultural contacts among mercenary communities in Saite and Persian Egypt', *Mediterranean Historical Review* 18, 1–31

Kessler, D. (1989) *Die heiligen Tiere und der König, Teil I*, Wiesbaden

Kessler, D. and Nur el-Din, A. (2005) 'Tuna al-Gebel. Millions of ibises and other animals', in Ikram 2005, 120–63

Kitchen, K. (1995) *The Third Intermediate Period (1100–650 BC)*, Warminster, 3rd edn

Le Rider, G. (2001) *La naissance de la monnaie. Pratiques monetaires de l'Orient ancient*, Paris

Lloyd, A. B. (1983) 'The Late Period, 664–323', in B. G. Trigger, B. J. Kemp, D. O'Connor and A. B. Lloyd (eds), *Ancient Egypt: A Social History*, Cambridge, 279–348

Lloyd, A. B. (2014) *Ancient Egypt: State and Society*, Oxford

Martin, G. T. (1981) *The Sacred Animal Necropolis at North Saqqara: The Southern Dependencies of the Main Temple Complex*, EES Excavation Memoirs, London

Masson, A. (2013–15a) 'Offering spoons', in Villing et al. 2013–15

Masson, A. (2013–15b) 'Foundation deposits', in Villing et al. 2013–15

Masson, A. (2013–15c) 'Stone vessels from Naukratis', in Villing et al. 2013–15

Masson, A. (2015) 'Cult and trade. A reflexion on Egyptian metal offerings from Naukratis', in Robinson and Goddio 2015, 71–88

Masson, A. (forthcoming a) 'Egyptian Naukratis: the early evidence', in A. Wodzińska (ed.), *Delta and Sinai Current Research: Proceedings of the Conference in the University of Warsaw, Warsaw, April 25–27, 2013*

Masson, A. (forthcoming b) 'Scarabs, scaraboids and amulets', in Villing et al. 2013–15

Meadows, A. (2015) 'Coin circulation and coin production at Thonis-Heracleion and in the Delta region in the Late Period', in Robinson and Goddio 2015, 121–35

Möller, A. (2000) *Naukratis: Trade in Archaic Greece*, Oxford Monographs on Classical Archaeology, Oxford

Moyer, I. S. (2011) *Egypt and the Limits of Hellenism*, Cambridge

Muhs, B. (2015) 'Money, taxes, and maritime trade in Late Period Egypt', in Robinson and Goddio 2015, 91–99

Nicholson, P. T. (2005) 'The sacred animal necropolis at North Saqqara. The cults and their catacombs', in Ikram 2005, 44–71

W.-D. Niemeier (2001) 'Archaic Greeks in the Orient: Textual and archaeological evidence', Bulletin of the American Schools of Oriental Research 322, 11–32

Panagiotopoulos, D. (2005) 'Chronik einer Begegnung. Ägypten und die Ägäis in der Bronzezeit', in H. Beck, P. C. Bol and M. Bückling (eds), Ägypten Griechenland Rom: Abwehr und Berührung, Frankfurt and Tübingen, 34–49

Pearce, S. J. K. (2007) The Land of the Body: Studies in Philo's Representation of Egypt, Tübingen

Pennington, B. and Thomas, R. I. (forthcoming) 'Palaeo-landscape reconstruction at Naukratis and the Canopic branch of the Nile', Journal of Archaeological Science

Petrie, W. M. F. (1886) Naukratis. Part I, 1884–5, Third Memoir of the Egypt Exploration Fund, London

Ray, J. D. (1976) The Archive of Hor, EES Texts from Excavations, London

von Recklinghausen, D. (2013–15) 'The decoration of the temple of Amun', in Villing et al. 2013–15 [http://www.britishmuseum.org/research/online_research_catalogues/ng/naukratis_greeks_in_egypt/material_culture_of_naukratis/amun_temple.aspx]

Robinson, D., Fabre, D. and Goddio, F. (forthcoming) 'Environment and agency in the formation of the Eastern Ship Graveyard in the Central Basin at Thonis-Heracleion, Egypt' in A. Caporaso and J. Steinmetz (eds), Formation Processes of Maritime Archaeological Landscapes, Berlin

Robinson, D. and Goddio, F. (eds) (2015) Thonis-Heracleion in Context, Oxford Centre for Maritime Archaeology, Monograph 8, Oxford

Rosloff, J. (1991) 'A one-armed anchor of c. 400 BCE from the Ma'agan Michael vessel, Israel. A preliminary report', IJNA 20.3, 223–26

Rutherford, I. C. (2003) 'Pilgrimage in Greco-Roman Egypt: New perspectives on graffiti from the Memnonion at Abydos', in C. Roemer and R. Matthews (eds), Ancient Perspectives on Egypt, Encounters with Ancient Egypt 7, London, 171–90

Saint-Pierre Hoffmann, C. (2012) 'Variations autour des offrandes égyptiennes d'Athéna Lindia: De l'époque archaïque à l'époque romaine', in V. Azoulay, F. Gherchanoc and S. Lalanne (eds), Le banquet de Pauline Schmitt Pantel, genre, mœurs et politique dans l'antiquité grecque et romaine, Paris, 376–98

Tanner, J. (2003) 'Finding the Egyptian in early Greek art', in R. Matthews and C. Roemer (eds), Ancient Perspectives on Egypt, London, 115–43

Thomas, R. I. (2013–15a) 'Egyptian Late Period figures in terracotta and limestone', in Villing et al. 2013–15

Thomas, R. I. (2015) 'Naukratis, "Mistress of ships", in context', in Robinson and Goddio 2015, 247–65

Thomas, R. I and Villing, A. (2013) 'Naukratis revisited 2012: integrating new fieldwork and old research', British Museum Studies in Ancient Egypt and Sudan 20, 81–125

Thomas, R. I. and Villing, A. (forthcoming) 'Return to Naukratis: New fieldwork at Kom Geif, 2012–2014', ASAE

Trethewey, K. (2001) 'Lead anchor-stock cores from Tektas Burnu, Turkey', IJNA 30.1, 109–14

van der Wilt, E. M. (2014) 'The Place of Lead in an Egyptian Port-City in the Late Period', DPhil thesis, University of Oxford

Vasunia, P. (2001) The Gift of the Nile. Hellenizing Egypt from Aeschylus to Alexander, Berkeley, CA

Villing, A. (2013) 'Egypt as a "market" for Greek pottery: Some thoughts on production, consumption and distribution in an intercultural environment', in A. Tsingarida and D. Viviers (eds), Pottery Markets in the Ancient Greek World (8th–1st centuries B.C.), Proceedings of the International Symposium held at the Université libre de Bruxelles, 19–21 June 2008, Études d'Archéologie 5, Brussels, 73–101

Villing, A. (2015) 'Egyptian–Greek exchange in the Late Period: The view from Nokradj-Naukratis', in Robinson and Goddio 2015, 229–46

Villing, A. and Schlotzhauer, U. (eds) (2006) Naukratis: Greek Diversity in Egypt. Studies on Greek Pottery and Exchange in the Eastern Mediterranean, British Museum Research Publication 162, London

Villing, A. and Thomas, R. I. (2013–15) 'The site of Naukratis: topography, buildings and landscape', in Villing et al. 2013–15

Villing, A., Bergeron, M., Bourogiannis, G., Johnston, A., Leclère, F., Masson, A. and Thomas, R. (2013–15) Naukratis: Greeks in Egypt. British Museum Online Research Catalogue [http://www.britishmuseum.org/research/online_research_catalogues/ng/naukratis_greeks_in_egypt.aspx]

Vittmann, G. (2003) Ägypten und die Fremden im ersten vorchristlichen Jahrtausend, Kulturgeschichte der antiken Welt 97, Mainz

Vittmann, G. (2006) 'Zwischen Integration und Ausgrenzung. zur Akkulturation von Ausländern im spätzeitlichen Ägypten,' in R. Rollinger and B. Truschnegg (eds), Altertum und Mittelmeerraum: Die antike Welt diesseits und jenseits der Levante. Festschrift für Peter W. Haider zum 60. Geburtstag, Oriens et Occidens 12, 561–95

van der Wilt, E. M. (2010) 'Lead weights and ingots from Heracleion-Thonis: An illustration of Egyptian trade relations with the Aegean', in A. Hudecz and M. Petrik (eds), Commerce and Economy in Ancient Egypt, BAR International Series 2131, Oxford, 157–64

van der Wilt, E. M. (2015) 'The weights of Thonis-Heracleion: Corpus, distribution, trade and exchange', in Robinson and Goddio 2015, 161–72

Winnicki, J. K. (2009) Late Egypt and her Neighbours: Foreign Population in Egypt

in the First Millennium BC, The Journal of Juristic Papyrology Supplement 12, Warsaw

Yoyotte, J. (1982–83) 'L'Amon de Naukratis', RdE 34, 129–36

Yoyotte, J. (2013) Histoire, géographie et religion de l'Égypte ancienne, Opera selecta, OLA 224, Leuven

Zivie, A. and Lichtenberg, R. (2005) 'The cats of the goddess Bastet', in Ikram 2005, 106–19

Selected references for featured objects in Chapter 2

p. 51 Tax and trade: The Decree of Saïs on the Heracleion stele
Agut-Labordère, D. (2009–10) 'Darius législateur et les sages de l'Égypte: un addendum au Livre des Ordonnances', in J. C. Moreno Garcia (ed.), Élites et pouvoir en Égypte ancienne, CRIPEL 28, 1–8; Agut-Labordère 2012, 353–73; von Bomhard 2012, 23, 78; von Bomhard 2015, 101–20.

p. 52 A Greek wine amphora from Egypt
Bîrzescu, I. (2012) Histria XV. Die archaischen und frühklassischen Transportamphoren, Bucharest; Guasch-Jané, M. R. (2008) Wine in Ancient Egypt: a Cultural and Analytical Study, Oxford; Johnston, A. (2013–15a) 'Greek transport amphorae', in Villing et al. 2013–15 [http://www.britishmuseum.org/research/online_research_catalogues/ng/naukratis_greeks_in_egypt/material_culture_of_naukratis/greek_transport_amphorae.aspx]; Leclère, F. and Spencer, J. (2014) Tell Dafana Reconsidered: The Archaeology of an Egyptian Frontier Town, British Museum Research Publication 199, London; Meeks, O. (1993) 'Oléiculture et viticulture dans l'Égypte pharaonique', in M.-C. Amouretti and J.-P. Brun (eds), La production du vin et de l'huile en Méditerrannée, BCH Suppl. 26, Athens, 3–38; Quaegebeur, J. (1990) 'Les rois saïtes amateurs de vin', Ancient Society 21, 241–71; Obbink, D. (2014) 'Two New Poems by Sappho', ZPE 189, 32–49; Poo, M.-C. (1995) Wine and Wine Offering in the Religion of Ancient Egypt, London and New York; Weber, S. (2012) 'Untersuchungen zur archaischen griechischen Keramik aus anderen ägypischen Fundorten', in U. Schlotzhauer and S. Weber, Die archaische griechische Keramik aus Naukratis und dem übrigen Ägypten, Archäologische Studien zu Naukratis III, Mainz, 195–432.

p. 53 An Athenian perfume bottle
Goddio and Fabre 2008; Grataloup 2015, 137–60, see: 140, 142, fig. 7.4.1; Hulin, L. (2009) 'Embracing the new: The perception of Cypriot pottery in Egypt', in D. Michaelides, V. Kassianidou and R. S. Merrillees (eds), Proceedings of the International Conference Egypt and Cyprus in Antiquity, Nicosia, 3–6 April 2003, Oxford, 40–47; van de Put, W. D. J. (2006) Corpus Vasorum Antiquorum, Amsterdam, Allard Pierson Museum 4 (The Netherlands 10), Amsterdam; Villing 2013, 73–101.

p. 54 Amulets and amulet moulds
Gorton, A. F. (1996) Egyptian and Egyptianizing Scarabs: A Typology of Steatite, Faience, and Paste Scarabs from Punic and Other

Mediterranean Sites, Oxford, 91–131; Hölbl, G. (2000) 'Die Problematik spätzeitlicher Aegyptiaca im östlichen Mittelmeerraum', in M. Görg and G. Hölbl (eds), Ägypten und der östliche Mittelmeerraum im 1. Jahrtausend v. Chr., Wiesbaden, 119–62; Masson, A. (2013–15d), 'New Year's flask', in Villing et al. 2013–15; Masson, A. (forthcoming b) 'Scarabs, scaraboids and amulets', in Villing et al. 2013–15; Petrie 1886, 35–37, pl. 41.

p. 56 Imported alabastron and drill cores
Hölbl, G. (1979) Beziehungen der ägyptischen Kultur zu Altitalien, Études préliminaires aux religions orientales dans l'empire romain 62/I, Leiden; Searight, A., Reade, J. and Finkel, I. (2008) Assyrian Stone Vessels and Related Material in the British Museum, Oxford; Verbanck-Piérard, A. et al. (2008) Parfums de l'antiquité: la rose et l'encens en Méditerranée, Morlanwelz-Mariemont; Masson 2013–15c.

p. 57 Tombstone of a Carian woman
Adiego, I.-J. (2007) The Carian Language, Leiden; Höckmann, U. (2001) '"Bilinguen": Zu Ikonographie und Stil der karisch-ägyptischen Grabstelen des 6. Jhs.v.Chr.', in U. Höckmann and D. Kreikenbom (eds), Naukratis: Die Beziehungen zu Ostgriechenland, Ägypten und Zypern in archaischer Zeit. Akten der Table Ronde in Mainz, 25.–27. November 1999, Möhnesee, 217–32; Kammerzell, F. (2001) 'Die Geschichte der karischen Minderheit in Ägypten', in U. Höckmann and D. Kreikenbom (eds), Naukratis: Die Beziehungen zu Ostgriechenland, Ägypten und Zypern in archaischer Zeit. Akten der Table Ronde in Mainz, 25–27. November 1999, Möhnesee, 233–55; Thompson, D. J. (2012) Memphis under the Ptolemies, 2nd edn, Princeton; Vittmann 2003, 198–92; Vittmann, G. (2005) 'Karische Stele', in H. Beck, P. C. Bol, and M. Bückling (eds), Ägypten Griechenland Rom: Abwehr und Berührung, Frankfurt and Tübingen, 484–85, no. 38; Vittmann 2006, 561–95.

On Carians: Haider, P. W. (1996) 'Griechen im Vorderen Orient und in Ägypten bis ca. 590 v. Chr.', in Ch. Ulf (ed.), Wege zur Genese griechischer Identität: Die Bedeutung der früarchaischen Zeit, Berlin, 59–115; Ray, J. D. (1995) 'Soldiers to Pharaoh: The Carians of southwest Anatolia', in J. M. Sasson (ed.), Civilizations of the Ancient Near East II, New York, 1185–94; Rumscheid, F. (ed.) (2009) Die Karer und die Anderen, Bonn.

p. 59 Ships and anchors from Thonis-Heracleion
Belov, A. (2015) 'Archaeological evidence for the Egyptian baris (Herodotus Historiae 2.96)' in Robinson and Goddio 2015, 29; Fabre, D. (2011) 'The shipwrecks of Heracleion-Thonis: A preliminary study', in Robinson and Goddio 2015, 13–32; Fabre, D. (2015) 'The ships of Thonis-Heracleion in context' in Robinson and Goddio 2015, 175–91; Fabre, D. and Belov, A. (2011) 'The shipwrecks of Heracleion-Thonis: An overview', in G. A. Belova (ed.), Achievements and Problems of Modern Egyptology. Proceedings of the International Conference. September 29–October 4, Moscow, Moscow, 107–18; Fabre, D. and Goddio, F. (2013) 'Thonis-Heracleion,

emporion of Egypt, recent discoveries and research perspectives: The shipwrecks', *Journal of Ancient Egyptian Interconnections*, 5(1), 1–8; Robinson, D. (2015) 'Ship 43 and the formation of the ship graveyard in the Central Port at Thonis-Heracleion' in Robinson and Goddio 2015, 211–25.

p. 60 Cypriot statuette of a seated goddess nursing a baby
Gardner, E. A. (1888), *Naukratis. Part II*, Sixth Memoir of the Egypt Exploration Fund, London, 57, pl. 14, fig. 7; Nick, G. (2006) *Zypro-ionische Kleinplastik aus Kalkstein und Alabaster*, Archäologische Studien zu Naukratis I, ed. U. Höckmann, Möhnesee, 68; Thomas, R. I. (2013–15c) 'Cypriot figures in terracotta and limestone' in Villing et al. 2013–15.

p. 61 Nude male figures: Cypriot nude male youth (*kouros*) and Cypriot sculpture of nude youth or hero wrestling a lion
Gardner, E. A. (1888) *Naukratis, Part II*, Sixth Memoir of the Egypt Exploration Fund, London (for British Museum 1888,0601.27 see: pp. 57, 85, pl. XIV); Höckmann, U. (2007) 'Zyprisch-griechische Kleinplastik: Kouroi, andere Figuren und plastisch verzierte Gefässe', in U. Höckmann and W. Koenigs, *Archäologische Studien zu Naukratis*, ed. U. Höckmann, Worms, 13–307 (for British Museum 1888,1006.1 see: pp. 176–77, no. N9); Jenkins, I. (2001) 'Archaic kouroi in Naucratis: the case for Cypriot origin', *American Journal of Archaeology* 105, 163–79; Möller 2000 (for British Museum 1888,0601.27 see: pp. 159–60, 162 note 597); Nick, G. (2006) *Zypro-ionische Kleinplastik aus Kalkstein und Alabaster*, Archäologische Studien zu Naukratis I, ed. U. Höckmann, Möhnesee (for British Museum 1888,0601.27 see: cat. 12, pp. 109–10; pp. 46–51; pl. 7); Thomas, R. I. (2013–15c) 'Cypriot figures in terracotta and limestone' in Villing et al. 2013–15. I. (2013–15d) 'Stone and terracotta figures from Naukratis: An introduction', in Villing et al. 2013–15.

p. 63 Architectural moulding from the Archaic Greek sanctuary of Apollo
Dyer, J. and Villing, A. (forthcoming) 'The polychromy of early Ionian architecture: analysis of pigments on architectural elements from the Archaic Apollo sanctuary at Naukratis'; Fontenrose, J. E. (1988) *Didyma: Apollo's Oracle, Cult, and Companions*, Oakland, CA; Herda, A. (2006) *Der Apollon-Delphinios-Kult in Milet und die Neujahrsprozession nach Didyma: Ein neuer Kommentar der sog. Molpoi-Satzung (Milet I 3 Nr.133)*, Milesische Forschungen 4, Mainz; Koenigs, W. (2007) 'Archaische griechische Bauteile', in U. Höckmann and W. Koenigs, *Archäologische Studien zu Naukratis* II, Worms, 311–84, see 328 no. 11, pls 14, 15 and 30; Möller 2000, 94–99; Petrie 1886, pl. 14.5; Villing, A. (2013–15) 'The material culture of Naukratis – an overview', in Villing et al. 2013–15, fig. 2.

p. 65 Votive female bust
Bowden, H. (1996) 'The Greek settlement and sanctuaries at Naukratis: Herodotus and archaeology', in M. H. Hansen and K. Raaflaub (eds), *More Studies in the Ancient Greek Polis*,

Historia Einzelschriften 108, Stuttgart, 17–37; Bresson 2000; Bresson, A. (2005) 'Naucratis: De l'Emporion à la cité', TOΠOI. *Orient-Occident* 12–13, 133–55; Höckmann, U. and Möller, A. (2006) 'The Hellenion at Naukratis; questions and observations', in Villing and Schlotzhauer 2006, 11–22; Hogarth, D. G., Edgar, C. C. and Gutch, C. (1898–99), 'Excavations at Naukratis', *The Annual of the British School at Athens* 5, 26–97; Malkin, I. (2011) *A Small Greek World*. Networks in the Ancient Mediterranean, Oxford; Möller 2000; Pébarthe, Ch. (2005) 'Lindos, l'Hellénion et Naucratis. Réflexions sur l'administration de l'emporion', TOΠOI. *Orient-Occident* 12/13, 157–81; Polinskaya, I. (2010) 'Shared sanctuaries and the gods of others: On the meaning of "common" in Herodotus 8.144', in R. M. Rosen and I. Sluiter (eds), *Valuing Others in Classical Antiquity*, Mnemosyne Supplements 323, Leiden and Boston, 43–70; Thomas, R. (2013–15b) 'Greek terracotta figures', in Villing et al. 2013–15 [http://www.britishmuseum.com/research/online_research_catalogues/ng/naukratis_greeks_in_egypt/material_culture_of_naukratis/greek_terracota_figures.aspx]; Thomas and Villing (forthcoming).

p. 66 Cypriot incense burner
Kiss, Z. (2008c) 'The scent of gods, an incense burner' in Goddio and Fabre 2008, 256–57; Ikram, S. 2005; Karageorghis, V. (1988) 'A stone statuette of a sphinx and a note on small limestone thymiateria from Cyprus', *Report of the Department of Antiquities Cyprus* 2, 89–93.

p. 66 Saucer with mythical beasts
von Bissing, F. W. (1942) 'Zu den griechisch-orientalischen Bleimedaillons aus Ionien', *Archäologischer Anzeiger*, 48–50.

p. 67 Head of a Cypriot statuette
Fabre, D. and Goddio, F. (2012) 'Une statuette chypriote découverte à Thônis-Héracléion', *Études et Travaux* (Warsaw) 25, 81–101; Heinz, S. (2013) 'The statuettes and amulets of Thonis-Heracleion', Vol. I, 57–58, Vol. II, 82–83, DPhil thesis, University of Oxford; Meadows 2015, 121–35.

p. 68 Votive box and mummy-case
Leitz, C. (2011) *Der Sarg des Panehemisis in Wien*, Studien zur spätägyptischen Religion 3, Wiesbaden; Masson 2015, 69–86; Petrie 1886, 41–42; Weiss, K. (2012) *Ägyptische Tier-und Götterbronzen aus Unterägypten: Untersuchungen zu Typus, Ikonographie und Funktion sowie der Bedeutung innerhalb der Kulturkontakte zu Griechenland*, Ägypten und Altes Testament 81, 720–21, Type T 5, pl. 40h, no. 723 and 799–800 pl. 51c, Type T 39, no. 1075.

p. 69 Ibis mummy
Kessler 1989; Martin 1981; Rawson, J. (1977) *Animals in Art*, London; Taylor, J. (2006) *Mummy – The Inside Story*, Catalogue accompanying the exhibitions held in Tokyo, 7 October, 2006–18 February, 2007 and Kobe, 17 March–17 June 2007, Tokyo.

p. 70 Pyramidal object
Goddio 2015, 15–54, see 18–19.

Chapter 3
Greek kings and Egyptian gods
Ashton, S.-A. (2001) *Ptolemaic Royal Sculpture from Egypt: The Interaction between Greek and Egyptian Traditions*, Oxford
Borgeaud, Ph. and Volokhine, Y. (2000) 'La formation de la légende de Sarapis: une approche transculturelle', *Archiv für Religionsgeschichte* 2, 37–76
Briant, P. (2002) *From Cyrus to Alexander: A History of the Persian Empire*, trans. Peter T. Daniels, Winona Lake
Bricault, L. (2006) *Isis, Dame des flots*, Ægyptiaca Leodiensia 7, Liège
Bricault, L., Versluys, M. J. and Meyboom, P. G. P. (2007) *Nile into Tiber: Egypt in the Roman World, Proceedings of the 3rd International Conference of Isis Studies, Leiden, May 11–14 2005*, Leiden and Boston
Brophy, E. (2014) 'Placing pharaohs and kings: Where were royal statues placed in Ptolemaic Egypt?', in Grieb, Nawotka and Wojciechowska 2014, 347–55
Carney, E. D. (2013) *Arsinoë of Egypt and Macedon: A Royal Life*, New York
Devauchelle, D. (2010) 'Osiris, Apis, Sarapis et les autres. Remarques sur les Osiris memphites au Ier millénaire av. J.-C.', in L. Coulon (ed.), *Le culte d'Osiris au Ier millénaire av. J.-C.: Découvertes et travaux récents*, BdE 153, Cairo, 33–38
Devauchelle, D. (2012) 'Pas d'Apis pour Sarapis!', in A. Gasse, Fr. Servajean and Chr. Thiers (eds), *Et in Ægypto et ad Ægyptum, Recueil d'études dédiées à Jean-Claude Grenier*, CENiM 5, Vol. 2, Montpellier, 213–26
Forgeau, A. (2008) 'Les reines dans l'Égypte pharaonique. Statut et représentations', in F. Bertholet, A. Bielman Sanchez and R. Frei-Stolba (eds), *Égypte – Grèce – Rome: Les différents visages des femmes antiques*, Berne, 3–24
Goddio, F. (2007a) *Underwater Archaeology in the Canopic Region in Egypt. The Topography and Excavation of Herakleion-Thonis and East Canopus (1996–2006)*, Oxford Centre for Maritime Archaeology Monograph 1, Oxford
Goddio, F. (2007b) *The Topography and Excavation of Heracleion-Thonis and East Canopus (1996–2006). Underwater Archaeology in the Canopic Region in Egypt*, Oxford Centre for Maritime Archaeology 1, Oxford
Goddio, F. and Fabre, D. (eds) (2008) *Egypt's Sunken Treasures*, Munich
Goddio, F. (2009) 'Introduction', in Thiers, C. (2009) *La Stèle de Ptolémée VIII Évergète II à Héracléion*, Underwater Archaeology in the Canopic Region in Egypt, Oxford Centre for Maritime Archaeology Monograph 4, Oxford, IX–XVII
Goddio, F. and Fabre, D. (eds) (2015) *Osiris. Egypt's Sunken Mysteries*, Paris
Goddio, F. (2015) 'The sacred topography of Thonis-Heracleion', in D. Robinson and F. Goddio (eds), *Heracleion in Context: The maritime economy of the Egyptian Late Period*, Oxford Centre for Maritime Archaeology 8, Oxford, 15–54

Grieb, V., Nawotka, K. and Wojciechowska, A. (2014) *Alexander the Great and Egypt. History, Art, Tradition*, Wiesbaden
Guermer, I. (2005) *Les cultes d'Amon hors de Thèbes. Recherches de géographie religieuse*. Bibliothèque de L'École des Hautes Études, Sciences Religieuses 123, Turnhout
Hölbl, G. (2001) *A History of the Ptolemaic Empire*, London and New York
Jenkins, I., Farge, C. and Turner, V. (2015) *Defining Beauty: The Body in Ancient Greek Art*, London
Kiss, Z. and Yoyotte, J. (2008) 'Torso of a Benefactor' in F. Goddio and D. Fabre (eds), *Egypt's Sunken Treasures*, Munich, 307.
Legras, B. (2014) 'Sarapis, Isis et le pouvoir lagide', in L. Bricault and M. J. Versluys (eds), *Power, Politics and the Cults of Isis*, Leiden, 95–115
Masson, O. (1977) 'Quelques bronzes égyptiens à inscription grecque', *RdE* 29, 53–67
McKenzie, J., Gibson, S. and Reyes, A. T. (2004) 'Reconstructing the Serapeum in Alexandria from archaeological evidence', *JRS* 94, 73–121
Parkinson, R. B. (2005) *The Rosetta Stone*, London
Pfeiffer, S. (2011) 'Herrscherlegitimität und Herrscherkult in den ägyptischen Tempeln griechisch-römischer Zeit', in D. von Recklinghausen and M. A. Stadler (eds), *KultOrte: Mythen, Wissenschaft und Alltag in den Tempeln Ägyptens*, Berlin, 116–41
Pfeiffer, S. (2008) 'The god Serapis, his cult and the beginnings of the ruler cult in Ptolemaic Egypt', in P. McKechnie and P. Guillaume (eds), *Ptolemy II Philadelphus and his World*, Boston, 387–408
Robinson, D. and Goddio, F. (eds) (2015) *Thonis-Heracleion in Context*, Oxford Centre for Maritime Archaeology, Monograph 8, Oxford
Robinson, D and Wilson, A. (eds) (2010) *Alexandria and the North-Western Delta*, Oxford Centre for Maritime Archaeology Monograph 5, Oxford
Romm, J. S. (2011) *Ghost on the Throne: The Death of Alexander the Great and the War for Crown and Empire*, New York
Robinson, Z. (2008) 'The Metalware from the Sanctuary Complex at Heracleion-Thonis', DPhil thesis, University of Oxford
Rowe, A. (1946) *Discovery of the Famous Temple and Enclosure of Serapis at Alexandria*, ASAE Suppl. 2, Cairo
Sabottka, M. (2008) *Das Serapeum in Alexandria: Untersuchungen zur Architektur und Baugeschichte des Heiligtums von der frühen ptolemäischen Zeit bis zur Zerstörung 391 n. Chr.*, Études alexandrines 15, Cairo
Smith, R. R. R. (1991) *Hellenistic Sculpture: A Handbook*, London
Stambaugh, J. E. (1972) *Sarapis under the Early Ptolemies*, Leiden
Stanwick, P. E. (2002) *Portraits of the Ptolemies: Greek Kings as Egyptian Pharaohs*, Austin

Thiers, C. (2008) 'Underlining the good deeds of a ruler – the stele of Ptolemy VIII', in F. Goddio and D. Fabre (eds), *Egypt's Sunken Treasures*, Munich, 134–137, 310

Thiers, C. (2009) *La stèle de Ptolémée VIII Évergète II à Héracléion*, Oxford Centre for Maritime Archaeology 4, Oxford

Vassiliou, E. D. (2009) 'Ptolemaic art and the legitimation of power', in D. Michaelides, V. Kassianidou and R. S. Merillees (eds), *Egypt and Cyprus in Antiquity*, Oxford, 151–60

Walker, S. and Higgs, P. (eds) (2001) *Cleopatra of Egypt*, London

Weinstein, J. M. (1973) *Foundation Deposits in Ancient Egypt*, Ann Arbor

Yoyotte, J. (2010) 'Osiris dans la région d'Alexandrie', in L. Coulon (ed.), *Le culte d'Osiris au Ier millénaire av. J.-C.: Découvertes et travaux récents*, BdE 153, Cairo, 33–38

Selected references for objects featured in Chapter 3

p. 86 Water-clock depicting Alexander the Great
Lippincott, K. (1999) *The Story of Time*, London, 134, no. 131; Walker and Higgs 2001, 38, no. 1; Stanwick, P. (2005) 'Wasseruhr mit dem Namen Alexanders des Großen', in H. Beck, P. C. Bol and M. Bückling, *Ägypten Griechenland Rom: Abwehr und Berührung*, Frankfurt and Tübingen, 548–49 no. 112.

p. 86 Coin portraying Alexander the Great
Fulińska, A. (2014) 'Ram horns of Alexander reconsidered' in Grieb, Nawotka and Wojciechowska 2014, 119–44; Kroll, J. (2007) 'The emergence of ruler portraiture on early Hellenistic coinage: The importance of being divine', in P. Schultz and R. von den Hoff (eds), *Early Hellenistic Portraiture: Image, Style, Context*, Cambridge, 113–22.

p. 87 Statue of Horus protecting pharaoh
Arnold, D. (1995) 'An Egyptian Bestiary', *Metropolitan Museum of Art Bulletin* 52 (4), 7–64; Holm-Rasmussen, T. (1979) 'On the statue cult of Nektanebos II', *Acta Orientalia* 40, 21–25; Hornung, E. and Bryan, B. M. (eds) (2002) *The Quest for Immortality. Treasures of Ancient Egypt*, Washington, D.C., National Gallery of Art, 171–72; Yoyotte, J.-Y. (1959) 'Nectanébo II comme faucon divin?', *Kêmi* 15, 70–74.

p. 88 Coins portraying Ptolemy I Soter I
Callataÿ, F. de (2005) 'L'instauration par Ptolémée Ier Sôter d'une économie monétaire fermée', in F. Duyrat and O. Picard (eds), *L'exception égyptienne? Production et échanges monétaires en Égypte hellénistique et romaine*, Études alexandrines 10, 117–34; Fulińska, A. (2014) 'Ram horns of Alexander reconsidered', in Grieb, Nawotka and Wojciechowska 2014, 119–44; Goddio and Fabre 2008; Kroll, J. (2007) 'The emergence of ruler portraiture on early Hellenistic coinage: The importance of being divine', in P. Schultz and R. von den Hoff (eds), *Early Hellenistic Portraiture: Image, Style, Context*,

Cambridge, 113–22; Meijer, F. and Van Nijf, O. (2015) *Trade, Transport and Society in the Ancient World. A Sourcebook*, New York, 2nd edn.

p. 88 Head of a pharaoh
Goddio and Fabre 2008; Josephson, J. A. (1997) *Egyptian Royal Sculpture of the Late Period 400–246 B.C.*, SDAIK 30, Mainz; Mysliwiec, K. (1988) *Royal Portraiture of the Dynasties XXI–XXX*, Mainz; Stanwick, P. E. (2002) *Portraits of the Ptolemies: Greek Kings as Egyptian Pharaohs*, Austin.

p. 93 Statue of Arsinoe II
Ashton 2001; Bing, P. (2002–3) 'Posidippus and the Admiral: Kallikrates of Samos in the Milan Epigrams', *Greek, Roman, and Byzantine Studies* 43, 243–66; Bricault 2006, 26, 28–29; Carney 2013, 78–79, 98–99, 106–7, 111–24; Forgeau 2008, 3–24; Goddio and Fabre 2008; Hölbl 2001; Quaegebeur, J. (1971) 'Documents concerning a Cult of Arsinoe Philadelphos at Memphis Cult of Arsinoe', *JNES* 30(4), 239–70.

p. 95 Queen (possibly Cleopatra III) dressed as Isis
Albersmeier, S. (2010) 'Statues of Ptolemaic queens from Alexandria, Canopus and Heracleion-Thonis', in Robinson and Wilson 2010, 191–201; Ashton, S.-A. (2001) *Ptolemaic Royal Sculpture from Egypt. The Interaction between Greek and Egyptian Traditions*, BAR 923, Oxford; Kiss, Z. (2008) 'A beauty from the depths. The dark queen', in Goddio and Fabre 2008, 121–23; Smith, R. R. R. (1988) *Hellenistic Royal Portraits*, Oxford; Stanwick, P. E. (2002) *Portraits of the Ptolemies: Greek Kings as Egyptian Pharaohs*, Austin.

p. 96 Stele of Ptolemy VIII Euergetes II
Goddio, F. (2015) 'The sacred topography of Thonis-Heracleion', in Robinson and Goddio 2015, 15–69; Grataloup, C. (2015) 'Thonis-Heracleion pottery of the Late Period: Tradition and influences', in Robinson and Goddio 2015, 137–60; Meadows, A. (2015) 'Coin circulation and coin production at Thonis-Heracleion and in the Delta region in the Late Period', in Robinson and Goddio 2015, 121–35; Thiers, C. (2008) 'Underlining the good deeds of a ruler—the stele of Ptolemy VIII', in Goddio and Fabre 2008, 134–37, 310; Thiers, C. (2009) *La stèle de Ptolémée VIII Évergète II à Héracléion*, Oxford Centre for Maritime Archaeology 4, Oxford.

p. 98 Statues of Ptolemaic king and queen
Albersmeier, S. (2002) *Untersuchungen zu den Frauenstatuen des ptolemäischen Ägypten*, Mainz, 284, cat. 8, pls 1a–b, 21 a–d; Albersmeier, S. (2010) 'Statues of Ptolemaic queens from Alexandria, Canopus and Heracleion-Thonis' in Robinson and Wilson 2010, 191–201; Libonati, E. (2010b) 'Egyptian statuary from the Abukir Bay: Ptolemaic and Roman finds from Herakleion and Canopus', Vol. I, DPhil thesis, University of Oxford, 116; Stanwick 2002, 59, 69; Yoyotte, J. (2008a) 'Over life-sized Ptolemaic ruling couple' in Goddio and Fabre 2008, 116–19.

p. 103 Statue of a fertility figure (probably Hapy)
Baines, J. (1985) *Fecundity Figures: Egyptian Personification and the Iconography of a Genre*, Warminster; Baines, J. (2004) 'Egyptian elite self-representation in the context of Ptolemaic rule' in W. Harris and G. Ruffini (eds), *Ancient Alexandria between Egypt and Greece*, Leiden, 33–61; Baines, J. (2008) 'Colossal and fertile – Hapy, the Inundation of the Nile' in Goddio and Fabre 2008, 100–5.

p. 105 Shrine of Amun, Lord of Gereb
Goddio, F. (2015) 'The sacred topography of Thonis-Heracleion', in Robinson and Goddio 2015, 15–54; Guermeur, I. (2005) *Les cultes d'Amon hors de Thèbes. Recherches de géographie religieuse*, Bibliothèque de l'École des Hautes Études, Sciences Religieuses 123, Turnhout, 143–48; Malaise, M. and Winand, J. (1993) 'Le racine grb et l'Amon-grb', *CdE* 74, 224–30; Yoyotte, J. (2004) 'Les trouvailles épigraphiques de l'Institut Européen d'Archéologie Sous-Marine dans la baie d'Abu Qîr', *Bulletin de la societé française d'égyptologie* 159, 29–40; Yoyotte, J. (2008) 'Naos of the temple of Amun-Gereb', in Goddio and Fabre 2008, 308.

p. 107 Plaque representing Amun as a ram
Fabre, D. (2014) 'La campagne de fouilles 2012 de l'IEASM à Thônis-Héracléion et « l'image vivante de culte » d'Amon', http://www.ieasm.org/downloads/IEASM_religion_Belier_Amon_df.pdf, 5–12; Goddio, F. (2015) 'The sacred topography of Thonis-Heracleion', in Robinson and Goddio 2015, 15–54; Meadows, A. (2008) 'Coin weight' in Goddio and Fabre 2008, 343.

p. 108 Sphinx
Goddio 2007, 28, 88–93, 118; Kiss, Z. (2008d) 'Sphinx (SCA 282)', in Goddio and Fabre 2008, 306; Libonati, E. (2010b) 'Egyptian Statuary from the Abukir Bay: Ptolemaic and Roman finds from Herakleion and Canopus', Vol. I, DPhil thesis, University of Oxford, 148–49.

p. 109 A temple benefactor
Kiss, Z. and Yoyotte, J. (2008) 'Torso of a benefactor', in Goddio and Fabre 2008, 307, no. 109; Libonati, E. (2010b) 'Egyptian statuary from the Abukir Bay: Ptolemaic and Roman finds from Herakleion and Canopus', Vol. I, DPhil thesis, University of Oxford, 184–84.

p. 112 Large brazier
Kiss, Z. (2008j) 'Large bronze brazier' in Goddio and Fabre 2008, 333; Robinson 2008, 224.

p. 112 Mirror
Derriks, C. (2001) *Les miroirs caratides Égyptiens en bronze, typologie, chronologie et symbolique*, Mainz, 6–9, 10–14; Goddio, F. (2015) 'The sacred topography of Thonis-Heracleion', in Robinson and Goddio 2015, 15–69; Kiss, Z. (2008e) 'Mirror', in Goddio and Fabre 2008, 324; Robinson 2008, 171–72, fig. 66.

p. 113 Bronze basins
Allen, J. P. (2005) *The Art of Medicine in Ancient Egypt*, New York, 18, no. 3; Blackman, A. M. (1998) *Gods, Priests and Men: Studies in the*

Religion of Pharaonic Egypt, London, 4; Dayagi-Mendels, M. (1989) *Perfumes and Cosmetics in the Ancient World*, Jerusalem, 17; Fabre, D. (2008b) 'Cults and rituals', in Goddio and Fabre 2008, 138–82; Goddio 2007); Goddio and Fabre 2008; Goddio, F. and Fabre, D. (eds) (2015) *Osiris. Egypt's Sunken Mysteries*, Paris; Moussa, A. M. and Altenmüller, H. (1977) *Das Grab des Nianchchnum und Chnumhotep*, Mainz; Robinson 2008.

p. 113 Achaemenid Persian bowls
Fabre, D. (2008c) 'Bowl', in Goddio and Fabre 2008, 327; Pfrommer, M. (1987) *Studien zu alexandrinischen und grossgriechischer Toreutik frühhellenistischer Zeit*, Berlin, 42; Robinson 2008, 99–100.

p. 116 Pharaoh with *khepresh* crown
Berlandini-Keller, J. (2015) 'Standing pharaoh with a *kheprech* crown', in Goddio and Fabre 2015, 86–87; Bothmer, B. V. (1960) *Egyptian Sculpture of the Late Period, 700 BC to AD 100*, New York, 88–89, no. 71 pl. 67, figs 172–73; Goddio, F. (2015) 'The sacred topography of Thonis-Heracleion', in Robinson and Goddio 2015, 15–54; Hill, M. (2004) *Royal Bronze Statuary from Ancient Egypt*, Leiden and Boston, 166–67, no. 32, pl. 65 (LPPt-20); Perdu, O. (2012) *Le crépuscule des pharaons, chefs-d-oeuvre des dernières dynasties égyptiennes*, Brussels, 176–79, 188–89, no. 92.

p. 119 Shrine with statuette and amulets
Andrews, C. (1994) *Amulets of Ancient Egypt*, London; Aufrère, S. (2013) '"Héraklès égyptien" et la maîtrise des eaux, de l'Achéloôs au Nil et au Bahr el-Youssef', in S. H. Aufrère and M. Mazoyer (eds), *Au confluent des cultures. Enjeux et maîtrise de l'eau*, Cahiers Kubaba, Paris, 1–36; von Bomhard, A. S. (2014a) 'Heracles and the Hone: About a foundation deposit from the temple of Thonis-Heracleion', *JEA* 100, 339–55; Fabre, D. (2008b) 'Cults and rituals', in Goddio and Fabre 2008, 138–82; Goddio 2007; Goddio, F. (2015) 'The sacred topography of Thonis-Heracleion', in Robinson and Goddio 2015, 15–54.

p. 120 Headdress of Khonsu-the-child
Abubakr, A. J. (1937) 'Untersuchungen über die ägyptischen Kronen', PhD thesis, Berlin, Glückstadt, Hamburg, New York; Bianchi, R. S. (2014) *Bronzes Égyptiens, Fondation Gandur pour l'art*, Berne; Goddio 2015; Goddio and Fabre 2008; Goddio and Fabre 2015; Heinz, S. (2013) 'The Statuettes and Amulets of Thonis-Heracleion, Vols I and II, DPhil thesis, University of Oxford; Kiss, Z. (2008g) 'Hem-hem crown of Khonsu' in Goddio and Fabre 2008, 322; Yoyotte, J. and Chuvin, P. (1988) 'Le Zeus Casios de Péluse à Tivoli, une hypothèse', *BIFAO* 88, 165–80, pls 14–17.

p. 122 Cypriot *hemistater* coin
Goddio, F. (2015) 'The sacred topography of Thonis-Heracleion', in Robinson and Goddio 2015, 15–54; Markou, E. (2011) *L'or des rois de Chypre: Numismatique et histoire à l'époque classique*, Meletemata 64, Athens, 147; Meadows, A. (2012) 'Review of E. Markou, L'Or des Rois de Chypre. Numismatique et historie à l'époque*

classique', *American Journal of Numismatics* 2nd ser. 24, 187–97; Yon, M. (1992) 'Heraklès à Chypre' in C. Bonnet and C. Annequin (eds), *Héraclès d'une rive à l'autre de la Mediterranée*, Brussels, 145–60; Yoyotte, J. and Lichocka, B. (2008) 'Cypriot hemistater' in Goddio and Fabre 2008, 351.

pp. 123–25 Gold jewellery: votive offerings?
Boardman, J. (2001) *Greek Gems and Finger Rings*, London; Bulsink, M. (2015) *Egyptian Gold Jewellery*, Turnhout; Goddio 2007; Goddio, F. and Fabre, D. (2015) *Osiris. Egypt's Sunken Mysteries*, Paris, 2015; Stolz, Y. (2008a) 'Lion-headed earring' in Goddio and Fabre 2008, 314; Stolz, Y. (2008b) 'Animal-headed earring' in Goddio and Fabre 2008, 314; Stolz, Y. (2008c) 'Ring with an engraved Victory' in Goddio and Fabre 2008, 315; Stolz, Y. (2008d) 'Ring with oval glass or stone cabochon' in Goddio and Fabre 2008, 316; Vernier, E., (1927) *Bijoux et orfèvrerie*, Catalogue general des antiquités du Musée du Caire, nos 52001–53855, Cairo; Williams, D. and Ogden, J. (1994) *Greek Gold Jewellery of the Classical World*, London, 198 no. 132, 232 no. 165.

p. 127 Colossal statue of the Apis bull
Ashton 2005; Borgeaud and Volokhine 2000; Empereur, J. Y. (2000) *Petit Guide du Musée Gréco-romain d'Alexandrie*, Alexandria, 6; Kayser, F. (1994) 'Recueil des inscriptions grecques et latines (non funéraires) d'Alexandrie impériale', BdE 108, Cairo, 176–79; Kessler, D. (1989) *Die Heiligen Tiere und der König*, Wiesbaden; Rowe, A. (1942) 'A short report on excavations of the Graeco-Roman Museum made during the season 1942 at "Pompey's Pillar"', *Bulletin de la Société royale d'archéologie d'Alexandrie* 35, 124–61; Savvopoulos, K. (2010) 'Alexandria in Aegypto. The use and meaning of Egyptian elements in Hellenistic and Roman Alexandria', in L. Bricault and M. J. Versluys (eds), *Isis on the Nile. Egyptian Gods in Hellenistic and Roman Egypt. Proceedings of the IVth International Conference of Isis Studies, Université de Liège, November 27–29 2008, Michel Malaise in honorem*, Leiden, 75–86

p. 128 Serapis statue
Bakhoum, S. (1971) 'Une statue en bois de Serapis au musée Gréco-Romain d'Alexandrie', *Archaeological & Historical Studies*, The Archaeological Society of Alexandria 4, 66–80, figs 1–6; Bergmann, M. (2010) 'Serapis im 3. Jahrhundert v. Chr.', in G. Weber (ed.), *Alexandreia und das ptolemäische Ägypten. Kulturbegegnungen in Hellenistischer Zeit*, Berlin, 109–35; Pfeiffer, S. (2008) 'The god Serapis, his cult and the beginnings of the ruler cult in Ptolemaic Egypt', in P. McKechnie and P. Guillaume (eds), *Ptolemy II Philadelphus and his World*, Boston, 387–408; Sabottka 2008.

p. 129 Foundation plaque from the Serapeum in Alexandria
Goddio and Fabre 2008; McKenzie, Gibson and Reyes 2004, 73–121, esp. 85; Montet, P. (1964) 'Le rituel de fondation des temples égyptiens', *Kêmi* 17, 74–100; Rowe 1946, 54–58; Sabottka

2008, 181–86, fig. 40, pl. 64; Weinstein 1973, 367–68, 370, 383–85, no. 165.

p. 130 Head of Serapis
Goddio 2007, 50–51, fig. 2.45, 50–57; Kiss, Z. (2008b) 'A guarantor for fertility, Serapis and Calathos' in Goddio and Fabre 2008, 174–76.

p. 133 Osiris-Canopus jar
Dunand, F. (2008) 'Priest bearing in his veiled hands an Osiris-Canopus jar', in Goddio and Fabre 2008, 160–63; Hardwick, T. (2008) 'Osiris-Canopus', in Goddio and Fabre 2008, 301; Kiss, Z. (2008a) 'A jar bringing hope for eternal life, The Osiris-Canopus' in Goddio and Fabre 2008, 62–65; Libonati, E. S. (2010a) 'Hydreios statues from the IEASM excavations in Aboukir Bay', in Robinson and Wilson 2010, 203–10; Pantalacci, L. (1981) 'Une conception originelle de la survie osirienne d'après les textes de Basse Époque', *Göttinger Miszellen* 52, 57–66; Quack, J. (2001) 'Die rituelle Erneuerung der Osirisfigurinen', *Die Welt des Orients* 31, 5–18; Raven, M. J. (1986) 'A rare type of Osiris Canopus', *Oudheidkundige mededelingen van het Rijksmuseum te Leiden* 66, 21–30.

p. 134 Head of Nectanebo II
Goddio and Fabre 2008; Josephson, J. A. (1997) *Egyptian Royal Sculpture of the Late Period 400–246 B.C.*, SDAIK 30, Mainz; Mysliwiec, K. (1988) *Royal Portraiture of the Dynasties XXI–XXX*, Mainz; Stanwick, P. E. (2002) *Portraits of the Ptolemies: Greek Kings as Egyptian Pharaohs*, Austin.

p. 137 Naos of the Decades
von Bomhard, A.-S. (2008) *The Naos of the Decades: Underwater Archaeology in the Canopic Region in Egypt*, Oxford Centre for Maritime Archaeology 3, Oxford; von Bomhard, A.-S. (2011) 'Le Naos des Décades. Puzzle archéologique et thématique', ENiM 4, 107–36; Habachi, L. and Habachi, B. (1952) 'The naos with the decades (Louvre D37) and the discovery of another fragment', *JNES* 11, 251–63; Leitz, C. (1995) *Altägyptische Sternuhren*, OLA 62, Leuven, 3–57; Virenque, H. (2006) 'Les quatre naos de Saft el-Henneh: Un rampart théologique construit par Nectanébo Ier dans le Delta oriental', *Égypte, Afrique et Orient* 42, 19–28; Yoyotte 1954.

Chapter 4
From myth to festivals
Aufrère, S. H. (1991) *L'univers minéral dans la pensée égyptienne*, BdE 105, Cairo
Aufrère, S. H. (1998) 'Parfums et onguents liturgiques du Laboratoire d'Edfou: compositions, codes végétaux et minéraux dans l'Égypte ancienne', in R. Gyselen (ed.), *Parfums d'Orient*, Res Orientales 11, Bures-sur-Yvette, 29–64
Aufrère, S. H. (2005a) 'Parfums et onguent liturgiques. Présentation des recettes d'Edfou', in S. H. Aufrère, *Encyclopédie religieuse de l'Univers végétal*, Orientalia Monspeliensia 16, Montpellier, 213–62
Aufrère, S. H. (2007) *Thoth, Hermès l'Égyptien. De l'infiniment grand à l'infiniment petit*, Paris

Assmann, J. (2008) 'Translating gods: Religion as a factor of cultural (un)translatability', in H. de Vries, *Religion: Beyond a Concept*, New York, 139–49
Baines, J. (1985) *Fecundity Figures. Egyptian Personification and the Iconology of a Genre*, Warminster and Chicago
Barguet, P. (1962) *Le papyrus N. 3176 (S) du Musée du Louvre*, BdE 37, Cairo
Burkert, W. (2004) *Babylon, Memphis, Persepolis: Eastern Contexts of Greek Culture*, Cambridge, MA
Cauville, S. (1997a) *Le temple de Dendara: 10, Les chapelles osiriennes*, 1. text; 2. plates, Cairo.
Cauville, S. (1997b) *Le temple de Dendara, Les chapelles osiriennes*, 1. Bibliothèque d'Étude 117, transcription et traduction; 2. Bibliothèque d'Étude 118, commentaire; 3. Bibliothèque d'Étude 119, index, Cairo
Chassinat, É. (1966) *Le mystère d'Osiris au mois de Khoiak* 1, Cairo
Chassinat, É. (1968) *Le mystère d'Osiris au mois de Khoiak* 2, Cairo
Coulon, L. (2010) 'Le culte osirien au 1er millénaire av. J.-C Une mise en perspective(s)', in L. Coulon (ed.), *Le culte d'Osiris au 1er millénaire av. J.-C. Découvertes at travaux récents*, Bibliothèque d'Étude 153, Le Caire, 1–17
Coulon, L. (2013) 'Osiris chez Hérodote', in L. Coulon, P. Giovannell-Jouanna and F. Kimmel-Clauzet (eds) *Hérodote et l'Égypte: regards croisés sur le livre II de l'enquête d'Hérodote*, Lyons, 167–90
Daressy, G. (1905–6) *Statues de divinités*, Catalogue général des antiquités du Musée du Caire nos 38001–39384, Cairo
Derchain, P. (1965) *Le Papyrus Salt 825 (B.M. 10051), rituel pour la conservation de la vie en Égypte*, Brussels
Dunand, F. (1986) 'Les associations dionysiaques au service du pouvoir lagide (IIIe s. av. J.-C.)', in *L'Association dionysiaque dans les sociétés anciennes*, Collection de l'École française de Rome 89, Rome, 85–103
Fabre, D. (2008b) 'Cults and rituals', in Goddio and Fabre 2008, 138–82
Frontisi-Ducroux, F. (1991) *Le Dieu-masqué. Une figure du Dionysos d'Athènes*, Paris and Rome
Goddio, F. (2010) 'Geophysical survey in the submerged Canopic region', in Robinson and Wilson 2010, 3–9
Goddio, F. (2015) 'The sacred topography of Thonis-Heracleion', in Robinson and Goddio 2015, 15–54
Goddio, F. and Fabre, D. (2008) *Egypt's Sunken Treasures*, Munich
Goddio, F. and Fabre, D. (2015) *Osiris, the Submerged Mysteries of Egypt*, Paris
Goyon, J.-Cl. (2013) 'Thèbes: Khonsou, Thot et la monarchie pharaonique après la Troisième Période de Transition. La fête de Thot du 19 du premier mois de l'année et les rites de confirmation du pouvoir royal à Karnak, Edfou et Philae (I)', in C. Thiers (ed.), *Documents de Théologies Thébaines Tardives (D3T 2)*, Montpellier, 33–93

Heinz, S. (2013) 'The statuettes and amulets of Thonis-Heracleion', Vols I and II, DPhil thesis, University of Oxford
Karageorghis, V. (1984) 'Dionysiaca and erotica from Cyprus', *Report of the Department of Antiquities Cyprus*, 214–20
Lavier, M.-C. (1989) 'Les mystères d'Osiris à Abydos d'après les stèles du Moyen Empire et du Nouvel Empire', in S. Schoske (ed.), *Akten des vierten internationalen Ägyptologen-Kongresses München 1985*, Studien zur altägyptischen Kultur Beihefte 3, Hamburg, 289–95
Lavier, M.-C. (1998) 'Les fêtes d'Osiris à Abydos au Moyen Empire et au Nouvel Empire', *Égypte, Afrique et Orient* 10, 27–33
Martín-Hernández, R. (2013) 'Herodotus' Egyptian Dionysos. A comparative perspective', in A. Bernabé, M. Herrero de Jáuregui, A. I. Jiménez San Cristóbal, R. Martín Hernández (eds), *Redefining Dionysos. MythosEikonPoiesis* Bd 5, Berlin and Boston, 250–61
Parker, R. (2005) *Polytheism and Society in Athens*, Oxford
Quack, J. F. (2000–1) 'Die rituelle Erneuerung der Osirisfiguren', Die Welt des Orients 31, 5–18
Quack, J. F. (2006) 'Das Grab am Tempeldromos. Neue Deutungen zu einem spätzeitlichen Grabtyp', in K. Zybelius-Chen, H. W. Fischer-Elfert (eds), *Von reichliche ägyptischem Verstande, Festschrift für Waltraud Guglielmi*, Wiesbaden 113–132
Rice, E. E. (1983) *The Grand Procession of Ptolemy Philadelphus*, Oxford
Robinson, D. and Goddio, F. (eds) (2015) *Thonis-Heracleion in Context*, Oxford Centre for Maritime Archaeology, Monograph 8, Oxford
Robinson, D. and Wilson, A. (eds) (2010) *Alexandria and the North–Western Delta*, Oxford Centre for Maritime Archaeology Monographs 5, Oxford
Thiers, C. (2009) *La Stèle de Ptolémée VIII Évergète II à Héracléion*, Underwater Archaeology in the Canopic Region in Egypt, Oxford Centre for Maritime Archaeology Monograph 4, Oxford
Thomas, R. (2013–15a) 'Egyptian Late Period figures in terracotta and limestone', in Villing et al. 2013–15 [http://www.britishmuseum.org/research/online_research_catalogues/ng/naukratis_greeks_in_egypt/material_culture_of_naukratis/late_period_figures.aspx]
Thomas, R. I. and Villing, A. (forthcoming) 'New fieldwork at Naukratis/Kom Ge'if, 2015', *ASAE*
Thompson, D. J. (2000) 'Philadelphus' procession: Dynastic power in a Mediterranean context', in L. Mooren (ed.), *Politics, Administration and Society in the Hellenistic and Roman World*, Studia Hellenistica 36, Leuven, 365–88
Vandier, J. (1961) *Le Papyrus Jumilhac*, Paris
Villing, A. and Schlotzhauer, U. (eds) (2006), *Naukratis: Greek Diversity in Egypt. Studies on Greek Pottery and Exchange in the Eastern Mediterranean*, British Museum Research Publication 162, London

Villing, A., Bergeron, M., Bourogiannis, G., Johnstone, A., Leclère, F., Masson, A. and Thomas, R. (2013–15) *Naukratis: Greeks in Egypt*, British Museum Online Research Catalogue. [www.britishmuseum.org/naukratis]
Yoyotte, J. (2010) 'Osiris dans la région d'Alexandrie', in L. Coulon (ed.), *Le culte d'Osiris au Ier millénaire av. J.-C.: Découvertes et travaux récents*, BdÉ 153, Cairo, 33–38

Selected references for objects featured in Chapter 4

p. 151 Standing statue of Osiris
von Bomhard, A. S. (2015d) 'Statue of Osiris' in Goddio and Fabre 2015, 60; Cauville, S. (1983) *La théologie d'Osiris à Edfou*, BdE 91, Cairo; Daressy 1905–6, 66–67, pl. XII; De Meulenaere, H. and Bothmer, B. V. (1969) 'Une tête d'Osiris du Musée du Louvre', *Kémi* 19, 9–16, fig. 12; El-Damaty, M. (2002) 'Statue of Osiris', in E. Hornung and B. M. Bryan (eds), *The Quest for Immortality, Treasures of Ancient Egypt*, Washington and Copenhagen, 169, no. 78.

p. 153 Isis and Osiris seated
Berlandini, J. (2015) 'Sitting statues of Osiris and Isis', in Goddio and Fabre 2015, 8–9, 184; Daressy (1905–6); El-Damaty, M. (2002a) 'Statue of Osiris', in E. Hornung and B. M. Bryan (eds), *The Quest for Immortality, Treasures of Ancient Egypt*, Washington, Copenhagen, 169, no. 78; El-Damaty, M. (2002b) 'Statue of Isis', in E. Hornung and B. M. Bryan (eds), *The Quest for Immortality, Treasures of Ancient Egypt*, Washington, Copenhagen, 170, no. 79; Perdu, O. (2013) 'L'Isis de Ptahirdis retrouvée', *RdE* 66, 93–133; Saleh, M. and Sourouzian, H. (1987) *Musée égyptien du Caire*, Mayence; Yoyotte, J. (1972) 'Petoubastis III', *RdE* 24, 216–23.

p. 154 Statuette of Isis holding Osiris
Berlandini-Keller, J. (2015a) 'Standing pharaoh with a *kheprech* crown', in Goddio and Fabre 2015, 86–87; Berlandini-Keller, J. (2015b) 'Statuette of Isis holding the Osirian figurine' in Goddio and Fabre 2015, 150–51; Berlandini-Keller, J. (forthcoming), '"La déesse au gisant", une enquête: de l'héliopolitaine-tentyrite Hathor-Nebethetepet à Isis en ses avatars de Selkis, Hededit el Ouhât', Cauville, S. (1997a); Cauville (1997b) Vol. 2. BdE 118; Daressy (1905–6), 218, pl. 44, no. 38 867; De Meulenaere, H. (2004) 'Sculptures dorées d'Abydos', *CdE* 79, 157–58, 81–88; Favard-Meeks, C. and Meeks, D. (2010) 'Les corps osiriens: Du *Papyrus du delta* au temple de Behbeit', in L. Coulon (ed.), *Le culte d'Osiris au Ier millénaire av. J.-C.: Découvertes et travaux récents*, BdE 153, Cairo, 39–48; Labrique, F. (2007) 'Ayn el-Mouftella: Osiris dans le Château de l'Or (Mission IFAO à Bahariya, 2002–2004)', in C. Cardin and J.-C. Goyon (eds), *Actes du Neuvième Congrès international des égyptologues*, OLA 150, Louvain, 1061–70; Mariette, A. (1880) *Catalogue général des monuments d'Abydos*, Paris, 15, no. 79.

p. 155 Cult statue of Osiris lying on a leonine bed, with Isis in the form of a kite
Amelineau, É. (1899) *Le tombeau d'Osiris*, Paris; Barucq, A. and Daumas, F. (1980) *Hymnes et prières de l'Égypte ancienne*, Paris; Berlandini-Keller, J. (2015) 'Cult statue of Osiris-Onnophris on a leonine bed, with Isis in a form of a bird of prey' in Goddio and Fabre 2015, 48–50; Cauville 1997b; Desroches-Noblecourt, C. (1953) '"Concubines du mort" et mères de famille au Moyen Empire. À propos d'une supplique pour une naissance', *BIFAO* 53, 7–47; Effland, A. (2013) 'Bis auf den heutigen Tag begab sich kein Mensch ... Umm el-Qa'ab', in I. Gerlach and D. Raue (eds), *Sanktuar und Ritual, Heilige Pfätze im archäologischen Befund*, 75–82; Effland, U. (2008) 'Das Gottesgrab. Der Gott Osiris in Umm el-Qaab/Abydos', *Sokar* 16, 6–17; Effland, U. (2013) 'Das Grab des Gottes Osiris in Umm el-Qa'ab/Abydos', in I. Gerlach and D. Raue (eds), *Sanktuar and Ritual, Heilige Pfätze im archäologischen Befund*, 321–30; Forgeau, A. (2010) *Horus-fils-d'Isis, la jeunesse d'un dieu*, BdE 150, Cairo.; Lavier 1989; Lavier 1998; Leahy, A. (1977) 'The Osiris "bed" reconsidered', *Orientalia* 46 (4), 424–34, pls 26–29; Moret, A. (1931) 'La légende d'Osiris à l'époque thébaine d'après l'hymne à Osiris du Louvre', *BIFAO* 30, 725–50; O'Connor, D. (2011) *Abydos, Egypt's First Pharaohs and the Cult of Osiris*, London.

p. 156 Statue of Osiris awakened
Assmann, J. (1977) *Das Grab der Mutirdis, Grabung im Asasif 1963–1970*, VI, Archäologische Veröffentlichun-gen 13, Mainz; Berlandini-Keller, J. (2002) 'Le "double-chaouabti gisant" des princes Ramsès et Khâemouaset', *RdE* 53, 5–59; Berlandini-Keller, J. (2015) 'Statuary of a wrapped "awakened" Osiris', in Goddio and Fabre 2015, 135–37; Cauville 1997b, Vol. 2, BdE 118; Daressy 1905–6, 114, no 38424, pl. 23; Favard-Meeks, C. (2009) 'Les couronnes d'Andjéty et le temple de Behbeit-el-Hagara', in I. Régen and F. Servajean (eds), *Verba manent*, CENIM 2, 137–43; Favard-Meeks, C. and Meeks, D. (2010) 'Les corps osiriens: Du Papyrus du Delta au temple de Behbeit', in L. Coulon (ed.), *Le culte d'Osiris au Ier millénaire av. J.-C. Découvertes et travaux récents, Actes de la table ronde internationale tenue à Lyon*, BdE 153, 39–48; Fazzini, R. (2002) 'Osiris resurrecting', in E. Hornung and B. M. Bryan (eds), *The Quest for Immortality, Treasures of Ancient Egypt*, Washington, Copenhagen, 177, no. 85; Josephson, J. (1992) 'Royal sculpture of the later Twenty-sixth Dynasty', *MDAIK* 48, 93–97; Koemoth, P. (2009) *Osiris-Mrjtj (le) Bien-Aimé*, Geneva; Mariette, A. (1872) *Monuments divers recueillis en Égypte et en Nubie*, Paris, 11–12, pl. 41; Mysliwiec, K. (1988) *Royal Portraiture of the Dynasties 21–30*, Mayence; Spencer, N. (2006) *A Naos of Nekhthorheb from Bubastis, Religious Iconography and Temple Building in the 30th Dynasty*, London; Vassilieva, O. (2010) 'Cairo statue of resurrecting Osiris (CG 38424), and related monuments', *Cultural Heritage of Egypt and Christian Orient* 5, 67–96.

p. 159 Stele of Horus
Berlandini-Keller, J. (2015) 'Stela of Horus on the crocodiles, with a receptacle in its base' in Goddio and Fabre 2015, 42–43, 170–71; Cauville 1997a; Cauville 1997b; Daressy, G. (1903) *Textes et dessins magiques*, Catalogue général des antiquités égyptiennes du Musée du Caire nos 9401–9449, Cairo; Gasse, A. (2004) *Stèles d'Horus sur les crocodiles*, Paris, 20–25, 171–73; Goyon, J.-C. (1981) 'L'eau dans la médecine pharaonique et copte', in P. Sanlaville and J. Métral (eds), *L'homme et l'eau en Méditerranée et au Proche Orient*, Séminaire de recherche 1979–1980, Lyon, 143–50; von Känel, F. (1984) *Les prêtres-ouab de Sekhmet, Les conjurateurs de Serket*, Bibliothèque de l'École pratique des hautes études 87, Paris; Koenig, Y. (1994) 'L'eau et la magie', in B. Menu (ed.), *Les problèmes institutionnels de l'eau en Égypte ancienne et dans l'Antiquité Méditerranéenne*, Cairo, 239–48; Lacau, P. (1922) 'Les statues "guérisseuses" dans l'ancienne Égypte', *Monuments Piot* 25 (1), 189–209; Magnanini, P. (1973) *Le Iscrizioni Fenicie dell'Oriente. Testi, Traduzioni, Glossari*, Istituto dei Studi del Vicino Oriente, Università di Roma, Rome; Ranke, H. (1935) *Die Ägyptischen Personennamen I, Verzeichnis der Namen*, Glückstadt; Rouffet, F. (2012) '*Hk3w, 3hw* et *md.t*, éléments essentiels d'un rituel égyptien', in A. Gasse (ed.), *Et in Aegypto et ad Aegyptum*, CENIM 5, Montpellier; Sternberg-el-Hotabi, H. (1999) *Untersuchungen zur Überlieferungsgeschichte der Horusstelen 1–2*, Ägyptische Abhandlungen 62, Wiesbaden; Zivie-Coche, C. (2003) 'Religion de l'Égypte ancienne', *Annuaire de l'École pratique des hautes études* 112, 135–43.

p. 160 Votive Horus falcon
Aubert, J. and Aubert, L. (2001) *Bronzes et or Égyptiens*, Paris, 234–35; Masson, A. (2015) 'Cult and trade. A reflection on Egyptian metal offerings from Naukratis', in Robinson and Goddio 2015, 71–88.

p. 161 Bead representing the eye of Horus
Aufrère, S. (2015a) 'Au pays de l'Oeil d'Horus et de l'Oeil d'Osiris ou l'Égypte comme regard du faucon divin', in M. Massiera, B. Mathieu and F. Rouffet (eds), *Taming the Wild*, CENIM 11, 31–47; Bulsink, M. (2015) *Egyptian Gold Jewellery*, Turnhout; Müller-Winckler, C. (1985) 'Udjatauge', *LÄ* 6, 824–26; Museo Civico Archeologico Bologna, Inventory no. MCA-EGI-Pal_0401 with references; Stolz, Y. (2008) 'Bead in the shape of an Eye of Horus or wedjat', in F. Goddio and D. Fabre (eds), *Trésors engloutis d'Égypte*, Paris, 316; Vernier, E. (1927) *Bijoux et orfèvrerie*, Catalogue general des antiquités égyptiennes du Musée du Caire, nos 52001–53855, Cairo.

p. 163 Osiris amulet and Libation ewer
Andrews, C. (1994) *Amulets of Ancient Egypt*, London; Goyon, G. (2004) *La découverte des trésors de Tanis*, Paris; Hope, C. A. (1989) *Gold of the Pharaohs: An Exhibition Provided by the Egyptian Antiquities Organisation*, Museum of Victoria, Queensland Art Gallery [Melbourne]; O'Connor, D. (2009) *Abydos: Egypt's First Pharaohs and the Cult of Osiris*, London.

p. 164 Osiris stele
Aufrère, S. (1999) 'Les végétaux sacrés de l'Égypte ancienne d'après les listes géographiques', in S. Aufrère (ed), *Encyclopédie religieuse de l'Univers végétal, Croyances phytoreligieuses de l'Égypte ancienne* I, Orientalia Monspeliensia X, Montpellier, 121–207; Aufrère, S. (2005b) 'A propos d'une stèle du Musée du Caire', *Encyclopédie religieuse de l'Univers végétal, Croyances phytoreligieuses de l'Égypte ancienne* III, Orientalia Monspeliensia XV, Montpellier, 307–12; Aufrère, S. (2013) 'Sacred trees and sacred snakes in priestly lists of Egyptian districts at the Graeco-Roman times: An overview", in M. Bauks and M. F. Meyer (eds), *Zur Kulturgeschichte der Botanik*, Trier, 10–35; Aufrère, S. (2015b) 'Stele of the Osirian mound', in Goddio and Fabre 2015, 154–55; Barguet 1962; Coulon, L., Leclère, F. and Marchand, S. (1995) '"Catacombes" osiriennes de Ptolémée IV à Karnak', *Cahiers de Karnak* 10, 205–51; Leclère, F. and Coulon, L. (1998) 'La nécropole osirienne de la "Grande Place" à Karnak', in C. Eyre (ed.), *Proceedings of the Seventh International Congress of Egyptologists*, OLA 82, Leuven, 649–59; Leitz, C. (2014) *Die Gaumonographien in Edfu und ihre Papyrusvarianten: ein überregionaler Kanon kultischen Wissens im spätzeitlichen Ägypten*, Wiesbaden.

p. 165 Head of a priest
Bianchi, R. S. (1988) 'The pharaonic art of Ptolemaic Egypt', in R. Fazzini and R. S. Bianchi (eds), *Cleopatra's Egypt. Age of the Ptolemies*, Brooklyn, 55–80; Goyon, J.-C. (1988) 'Ptolemaic Egypt: Priests and the traditional religion', in R. Fazzini and R. S. Bianchi (eds), *Cleopatra's Egypt. Age of the Ptolemies*, Brooklyn, 29–40; Hölbl, G. (2001) *A History of the Ptolemaic Empire*, London; Sauneron, S. (2000) *The Priests of Ancient Egypt*, Ithaca, NY (new edn).

p. 168 Making the figures of Osiris *vegetans*
Cauville, S. (1997b) *Le temple de Dendara, Les chapelles osiriennes*, vol. 1. Bibliothèque d'Étude 117, transcription et traduction, Le Caire; Chassinat, É. (1966) *Le mystère d'Osiris au mois de Khoiak*, Le Caire.

p. 169 Osiris *vegetans* figure in a falcon-headed coffin
Centrone, M. C. (2009) *Egyptian Corn-mummies: A Class of Religious Artefacts Catalogued and Systematically Analyzed*, Saarbrücken; Coulon, L., Leclère, F., and Marchand, S., (1995) '"Catacombes" osiriennes de Ptolémée IV à Karnak. Rapport préliminaire de la campagne de fouilles 1993', *Cahier de Karnak* 10, 205–51; Raven, M. J. (1982) 'Corn-mummies', *Oudheidkundige Mededelingen vit het Rijksmuseum van Oudheden* 63, 7–38.

p. 170 Osiris brick
Tooley, A. M. J. (1996) 'Osiris bricks', *JEA* 82, 167–79.

p. 171 'Garden tank' under excavation
Cauville 1997b, Vol. 1, BdE 117, 15–16; Cauville, S. (1981) 'Chentayt et Merkhetes, des avatars d'Isis et Nephthys', *BIFAO* 81, 21–40; Chassinat, É. (1966) *Le mystère d'Osiris au mois de Khoiak*, Cairo, 53–54; Goddio, F. (2015) 'The sacred topography of Thonis-Heracleion', in Robinson

and Goddio 2015, 15–54, and for Osirian rites linked to royal power, 34–35; Yoyotte, J. (2008f) 'Vat' in Goddio and Fabre 2008, 313; Yoyotte, J. (2013) *Histoire, géographie et religion de l'Égypte ancienne, Opera selecta,* Textes édités et indexés par I. Guermeur, OLA 224, Leuven, 385–92, 397–400, 403–6.

p. 172 Shallow dish (*phiale*)
Goddio, F. (2007), *The Topography and Excavation of Heracleion-Thonis and East Canopus (1996–2006).* Underwater Archaeology in the Canopic Region in Egypt, Oxford Centre for Maritime Archaeology 1, Oxford, 92–93, figs 3.40–3.41, 271–72; Goddio, F. (2015) 'The sacred topography of Thonis-Heracleion', in Robinson and Goddio 2015, 15–54; Kiss, Z. (2008h). 'Phiale' in Goddio and Fabre 2008, 313–14; Robinson, Z. (2008) 'The metalware from the sanctuary complex at Heracleion-Thonis', DPhil thesis, University of Oxford.

p. 173 Pail (*situla*)
von Bissing, F. W. (1901) *Metallgefässe,* Catalogue général des antiquités égyptiennes du Musée du Caire nos 3426–3587, Vienne, 9–31; Cauville 1997b, Vol. 1, BdE 117; Chassinat 1966, 54, 211–13; Goddio, F. (2015) 'The sacred topography of Thonis-Heracleion', in Robinson and Goddio 2015, 15–54; Goddio and Fabre 2015; Green, C. (1987) *The Temple Furniture from the Sacred Animal Necropolis at North Saqqâra,* London, 66–115; Grenier, J.-C. (2002) *Les bronzes du Museo Gregoriano Egizio,* Vatican City, 197–208, pls 56–57; Lichtheim, M. (1947) 'Situla no, 11395 and some remarks on Egyptian situlae', *JNES* 6(3), 169–79; Robinson, Z. (2008) 'The metalware from the sanctuary-complex at Heracleion-Thonis', PhD thesis, University of Oxford.

p. 174 The Osiris-Sokar figure: sacred recipes
Aufrère, S. H. (1991) *L'univers minéral dans la pensée égyptienne,* Bibliothèque d'Étude 105, Le Caire; Aufrère, S. H. (1998) 'Parfums et onguents liturgiques du Laboratoire d'Edfou: compositions, codes végétaux et minéraux dans l'Égypte ancienne', in R. Gyselen (ed.), *Parfums d'Orient,* Res Orientales 11, Bures-sur-Yvette, 29–64; Aufrère, S. H. (2005) 'Parfums et onguent liturgiques. Présentation des recettes d'Edfou', in S. H. Aufrère, *Encyclopédie religieuse de l'Univers végétal,* Orientalia Monspeliensia 16, Montpellier, 213–262.; Aufrère, S. H. (2007) *Thoth, Hermès l'Égyptien. De l'infiniment grand à l'infiniment petit,* Paris; Chassinat, É. (1966) *Le mystère d'Osiris au mois de Khoiak,* Le Caire; Derchain, P. (1965) *Le Papyrus Salt 825 (B.M. 10051), rituel pour la conservation de la vie en Égypte,* Bruxelles; Vandier J. (1961) *Le Papyrus Jumilhac,* Paris.

p. 175 Ladle (*simpulum*) with *wedjat*-eye
Bénazeth, D. (1992) *L'art du métal au début de l'ère chrétienne,* Paris, 71; Cauville 1997b, Vol. 1, BdE 117, 1, 20; Chassinat 1966, 59–60, pl. 7, col. 118; Chassinat 1968, 776; Goddio, F. (2015) 'The sacred topography of Thonis-Heracleion', in Robinson and Goddio 2015, 15–54; deposition of *simpula*, 29–33; Goddio and Fabre 2015, 38–39; Hayes, J. W. (1984) *Greek, Roman and*

Related Metalware in the Royal Ontario Museum, Toronto, 61 no. 9; Mariette, A. (1873) *Denderah, tome 4, planches,* Paris, pl. 38, col. 118; Robinson, Z, (2008) 'The metalware from the sanctuary-complex at Heracleion-Thonis', DPhil thesis, University of Oxford, 60–61, 71.

p. 176 Incense burner and shovel
Goddio, F. (2007) *The Topography and Excavation of Heracleion-Thonis and East Canopus (1996–2006).* Underwater Archaeology in the Canopic Region in Egypt, Oxford Centre for Maritime Archaeology 1, Oxford, 99; Kiss, Z. (2008i) 'Incense burner', in Goddio and Fabre 2008, 333; Kiss, Z. (2008j) 'Large bronze brazier' in Goddio and Fabre 2008, 333; Ragheb, A. (2008) 'Shovel', in Goddio and Fabre 2008, 335; Robinson, Z. (2008) 'The metalware from the sanctuary-complex at Heracleion-Thonis', DPhil thesis, University of Oxford, 205 fig. 76 and 219 fig. 82, 221–22, 206–7.

p. 177 Fragment of an incense burner
Chassinat 1968; Green, C. I. (1987) *The temple furniture from the sacred animal necropolis at North Saqqâra 1964–1976,* MEES 35, London; Moret, A. (1902) *Le rituel du culte divin journalier en Egypte,* Paris; Seipel, W. (1989) Ägypten: Götter, Gräber und die Kunst. 4000 Jahre Jenseitsglaube, Vol. 1 Linz, 186, no. 151.

p. 178 Bronze box
von Bomhard, A. S. (2014a) 'Heracles and the Hone: about a foundation deposit from the temple of Thonis-Heracleion', *JEA* 100, 339–55; Goddio, F. (2015) 'The sacred topography of Thonis-Heracleion', in Robinson and Goddio 2015, 15–54.

p. 179 Lamp
Fabre, D. and Kiss, Z. (2008k) 'Lamp', in Goddio and Fabre 2008, 332; Goddio, F. (2007) *The Topography and Excavation of Heracleion-Thonis and East Canopus (1996–2006),* Oxford Centre for Maritime Archaeology 1, Oxford, 124–25; Goddio, F. (2015) 'The sacred topography of Thonis-Heracleion' in Robinson and Goddio 2015, 15–54; Grenier, J.-C. (2002) *Les bronzes du Museo Gregoriano Egizio,* Città del Vaticano; Robinson, Z. (2008) 'The metalware from the sanctuary-complex at Heracleion-Thonis', DPhil thesis, University of Oxford.

p. 181 Pectoral
Goyon, G. (2004) *La découverte des trésors de Tanis,* Paris, 2004; Hope, C. A. (1989) *Gold of the Pharaohs: An Exhibition Provided by the Egyptian Antiquities Organisation,* Museum of Victoria, Queensland Art Gallery [Melbourne]; Hornung, E. and B. M. Bryan (eds) (2002) *The Quest for Immortality. Treasures of Ancient Egypt,* Washington, D.C. National Gallery of Art; Stierlin, H. (1997) *The Gold of the Pharaohs,* Paris.

p. 183 Lead votive barques
Fabre, D. (2008b), 'Cults and rituals', Goddio and Fabre 2008, 145–47; Heinz, S. (2013) *The Statuettes and Amulets of Thonis-Heracleion,* Vols I and II, DPhil thesis, University of Oxford, Vol. I, 73–77.

p. 184 Figurehead
Abitz, F. (1979) *Statuetten in Schreinen als Grabbeigaben in den ägyptischen Königsgräbern der 18. und 19. Dynastie,* Ägyptologische Abhandlungen 35, Wiesbaden; von Bomhard, A. S. (2012) *The Decree of Sais,* Underwater Archaeology in the Canopic Region in Egypt, Oxford Centre for Maritime Archaeology 7, Oxford; von Bomhard, A. S. (2014b) 'Le début du Livre de Nout', *ENM* 7, 79–123; Germond, P. (2002-3) 'En marge du bestiaire: Un drôle de canard', *Bulletin de la Société d'Égyptologie de Genève* 25, 75–94; Goddio and Fabre 2015; Graindorge, C. (1996) 'La quête de la lumière au mois de Khoiak: Une histoire d'oies', *JEA* 82, 83–105; Jequier, G. (1921) *Les frises d'objets des sarcophages du Moyen Empire,* Mémoires publiés par les membres de l'Institut français d'archéologie orientale du Caire 47, Cairo; Petrie, W.M.F. (1920) *Prehistoric Egypt,* British School of Archaeology and Egyptian Research Account 31, London; Vandier d'Abbadie, J. (1973) 'Le cygne dans l'Égypte ancienne', *RdE* 25, 35–49; van de Walle, B. (1984) 'Schwan', *LÄ* 5, 755–57.

p. 185 Greek-style lamps from Athens and Alexandria
Bailey, D. (1988) *A Catalogue of the Lamps in the British Museum,* Vol. 3. London; Thomas, R. I. (2013–15e) 'Lamps in terracotta and bronze', in Villing et al. 2013–15.

p. 187 Anubis and Horus emblems
Baines 1985, 41–43; Goddio and Fabre 2015, 118.

p. 189 Offering dishes
Goddio, F. (2007) *The Topography and Excavation of Heracleion-Thonis and East Canopus (1996–2006).* Underwater Archaeology in the Canopic Region in Egypt, Oxford Centre for Maritime Archaeology 1, Oxford, 105; Lacau, P. and Lauer, J. Ph. (1959) *La pyramide à degrés IV, Inscriptions gravées sur les vases,* Cairo; du Mesnil du Buisson, R. (1935) *Les noms et signes égyptiens désignant des vases ou objets similaires,* Paris, 64–65, 93–94.

p. 190 *Sistrum* (rattle)
Duquesne, T. (2002) 'Sistrum', in E. Hornung and B.M. Bryan (eds), *The Quest for Immortality, Treasures of Ancient Egypt,* Washington, Copenhagen, 2002, 117, no. 33; Ziegler, C. (1979) *Catalogue des instruments de musique égyptiens, catalogue du Musée du Louvre, Département des Antiquités Égyptiennes,* Paris, 31–62; Ziegler, C. (1984) 'Sistrum', *LÄ* 5, cols 959–63.

p. 192 Statuettes of Osiris
Fabre, D. (2008) 'Statuettes of Osiris' in Goddio and Fabre 2008, 67, 148, 283; Goddio, F. (2015) 'The sacred topography of Thonis-Heracleion', in Robinson and Goddio 2015, 15–54; Goddio and Fabre 2015; Heinz, S. (2013) 'The statuettes and amulets of Thonis-Heracleion', Vols I and II, D.Phil thesis, University of Oxford, Vol. I 37–42, Vol. II 30–43.

p. 197 Divine beard from a statue
Davies, S. (2007) 'Bronzes from the sacred animal necropolis at North Saqqara', in H. Marsha and

D. Schorsch (eds), *Gifts for the Gods: Images from Egyptian Temples,* Metropolitan Museum of Art. New York, 174–87; Goddio and Fabre 2008, 2nd revised edition, no. 211; Weiss, K. (2012) *Ägyptische Tier– und Götterbronzen aus Unterägypten: Untersuchungen zu Typus, Ikonographie und Funktion sowie der Bedeutung innerhalb der Kulturkontakte zu Griechenland,* Ägypten und Altes Testament 81, Wiesbaden, 39, fig. 5.1; Wuttmann, M., L. Coulon, and F. Gombert (2008) 'An assemblage of bronze statuettes in a cult context: The temple of 'Ayn Manawir (Kharga Oasis)', in M. Hill and D. Schorsch (eds), *Offrandes aux dieux d'Égypte. Catalogue de l'exposition à la Fondation P. Gianadda.* Martigny, Suisse, Lausanne, 167–73.

p. 199 Statuettes of Isis
von Bomhard, A. S. (2014a) 'Heracles and the Hone: About a foundation deposit from the temple of Thonis-Heracleion', *JEA* 100, 339–55; Fabre, D. (2008d) 'Heracleion-Thonis: customs station and Emporion', in F. Goddio and D. Fabre (eds), *Egypt's Sunken Treasures,* Munich, 218–234; Goddio, F. (2015) 'The sacred topography of Thonis-Heracleion', in D. Robinson and F. Goddio (eds), *Heracleion in Context: The maritime economy of the Egyptian Late Period,* Oxford Centre for Maritime Archaeology 8, Oxford, 15–54; Goddio, F. and Fabre, D. (2008) *Egypt's Sunken Treasures,* Munich; Heinz, S. (2013) 'The Statuettes and amulets of Thonis-Heracleion', Vols I and II, DPhil thesis, University of Oxford.

p. 200 Statuettes of Harpokrates
von Bomhard, A. S. (2014a) 'Heracles and the Hone: About a foundation deposit from the temple of Thonis-Heracleion', *JEA* 100, 339–55; Fabre, D. (2008e) 'Statuettes of Harpokrates', in Goddio and Fabre 2008, 318, 339; Goddio, F. (2015) 'The sacred topography of Thonis-Heracleion', in Robinson and Goddio 2015, 15–54; Goddio and Fabre 2008; Heinz, S. (2013) 'The statuettes and amulets of Thonis-Heracleion', Vols I and II, D.Phil thesis, University of Oxford; Malaise, M. (1991) 'Harpocrate au pot', in U. Verhoeven and E. Graefe, *Religion und Philosophie im alten Ägypten, Festgabe für Philippe Derchain,* OLA 39, 219–32; Yoyotte J. and Chuvin P. (1988) 'Le Zeus Casios de Péluse à Tivoli, une hypothèse', *BIFAO* 88, 165–80, pls 14–17.

p. 201 Small container with offering
Goddio, F. (2007) *The Topography and Excavation of Heracleion-Thonis and East Canopus (1996–2006).* Underwater Archaeology in the Canopic Region in Egypt, Oxford Centre for Maritime Archaeology 1, Oxford; Goddio, F. (2015) 'The sacred topography of Thonis-Heracleion', in Robinson and Goddio 2015, 15–54; see 33 and n. 153; Goddio and Fabre 2008, 193, 341; Quack, J. F. (2000–1) 'Die rituelle Erneuerung der Osirisfigurinen', *Die Welt des Orients* 31, 5–18.

p. 203 Offering table
Baines 1985; Goddio, F. (2015) 'The sacred topography of Thonis-Heracleion', in Robinson and Goddio 2015, 15–54; Goddio and Fabre 2015; Heinz, S. (2013), 'The statuettes and amulets of Thonis-Heracleion', Vols I and II, D.Phil thesis,

University of Oxford; Libonati, E. (2008) 'Offering table' in Goddio and Fabre 2008, 297.

p. 203 Model of an offering table
Goddio and Fabre 2015; Masson, A. (2013–15) 'Bronze votive offerings', in Villing et al. 2013–15; Teeter, E. (1994) 'Bronze votive offering tables', in D. P. Silverman (ed.), *For His Ka. Essays Offered in Memory of Klaus Baer*, Chicago, 255–65.

p. 204 Bes vase
Dasen, V. (1993) *Dwarfs in Ancient Egypt and Greece*, Oxford Monographs on Classical Archaeology, Oxford; Defernez, C. (2009) 'Les vases Bès à l'époque perse (Égypte-Levant), Essai de classification', in P. Briant and M. Chauveau (eds), *Organisation des pouvoirs et contacts culturels dans les pays de l'empire achéménide*, Persika 14, Paris, 153–215; Malaise, M. (2004) 'Bès et la famille isiaque', *CdE* 79, 266–92.

p. 204 Figure of Bes as a warrior
Bailey, D. (2008) *Catalogue of the Terracottas in the British Museum, Vol. 4: Ptolemaic and Roman Terracottas from Egypt*, London; Dasen, V. (1993) *Dwarfs in Ancient Egypt and Greece*, Oxford Monographs on Classical Archaeology, Oxford; Dunand, F. (1990) *Catalogue des terre cuites gréco-romaines d'Égypte: Musée du Louvre*, Paris; Thomas, R. (2013–15) 'Ptolemaic and Roman figures, models and coffin-fittings in terracotta', in Villing et al. 2013–15.

p. 206 Bes vase
Dasen, V. (1993) *Dwarfs in Ancient Egypt and Greece*, Oxford Monographs on Classical Archaeology, Oxford; Defernez, C. (2011) 'Four Bes vases from Tell el-Herr (North-Sinai): Analytical description and correlation with the goldsmith's art of Achaemenid tradition', in D. Aston, B. Bader, C. Gallorini, P. Nicholson, and S. Buckingham (eds), *Under the Potter's Tree. Studies in Ancient Egypt Presented to Janine Bourriau on the Occasion of her 70th Birthday*, OLA 204, 287–323.

p. 206 Vase fragment depicting Bes, Serapis and Isis
Bianchi, R., R. A. Fazzini and J. Quagebeur (eds) (1988) *Cleopatra's Egypt. Age of the Ptolemies*, Brooklyn; Borgeaud, Ph., and Y. Volokhine (2000) 'La formation de la légende de Sarapis: une approche transculturelle', *Archiv für Religionsgeschichte* 2, 37–76; Legras, B. (2014) 'Sarapis, Isis et le pouvoir lagide', in L. Bricault and M. J. Versluys (eds), *Power, Politics and the Cults of Isis*, Leiden, 95–115; Stambaugh, J. E. (1972) *Sarapis Under the Early Ptolemies*, Leiden.

p. 207 Statue of Taweret
Coulon, L. (2009) 'Un dieu mort florissant: Osiris à Karnak', *Religions et histoire* 29, 44–49; Payraudeau, F. (forthcoming) 'The chapel of Osiris Nebdjet/Padedankh in north-Karnak', *Cahiers de Karnak*; Pinch, G. (2004) *Egyptian Mythology: A Guide to the Gods, Goddesses, and Traditions of Ancient Egypt*, 2nd edn, Oxford, 142; Roeder, G. (1914) *Naos, CGC*, Leipzig, 106–9; Thiers, C. (2013) 'La chapelle d'Ipet la Grande

/ Époëris sur le parvis du temple de Louqsor. Relecture d'une stèle kouchite', in Chr. Thiers (ed.), *Documents de Théologies Thébaines Tardives (D3T 2)*, CENIM 8, 149–76; see 163–66 for birthplace of Osiris.

p. 209 Bust of Neilos, god of the Nile
Bakhoum, S. (1999) *Dieux égyptiens à Alexandrie sous les Antonins*, Paris; Görg, M. (1988) 'Neilos und Domitian. Ein Beitrag zur spätantiken Nilgott-Ikonographie', in M. Görg (ed.), *Religion im Erbe Ägyptens*, Ägypten und Altes Testament 14, Wiesbaden, 65–82; Jentel, M. O. (1992) 'Neilos', *Lexicon iconographicum mythologiae classicae* VI, 720–26; Kiss, Z. (2010) 'Le dieu Nil Hellénistique – A propos d'une sculpture de Canope', in Robinson and Wilson 2010, 211–18; Smith, R. R. R. (2008) 'As grey as the fertile riverbed, Father Nile', in Goddio and Fabre 2008, 80–83.

p. 211 Phallic representations of Horus-the-child (Harpokrates)
Thomas, R. I. (2013–15d) 'Stone and terracotta figures from Naukratis: An introduction', in Villing et al. 2013–15; Thomas, R. I. (2013–15a) 'Egyptian Late Period figures in terracotta and limestone', in Villing et al. 2013–15.

p. 212 Gilded and painted figure of Egyptian goddess, probably Hathor
Thomas, R. I. (2013–15a) 'Egyptian Late Period figures in terracotta and limestone', in Villing et al. 2013–15.

p. 212 Terracotta figure of Isis-Bubastis wearing festival dress
Bailey, D. M. (2008) *Catalogue of the Terracottas in the British Museum 4: Ptolemaic and Roman Terracottas from Egypt*, London; Thomas, R. I. (2013–15f) 'Ptolemaic and Roman figures, models and coffin-fittings in terracotta', in Villing et al. 2013–15.

p. 213 Plaque of Isis-Hathor standing within a shrine
Bailey, D. M. (2008) *Catalogue of the Terracottas in the British Museum 4: Ptolemaic and Roman Terracottas from Egypt*, London; Barrett, C. E. (2011) *Egyptianizing Figurines from Delos: A Study in Hellenistic Religion*, Leiden, 308–9; Redford, D. B., Sternberg-el-Hotabe, H. and Redford, S. (1991) 'Three seasons in Egypt: the first season of excavations at Mendes (1991)', *Journal of the Society for the Study of Egyptian Antiquities* 18, 1–79; Thomas, R. I. (2013–15a) 'Egyptian Late Period figures in terracotta and limestone', in Villing et al. 2013–15.

p. 214 East Greek *situla* with struggle between Apollo/Horus and Typhon/Seth
Leclère, F. and J. Spencer (2014) *Tell Dafana Reconsidered: The Archaeology of an Egyptian Frontier Town*, British Museum Research Publication 199, London; Petrie, W. M. F. (1888) *Tanis 2: Nebesheh (Am) and Defenneh (Tahpanhes)*, London; Villing, A. (2014) 'Situle à figures noires', in A. Coulié and M. Filimonos-Tsopotou, *Rhodes, une île grecque aux portes de l'Orient*, Paris, 296; Weber, S. (2012) 'Untersuchungen zur archaischen griechischen

Keramik aus anderen ägyptischen Fundorten', in U. Schlotzhauer and S. Weber, *Griechische Keramik des 7. und 6. Jhs. v. Chr. aus Naukratis und anderen Orten in Ägypten* (Archäologische Studien zu Naukratis III, ed. U. Höckmann), Mainz, 195–432. On the Contendings of Horus and Seth: Fairman, H. W. (1974) *The Triumph of Horus: An Ancient Egyptian Sacred Drama*, London; Moyer, I. S. (2011) *Egypt and the Limits of Hellenism*, Cambridge.

p. 215 Ritual bucket with Greek inscription on handle
Cox, Z. (2008) 'Situla with Greek inscription on handle', in Goddio and Fabre 2008, 328; Hayes, J. W. (1984) *Greek, Roman, and Related Metalware in the Royal Ontario Museum: A Catalogue*, Toronto; Jenkins, I. (1994) 'The masks of Dionysos/Pan-Osiris-Apis', *Jahrbuch des Deutschen Archäologischen Instituts* 109, 273–99; Robinson, Z. (2010) 'Living with metals in Hellenistic Egypt – New finds from Heracleion-Thonis', in Robinson and Wilson 2010, 219–31.

p. 217 Hermes relief
Smith, A. H. (1892) *Catalogue of Greek Sculpture in the British Museum*, London, no. 2205; Fuchs, W. (1959) *Die Vorbilder der neuattischen Reliefs*, Berlin, 171; Smyth, Captain W. H. (1851) *Aedes Hartwellianae: or, Notices of the manor and mansion of Hartwell*, London, 192–93; Zagdoun, M.-A. (1989) *La sculpture archaïsante dans l'art hellénistique et dans l'art romain du Haut-Empire*, Paris, 91–93 (for comparable archaizing reliefs of Hermes).

p. 218 Silver goblet
Adriani, A. (1939) *Le Goblet en argent des amours vendangeurs du muse d'Alexandrie*, Alexandria; Baratte, F. (1996) 'Dionysos en Chine: Remarques à propos de la coupe en argent de Beitan', *Art Asiatique* 51, 142–47; Boussac, M.-F. (1998) in M. Rausch (ed.), *La Gloire d'Alexandrie*, exhibition catalogue Petit Palais, Paris, 162, no. 104; Walker, S. and P. Higgs (eds) (2001) *Cleopatra of Egypt. From History to Myth*, British Museum exhibition catalogue, London, 91.

Chapter 5
Egypt and Rome
Adlington, W. and Gaselee, S. trans. (1924) *Apuleius The Golden Ass*. The Loeb Classical Library, London

Adriani, A. (1940) *Annuaire du Musée Gréco-Romain (1935–1939)*, Alexandria

Adriani, A. (1963–66) *Repertorio d'arte dell' Egitto greco-romano, Serie C*, Vols 1–2, Palermo

Alfano, C. (2001) 'Egyptian influences in Italy', in S. Walker and P. Higgs (eds), *Cleopatra of Egypt*, London, 276–91

Bagnall, R. S. (1993) *Egypt in Late Antiquity*, Princeton, NJ

Bagnall, R. and Rathbone, D. W. (2004) *Egypt from Alexander to the Early Christians. An Archaeological and Historical Guide*, Los Angeles and London

Beard, M., North, J. and Price, S. (1998) *Religions of Rome: Vol. 1, A History*, Cambridge

Cumont, F. (1911.) *The Oriental Religions in Roman Paganism*. Chicago

Dow, S. and Upson, F. S. (1944) 'The foot of Sarapis', *Hesperia* 13(1), 58–77

Goddio, F., Bernand, A., Bernand, É., Darwish, I., Kiss, Z. and Yoyotte, J. (1998) *Alexandria. The Submerged Royal Quarters*, London

Goddio, F. and Fabre, D. (eds) (2008) *Egypt's Sunken Treasures*, Munich

Goddio, F. and Fabre, D. (eds) (2015) *Osiris. Egypt's Sunken Mysteries*, Paris

Goodburn, R., Wright, R. P., Hassall, M. W. C. and Tomlin, R. S. O., (1976) 'Roman Britain in 1975', *Britannia* 7, 290–392

Grenier, J-C. (2008) *L'Osiris Antinoos*, CENIM 1, Montpellier

Guarducci, M. (1974) *Epigrafia Graeca* III, Rome

Hassan, F., El-Abbadi, M., Abdel-Fattah, A., and Seif el-Din, M. (2002) *Alexandria: Graeco-Roman Museum, a Thematic Guide*, Alexandria

Hill, D. K. (1946) 'Material on the cult of Sarapis', *Hesperia* 15(1), 60–72

Klotz, D. (2012) 'Caesar in the Temple of Amun: Egyptian temple construction and theology in Roman Thebes', *Monographies reine Elisabeth* 15

Lambert, R. (1984) *Beloved and God: The Story of Hadrian and Antinous*. New Jersey

McKenzie, J. (2007) *The Architecture of Alexandria and Egypt 300 BC–AD 700*, New Haven

Meadows, A. (2001) 'Sins of the fathers: The inheritance of Cleopatra, last queen of Egypt', in S. Walker and P. Higgs (eds), *Cleopatra of Egypt*, London, 22–31

Montserrat, D. (1998) 'Pilgrimage to the shrine of SS Cyrus and John at Menouthis in late Antiquity', in D. Frankfurter (ed.), *Pilgrimage and Holy space in late Antique Egypt*. Brill Leiden, 257–279

Naerebout, F. (2007) 'The temple at Ras el-Soda. Is it an Isis temple? Is it Greek, Roman, Egyptian, or neither? And so what?', in L. Bricault, P. G. P. Meyboom and M. J. Versluys (eds), *Nile into Tiber. Egypt in the Roman World. Proceedings of the IIIrd International Conference of Isis Studies*, Leiden, 506–54

O'Connell, E. R. (2015) 'Roman Egypt: Introduction' in Fluck, C., Helmecke, G. and O'Connell, E. R. (eds), *Egypt: Faith After the Pharaohs*, London

Petridou, G. (2009) 'Artemidi to ichnos: Divine feet and hereditary priesthood in Pisidian Pogla', *Anatolian Studies* 59, 81–93

Rendall, G. H. (trans.) (1998) *Minucius Felix Octavius*. The Loeb Classical Library, Bury St Edmonds

Tiradritti, F. (1997) *Iside: il mito, il mistero, la magia*, Milan

Versluys, M. J. (2007) 'Aegyptiaca Romana: The widening debate', in L. Bricault, P. G. P. Meyboom and M. J. Versluys (eds), *Nile into Tiber. Egypt in the Roman World. Proceedings of the IIIrd International Conference of Isis Studies*, Leiden, 1–10

Vout, C. (2005) 'Antinous, archaeology and history', *JRS* 95, 80–96

Williams, J. H. C. (2001) '"Spoiling the Egyptians": Octavian and Cleopatra', in S. Walker and P. Higgs (eds), *Cleopatra of Egypt*, London, 192–93

Selected references for objects featured in Chapter 5

p. 227 Roman relief of a Nile scene with two lovers, possibly Cleopatra VII and Mark Antony
Walker, S. and Higgs, P. (eds) (2001) *Cleopatra of Egypt*, London, 336, no. 356.

p. 228 Priest with Osiris-Canopus jar
Bianchi, R. (1988) *Cleopatra's Egypt: Age of the Ptolemies*, Brooklyn, 248–49 no. 136; Dunand, F. (1998) 'Priest bearing an 'Osiris-canopus' in his veiled hands', in Goddio et al. 1998, 189–94; Dunand, F. (2008) 'The fear of a forbidden contact – Priest with Osiris-Canopus', in Goddio and Fabre 2008, 160–62; Goddio, F. (2007) *The Topography and Excavation of Heracleion-Thonis and East Canopus (1996–2006)*, Oxford Centre for Maritime Archaeology Monograph 1, Oxford, 50–53; Goddio, F. (2008) 'Rediscovered sites', in Goddio and Fabre 2008, 26–48; Goddio, F. and Darwish, I. (1998) 'The topography of

the submerged royal quarters of the Eastern Harbour of Alexandria' in Goddio et al. 1998, 1–52; Kiss, Z. (1998) 'The sculptures', in Goddio et al. 1998, 169–88; Kiss, Z. (2008a) 'A jar bringing hope for eternal life, The Osiris-Canopus', in Goddio and Fabre 2008, 62–65; Libonati, E. (2010a) 'Hydreios statues from the IEASM excavations in Aboukir Bay', in Robinson, D. and Wilson, A. (eds), *Alexandria and the North-Western Delta*, Oxford Centre for Maritime Archaeology Monograph 5, Oxford 203–10; Libonati, E. (2010b) 'Egyptian statuary from the Aboukir Bay: Ptolemaic and Roman finds from Herakleion and Canopus', DPhil thesis, University of Oxford; Quack, J. F. (2003) 'Zum ägyptischen Kult im Iseum Campense in Rom', in C. Metzner-Nebelsick (ed.), *Rituale in der Vorgeschichte, Antike und Gegenwart. Studien zur vorderasiatischen, prähistorischen und klassischen Archäologie, Ägyptologie, alten Geschichte, Theologie und Religionswissenschaft. Interdisziplinäre Tagung vom 1.-2. Februar 2002 an der Freien Universität Berlin*, Rahden, 57–66.

pp. 232–33 Pair of sphinxes
Goddio, F. and Darwish, I. 1998 'The topography of the submerged royal quarters of the Eastern

Harbour of Alexandria', in Goddio et al. 1998, 41; Kiss, Z. (1998) 'The sculptures', in Goddio et al. 1998, 169, 173–74; Kiss, Z. (2008d) 'Sphinx', in Goddio and Fabre 2008, 356; Kiss, Z. (2008l) 'Sphinx (Ptolemy XII)', in Goddio and Fabre 2008, 357.

p. 234 Intaglio ring
Delatte, A. and Derchain, P. (1964) *Les intailles magiques gréco-égyptiennes*, Paris, 191–92, no. 254 bis; Goddio et al. 1998, 28–43; Philipp, H. (1986) *Mira et Magica*, Berlin, 54; Sandrin, P., Belov A. and Fabre, D. (2013) 'The Roman shipwreck of Antirhodos Island in the *Portus Magnus* of Alexandria, Egypt', *IJNA* 42(1), 44–59.

p. 234 Bust of Serapis
Bagnall and Rathbone 2004, 59–62; Hassan et al. 2002, 40–41; McKenzie 2007, 53–56, 195–203; Tiradritti 1997, 164, pl. IV.9–10.

p. 235 Bust of Isis in Roman style
Tiradritti 1997.

p. 237 Osiris-Canopus jars
Hassan et al. 2002, 108; Goddio and Fabre 2015, 158–59.

p. 238 Marble votive foot dedicated by Isidoros to Isis or Serapis
Adriani 1940, 136–38; Dow and Upson 1944; Goddio and Fabre 2015, 209; Guarducci 1974, 73–74; Hassan et al. 2002, 73; Hill 1946, 60–72; Naerebout 2007; Petridou 2009, 81–93; Tiradritti 1997, 224, pl. IV.205.

p. 239 Roman lamp handle with Isis nursing Harpokrates (Horus-the-child)
Bailey, D. (1988) *Catalogue of the Lamps in the British Museum, I–IV*, London, Q2007–Q2010.

p. 240 Bronze head of a private individual
Lahusen, G. and Formigli, E. (2001) *Römische Bildnisse aus Bronze: Kunst und Technik*, Munich, 209–210; Bülow-Jacobsen, A. (1996) 'Archaeology and philology on Mons Claudianus 1987–1993', ΤΟΠΟΙ. *Orient-Occident* 6(2), 721–30; McKenzie 2007, 184.

p. 241 Statue of Antinous
Breccia, E. (1932) *Le Musée Gréco-Romain 1925–1931*, Bergamo, 14-20, pls II–IX; Savvopoulos, K., Bianchi, R. and Hussein, Y. (2013) *The Oman Toussoun Collection in the Graeco-Roman Museum*, Graeco-Roman Museum Series 2, Alexandria; Vout2005, 82, 94.

List of exhibits

Each object is followed by its date and findspot, materials and principal dimensions, museum and registration number (where available) and page reference if illustrated in this catalogue. The list corresponds in most cases to the order of the exhibits at the British Museum showing. Objects from the IEASM excavations are indicated as such.

Details correct at time of printing.

L. = length | H. = height | W. = width |
D. = depth | Diam. = diameter | Wt = weight

List of lenders

The British Museum would like to thank all the lenders to the exhibition for their generosity:

Ashmolean Museum, Oxford

Bibliotheca Alexandrina Antiquities Museum, Alexandria

Egyptian Museum, Cairo

Fitzwilliam Museum, Cambridge

Graeco-Roman Museum, Alexandria

Maritime Museum, Alexandria

National Museum of Alexandria

Chapter 1
Rediscovering Thonis-Heracleion and Canopus

Statue of Hapy, 4th or 3rd century BC
Thonis-Heracleion, Egypt
Red granite. H. 5.4 m | W. 1.05 m | D. 90 cm
Maritime Museum, Alexandria SCA 281
IEASM excavations
Illustrated pp. 23, 102–103

Ladle, 6th–2nd century BC
Thonis-Heracleion, Egypt
Bronze. H. 50.7 cm | Diam. 4.2 cm
Maritime Museum, Alexandria SCA 397
IEASM excavations
Not illustrated

Ladle, 6th–2nd century BC
Thonis-Heracleion, Egypt
Bronze. H. 50.5 cm | Diam. 6.1 cm
Maritime Museum, Alexandria SCA 579
IEASM excavations
Not illustrated

Ladle, 6th–2nd century BC
Thonis-Heracleion, Egypt
Bronze. H. 46.5 cm | Diam. 5.3 cm
Maritime Museum, Alexandria SCA 1071
IEASM excavations
Not illustrated

Ladle, 6th–2nd century BC
Thonis-Heracleion, Egypt
Bronze. H. 43.9 cm | Diam. 4.4 cm
Maritime Museum, Alexandria SCA 1043
IEASM excavations
Not illustrated

Ladle, 6th–2nd century BC
Thonis-Heracleion, Egypt
Bronze. H. 51.8 cm | Diam 4.2 cm
Maritime Museum, Alexandria SCA 1034
IEASM excavations
Not illustrated

Ladle, 6th–2nd century BC
Thonis-Heracleion, Egypt
Bronze. H. 49.2 cm | Diam. 5.8 cm
Maritime Museum, Alexandria SCA 909
IEASM excavations
Not illustrated

Ladle, 6th–2nd century BC
Thonis-Heracleion, Egypt
Bronze. H. 52.2 cm | Diam. 6.7 cm
National Museum of Alexandria 296, SCA 395
IEASM excavations
Not illustrated

Ladle, 6th–2nd century BC
Thonis-Heracleion, Egypt
Bronze. H. 51.9 cm | Diam. 6.5 cm
Maritime Museum, Alexandria SCA 1095
IEASM excavations
Not illustrated

Bowl, 5th–4th century BC
Thonis-Heracleion, Egypt
Bronze. H. 9.4 cm | Diam. 13.4 cm
Maritime Museum, Alexandria SCA 916
IEASM excavations
Not illustrated

Bowl, 5th–4th century BC
Thonis-Heracleion, Egypt
Bronze. H. 9.3 cm | Diam. 12.1 cm
Maritime Museum, Alexandria SCA 391
IEASM excavations
Not illustrated

Bowl, 5th–4th century BC
Thonis-Heracleion, Egypt
Bronze. H. 6.5 cm | Diam. 12.7 cm
Maritime Museum, Alexandria SCA 940
IEASM excavations
Not illustrated

Bowl, 5th–4th century BC
Thonis-Heracleion, Egypt
Bronze. H. 9.8 cm | Diam. 15.5 cm
Maritime Museum, Alexandria SCA 1045
IEASM excavations
Not illustrated

Bowl, 5th–4th century BC
Thonis-Heracleion, Egypt
Bronze. H. 6.5 cm | Diam. 13.1 cm
Maritime Museum, Alexandria SCA 964
IEASM excavations
Not illustrated

Bowl, 5th–4th century BC
Thonis-Heracleion, Egypt
Bronze. H. 7.2 cm | Diam. 11.2 cm
Maritime Museum, Alexandria SCA 390
IEASM excavations
Not illustrated

Bowl, 5th–4th century BC
Thonis-Heracleion, Egypt
Bronze. H. 7.8 cm | Diam. 11.7 cm
Maritime Museum, Alexandria SCA 897
IEASM excavations
Not illustrated

Bowl, 5th–4th century BC
Thonis-Heracleion, Egypt
Bronze. H. 6.5 cm | W. 4 cm | Diam. 12.6 cm
Maritime Museum, Alexandria SCA 961
IEASM excavations
Not illustrated

Dish, 5th–2nd century BC
Thonis-Heracleion, Egypt
Bronze. H. 13 cm | Diam. 41.5 cm
Maritime Museum, Alexandria SCA 222
IEASM excavations
Not illustrated

Incense burner, 6th–2nd century BC
Thonis-Heracleion, Egypt
Bronze. H. 7.8 | W. 8.6 cm | Diam. 7.6 cm
Maritime Museum, Alexandria SCA 1058
IEASM excavations
Not illustrated

Spoon, 6th–2nd century BC
Thonis-Heracleion, Egypt
Bronze. L. 25.2 | Diam. 10.4 cm
Maritime Museum, Alexandria SCA 915
IEASM excavations
Not illustrated

Chapter 2
Egypt and Greece: early encounters

Stele of Thonis-Heracleion, 380 BC
Thonis-Heracleion, Egypt
Black Granite. H. 1.99 m | W. 0.88 cm | D. 0.33 cm
National Museum of Alexandria 285, SCA 277
IEASM excavations
Illustrated pp. 32, 50–1

Coin, 450–406 BC
Naukratis, Egypt
Silver. Wt 16.73 g
British Museum 1905,0309.3
Illustrated p. 36

Coin, 450–406 BC
Naukratis, Egypt
Silver. Wt 16.76 g
British Museum 1905,0309.2
Illustrated p. 36

Coin, 450–406 BC
Naukratis, Egypt
Silver. Wt 16.54 g
British Museum 1905,0309.1
Illustrated p. 36

Wine amphora, 550–500 BC
Tell Dafana, Egypt
Pottery. H. 75 cm
British Museum EA 22343
Illustrated p. 52

Perfume bottle, c. 410–400 BC
Thonis-Heracleion, Egypt
Pottery. H. 8.3 cm | Diam. 5.4 cm
National Museum of Alexandria 287, SCA 247
IEASM excavations
Illustrated p. 53

Scarab mould, 600–570 BC
Naukratis, Egypt
Terracotta. H. 1.2 cm | Diam. 3.1–3.2 cm
British Museum 1965,0930.902
Illustrated pp. 54–55

Scarab mould, 600–570 BC
Naukratis, Egypt
Terracotta. Diam. 2.8 cm
British Museum 1965,0930.917
Illustrated pp. 54–55

Scarab mould, 600–570 BC
Naukratis, Egypt
Terracotta. H. 4 cm | Diam. 4 cm
British Museum 2012,5020.1
Illustrated pp. 54–55

Scarab mould, 600–570 BC
Naukratis, Egypt
Terracotta. Diam. 3.2 cm
British Museum EA 26902
Illustrated pp. 54–55

Amulet mould, 600–570 BC
Naukratis, Egypt
Terracotta. W. 2.85 cm | D. 1.7 cm
British Museum 1920,0417.2
Illustrated pp. 54–5

Amulet mould, 600–570 BC
Naukratis, Egypt
Terracotta. L. 4.6 cm | W. 4 cm
British Museum EA 26918
Illustrated pp. 54–55

Scarab, 600–570 BC
Naukratis, Egypt
Terracotta. L. 1 cm | W. 0.7 cm
British Museum EA 66452
Illustrated pp. 54–55

Scarab, 600–570 BC
Naukratis, Egypt
Terracotta. W. 1.25 cm | D. 1.45 cm
British Museum EA 29961
Illustrated pp. 54–55

Scarab, 600–570 BC
Naukratis, Egypt
Terracotta. W. 1 cm | D. 1.35 cm
British Museum EA 27570
Illustrated pp. 54–55

Scarab, 600–570 BC
Naukratis, Egypt
Terracotta. W. 0.8 cm | D. 1.2 cm
British Museum EA 66487
Illustrated pp. 54–55

Scaraboid, 600–570 BC
Naukratis, Egypt
Terracotta. H. 0.7 cm | Diam. 1.35 cm
British Museum EA 66443
Illustrated pp. 54–55

Scaraboid, 600–570 BC
Naukratis, Egypt
Terracotta. D. 1.1 cm | Diam. 0.95 cm
British Museum EA 30705
Illustrated pp. 54–55

Scaraboid, 600–570 BC
Naukratis, Egypt
Terracotta. W. 1.05 cm | D. 1.15 cm
British Museum EA 66493
Illustrated pp. 54–55

Scaraboid, 600–570 BC
Naukratis, Egypt
Terracotta. W. 1 cm | D. 1.4 cm
British Museum EA 66514
Illustrated pp. 54–55

Alabastron, Hellenistic (323–31 BC)
Egypt
Alabaster, H. 20.3 cm
British Museum 1895,1020.5
Illustrated p. 56

Drill cores, late 6th–early 5th century AD
Naukratis, Egypt
Calcite, H. 0.8–3 cm
British Museum EA 27628
Illustrated p. 56

**Plaque with Horus name of Psamtik I
(r. 664–610 BC)**
Thonis-Heracleion, Egypt
Bronze, H. 11 cm | W. 7 cm | D. 3.3 cm
Maritime Museum, Alexandria SCA 1392
IEASM excavations
Illustrated p. 33

Votive stela, 525–500 BC
Naukratis, Egypt
Limestone, H. 39 cm | W. 30 cm
British Museum 1900,0214.21
Illustrated p. 38

Tombstone of a Carian woman, 540/530 BC
Saqqara, Egypt
Limestone, H. 63 cm | W. 31 cm | D. 10 cm
British Museum EA 67235
Illustrated p. 57

Lekane of Sostratos, late 7th century BC
Chios, Greece
Ceramic, H. 17.7 cm | Diam. 38.8 cm
British Museum 1888,0601.456
Illustrated p. 42

Cypriot statuette of Isis nursing Horus, c.550 BC
Naukratis, Egypt
Limestone, H. 11.9 cm | W. 7.5 cm | L. 5.1 cm
British Museum 1888,0601.31
Illustrated p. 60

**Cypriot figure of a youth or hero wrestling
a lion, 600–560 BC**
Naukratis, Egypt
Limestone, H. 21.3 cm | W. 6.4 cm | L. 4.2 cm
British Museum 1888,0601.27
Illustrated p. 61

Cypriot nude male youth, c. 580–560 BC
Naukratis, Egypt
Alabaster, H. 25.7 cm | W. 8.8 cm | D. 4.4 cm
British Museum 1888,1006.1
Illustrated p. 61

Cypriot horse-and-rider figure, c. 600–525 BC
Naukratis, Egypt
Terracotta, H. 9.8 cm | W. 4.3 cm | L. 9.4 cm
British Museum 1911,0606.1
Illustrated p. 43

Fragment of cornice, c. 530–510 BC
Naukratis, Egypt
Marble, H. 22 cm | W. 13 cm | L. 8 cm
British Museum 1886,0401.41
Illustrated p. 63

Votive female bust, 450–350 BC
Naukratis, Egypt
Terracotta, H. 17.8 cm | W. 18.3 cm
Fitzwilliam Museum GR.3.1898
Illustrated p. 65

**Egyptian figure of Horus the child on a horse,
450–350 BC**
Naukratis, Egypt
Limestone, W. 10 cm | Diam. 11.75 cm
British Museum 1900,0214.27
Illustrated p. 43

Incense burner, early 5th century BC
Thonis-Heracleion, Egypt
Limestone, H. 24.2 cm | W. 9 cm |
Diam. of Bowl 13.5 cm
National Museum of Alexandria 291, SCA 270
IEASM excavations
Illustrated p. 66

**Head of Cypro-Phoenician god Baal,
late 5th–early 4th century BC**
Thonis-Heracleion, Egypt
Limestone, H. 12.9 cm | W. 8.9 cm | D. 8.2 cm
Maritime Museum, Alexandria SCA 1394
IEASM excavations
Illustrated p. 67

Saucer with mythical beasts, 6th–4th century BC
Thonis-Heracleion, Egypt
Lead, Diam. 5 cm
Maritime Museum, Alexandria SCA 907
IEASM excavations
Illustrated p. 66

Pyramidal object, Amasis (570–526 BC)
Thonis-Heracleion, Egypt
Bronze, H. 13 cm | W. 8.5 cm
Maritime Museum, Alexandria SCA 1575
IEASM excavations
Illustrated pp. 70–71

Plaque, Amasis (570–526 BC)
Thonis-Heracleion, Egypt
Bronze, L. 10 cm | L. 8.5 cm
Maritime Museum, Alexandria SCA 1310
IEASM excavations
Illustrated p. 47

Sarcophagus, 26th dynasty (664–525 BC)
Thonis-Heracleion, Egypt
Limestone, L. 35 cm
Maritime Museum, Alexandria SCA 1513
IEASM excavations
Illustrated p. 46

Sarcophagus, 26th dynasty (664–525 BC)
Thonis-Heracleion, Egypt
Limestone, W. 36 cm
Maritime Museum, Alexandria SCA 1514
IEASM excavations
Illustrated p. 46

Sarcophagus, 26th dynasty (664–525 BC)
Thonis-Heracleion, Egypt
Limestone, W. 37 cm
Maritime Museum, Alexandria SCA 1517
IEASM excavations
Illustrated p. 46

Ibis figure, 6th–2nd century BC
Thonis-Heracleion, Egypt
Bronze, W. 8.8 cm | H. 10 cm | D. 3.3 cm
Maritime Museum, Alexandria SCA 1087
IEASM excavations
Illustrated p. 47

Ibis mummy, Ptolemaic Period (332–31 BC)
Saqqara, Egypt
Linen and resin, H. 42 cm | Diam. 16 cm
British Museum 1971,0227.153
Illustrated p. 69

**Votive box with eel,
c. late 5th–early 4th century BC**
Naukratis, Egypt
Bronze, H. 3.5 cm | W. 2.7 cm | L. 35.5 cm
British Museum EA 27581
Illustrated p. 68

**Mummy case for a mongoose,
c. late 5th–early 4th century BC**
Naukratis, Egypt
Bronze, H. 31.5 cm | W. 10.2 cm | D. 9.8 cm
British Museum EA 16040
Illustrated p. 68

**Sculptor's model in the shape of a ram,
450–350 BC**
Naukratis, Egypt
Limestone, W. 10.2 cm | H. 6.9 cm | D. 11.35 cm
British Museum EA 27528
Illustrated p. 44

Chapter 3
Greek kings and Egyptian gods

**Posthumous portrait of Alexander the Great,
2nd–1st century BC**
Alexandria, Egypt
Marble, H. 37 cm
British Museum 1872,0515.1
Illustrated p. 73

**Water-clock depicting Alexander the Great,
331–323 BC**
Tell el-Yahudiya, Egypt
Black granodiorite, H. 37 cm | W. 38 cm
British Museum EA 933
Illustrated p. 86

**Coin portraying Alexander the Great,
late 4th century BC**
Minted in Alexandria, Egypt
Silver, Diam. 3 cm
British Museum 1876,0505.33
Illustrated p. 86

Statue of Horus protecting pharaoh, c. 350 BC
Unknown findspot, Egypt
Limestone and glass, H. 55 cm | W. 19 cm |
D. 42 cm
Egyptian Museum, Cairo JE33262
Illustrated p. 87

Royal head, c. 2nd–1st century BC
Canopus, Egypt
Quartzite, H. 38 cm | W. 31.5 cm | D. 34.5 cm
Bibliotheca Alexandrina Antiquities Museum
SCA 166
IEASM excavations
Illustrated p. 76

Head of a pharaoh, 3rd century BC
Canopus, Egypt
Granodiorite, H. 35 cm | W. 30 cm | D. 29 cm
Bibliotheca Alexandrina Antiquities Museum
SCA 167
IEASM excavations
Illustrated pp. 89, 90–1

Coin portraying Ptolemy I (305–247 BC)
Thonis-Heracleion, Egypt
Gold, Diam. 10 mm
Graeco-Roman Museum, Alexandria SCA 304
IEASM excavations
Illustrated p. 88

Coin portraying Ptolemy I (305–247 BC)
Thonis-Heracleion, Egypt
Gold, Diam. 11 mm
Graeco-Roman Museum, Alexandria SCA 307
IEASM excavations
Illustrated p. 88

Coin portraying Ptolemy I (305–247 BC)
Thonis-Heracleion, Egypt
Gold, Diam. 10 mm
Graeco-Roman Museum, Alexandria SCA 313
IEASM excavations
Illustrated p. 88

Coin portraying Ptolemy I (305–247 BC)
Thonis-Heracleion, Egypt
Gold, Diam. 10 mm
Graeco-Roman Museum, Alexandria SCA 318
IEASM excavations
Illustrated p. 88

Coin portraying Ptolemy I (305–247 BC)
Thonis-Heracleion, Egypt
Gold, Diam. 9 mm
Graeco-Roman Museum, Alexandria SCA 312
IEASM excavations
Illustrated p. 88

Statue of Arsinoe II, 3rd century BC
Canopus, Egypt
Black granodiorite, H. 1.5 m | W. 55 cm | D. 28 cm
Bibliotheca Alexandrina Antiquities Museum
SCA 208
IEASM excavations
Illustrated p. 93

**Statue of a queen (possibly Cleopatra III)
dressed as Isis, 2nd century BC**
Thonis-Heracleion, Egypt
Granodiorite, H. 2.2 m | W. 60 cm | D. 40 cm
National Museum of Alexandria 286, SCA 283
IEASM excavations
Illustrated pp. 94–5

**Statue of a Ptolemaic king, Early Ptolemaic
period, possibly reign of Ptolemy II**
Thonis-Heracleion, Egypt
Red granite, H. 5 m | W. 1.5 m | D. 75 cm
Maritime Museum, Alexandria SCA 279
IEASM excavations
Illustrated pp. 98–101

**Statue of a Ptolemaic queen, Early Ptolemaic
period, possibly reign of Ptolemy II**
Thonis-Heracleion, Egypt
Red granite, H. 4.9 m | W. 1.2 m | D. 75 cm
Maritime Museum, Alexandria SCA 280
IEASM excavations
Illustrated pp. 77, 97

Naos of Amun-Gereb, 4th–2nd century BC
Thonis-Heracleion, Egypt
Pink granite, H. 1.74 m | W. 1 m | D. 93 cm
Maritime Museum, Alexandria SCA 457
IEASM excavations
Illustrated pp. 104–5

Crown of Amun, 4th–2nd century BC
Thonis-Heracleion, Egypt
Bronze, H. 15.1 cm | W. 22.5 cm | D. 18.5 cm
Maritime Museum, Alexandria SCA 967
IEASM excavations
Illustrated p. 106

**Plaque representing Amun as a ram,
6th century BC**
Thonis-Heracleion, Egypt
Limestone, H. 9 cm | L. 11.5 cm | D. 0.4 cm
Maritime Museum, Alexandria SCA 1579
IEASM excavations
Illustrated p. 107

**Statue of a temple benefactor,
4th–2nd century BC**
Thonis-Heracleion, Egypt
Granodiorite, H. 64 cm | W. 20 cm | D. 22 cm
Maritime Museum, Alexandria SCA 455
IEASM excavations
Illustrated p. 109

Statue of a sphinx, 4th century BC
Thonis-Heracleion, Egypt
Granodiorite, H. 98 cm | W. 58 cm | L. 1.47 m
Maritime Museum, Alexandria SCA 282
IEASM excavations
Illustrated p. 108

**Statuette of a pharaoh, 26th–29th dynasty
(664–380 BC)**
Thonis-Heracleion, Egypt.
Bronze, H. 21 cm | W. 5.5 cm | D 5.8 cm
Maritime Museum, Alexandria SCA 1305
IEASM excavations
Illustrated pp. 116–17

Basin, 4th–2nd century BC
Thonis-Heracleion, Egypt
Bronze, H. 7 cm | Diam. 25.2 cm
Maritime Museum, Alexandria SCA 1011
IEASM excavations
Not illustrated

Basin, 4th–2nd century BC
Thonis-Heracleion, Egypt
Bronze, H. 11.9 cm | Diam. 42.1 cm
Maritime Museum, Alexandria SCA 911
IEASM excavations
Illustrated p. 113

Basin, 4th–2nd century BC
Thonis-Heracleion, Egypt
Bronze, H. 13.3 cm | Diam. 25.8 cm
Maritime Museum, Alexandria SCA 899
IEASM excavations
Not illustrated

Basin, 4th–2nd century BC
Thonis-Heracleion, Egypt
Bronze, H. 17 cm | Diam. 25.3 cm
Maritime Museum, Alexandria SCA 900
IEASM excavations
Illustrated p. 113

Bowl, 5th–4th century BC
Thonis-Heracleion, Egypt
Bronze, H. 7.3 cm | Diam. 14.6 cm
Maritime Museum, Alexandria SCA 928
IEASM excavations
Not illustrated

Bowl, 5th–2nd century BC
Thonis-Heracleion, Egypt
Bronze, H. 6.5 cm | Diam. 12.5 cm
Maritime Museum, Alexandria SCA 586
IEASM excavations
Not illustrated

Bowl, 5th–4th century BC
Thonis-Heracleion, Egypt
Bronze, Diam. 14 cm
Maritime Museum, Alexandria SCA 1380
IEASM excavations
Not illustrated

Bowl, 5th–2nd century BC
Thonis-Heracleion, Egypt
Bronze, H. 8.2 cm | Diam. 10.6 cm
Maritime Museum, Alexandria SCA 216
IEASM excavations
Illustrated p. 113

Bowl, 5th–4th century BC
Thonis-Heracleion, Egypt
Bronze, H. 8.5 cm | Diam. 9.6 cm
Maritime Museum, Alexandria SCA 904
IEASM excavations
Illustrated pp. 114–15

Goblet, 5th–4th century BC
Thonis-Heracleion, Egypt
Bronze, H. 13 cm | Diam. 9.7 cm
Maritime Museum, Alexandria SCA 992
IEASM excavations
Not illustrated

Goblet, 5th–4th century BC
Thonis-Heracleion, Egypt
Bronze, H. 14.5 cm | Diam. 11 cm
Maritime Museum, Alexandria SCA 987
IEASM excavations
Not illustrated

Brazier, 4th century BC
Thonis-Heracleion, Egypt
Bronze, H. 23 cm | Diam. 46 cm
Maritime Museum, Alexandria SCA 912
IEASM excavations
Illustrated p. 112

Incense burner, 4th–2nd century BC
Thonis-Heracleion, Egypt
Bronze, H. 8 cm | Diam. 13 cm
Maritime Museum, Alexandria SCA 1086
IEASM excavations
Illustrated p. 111

Bowl, 4th–2nd century BC
Thonis-Heracleion, Egypt
Bronze, H. 6.8 cm | Diam. 50.1 cm
Maritime Museum, Alexandria SCA 993
IEASM excavations
Not illustrated

Pot, 4th–2nd century BC
Thonis-Heracleion, Egypt
Bronze, H. 18 cm | Diam. 27.9 cm
Maritime Museum, Alexandria SCA 407
IEASM excavations
Illustrated p. 111

Bowl, 4th–2nd century BC
Thonis-Heracleion, Egypt
Bronze, H. 9.6 cm | Diam. 25.2 cm
Maritime Museum, Alexandria SCA 406
IEASM excavations
Illustrated p. 111

Oil lamp, 4th–2nd century BC
Thonis-Heracleion, Egypt
Bronze, H. 2.4 cm | W. 5.8 cm | L. 14.1 cm
Maritime Museum, Alexandria SCA 1568
IEASM excavations
Illustrated p. 110

Mirror, 4th–2nd century BC
Thonis-Heracleion, Egypt
Bronze, L. 19.8 cm | Diam. 15 cm
Maritime Museum, Alexandria SCA 985
IEASM excavations
Illustrated p. 112

Mirror, 4th–2nd century BC
Thonis-Heracleion, Egypt
Bronze, H. 15.1 cm | Diam. 11.9 cm
Maritime Museum, Alexandria SCA 1016
IEASM excavations
Not illustrated

Naos of Khonsu-the-Child, 4th–2nd century BC
Thonis-Heracleion, Egypt
Pink granite, H. 110 cm | W. 53 cm | D. 63 cm
Maritime Museum, Alexandria SCA 456
IEASM excavations
Illustrated p. 80

**Headdress of Khonsu-the-Child,
4th–3rd century BC**
Thonis-Heracleion, Egypt
Bronze, H. 15 cm | W. 10 cm
Maritime Museum, Alexandria SCA 401
IEASM excavations
Illustrated pp. 120–21

Statue of Khonsu, Late Period (664–332 BC)
Thonis-Heracleion, Egypt
Bronze, H. 21.5 cm | W. 6.5 cm
National Museum of Alexandria 294, SCA 387
IEASM excavations
Illustrated p. 122

**Statue of Khonsu as a falcon,
6th–2nd century BC**
Thonis-Heracleion, Egypt
Black granite, H. 68 cm | W. 23 cm | D. 54 cm
Maritime Museum, Alexandria SCA 278
IEASM excavations
Not illustrated

Statuette of Harpokrates, 4th–2nd century BC
Thonis-Heracleion, Egypt
Bronze, H. 18 cm | W. 4 cm
Maritime Museum, Alexandria SCA 1268
IEASM excavations
Illustrated p. 122

Head of Herakles, 6th century BC
Naukratis, Egypt
Terracotta, H. 7.5 cm | W. 6.8 cm | D. 7.5 cm
British Museum 1886,0401.1402
Illustrated p. 79

Coin, 355/354 or 354/353 BC
Thonis-Heracleion, Egypt
Gold, Diam. 1.37 cm
National Museum of Alexandria SCA 287
IEASM excavations
Illustrated p. 122

**Amulet in the shape of a *uraeus*, 30th dynasty
(380–342 BC)**
Thonis-Heracleion, Egypt
Faience, H. 4.15 cm | W. 2.2 cm | D. 1.1 cm
Maritime Museum, Alexandria SCA 552
IEASM excavations
Illustrated pp. 118–19

Faience plaque, 30th dynasty (380–342 BC)
Thonis-Heracleion, Egypt
Faience, L. 8.4 cm | W. 3.6 cm | H. 1 cm
Maritime Museum, Alexandria SCA 560
IEASM excavations
Illustrated pp. 118–19

Naos, 30th dynasty (380–342 BC)
Thonis-Heracleion, Egypt
Wood, H. 13 cm | W. 6 cm
Maritime Museum, Alexandria SCA 583
IEASM excavations
Illustrated pp. 118–19

**Papyrus-shaped amulet, 30th dynasty
(380–342 BC)**
Thonis-Heracleion, Egypt
Faience, H. 13 cm | W. 3.6 cm
Maritime Museum, Alexandria SCA 565
IEASM excavations
Illustrated pp. 118–19

***Wedjat*-eye amulet, 30th dynasty (380–342 BC)**
Thonis-Heracleion, Egypt
Faience, H. 4 cm | W. 5 cm | D. 0.9 cm
National Museum Alexandria 303, SCA 558
IEASM excavations
Illustrated pp. 118–19

Figurine of Khonsu, 30th dynasty (380–342 BC)
Thonis-Heracleion, Egypt
Faience, H. 7.8 cm | W. 2.2 cm | D. 1.8 cm
National Museum, Alexandria SCA 562
IEASM excavations
Not illustrated

Figure of Shu, 30th dynasty (380–342 BC)
Thonis-Heracleion, Egypt
Faience, H. 5.5 cm | W. 1.4 cm | D. 1.3 cm
Maritime Museum, Alexandria SCA 553
IEASM excavations
Not illustrated

Double-vase amulet, 30th dynasty (380–342 BC)
Thonis-Heracleion, Egypt
Faience, H. 7.3 cm | W. 3.2 cm | D. 1.6 cm
National Museum of Alexandria SCA 559
IEASM excavations
Illustrated pp. 118–19

Earring, 4th–2nd century BC
Thonis-Heracleion, Egypt
Gold, Diam. 3.2 cm
National Museum of Alexandria 1611, SCA 1408
IEASM excavations
Illustrated p. 124

Earring, 4th–2nd century BC
Thonis-Heracleion, Egypt
Gold, Diam. 1.9 cm | D. 3.8 cm
National Museum of Alexandria 318, SCA 288
IEASM excavations
Illustrated p. 124

Earring, 4th–2nd century BC
Thonis-Heracleion, Egypt
Gold, Diam. 1.9 cm
Graeco-Roman Museum, Alexandria 32231,
SCA 298
IEASM excavations
Illustrated p. 124

Earring, 4th–2nd century BC
Thonis-Heracleion, Egypt
Gold, Diam. 2.5 cm
National Museum of Alexandria 1623, SCA 14372
IEASM excavations
Illustrated p. 124

Earring, 4th–2nd century BC
Thonis-Heracleion, Egypt
Gold, D. 0.83 cm | Diam. 2.6 cm
Graeco-Roman Museum, Alexandria 32230,
SCA 297
IEASM excavations
Illustrated p. 124

Ring with engraved Nike, 4th–2nd century BC
Thonis-Heracleion, Egypt
Gold, Diam. 2.8 cm
National Museum of Alexandria 314, SCA 286
IEASM excavations
Illustrated p. 125

Ring, engraved, 4th–2nd century BC
Thonis-Heracleion, Egypt
Gold, Diam. 1.3 cm
National Museum of Alexandria 1599, SCA 1344
IEASM excavations
Illustrated p. 125

Earring, 4th–2nd century BC
Thonis-Heracleion, Egypt
Gold, Diam. 1.71 cm
Graeco-Roman Museum, Alexandria 32239,
SCA 308
IEASM excavations
Illustrated p. 125

Ring, 4th–2nd century BC
Thonis-Heracleion, Egypt
Gold, Diam. 1.56 cm
Graeco-Roman Museum, Alexandria 32344,
SCA 1128
Illustrated p. 125

Ring, 4th–2nd century BC
Thonis-Heracleion, Egypt
Gold, glass or stone, Diam. 2.68 cm
National Museum of Alexandria 315, SCA 290
IEASM excavations
Illustrated p. 125

Bird-shaped pendant, 4th–2nd century BC
Thonis-Heracleion, Egypt
Gold, L. 1.7 cm
National Museum of Alexandria 1558, SCA 1204
IEASM excavations
Illustrated p. 125

***Uraeus*, 4th–2nd century BC**
Thonis-Heracleion, Egypt
Gold, L. 3.8 cm
National Museum of Alexandria SCA 14333
IEASM excavations
Illustrated p. 125

Pendant, 4th–2nd century BC
Thonis-Heracleion, Egypt
Gold, Diam. 2 cm
National Museum of Alexandria 1621, SCA 14174
IEASM excavations
Illustrated p. 124

**Statue of Apis bull, AD 117–138
(reign of emperor Hadrian)**
Alexandria, Egypt
Black diorite, H. 1.9 m | L. 2.05 m |
W. 89.0 cm
Graeco-Roman Museum, Alexandria 351
Illustrated pp. 126–7

Statuette of Apis bull, 500–450 BC
Memphite region, Egypt
Bronze, H. 10 cm | L. 8.7 cm
British Museum 1898,0225.1
Illustrated p. 82

Statue of Osiris, Ptolemaic Period (332–31 BC)
Minia, Egypt
Sycamore wood, H. 1.52 m | W. 44 cm
Bibliotheca Alexandrina Antiquities Museum 633
Illustrated p. 84

Statue of Serapis, 2nd century BC
Theadelphia, El-Fayum, Egypt
Sycamore wood, H. 1.81 m
Graeco-Roman Museum, Alexandria 23352
Illustrated p. 128

Bust of Serapis, 2nd century BC
Alexandria, Egypt
Marble, H. 81 cm
Graeco-Roman Museum, Alexandria, 22158
Illustrated p. 81

Foundation plaque, Ptolemy IV (221–204 BC)
Alexandria, Egypt
Gold, L. 12 cm
Graeco-Roman Museum, Alexandria P.10035
Illustrated p. 129

**Amulet in the shape of a temple,
Ptolemaic Period (332–31 BC)**
Canopus, Egypt
Lead, L. 1.2 cm
Maritime Museum, Alexandria SCA 470
IEASM excavations
Illustrated p. 85

Osiris-Canopus jar, 1st–2nd century AD
Canopus, Egypt
Marble, H. 37.5 cm | Diam. 21 cm
Bibliotheca Alexandrina Antiquities Museum
SCA 205
IEASM excavations
Illustrated pp. 132–33

**Amulet in the shape of an Osiris-Canopus jar,
30 BC–AD 395**
Canopus, Egypt
Bronze, H. 6 cm | W. 2.2 cm | D. 1.9 cm
Maritime Museum, Alexandria SCA 471
IEASM excavations
Illustrated p. 133

**Head of Serapis with *Kalathos*, 2nd century BC
(head) and Roman? (*Kalathos*)**
Canopus, Egypt
Marble, H. 83 cm | W. 34 cm | D. 34 cm
Bibliotheca Alexandrina Antiquities Museum
SCA 169 and SCA 206
IEASM excavations
Illustrated pp. 130–31

Head of Nectanebo II, 360–342 BC
Canopus, Egypt
Granodiorite, H. 37 cm | W. 17 cm | D. 14 cm
Bibliotheca Alexandrina Antiquities Museum
SCA 168
IEASM excavations
Illustrated pp. 134–35

**Naos of the Decades, 380–362 BC
(reign of Nectanebo I)**
Canopus, Egypt
Black granite, H. 1.3 m | W. 0.87 m
Graeco-Roman Museum, Alexandria
(JE 25774, and SCA 161, 163, 162, 164 (IEASM
excavations))
Illustrated pp. 136–7

Chapter 4
From myth to festivals

Statue of Osiris, 26th dynasty (664–525 BC)
Medinet Habu, Egypt
Greywacke, H. 1.5 m | W. 24.5 cm | D. 43 cm
Egyptian Museum, Cairo JE 30997, CG 38231
Illustrated p. 151

Statue of Osiris, 570–526 BC (reign of Amasis)
Saqqara, Egypt
Greywacke, H. 90 cm | W. 28 cm | D. 46.5 cm
Egyptian Museum, Cairo CG 38358
Illustrated p. 153

Statue of Isis, 570–526 BC (reign of Amasis)
Saqqara, Egypt
Greywacke, H. 90 cm | W. 20 cm | D. 45 cm
Egyptian Museum, Cairo CG 38884
Illustrated p. 152

**Osiris stele, 30th dynasty to Ptolemaic Period
(380–31 BC)**
Karnak, Egypt
Sandstone, H. 60 cm | W. 38 cm
Egyptian Museum, Cairo PV.2014.18
Illustrated p. 164

False door, Late Period (664–332 BC)
Saïs, Egypt
Limestone, H. 37 cm | W. 25 cm
Bibliotheca Alexandrina Antiquities Museum 587,
CG 42879
Illustrated p. 140

**Statuette of Isis with Osiris, 25th dynasty
(760–656 BC)**
Abydos, Egypt
Limestone, H. 19.5 cm
Egyptian Museum, Cairo CG 38867
Illustrated p. 154

Osiris on bed, 13th dynasty? (c. 1800–1650 BC)
Abydos, Egypt
Basalt, H. 1.1 m | L. 1.78 m | D. 89 cm
Egyptian Museum, Cairo JE 32090
Illustrated p. 155

**Statue of Osiris Awakening, 26th dynasty
(664–525 BC), perhaps reign of Apries
(580–570 BC)**
Horbeit, Egypt
Gneiss, gold, electrum, bronze, H. 29.5 cm |
L. 55.5 cm | D. 18 cm
Egyptian Museum, Cairo CG 38424
Illustrated pp. 156–7

**Osiris amulet, 22nd dynasty
(reign of Osorkon II, 874–850 BC)**
Tanis, Egypt
Gold, H. 8.2 cm
Egyptian Museum, Cairo JE 87146
Illustrated p. 163

**Ewer, 21st dynasty, reign of Amenemope
(993–984 BC)**
Tanis, Egypt
Gold, H. 20 cm
Egyptian Museum Cairo JE 86098
Illustrated p. 163

Horus falcon, 26th–30th dynasty (664–343 BC)
Buto, Egypt
Bronze, H. 15 cm | W. 5 cm | D. 15 cm
Graeco-Roman Museum, Alexandria 247
Illustrated p. 160

Wedjat-eye amulet, 26th–30th dynasty
Thonis-Heracleion, Egypt
Gold, L. 0.82 cm | H. 0.68 cm | D. 0.18 cm
Graeco-Roman Museum, Alexandria 32339,
SCA 1123
IEASM excavations
Illustrated p. 161

Magic stela of Horus, 30th dynasty (380–343 BC)
Tell el-Qalâh, Egypt
Greywacke and limestone, H. 93 cm (total) |
H. (of stele) 61 cm
Egyptian Museum, Cairo JE 33264,
CG 9402.1 and 2
Illustrated pp. 158–9

Osiris brick, c. 950–350 BC
Said to be from Thebes, Egypt
Terracotta, L. 24.9 cm | W. 12.4 cm | H. 6.1 cm
Ashmolean Museum, Oxford 1991.18
Illustrated p. 170

**Osiris-vegetans figure, 8th–7th century BC
Tihna el-Gebel/Akoris, Egypt**
Sycamore wood, earth and grain,
L. (of coffin) 61.5 cm
Egyptian Museum, Cairo JE 36539 (A, B, and C)
Illustrated p. 169

Head of Berenike II, 3rd century BC
Canopus, Egypt
Diorite, H. 13.7 cm | W. 11.4 cm | D. 9 cm
Bibliotheca Alexandrina Antiquities Museum
SCA 204
IEASM excavations
Illustrated p. 144

Head of a priest, Ptolemaic Period (332–31 BC)
Alexandria, East harbour, Egypt
Granodiorite, H. 21.8 cm | W. 13.6 cm | D. 17 cm
Maritime Museum, Alexandria SCA 1398
IEASM excavations
Illustrated pp. 165–67

'Garden tank', 4th–2nd century BC
Thonis-Heracleion, Egypt
Pink granite, H. 63 cm | W. 90 cm | L. 205 cm
Maritime Museum, Alexandria SCA 459
IEASM excavations
Illustrated p. 171

**Pail (situla), 4th–2nd century BC
Thonis-Heracleion, Egypt**
Bronze, H. 15.6 cm | Diam. 5.6 cm
Maritime Museum, Alexandria SCA 1604
IEASM excavations
Illustrated p. 173

Shallow dish, 6th–2nd century
Thonis-Heracleion, Egypt
Gold, H. 1.5 cm | Diam. 18.9 cm
National Museum of Alexandria 313, SCA 296
IEASM excavations
Illustrated p. 172

Strainer, 4th–2nd century BC
Thonis-Heracleion, Egypt
Bronze, H. 17.6 cm | Diam. 8.6 cm
Maritime Museum, Alexandria SCA 1063
IEASM excavations
Illustrated p. 173

Strainer, 4th–2nd century BC
Thonis-Heracleion, Egypt
Bronze, H. 9.1 cm | D. 22 cm | Diam. 9.1 cm
Maritime Museum, Alexandria SCA 1062
IEASM excavations
Illustrated p. 173

Ladle, 4th–2nd century BC
Thonis-Heracleion, Egypt
Bronze, L. 26.5 cm | Diam. 6.1 cm
Maritime Museum, Alexandria SCA 1064
IEASM excavations
Illustrated p. 173

Bowl, 5th–4th century BC
Thonis-Heracleion, Egypt
Bronze, H. 5.5 cm | Diam. 9 cm
Maritime Museum, Alexandria SCA 1228
IEASM excavations
Not illustrated

Oil lamp, 4th–2nd century BC
Thonis-Heracleion, Egypt
Bronze, L. 15.3 cm | Diam. 6.0 cm
Maritime Museum, Alexandria SCA 1307
IEASM excavations
Not illustrated

Lamp, 4th–2nd century BC
Thonis-Heracleion, Egypt
Bronze, L. 36.4 cm | W. 2.3 cm | D. 1.1 cm
(SCA 1024) and L. 13.2 cm | W. 7.6 cm |
H. 11 cm (SCA 1028)
Maritime Museum, Alexandria SCA 1024
and SCA 1028
IEASM excavations
Illustrated p. 179

Mortar, 4th–2nd century BC
Thonis-Heracleion, Egypt
Granodiorite, H. 30 cm | Diam. 32 cm
Maritime Museum, Alexandria SCA 367
IEASM excavations
Illustrated p. 175

Pestle, 4th–2nd century BC
Thonis-Heracleion, Egypt
Granodiorite, L. 27 cm | W. 9.2 cm
Maritime Museum, Alexandria SCA 269
IEASM excavations
Illustrated p. 175

Incense burner, 4th–2nd century BC
Thonis-Heracleion, Egypt
Bronze, H. 9.6 cm | Diam. 8.7 cm
Maritime Museum, Alexandria SCA 1073
IEASM excavations
Illustrated p. 176

Spoon, 4th–2nd century BC
Thonis-Heracleion, Egypt
Bronze, L. 20.3 cm | Diam. (scoop) 10.2 cm
Maritime Museum, Alexandria SCA 1057
IEASM excavations
Illustrated p. 176

Fragment of incense burner, 5th–2nd century BC
Thonis-Heracleion, Egypt
Bronze, H. 4 cm | L. 4.3 cm | D. 2.5 cm
Maritime Museum, Alexandria SCA 1569
IEASM excavations
Illustrated p. 177

Ladle, 5th–2nd century BC
Thonis-Heracleion, Egypt
Bronze, L. 50.4 cm | Diam. 6.1 cm
Maritime Museum, Alexandria SCA 220
IEASM excavations
Illustrated p. 175

Wedjat-eye amulet, 4th–2nd century BC
Thonis-Heracleion, Egypt
Gold, D. 0.8 cm
National Museum of Alexandria 1610, SCA 1405
IEASM excavations
Not illustrated

Bowl, 4th century BC
Thonis-Heracleion, Egypt
Silver, H. 6.4 cm, Diam. 11 cm
Maritime Museum, Alexandria SCA 951
IEASM excavations
Illustrated p. 175

Vase, 6th–2nd century BC
Thonis-Heracleion, Egypt
Bronze, H. 10.3 cm | Diam. 5.1 cm
Maritime Museum, Alexandria SCA 1010
IEASM excavations
Not illustrated

Spoon, 4th–2nd century BC
Thonis-Heracleion, Egypt
Bronze, D. 27 cm | Diam. 10.2 cm
Maritime Museum, Alexandria SCA 1044
IEASM excavations
Not illustrated

Box, 4th–2nd century BC
Thonis-Heracleion, Egypt
Bronze, L. 6.9 cm | W. 5.1 cm | H. 3.6 cm
Maritime Museum, Alexandria SCA 1605
IEASM excavations
Illustrated p. 178

Incense burner, 4th–2nd century BC
Thonis-Heracleion, Egypt
Bronze, H. 7.9 cm | Diam. 10.4 cm
Maritime Museum, Alexandria SCA 392
IEASM excavations
Illustrated p. 176

Coal shovel, 4th–2nd century BC
Thonis-Heracleion, Egypt
Bronze, L. 22.6 cm | W. (scoop) 3.8 cm
Maritime Museum, Alexandria SCA 580
IEASM excavations
Illustrated p. 176

Tongs, 4th–2nd century BC
Thonis-Heracleion, Egypt
Bronze, W. 1 cm | D. 46.1 cm
Maritime Museum, Alexandria SCA 943
IEASM excavations
Not illustrated

Pectoral, 22nd dynasty,
(reign of Shoshenq I, 943–922 BC)
Tanis, Egypt
Gold, lapis lazuli and glass paste, H. 19 cm |
W. 37.5 cm
Egyptian Museum, Cairo JE 72171
Illustrated pp. 180–81

Votive barge, 4th–2nd century BC
Thonis-Heracleion, Egypt
Lead, H. 6.5 cm | L. 44.5 cm | W. 3.7 cm
Maritime Museum, Alexandria SCA 1072
IEASM excavations
Not illustrated

Votive barge, 4th–2nd century BC
Thonis-Heracleion, Egypt
Lead, L. 37.3 cm | W. 3.3 cm | H. 6.2 cm
Maritime Museum, Alexandria SCA 1039
IEASM excavations
Not illustrated

Votive barge, 6th–2nd century BC
Thonis-Heracleion, Egypt
Lead, L. 9 cm | H. 3.2 cm | W. 21 cm
Maritime Museum, Alexandria SCA 1574
IEASM excavations
Not illustrated

Votive barge, 6th–2nd century BC
Thonis-Heracleion, Egypt
Lead, L. 35 cm | H. 7 cm | W. 3 cm
Maritime Museum, Alexandria SCA 1583
IEASM excavations
Not illustrated

Votive barge, 4th–2nd century BC
Thonis-Heracleion, Egypt
Lead, L. 59 cm
Maritime Museum, Alexandria SCA 1591
IEASM excavations
Illustrated p. 183

Votive barque, 4th–2nd century BC
Thonis-Heracleion, Egypt
Lead, L. 61.5 cm
Maritime Museum, Alexandria SCA 1607
IEASM excavations
Illustrated p. 183

Votive barge, 4th–2nd century BC
Thonis-Heracleion, Egypt
Lead, L. 62 cm
Maritime Museum, Alexandria SCA 1606 and 1617
IEASM excavations
Illustrated p. 183

Votive barge, 4th–2nd century BC
Thonis-Heracleion, Egypt
Lead, L. 21.5 cm | H. 6.4 cm | W. 3 cm
Maritime Museum, Alexandria SCA 1017
IEASM excavations
Not illustrated

Waterfowl figurehead (of votive barge),
4th century BC
Thonis-Heracleion, Egypt
Bronze, H. 17 cm | W. 8.6 cm
Maritime Museum, Alexandria SCA 1592
IEASM excavations
Illustrated p. 184

Oil lamp, Late Period (664–332 BC)
Thonis-Heracleion, Egypt
Lead, Diam. 7 cm
Maritime Museum, Alexandria SCA 998
IEASM excavations
Not illustrated

Oil lamp, end of 4th century BC
Thonis-Heracleion, Egypt
Pottery, L. 10.5 cm, H. 5.5 cm | Diam. 4 cm
Maritime Museum, Alexandria SCA 1506
IEASM excavations
Not illustrated

Oil lamp, 350–200 BC
Thonis-Heracleion, Egypt
Pottery, L. 8.5 cm | H. 2.6 cm | Diam. 5.9 cm
Maritime Museum, Alexandria SCA 1584
IEASM excavations
Illustrated p. 185

Oil lamp,
end of 6th–beginning of 5th century BC
Thonis-Heracleion, Egypt
Pottery, H. 2.2 cm | Diam. 5.2 cm
Maritime Museum, Alexandria SCA 598
IEASM excavations
Not illustrated

Oil lamp, 350–300 BC
Thonis-Heracleion, Egypt
Pottery, H. 4.3 cm | Diam. 3.4 cm
Maritime Museum, Alexandria SCA 342
IEASM excavations
Not illustrated

Oil lamp, mid 4th–early 3rd century BC
Thonis-Heracleion, Egypt
Pottery, L. 7 cm | H. 2.5 cm | Diam. 5 cm
Maritime Museum, Alexandria SCA 1587
IEASM excavations
Illustrated p. 185

Oil lamp, mid 4th–early 3rd century BC
Thonis-Heracleion, Egypt
Pottery, L. 7.5 cm | H. 2.8 cm | Diam. 5.4 cm
Maritime Museum, Alexandria SCA 1589
IEASM excavations
Illustrated p. 185

Oil lamp, mid 4th–early 3rd century BC
Thonis-Heracleion, Egypt
Pottery, D. 5.7 cm
Maritime Museum, Alexandria SCA 856
IEASM excavations
Not illustrated

Oil lamp, mid 4th–early 3rd century BC
Thonis-Heracleion, Egypt
Pottery, L. 4.7 cm | H. 2.9 cm
Maritime Museum, Alexandria SCA 1594
IEASM excavations
Illustrated p. 185

Oil lamp, mid 4th–early 3rd century BC
Thonis-Heracleion, Egypt
Pottery, L. 9 cm
Maritime Museum, Alexandria SCA 1324
IEASM excavations
Illustrated p. 185

Anubis emblem, 4th century BC
Thonis-Heracleion, Egypt
Bronze, H. 18 cm | W. 22.7 cm | D. 3.7 cm
Maritime Museum, Alexandria SCA 975
IEASM excavations
Illustrated p. 187

Anubis emblem, 4th century BC
Thonis-Heracleion, Egypt
Bronze, H. 8.6 cm | W. 4.7 cm | D. 2.7 cm
Maritime Museum, Alexandria SCA 981
IEASM excavations
Illustrated p. 187

Horus emblem, 4th century BC
Thonis-Heracleion, Egypt
Bronze, H. 6.9 cm | W. 4.2 cm | D. 1.4 cm
Maritime Museum, Alexandria SCA 997
IEASM excavations
Illustrated p. 187

Votive barge, 4th century BC
Thonis-Heracleion, Egypt
Lead, D. 12.1 cm | W. 1.6 cm
Maritime Museum, Alexandria SCA 405
IEASM excavations
Not illustrated

Offering dish, 6th–2nd century BC
Thonis-Heracleion, Egypt
Granodiorite, Diam. 46 cm
Maritime Museum, Alexandria SCA 265
IEASM excavations
Illustrated p. 189

Mortar, 6th–2nd century BC
Thonis-Heracleion, Egypt
Black granite, H. 6 cm | Diam. 31.5 cm
Maritime Museum, Alexandria SCA 373
IEASM excavations
Not illustrated

Offering dish, 6th–2nd century BC
Thonis-Heracleion, Egypt
Quartzite, Diam. 46 cm
Maritime Museum, Alexandria SCA 374
IEASM excavations
Illustrated p. 189

Mortar, 6th– 2nd century BC
Thonis-Heracleion, Egypt
Pink granite, H. 5 cm | Diam. 28.5 cm
Maritime Museum, Alexandria SCA 358
IEASM excavations
Not illustrated

Offering dish, 6th–2nd century BC
Thonis-Heracleion, Egypt
Granodiorite, H. 6 cm | Diam. 35 cm
Maritime Museum, Alexandria SCA 362
IEASM excavations
Not illustrated

Offering dish, 6th–2nd century BC
Thonis-Heracleion, Egypt
Granodiorite, Diam. 30.5 cm
Maritime Museum, Alexandria SCA 1091
IEASM excavations
Illustrated p. 189

Offering dish, 6th–2nd century BC
Thonis-Heracleion, Egypt
Granodiorite, Diam. 33 cm
Maritime Museum, Alexandria SCA 1280
IEASM excavations
Illustrated p. 189

Offering dish, 6th–2nd century BC
Thonis-Heracleion, Egypt
Granodiorite, Diam. 34 cm
Maritime Museum, Alexandria SCA 360
IEASM excavations
Not illustrated

Offering dish, 6th–2nd century BC
Thonis-Heracleion, Egypt
Granodiorite, H. 6 cm | Diam. 34 cm
Maritime Museum, Alexandria SCA 1620
IEASM excavations
Not illustrated

Offering table, 4th–2nd century BC
Thonis-Heracleion, Egypt
Black granite, D. 61.5 cm | H. 17 cm | W. 59 cm
Maritime Museum, Alexandria SCA 1163
IEASM excavations
Not illustrated

Ladle, 6th–2nd century BC
Thonis-Heracleion, Egypt
Bronze, L. 55.4 cm | Diam. 6.9 cm
Maritime Museum, Alexandria SCA 478
IEASM excavations
Illustrated p. 189

Ladle, 6th–2nd century BC
Thonis-Heracleion, Egypt
Bronze, L. 52.3 cm | Diam. 5.6 cm
Maritime Museum, Alexandria SCA 931
IEASM excavations
Illustrated p. 189

Ladle, 6th–2nd century BC
Thonis-Heracleion, Egypt
Bronze, L. 56.8 cm | Diam. 4.1 cm
Maritime Museum, Alexandria SCA 1014
IEASM excavations
Illustrated p. 189

Ladle, 6th–2nd century BC
Thonis-Heracleion, Egypt
Bronze, L. 53.8 cm | W. 20 cm | Diam. 4.2 cm
Maritime Museum, Alexandria SCA 1042
IEASM excavations
Illustrated p. 189

Ladle, 6th–2nd century BC
Thonis-Heracleion, Egypt
Bronze, L. 44.5 cm | Diam. 7.4 cm
Maritime Museum, Alexandria SCA 1032
IEASM excavations
Illustrated p. 189

Bell, 6th–2nd century BC
Thonis-Heracleion, Egypt
Bronze, H. 7.5 cm | W. 5.2 cm | Diam. 4.3 cm
Maritime Museum, Alexandria SCA 388
IEASM excavations
Illustrated p. 190

Bell, 6th–2nd century BC
Thonis-Heracleion, Egypt
Bronze, H. 7.4 cm | W. 5.2 cm | Diam. 4.5 cm
Maritime Museum, Alexandria SCA 385
IEASM excavations
Illustrated p. 190

Bell, 6th–2nd century BC
Thonis-Heracleion, Egypt
Bronze, H. 9.4 cm | Diam. 7.2 cm
Maritime Museum, Alexandria SCA 1381
IEASM excavations
Illustrated p. 190

Sistrum (rattle), 4th–2nd century BC
Thonis-Heracleion, Egypt
Bronze, L. 14.4 cm | W. 4.4 cm
Maritime Museum, Alexandria SCA 1619
IEASM excavations
Illustrated p. 191

Fragment of a sistrum, 6th–2nd century BC
Thonis-Heracleion, Egypt
Bronze, H. 2.7 cm | W. 4 cm | D. 12 cm
Maritime Museum, Alexandria SCA 906
IEASM excavations
Illustrated p. 191

Fragment of a sistrum, 6th–2nd century BC
Thonis-Heracleion, Egypt
Bronze, H. 14 cm | W. 4 cm | D. 1.2 cm
Maritime Museum, Alexandria SCA 581
IEASM excavations
Illustrated p. 191

Sistrum (rattle), Ptolemaic period (332–31 BC)
Unknown provenance, Egypt
Gilded wood, H. 16 cm | W. 4.5 cm
Egyptian Museum, Cairo JE 67887
Illustrated p. 190

Stele of Ptolemy VIII, 2nd century BC
Thonis-Heracleion, Egypt
Red granite. H. 6.1 m | W. 3.1 m | D. 40 cm
Maritime Museum, Alexandria SCA 529
IEASM excavations
Illustrated pp. 96–7

Statuette of Osiris, Late Period (664–332 BC)
Thonis-Heracleion, Egypt
Bronze and gold, H. 26.5 cm | W. 7.2 cm | D. 4.3 cm
Maritime Museum, Alexandria SCA 1267
IEASM excavations
Illustrated pp. 192–5

Statuette of Osiris, 6th–2nd century BC
Thonis-Heracleion, Egypt
Bronze, H. 21 cm | W. 4.3 cm | D. 2.2 cm
Maritime Museum, Alexandria SCA 1081
IEASM excavations
Illustrated p. 192

Statuette of Osiris, 6th–2nd century BC
Thonis-Heracleion, Egypt
Bronze, H. 30.5 cm | W. 7.6 cm | D. 6 cm
Maritime Museum, Alexandria SCA 1266
IEASM excavations
Illustrated p. 192

Statuette of Osiris, 6th–2nd century BC
Thonis-Heracleion, Egypt
Bronze, H. 9 cm | W. 2.3 cm | D. 1.1 cm
Maritime Museum, Alexandria SCA 1255
IEASM excavations
Not illustrated

Statuette of Osiris, 6th–2nd century BC
Thonis-Heracleion, Egypt
Bronze, H. 9 cm | W. 2.7 cm | D. 0.7 cm
Maritime Museum, Alexandria SCA 1004
IEASM excavations
Not illustrated

Statuette of Osiris, 6th–2nd century BC
Thonis-Heracleion, Egypt
Bronze, H. 9.5 cm | W. 2.5 cm | D. 1.5 cm
Maritime Museum, Alexandria SCA 1563
IEASM excavations
Not illustrated

Amulet of Osiris-Sokar, 4th–2nd century BC
Thonis-Heracleion, Egypt
Bronze, H. 6.6 cm | W. 2 cm | D. 0.7 cm
Maritime Museum, Alexandria SCA 1616
IEASM excavations
Illustrated p. 197

Head of Osiris, Late Period (664–332 BC)
Thonis-Heracleion, Egypt
Bronze, H. 5.5 cm | W. 1.5 cm | D. 2 cm
Maritime Museum, Alexandria SCA 926
IEASM excavations
Illustrated p. 196

Divine beard, late 7th–4th century BC
Thonis-Heracleion, Egypt
Bronze, H. 16.6 cm | W. 4.5 cm
Maritime Museum, Alexandria SCA 1079
IEASM excavations
Illustrated p. 197

Head of a duck, 6th–2nd century BC
Thonis-Heracleion, Egypt
Bronze, L. 12 cm | W. 2.4 cm | D. 2.8 cm
Maritime Museum, Alexandria SCA 1561
IEASM excavations
Not illustrated

Statuette of Isis, 4th–2nd century BC
Thonis-Heracleion, Egypt
Bronze, H. 9.2 cm | W. 1.5 cm | D. 0.7 cm
Maritime Museum, Alexandria SCA 1576
IEASM excavations
Not illustrated

Statuette of Isis, 6th–2nd century BC
Thonis-Heracleion, Egypt
Bronze, H. 15.5 cm | W. 3.6 cm | D. 1.6 cm
Maritime Museum, Alexandria SCA 1306
IEASM excavations
Not illustrated

Statuette of Isis, 6th–2nd century BC
Thonis-Heracleion, Egypt
Bronze, H. 12.3 cm | W. 2.8 cm
Maritime Museum, Alexandria SCA 972
IEASM excavations
Illustrated p. 199

Statuette of Isis, 6th–2nd century BC
Thonis-Heracleion, Egypt
Faience, H. 7 cm | W. 2.1 cm
Maritime Museum, Alexandria SCA 522
IEASM excavations
Illustrated p. 199

Statuette of Harpokrates, 5th–2nd century BC
Thonis-Heracleion, Egypt
Bronze, H. 9.5 cm | W. 2.7 cm
Maritime Museum, Alexandria SCA 995
IEASM excavations
Illustrated p. 200

Statuette of Harpokrates, 6th–2nd century BC
Thonis-Heracleion, Egypt
Bronze, H. 9.5 cm | W. 1.8 cm | D. 1.2 cm
Maritime Museum, Alexandria SCA 1572
IEASM excavations
Not illustrated

Model of an offering table, 6th–2nd century BC
Thonis-Heracleion, Egypt
Bronze, H. 5.1 cm | W. 4.6 cm | D. 0.4 cm
Maritime Museum, Alexandria SCA 1250
IEASM excavations
Illustrated p. 203

Offering table, 4th–2nd century BC
Thonis-Heracleion, Egypt
Granodiorite, H. 64 cm | W. 63 cm | D. 19 cm
Maritime Museum, Alexandria SCA 1257
IEASM excavations
Illustrated p. 202

Statuette of Harpokrates, 6th–2nd century BC
Thonis-Heracleion, Egypt
Bronze, H. 3.3 cm | W. 1.3 cm
Maritime Museum, Alexandria SCA 423
IEASM excavations
Illustrated p. 200

Statuette of Harpokrates, 6th–2nd century BC
Thonis-Heracleion, Egypt
Lead, H. 4 cm | W. 2.6 cm
Maritime Museum, Alexandria SCA 925
IEASM excavations
Illustrated p. 200

Figure of an owl?, 6th–2nd century BC
Thonis-Heracleion, Egypt
Bronze, H. 9.2 cm | W. 1.5 cm | D. 0.7 cm
Maritime Museum, Alexandria SCA 1050
IEASM excavations
Illustrated p. 201

Harpokrates, 6th–2nd century BC
Thonis-Heracleion, Egypt
Lead, H. 4.2 cm | W. 2.9 cm | D. 2 cm
Maritime Museum, Alexandria SCA 1052
IEASM excavations
Illustrated p. 201

Miniature bowl, 6th–2nd century BC
Thonis-Heracleion, Egypt
Lead, H. 2 cm | D. 0.3 cm | Diam. 7.7 cm
Maritime Museum, Alexandria SCA 1053
IEASM excavations
Illustrated p. 201

Miniature vessel, 6th–2nd century BC
Thonis-Heracleion, Egypt
Lead, H. 4.9 cm | W. 3 cm | D. 1.5 cm
Maritime Museum, Alexandria SCA 1051
IEASM excavations
Illustrated p. 201

Lid of small box, 6th–2nd century BC
Thonis-Heracleion, Egypt
Lead, H. 3.5 cm | Diam. 5 cm
Maritime Museum, Alexandria SCA 938
IEASM excavations
Illustrated p. 201

Small box with lid, 6th–2nd century BC
Thonis-Heracleion, Egypt
Lead, H. 3.5 cm | Diam. 5 cm
Maritime Museum, Alexandria SCA 939
IEASM excavations
Illustrated p. 201

Miniature vase, 6th–2nd century BC
Thonis-Heracleion, Egypt
Lead, H. 2.5 cm | Diam. 3.3 cm
Maritime Museum, Alexandria SCA 923
IEASM excavations
Illustrated p. 201

Small container, 6th–2nd century BC
Thonis-Heracleion, Egypt
Lead, H. 4 cm | Diam. 5 cm
Maritime Museum, Alexandria SCA 914
IEASM excavations
Not illustrated

Miniature head rest, 6th–2nd century BC
Thonis-Heracleion, Egypt
Lead, H. 1.8 cm | D. 2.6 cm
Maritime Museum, Alexandria SCA 1005
IEASM excavations
Not illustrated

Container, 6th–2nd century BC
Thonis-Heracleion, Egypt
Lead, H. 2.8 cm | D. 7 cm
Maritime Museum, Alexandria SCA 1077
IEASM excavations
Illustrated p. 201

Bes vase, Late 5th–mid-4th century BC
Thonis-Heracleion, Egypt
Lead, H. 7.5 cm | W. 2.8 cm | D. 1.3 cm
Maritime Museum, Alexandria SCA 1234
IEASM excavations
Illustrated p. 204

Figure of Bes, 3rd–2nd century BC
Thonis-Heracleion, Egypt
Terracotta, H. 25 cm | W. 15 cm | D. 5 cm
Maritime Museum, Alexandria SCA 1586
IEASM excavations
Illustrated pp. 204–5

Bes vase, 5th–4th century BC
Thonis-Heracleion, Egypt
Bronze, H. 9.5 cm | W. 11.9 cm
Maritime Museum, Alexandria SCA 1235
IEASM excavations
Illustrated p. 206

Fragment of a vase depicting Bes, Serapis and Isis, 3rd–2nd century BC
Thonis-Heracleion, Egypt
Pottery, H. 6 cm
Maritime Museum, Alexandria SCA 1588
IEASM excavations
Illustrated p. 206

Statue of Taweret, 664–610 BC (reign of Psamtik I)
Luxor (North Karnak), Egypt
Greywacke, H. 96 cm | W. 26 cm | D. 38 cm
Egyptian Museum, Cairo CG 39145
Illustrated p. 207

Bust of Neilos, 2nd century AD
Canopus, Egypt
Greywacke, H. 67 cm | W. 56 cm | D. 30 cm
Maritime Museum, Alexandria SCA 842
IEASM excavations
Illustrated pp. 2–3, 208–9, and on the back cover

Phallic figurine, 4th–2nd century BC
Thonis-Heracleion, Egypt
Limestone, H. 4.3 cm | L. 8.6 cm
Maritime Museum, Alexandria SCA 1590
IEASM excavations
Illustrated p. 211

Phallic figurine, 4th–2nd century BC
Thonis-Heracleion, Egypt
Limestone, H. 14 cm | W. 5 cm
National Museum of Alexandria 293, SCA 383
IEASM excavations
Illustrated p. 211

Figurine of Egyptian goddess, c. 400–200 BC
Naukratis, Egypt
Limestone, H. 13.1 cm | W. 5.1 cm
British Museum EA 68814
Illustrated p. 212

Plaque with naked goddess, c. 400–300 BC
Naukratis, Egypt
Terracotta, H. 9.5 cm | W. 8.4 cm
British Museum 1885,1010.28
Illustrated p. 213

Figurine of Isis-Bubastis, c. 300–100 BC
Naukratis, Egypt
Terracotta, H. 24.5 cm | W. 8.2 cm
British Museum 1886,0401.1451
Illustrated p. 212

Pendant, 4th–2nd century BC
Thonis-Heracleion, Egypt
Gold, H. 1.2 cm | W. 0.9 cm | D. 0.5 cm
Graeco-Roman Museum, Alexandria 32338, SCA 1122
IEASM excavations
Not illustrated

Goblet, early 1st/2nd century AD
Hermopolis Magna/El Ashmunein, Egypt
Gilded silver, H. 13 cm
Graeco-Roman Museum, Alexandria 24201
Illustrated pp. 218–19

Vase, late 1st century BC
Alexandria, Egypt
Pottery, H. 16 cm | Diam. 11 cm
Maritime Museum, Alexandria SCA 1608
IEASM excavations
Illustrated pp. 148–9

East Greek situla (jar), 600–570 BC
Tell Dafana, Egypt
Pottery, H. 53.6 cm | Diam. 26.7 cm
British Museum 1888,0208.1
Illustrated p. 214

***Pyxis* (vessel), c. 350 BC**
Thonis-Heracleion, Egypt
Pottery, H. 15.5 cm | Diam. 17 cm
Maritime Museum, Alexandria SCA 590
IEASM excavations
Not illustrated

***Stamnos*, 470–450 BC**
Vulci, Italy
Pottery, H. 34.3 cm
British Museum 1856,0512.14
Illustrated p. 147

Ladle, 6th–2nd century BC
Thonis-Heracleion, Egypt
Bronze, L. 51.7 cm | Diam. 4.5 cm
Maritime Museum, Alexandria SCA 936
IEASM excavations
Not illustrated

Ritual pail, c. 4th–2nd century BC
Thonis-Heracleion, Egypt
Bronze, H. 25 cm | Diam. 28.5 cm
National Museum of Alexandria 310, SCA 223
IEASM excavations
Illustrated p. 215

Hermes relief, early 1st century BC
Canopus, Egypt
Granite or basalt, H. 1.21 m | W. 0.79 m
British Museum 1848,1014.1
Illustrated p. 217

**Chapter 5
Egypt and Rome**

Roman relief, c. 30 BC–AD 100
Probably from Italy
Marble, H. 35 cm | W. 40 cm | D. 5.5 cm
British Museum 1865,1118.252
Illustrated p. 227

Sphinx, 1st century BC
Alexandria, Egypt
Granodiorite, H. 75 cm | L. 1.4 m
National Museum of Alexandria 284, SCA 451
IEASM excavations
Illustrated p. 233

Priest with Osiris-Canopus jar, 1st century BC–2nd century AD
Alexandria, Egypt
Black Granite, H. 122 cm
National Museum of Alexandria 282, SCA 449
IEASM excavations
Illustrated pp. 220, 228–9

Sphinx, 1st century BC
Alexandria, Egypt
Granodiorite, H. 70 cm | L. 1.5 m
National Museum of Alexandria 283, SCA 450
IEASM excavations
Illustrated pp. 231–2

Ring, end of 1st century BC–1st century AD
Alexandria, Egypt
Gold and chalcedony, Diam. (of ring) 2.95 cm | Diam. (of setting) 1.8 cm
Bibliotheca Alexandrina Antiquities Museum SCA 84
IEASM excavations
Illustrated p. 234

***Patera* (libation bowl), 1st century AD**
Alexandria, Egypt
Bronze, L. 38 cm | W. 21 cm
Maritime Museum, Alexandria SCA 1618
IEASM excavations
Not illustrated

Bust of Serapis, Roman (AD 1–100)
Unknown provenance, acquired in Egypt
Alabaster, H. 27 cm
Graeco-Roman Museum, Alexandria 23925
Illustrated p. 234

Bust of Isis, AD 150–200
Cyrene, Libya
Alabaster, H. 30 cm
British Museum 1861,1127.83
Illustrated p. 235

Lamp with Isis nursing Harpokrates, c. AD 100–200
Faversham, United Kingdom
Ceramic, H. 7.7 cm
British Museum 1984,1004.3
Illustrated p. 239

Osiris-Camopus jar, AD 150–200
Ras el-Soda, Egypt
Marble, H. 95 cm
Graeco-Roman Museum, Alexandria 25786
Illustrated p. 237

Foot on column, AD 150–200
Ras el-Soda, Egypt
Marble, H. (stand) 1.02 m | H. (foot) 28 cm | W. 42.5 cm
Graeco-Roman Museum, Alexandria 25788 and 25789
Illustrated p. 238

Osiris-Camopus jar, AD 150–200
Ras el-Soda, Egypt
Marble, H. 1.07 m
Graeco-Roman Museum, Alexandria 25787
Illustrated p. 237

Head of a private Individual, 2nd century AD?
Qena, Egypt
Bronze, H. 38 cm
Graeco-Roman Museum, Alexandria 22902
Illustrated p. 240

Statue of Antinous, 4th–2nd century AD
Canopus, Egypt
Limestone, H. 45 cm
Graeco-Roman Museum, Alexandria 22829
Illustrated p. 241

List of contributors

Franck Goddio [FG] is President of the European Institute for Underwater Archaeology (IEASM), and director of the excavations that in 2000 uncovered the city of Thonis-Heracleion, 7 km off the Egyptian shore, and the submerged part of Canopus in Abukir Bay. He has published numerous scientific works and popular books on his discoveries

Dr Aurélia Masson-Berghoff [AMB] is the curator of the exhibition *Sunken cities: Egypt's lost worlds* at the British Museum. She is the Egyptologist for the British Museum research project *Naukratis: Greeks in Egypt*. Since 2000, she has directed and participated in numerous archaeological missions in Egypt and Sudan, particularly in the Theban region

Dr Damian Robinson [DJR] is the Director of the Oxford Centre for Maritime Archaeology at the University of Oxford, where he lectures on maritime and classical archaeology. He works extensively with the European Institute for Underwater Archaeology (IEASM) and is excavating one of the ships in the harbour at Thonis-Heracleion

Dr Ross Thomas [RT] is an archaeologist and project curator at the British Museum and has been directing new fieldwork at Naukratis since 2012 on behalf of the project *Naukratis: Greeks in Egypt*. He has worked extensively on the archaeology of the Hellenistic and Roman east and their neighbours

Dr Alexandra Villing [AV] is a Classical archaeologist, curator at the British Museum and director of the project *Naukratis: Greeks in Egypt*. She has published widely on the art and religion of Archaic and Classical Greece and the relations between the Greeks and their Eastern neighbours

Dr Sydney H. Aufrère [SA] is director of research at the French National Centre of Scientific Research (CNRS) and has written numerous books and articles, especially on naturistic thought and the transmission of priestly science in ancient Egypt

Dr Jocelyne Berlandini-Keller [JB] is a research fellow at the French National Centre of Scientific Research (CNRS) and at Sorbonne (Paris IV) University, and has extensive field experience. She has published numerous scientific works in the fields of magic-religious beliefs, history and art in ancient Egypt

Dr A.-S. von Bomhard [ASvB] is a member of the European Institute for Underwater Archaeology (IEASM) specializing in Egyptology and ancient Egyptian astronomy. She has published numerous books and articles in English, French and German

Dr David Fabre [DF] is an Egyptologist whose PhD focused on the organization of maritime trade in ancient Egypt. He participated in the French excavations at Tanis and has been collaborating with the European Institute for Underwater Archaeology (IEASM) since 2005

Professor Zsolt Kiss [ZK] has been the Head of the Department of Classical Mediterranean Cultures of the Polish Academy of Science, Warsaw since 2010. He has been collaborating with the European Institute for Underwater Archaeology (IEASM) since 1996

Dr Daniela Rosenow [DR] is project curator of the exhibition *Sunken cities: Egypt's lost worlds* at the British Museum. She has previously worked at UCL's Institute of Archaeology and has participated in numerous international fieldwork projects in Egypt. Her research interests include Late Period and Graeco-Roman Egypt and the study of ancient glass

Dr Mervat Seif el-Din [MSD] is a specialist in Graeco-Roman Egypt. Once the lead curator of the Graeco-Roman Museum in Alexandria, she is now in charge of the scientific research in the museums of Alexandria (Egyptian Ministry of State Antiquities). Since 2010, she has been responsible for the publication of the objects recently discovered in Alexandria's Bubasteion

Professor Jean Yoyotte [JY] (1927–2009) held the Chair of Egyptology at the Collège de France. A specialist of the Late Period, he focused on the major cities of the Nile Delta, especially Naukratis and then Thonis-Heracleion after its discovery by the European Institute for Underwater Archaeology (IEASM)

Dr Sanda Heinz [SH], Oxford Centre for Maritime Archaeology, University of Oxford, former Hilti Foundation Student

Dr Emma Libonati [EL], University College London (formerly University of Oxford)

Professor Barbara Lichocka [BL], Department of Classical Mediterranean Cultures, Polish Academy of Science, Warsaw

Professor Andrew Meadows [AM], New College and Faculty of Classics, University of Oxford

Dr Zöe Robinson [ZR], former Hilti Foundation Student, Oxford Centre for Maritime Archaeology, University of Oxford

Dr Yvonne Stolz [YS], Institute of Byzantine Studies, Ludwig Maximilian University of Munich, former Hilti Foundation Student, Oxford Centre for Maritime Archaeology, University of Oxford

Professor Christophe Thiers [CT], Centre franco-égyptien d'études des temples de Karnak

Acknowledgments

The editors warmly thank the authors for their essays and object descriptions included in this book, and gratefully acknowledge the following for their support:

For the British Museum, colleagues across a range of departments, in particular Neal Spencer, John Taylor, Claire Thorne and Evan York and his Collection Management team (Department of Ancient Egypt and Sudan), Lesley Fitton, Peter Higgs, Ian Jenkins, Thomas Kiely, Kate Morton and Alex Truscott (Department of Greece and Rome), Emma Poulter, Chris Manning, Chris Michaels and Patricia Wheatley (Department of Digital and Publishing), Jane Batty (Department of Learning and National Partnerships), Karen Birkhoelzer, Joanne Dyer and Fleur Shearman (Department of Conservation and Scientific Research), Jane Bennett, Elizabeth Bray, Caroline Ingham and Carolyn Marsden-Smith (Department of Exhibitions), Darrel Day, Christopher Stewart and George Benson (Registrar's Office), Amelia Dowler (Department of Coins and Medals), Benjamin Ward and Hannah Boulton (Press Office), Kathryn Havelock (Marketing) and Clara Potter (British Museum Company).

Research on Naukratis had been supported by grants from the Leverhulme Trust (Research Project Grant F/100 052/E), Chris Levett, the Shelby White and Leon Levy Program for Archaeological Publications, the Honor Frost Foundation, the British Academy, Reckitt Fund, and the Institute of Classical Studies, London. We would also like to express our gratitude to the many academic collaborators, museum curators, scientists, student volunteers, and colleagues across the British Museum and in partner institutions who have generously assisted the British Museum's *Naukratis: Greeks in Egypt* project.

The ongoing support of colleagues in the Ministry of Antiquities is gratefully acknowledged for both the exhibition in London and research fieldwork, particularly the Minister of State for Antiquities, Dr Mamdouh el-Damaty, but also Dr Hisham el-Leithy (Director of Scientific Publications Department). We are indebted to our Egyptian colleagues from Damanhur Inspectorate, particularly its director Ahmed Kamel el-Adham, for their active help on the fieldwork at Naukratis.

We would also like to thank His Excellency Nasser Kamel, Egyptian Ambassador to the United Kingdom, and his colleagues, for their support of the exhibition.

The 3D reconstruction of Naukratis was created by Grant Cox (ArtasMedia), supervised by Ross Thomas and based on information provided by Ross Thomas, Alexandra Villing, Aurélia Masson-Berghoff, Manuela Lehmann Ben Pennington and Wolf Koenigs. The reconstruction drawings of the Egyptian sanctuary and Apollo temple at Naukratis were prepared by Kate Morton based on information provided by Aurélia Masson-Berghoff and François Leclère (Egyptian sanctuary) and Wolf Koenigs and Alexandra Villing (Apollo temple).

The 3D design of the exhibition is the result of the excellent work of Sylvain Roca and Nicolas Groult, while we gratefully acknowledge James Alexander (Jade Design) for the graphic design.

Special thanks go to the publisher of the catalogue, Thames & Hudson – in particular Sophy Thompson, Julian Honer, Amanda Vinnicombe, Jen Moore, Johanna Neurath, Maggi Smith (Sixism Limited), Carolyn Jones, Susanna Ingram, Sophie Neve and Ben Plumridge.

For the Institut Européen d'Archéologie Sous-Marine (IEASM), Franck Goddio, President of the European Institute for Underwater Archeology, Director of excavations and co-curator of the exhibition in London, wishes to express his profound gratitude to lenders, institutions and individuals who have contributed to the success of the excavations in Egypt, to the scientific studies and the creation of the exhibition as well as the catalogue, and especially to the Hilti Foundation, which has supported him for almost twenty years and without whose assistance the excavations, scientific studies, conservation and exhibition could not have been accomplished.

Particular thanks go to:
in Egypt
Pr. Dr Mamdouh Eldamaty, Minister of Antiquities of the Arab Republic of Egypt
Nachwa Gaber, Technical Director at the minister's office

Elham Salah, Director General of the museums in Egypt and Director General of Exhibitions

Dr Mohamed Mostafa Abdelmaguid, Director of the underwater archaeology department

Dr Nadia Khadr, Director of the National Museum of Alexandria and the Graeco-Roman Museum of Alexandria

Samia Rachwane, Director of the museum of the Bibliotheca Alexandrina

Mahmoud el Halwagy, Director of the Egyptian Museum, Cairo

and the Coast Guard, the Egyptian Navy and the Egyptian archaeologists and inspectors of the Ministry of Antiquities, without whom the excavations in Egypt would not be possible.

in France
Ministry of Foreign Affairs, Ministry of Culture and Communications:

André Parant, French Ambassador at the Arab Republic of Egypt and his staff

All participants in the survey missions, the archaeological excavations, and the studies of the IEASM:

Amani Badr, Coordination
David Fabre, Egyptologist, IEASM
Catherine Grataloup, ceramicist, IEASM
Anne-Sophie von Bomhard, Egyptologist, IEASM

Andrew Meadows, Professor of Ancient History, New College, University of Oxford

Jocelyne Berlandini-Keller, research fellow, CNRS
Sylvie Cauville, Research Director, CNRS
Sydney H. Aufrère, Research Director, CNRS

in the UK
The team at the Oxford Centre for Maritime Archaeology, University of Oxford:

Damian Robinson, Director
Linda Hulin, Research Officer
and Elsbeth van der Wilt, Sanda Heinz, Emma Libonati, Yvonne Petrina, and Zoe Robinson whose doctoral theses focused on the archaeological artefacts from the IEASM excavations.

Illustration credits

Index

Page numbers in *italic* refer to illustrations